Clothing, Food, and Travel

This book explores the material and cultural history of the Ming Dynasty based on the Chinese magnum opus *Xingshi Yinyuan Zhuan* (literally, The Story of a Marital Fate to Awaken the World), written under the pseudonym of the seventeenth-century writer Xizhou Sheng.

The novel weaves into its narrative, through the characters' personalities and the events it illustrates, important details of Ming material life. Through the literary snapshot of the Ming material culture as reflected in *Xingshi Yinyuan Zhuan*, this work investigates the practices and customs of clothing, food, and travel, three of the "four major concerns of the people's livelihoods," known as *yishizhuxing* in Chinese. While frequenting economic dimensions and probing the impact that Ming politics had on the ethos and social economy of the period, it sheds significant light on folk customs, legal and religious practices, and the status of women, among other issues.

This work aims to enrich the current Western scholarship, done primarily by Timothy Brook, Craig Clunas, and Glen Dudbridge, on Ming material culture. The book will be of great value to students and scholars of East Asian Studies, Chinese literature, and those interested in the history of material culture in general.

Liu Xiaoyi is a professor at the School of Literature, Shandong University, China. She also serves on the Expert Committee of the Shandong Translators Association. She received both her M.A. and Ph.D. degrees from the Dept. of East Asian Studies, University of Arizona. She has published 18 CSSCI and English papers, 5 Chinese monographs, and hosted national and ministerial translation projects. Her bilingual collection, *The Past Lingers*, presents her own lyrical writings with English translations and Shakespeare's sonnets in localization rendering.

Clothing, Food, and Travel
Ming Material Culture as Reflected in Xingshi Yinyuan Zhuan

Liu Xiaoyi

LONDON AND NEW YORK

Supported by Chinese Fund for the Humanities and Social Sciences.

First published 2024
by Routledge
4 Park Square, Milton Park, Abingdon, Oxon OX14 4RN

and by Routledge
605 Third Avenue, New York, NY 10158

Routledge is an imprint of the Taylor & Francis Group, an informa business

© 2024 Liu Xiaoyi

The right of Liu Xiaoyi to be identified as author of this work has been asserted in accordance with sections 77 and 78 of the Copyright, Designs and Patents Act 1988.

All rights reserved. No part of this book may be reprinted or reproduced or utilised in any form or by any electronic, mechanical, or other means, now known or hereafter invented, including photocopying and recording, or in any information storage or retrieval system, without permission in writing from the publishers.

Trademark notice: Product or corporate names may be trademarks or registered trademarks, and are used only for identification and explanation without intent to infringe.

English Version by permission of Shanghai Chinese Classics Publishing House Co., Ltd.

British Library Cataloguing-in-Publication Data
A catalogue record for this book is available from the British Library

ISBN: 978-1-032-52325-5 (hbk)
ISBN: 978-1-032-52326-2 (pbk)
ISBN: 978-1-003-40614-3 (ebk)

DOI: 10.4324/9781003406143

Typeset in Times New Roman
by Apex CoVantage, LLC

Contents

	Introduction	1
1	The Clothing Culture and Clothing Choices of the Ming People	29
2	Luxury Consumption and the Financial System	75
3	Food Cultures of the Ming	114
4	Traveling Cultures of the Ming	150
	Conclusion	191
	Index	*199*

Introduction

1. An Outline of *Xingshi Yinyuan Zhuan*

Xingshi Yinyuan Zhuan 醒世姻缘传 (English title *The Story of a Marital Fate to Awaken the World*; hereafter *XSYYZ* or "the Novel") is an epic classical Chinese novel written in the late imperial period. Its author, writing under the pseudonym of Xizhou Sheng (Scholar of the Western Zhou 西周生), has been surmised by later researchers to have been a literatus who lived during the late Ming and possibly into the early Qing. He was considered well-exposed to the Shandong culture and dialect, and familiar with late Ming officialdom operations. The content and dramatis personae within the Novel, however, fall into a narrative frame identifiably Ming, ranging from Zhengtong (1436–1449) to Chenghua (1465–1487) in its setting.

A 100-chapter, 100,000-character magnum opus, the Novel primarily concerns itself with what the author deems a curious reversal of power dynamics and relations in the institution of marriage: henpecking. Two uneven plots—largely independent of each other and only loosely connected by the threads of karmic reincarnation—constitute its framework. The Chao plot, ranging from Chapter 1 to Chapter 22, tells the story of the rise and fall of the Chao family of Wucheng 武城, Shandong. The only son of the Chaos, Chao Yuan, besides having committed many a moral offense, including driving his primary wife *nee* Ji to suicide, also ruthlessly kills a fox spirit, who thereupon vows revenge. The major Chao plot ends in Chapter 22. At this point, through the intercession of the fox spirit, cosmic retribution visits Chao Yuan, causing him to be killed by the husband of a woman with whom he is having an affair. Yet the remainder of the Chao plot, designed to exalt the benevolent conduct of Madame Chao and Chao Yuan's half-brother, Chao Liang, continues through the remaining chapters and is primarily concerned with the Di plot. The Di family lives in Mingshui, Shandong, geographically not far from where the Chao plot occurs. In the Di plot, the author expounds on how an unhappy marriage is doomed by fate and why a man's suffering from a tyrannical wife is a consequence of his sins committed in a previous life. In his second life, Chao Yuan is reincarnated into Di Xichen, the only son of an affluent peasant family. The fox spirit he kills, Xue Sujie, is reborn as the daughter of a wealthy family who relocates to Mingshui. Xichen's father, Old Di, amasses his fortune through arduous work and frugality, and Sujie's father, Old Xue, an unsuccessful

DOI: 10.4324/9781003406143-1

Confucian scholar in his retirement, runs a cloth store to make his living. Xichen's first marriage to Sujie and his second to Jijie, the daughter of his old landlady and the reincarnation of *nee* Ji, turn out to be nightmarish ones. With a mixed sense of delight, curiosity, and stern, upright Confucian sentiment, the author expounds on the domestic squabbles, condemning both henpecked husband and fierce wife alike.

Much as constituent fibers decide the quality of a textile piece, the success of historiographies and novels is delivered by the warp and weft of the details. Narrations of a constellation of brilliant particulars always excel. *XSYYZ* falls into the category of the latter but functions as the former. As the narrative unwinds, the Novel is inclined to devote massive attention to material details, both in the personalities and the events it illustrates. Eventually, *XSYYZ* evolves into a comprehensive, panoramic portrait of seventeenth-century China. The narrative strategy, admittedly, is very much against the author's intention: satirizing tyrannical wifery.

In *XSYYZ*, fiction and history converge in many places, most unmistakably in the recording of the Tumu Fort Incident 土木堡事变, where the author expounds on the ins and outs of the event, the panic it caused among Ming bureaucrats, and the remedial measures taken by the government in its aftermath. Although the Novel treats no other historic event with equal length and details, when the flow of the narrative necessitates recording or referencing significant Ming events or policies, the author's pen does not flinch. Jingdi's ascending to the throne, the purge of the powerful eunuch Wang Zhen 王振, Yingzong's reinstatement, and the "single whip" tax reform are all truthfully rendered. The unrestrained pen indicates that the author does not need to resort to innuendo and insinuation. Nevertheless, the historical fidelity of the Novel does not lie in its unabridged recording of historical events—if so, the author would have been reduced to no more than an amanuensis. It is the rich, descriptive details rendering the landscape of Ming material life that make *XSYYZ* stand out from other works and make it an invaluable source for historical studies.

In December 1931, Hu Shih completed one of his most striking textual research works, "The Textual Research on *Xingshi Yinyuan Zhuan*." Approaching the conclusion, Hu Shih's remarks went beyond a literary and textual evaluation of the masterpiece, addressing its value regarding the broader context of studies of social economy, historiography, and folk culture.

> Those who read the Novel should read it this way so as to be regarded as having a historical vision. Had we been equipped with such a historical vision, not only would we be able to recognize the significance of the book, that it befits itself in the category of "the five greatest Chinese magnum opuses"—as Xu Zhimo has suggested—but also appreciate the richness and details of the historical culture this book presents to us. I can assure you, my reader: future historians of seventeenth-century Chinese social customs are to study this book, and so are the future scholars of seventeenth-century educational history to include this book in their bibliographies. Researchers of the seventeenth-century Chinese economy whose studies pertain to grain prices, informatics of natural disasters, costs of official titles, etc., will need to focus their efforts on this book, and so will those who study the history

of seventeenth-century political corruption and the suffering of the people's livelihood, as well as the scholars of religious studies.[1]

Ninety years have passed since Hu Shih made his groundbreaking statement. Still, the respect due from academia, or a proper awareness from the populace towards *XSYYZ*, on which Hu and his friend Xu Zhimo had placed so much confidence, has yet come into being. The Novel is still regarded as a second-rate entry in the view of most literary critics; it is less known, read, and studied than any of the Four Chinese Classical Novels: *A Dream of Red Mansions* 红楼梦, *Journey to the West* 西游记, *Romance of the Three Kingdoms* 三国演义, and *Water Margin* 水浒传. It is outmatched by *Jin Ping Mei* 金瓶梅 and less famous than *The Scholars* 儒林外史 or *Strange Tales from a Chinese Studio* 聊斋志异. The contemporary reader easily confuses the title *Xingshi Yinyuan Zhuan* with that of the modern novelist Zhang Henshui's 张恨水 *Fate in Tears and Laughter* 啼笑因缘, a romance backdropped in 1920s Beijing. Sometimes, it would be juxtaposed to and introduced along with the late imperial pornographic novels such as *Rou Putuan* 肉蒲团 and *Ruyijun Zhuan* 如意君传 by benefit-seeking publishers—a selling point it justifiably deserves, for the Novel does boast some graphic depictions of sex, though reducing it to sheer pornography is both unfair and denigrating. The likeness between its title, *The Story of a Marital Fate to Awaken the World*, and that of the *Lasting Words to Awaken the World* 醒世恒言, a collection from *Collections of Short Stories and Two Collections of Surprising Stories* 三言二拍, would on occasion cause the reader to mistake it for works by Ming literatus Feng Menglong 冯梦龙.

The Novel does excel in at least one aspect. It has aroused the interest of linguists and dialectologists on the merits of its vernacular features; long regarded as a treasure trove of Shandong dialects, it has become one of the favorite books for linguistic treasure hunts. A casual indexing from Wanfang Data 万方数据,[2] one of China's largest databases of academic journals, renders 183 search results, the majority of which are linguistics-related.

Lu Xun, in the writing of his renowned *A Brief History of Chinese Fiction* 中国小说史略,[3] failed to mention *XSYYZ* at all. The absence almost constituted a blunder or, at least, undermined his critical work's completeness. Did Lu Xun loathe the Novel's overemphasis on female subordination and its didactic tone? We will never know. Despite his stand on individual liberty and gender equality, and aside from his aversion to arranged marriages, Lu Xun seldom allowed his personal preferences to overrule the significance of a literary work. Discretion was used when he selected works of fiction for his critic's list, of which comprehensiveness was a dominant factor. Even stereotyped "talented scholar-beauty" 才子佳人 works like *Pinhua Baojian* 品花宝鉴 and *Pingshan Lengyan* 平山冷燕 were reviewed and critiqued at considerable length. Lu Xun would make fair comments based on a work's literary merits. Later, in a letter to his friend Qian Xuantong 钱玄同 regarding his negligence regarding *XSYYZ*, he explained:

> I have heard about the book *Xingshi Yinyuan Zhuan*, which is also known as *The Bad Marriage* 恶姻缘; as to its exact original title, I do not know.

I have read it sketchily and found it verbose and repetitious; though a completed work, its theme goes no further than karmic retribution. Its depiction of trivial matters of the household is, nevertheless, far superior to the likes of *Pingshan Lengyan*. I have not finished reading this work because of my remissness rather than its lack of attraction.[4]

The significance of Lu Xun's *A Brief History of Chinese Fiction* to the studies of Chinese fiction, classic or modern, can never be overstated. To sum up, *XSYYZ* continued to be denied membership in the elite club of Chinese classics until the early 1930s, when its reputation began to rise. Owing to the promotion of Shanghai's Yadong Library, the Novel was re-punctuated and reprinted in 1933, with Xu Zhimo prefacing and Hu Shih post-scripting it with his 30,000-word textual research. Following its modern debut, Zhou Zhenfu 周振甫 and Sun Kaidi 孙楷第, experts of Chinese classical literature, both shared their comments on the Novel, thus inspiring increased interest in the related studies. Unfortunately, this long-awaited academic focus was soon overwhelmed by the urgent theme of national survival. The 1937 Japanese invasion had crushed "the last peaceful study table in Beiping," dispersing scholars to impoverished countries and underdeveloped border provinces. No large-scale discussions about the Novel were brought up before the end of the anti-Japanese war in 1945. After 1949 and before the Cultural Revolution, the academic community in mainland China demonstrated some interest in the Novel's unknown authorship. Among those papers, two were noteworthy: Lu Dahuang's 路大荒 rebuttal to Hu Shih's hypothesis identifying the author Xizhou Sheng as Pu Songling[5] and Wang Shouyi's 王守义 textual research on the periodization of the Novel.[6] The Cultural Revolution decade resulted in barren, rusty academia in China. It was not until the 1980s that the gradual rehabilitation of *XSYYZ* studies started to generate quality papers like those of Xu Fuling 徐复岭, who ascribed the authorship to Jia Fuxi 贾凫西, a late Ming vernacular *Ci* lyric composer,[7] and of Zhang Qingji 张清吉, who argued that Ding Yaokang 丁耀亢, a late Ming *jinshi* scholar, was the real author.[8]

In addition, Jin Xingyao 金性尧 proposed that the author was not Pu Songling, but Zhangqiu,[9] and Tong Wanzhou 童万周 argued that the author might be a long-time follower of Li Cuiran 李粹然.[10] More recently, Liu Hongqiang 刘洪强 has stated that the author is a Zhangqiu scholar.[11] Unfortunately, due to the poor communication between academics on both sides of the Taiwan Strait before and after the Cultural Revolution, we cannot determine whether the various early hypotheses were inspired by relevant research by scholars on the other side of the Strait. For example, the "Ding Yaokang hypothesis" was first proposed in the mainland in 1962 in *A History of Chinese Literature*,[12] compiled by the Institute of Literature of the Chinese Academy of Social Sciences, and was later developed by Tian Pu 田璞[13] and Zhang Qingji in the mid-to-late 1980s. However, scholars in Taiwan, namely Wang Sucun 王素存[14] and Liu Jieping 刘阶平,[15] had put forward this hypothesis early on.

However creative those papers may be, it ought to be pointed out that the most serious works about *XSYYZ*—from the 1930s onwards—were overwhelmingly textual research. Following Hu Shih's lead, scholars' endeavors and undertakings were absorbed by intense arguments about authorship, versions, and periodization. That such a highly respected figure in Chinese intellectual history would roll up his sleeves, write some 30,000 words to address the unknown authorship, and bring up the hypothesis that Pu Songling was the author had only boosted this trend, though not in a plausible way. Hu's hypothesis, by any measure, was not based on solid, infallible evidence—as was the case with his *Textual Research on A Dream of Red Mansions* 红楼梦考证, which had much success in identifying Cao Xueqin 曹雪芹 as the ultimate author. Nevertheless, the fallibility of his "Pu Songling hypothesis" has been, in a strange way, very entertaining for academia, in both the past and present. Putting agreement or disagreement on such a proposition aside, the glamour of being part of a project initiated by a master scholar is tempting. It draws talents to become textual researchers, many of whom have willingly ignored Hu Shih's closing remarks that *XSYYZ* is more socio-economically and historically valuable than it is textually and literarily.

Even Hu Shih himself detoured from the path of methodology he originally had begun to tread. Not so different from later textual researchers, Hu also pounded heavily on the Novel's textology, authorship, and versions. Having approbated the studies of the "history of the seventeenth-century Chinese social customs" eagerly, Hu Shih indulged in textual research in his late years. He was perceived by his biographer Jerome Grieder as "a disappointing figure, vaingloriously parading the reputation earned in an earlier and more propitious era." Yet in the same vein, Grieder also sees him as "a profoundly disappointed man."[16] Many researchers of Hu Shih, his favorite disciples included, ascribed Hu's failure to ascend to a higher academic level to his lifelong fondness for textology.[17] Given the profound influence Hu Shih had on Chinese academics, particularly the studies of *XSYYZ*, Hu's penchant for textology and its subsequent detrimental effects must be made known first.

The zeal for engaging in textology, not only of Hu Shih but also of Chinese researchers in general, is rarely shared by their Western counterparts. Andrew Plaks dismisses the "Pu Songling hypothesis" by Hu Shih as "discredited," "inconclusive," and "fanciful," and that of Hu's detractors as "equally based on circumstantial grounds, and do(ing) little to clear up the issue."[18] Yenna Wu 吴燕娜, while acknowledging the contribution made by Sun Kaidi in identifying the Novel's latest possible date of completion as 1661, states, "no hard evidence is available to resolve the controversy on authorship."[19]

Taiwanese scholars Chun-shu Chang 张春树 and his wife Shelley Hsueh-lun Chang 骆雪伦, both of the University of Michigan, are familiar with the controversy over the authorship of *XSYYZ*. They have taken a chronological approach to the controversial issue, with brief comments on the main arguments in each period. As they come from Taiwan, they can also comment on the findings of scholars from Taiwan, as in the case of Zhu Yanjing's 朱燕静 master's thesis at National Taiwan University in 1978, which refutes both the "Pu Songling hypothesis" and the "Ding Yaokang hypothesis."[20] Chun-shu Chang and Shelley Hsueh-lun Chang argue that, although Hu Shih's "Pu Songling hypothesis" has been challenged, "there is no external evidence to prove it is wrong, and internal evidence only points to vague suppositions, such as the 'Ding Yaokang hypothesis.'" Mr. and Mrs. Chang emphasize textual research of a scientific experimental nature. Their article refers to a 1985 study by Taiwanese scholar Chen Bingzao 陈炳藻, which uses the computer to analyze the differences between the nouns used in Pu Songling's slang music and *XSYYZ*.[21] It also recommends another study that uses purely grammatical analysis to compare the differences between the two texts. The Changs come to the verdict that these two studies could prove the difference between the writing styles of Pu Songling and Xizhou Sheng. Therefore Up untill then, the "Pu Songling hypothesis" was "proven problematic."[22]

Glen Dudbridge 杜德桥, a British scholar and a long-time teacher at both Cambridge and Oxford Universities, tries to use Sujie's Mount Tai pilgrimage as a source for his study of seventeenth-century folk travel in China. In terms of his long paper *A Pilgrimage in Seventeenth-Century Fiction: T'ai-shan and the Hsing-shih yin-yüan chuan*, published in the *T'oung Pao* in 1991,[23] he is well-versed in the versions and authorship research on *XSYYZ* in mainland China, Taiwan, and overseas. In *XSYYZ* studies, usually not considered prominent, versions and authorship research have always been quite "prominent" in the academic community on both sides of the Taiwan Strait. As early as the 1980s and early 1990s, overseas researchers had the advantage of broader information access and could review various research results. Still, no one specialized in them, let alone proposed an innovative authorship hypothesis. It is indeed a thought-provoking phenomenon.

One of the most popular activities in studying Chinese classical novels is formulating innovative hypotheses about authorship; the more famous the novel, the more intense the hypotheses. Researchers mainly focus on three outstanding works: *A Dream of Red Mansions*, *Jin Ping Mei*, and *XSYYZ*. Such innovative hypotheses, however, often cite only one or two similarities between the real author and the hypothetical author and give far-fetched evidence without logical persuasiveness. According to Yan Zhong 严中, a Nanjing scholar of *A Dream of Red Mansions*, 63 people, in addition to Cao Xueqin, have been considered to be the author of *A Dream of Red Mansions* by various researchers since the beginning of the Qianlong fifties (1785). What underlies this phenomenon is, in fact, a chain of interests in the research of *A Dream of Red Mansions*, which has enticed laypeople to take a share. For example, Mao Lianquan 冒廉泉, a descendant of Mao Pijiang 冒辟疆, wanted to prove that the author of *A Dream of Red Mansions* was Mao Pijiang since he saw that the copyright of *A Dream of Red Mansions* was "a matter of interest." He said:

> *A Dream of Red Mansions* and other works of Cao Xueqin, researched and verified by Hu Shih, are printed in millions of copies each year. Red Mansions and other attractions of Cao Xueqin identified by Hu Shih, receive tens of millions of visitors each year, forming a huge industrial chain and interest group.... Discrediting Hu Shih's identification that Cao Xueqin is the author of *A Dream of Red Mansions* and arguing for Mao Pijiang penning *A Dream of Red Mansions* with the pseudonym Cao Xueqin will affect the vital interests of many regions and groups.[24]

The unknown authorship troubles us less, however, than the issue of an obscure periodization that has been a Gordian knot in my construction of this work. Duan Jiangli 段江丽, Xia Wei 夏薇, Zou Zongliang 邹宗良, and Xu Fuling all engaged in the discussion on when the Novel was written. Nevertheless, we deem Yang Dongfang's 杨东方 viewpoint the most just and sound:

> There is still a lack of material evidence dating the book, so we can only say in general that it is a work of the late Ming and early Qing dynasties, which is the most appropriate and desirable attitude.[25]

As such, we must establish a timeline in history to accommodate the context of the narrative. Hu Shih's identification of Pu Songling (1640–1715) as the author inevitably stamped on the Novel the mark of the seventeenth century, which had witnessed the regime transition from Ming to Qing. Yet the seventeenth century was a turbulent time. Split by the Qing conquest of 1644, the former and the latter half of the century were drastically different regarding their social constitutions. Their ethoses were mutually opposing. The late Ming was a captive of material culture, eschatological and concupiscent in terms of the living style of the middle and upper classes, and quite ignorant of the heightened sufferings of the poor. The early Qing was a period of political and moral reconstruction, which gave the material culture a tinge of puritanism, but the livelihood of the lower stratum of the society was certainly improved. Judging from the richness of the material culture depicted, and on the grounds of the absence of even the slightest hint of dynastic change in the Novel, one can reasonably argue that it was written at least 50 years prior to the anachronistic "Pu Songling as the author" periodization.

In the sixth chapter of *XSYYZ*, a couplet is cited in the narration of the birthday feast of Wang Zhen, a eunuch of the Silijian (the Imperial Ceremony Office 司礼监), which reads, "The Emperor's grace is as deep as the sea; The minister's integrity is as heavy as a mountain." The couplet was composed by Hong Chengchou 洪承畴 during the period when he was enjoying the grace of Chongzhen (1628–1644). Hong later surrendered to the Qing after the Battle of Songjin in 1642. In addition, there is a reference to Li Cuiran, a stationed deputy envoy, providing relief to the victims in Xiujiang 绣江 (Zhangqiu) in the 31st chapter. Li Cuiran was a real person in the late Ming dynasty, having served as a magistrate in Zichuan from the first to the third year of the Tianqi era (1621–1623). The central part of Xizhou Sheng's life would have been in the first half of the seventeenth century. It is possible that he lived through the overthrow of the Ming by the Qing. There are three possible reasons why this significant historical fact is not reflected in the Novel: the first is to avoid political disaster, the second is that this historical event is irrelevant to the theme of the *XSYYZ*, and the third is that the main body of the Novel was already completed around the time of the Qing soldiers' entry into the country.

2. The Merits of *XSYYZ* and its Value as a Historical Reference

Not many classical Chinese novels are eligible to be labeled as "panoramic novels." Even fewer boast the most penetrating insights and the best literary techniques that combine to illustrate the societies from which they were derived. The twin crown jewels in this category are *A Dream of Red Mansions* and *Jin Ping Mei*. However, three characteristics of *XSYYZ* have made it different from, and in a sense superior to, the classics mentioned above:

First, *XSYYZ* is a full-fledged novel. It has a persistent and independent theme running through the entire composition. The plots (divided into two parallel episodes) are generic and creative, unlike *Jin Ping Mei's* scrounging of its opening plot from *Water Margin*, or the *Romance of the Three Kingdoms'* basing its composition on the long-circulated vernacular scripts.

Second, *XSYYZ* is a completed novel by the same author. It thus boasts better continuity, integrity, and consistency than the half-finished *A Dream of Red Mansions* or other novels adulterated by the hands of too many editors and re-writers.

Third, *XSYYZ* is an example of a Ming writer addressing Ming concerns in a Ming setting. None of the great pre-modern novels can claim such an unparalleled contemporaneity. For all its comprehensiveness in covering the Ming society, *Jin Ping Mei* lays its fictional backdrop in the Northern Song. In contrast, *A Dream of Red Mansions* declares that "no specific dynasty is referenced" at its opening. On the other hand, the author Xizhou Sheng—whoever he might be—is himself a living encyclopedia of his society and breathing history of the Ming dynasty, which he addresses with much pride as *Guo Chao* 国朝, the National Dynasty. From the unaltered recording of a series of historical events, including the Tumu Fort Incident, the reader can reasonably deduce the author's freedom to express himself. That he comments on contemporary politics substantially means that the censoring system was less rigid, and the notorious literary inquisition might not have come into term—which constitutes another piece of evidence for the Novel's Ming attributes.

Some significant developments were taking effect that began to change the shape of the fiction genre. The last few decades of the Ming saw the gradual growth of a more broad-based audience for printed colloquial fiction, which included fine editions of vernacular plays and short stories published by the studios of Feng Menglong. As to saga novels, the Jiajing (1522–1566) and Wanli (1573–1620) reigns of the sixteenth century witnessed the completion of the four undisputed Ming masterpieces due to the appearance of *Xingshi Yinyuan Zhuan*.[26]

A well-known fact about the composition of *A Dream of Red Mansions* is that Cao Xueqin, in attempting to avoid the Qing literary inquisition, had to, in many circumstances, resort to innuendos and enantiosis, leaving a labyrinth of mysteries behind his work. Much as today's reader enjoys deciphering the "Cao Xueqin codes," he is compelled to simultaneously accept the work's discounted historical fidelity. Fortunately, this is not the case with *XSYYZ*. A work born from a loose censorial environment is bound to render more accurate, richer details of the society in which its contents dwell. When circumstances do not necessitate the author to harbor criticisms of his society under the cover of allusions and insinuations, its historical—albeit not necessarily literary—value is usually higher than those written under the jaws of literary imputation.

Still, a novel's value as a historical reference is not guaranteed simply through its sheer luck of escaping censorship. Instead, the rich details it weaves into every fiber of its composition make it appealing to historical researchers.

However, to what extent can a historian excurse into the territory of literature? How does one justify that his or her study could have been founded on the seemingly inexhaustible warehouse of historical materials, but he or she instead ventured into the field of literature to unearth history anyway? Should such a situation arise, how does one distinguish his or her research from the literary critiques made of the same work? Those questions are what this book is determined to address, and the answers to which lay scattered along the trail this project travels. The previous scholarship by Glen Dudbridge has also puzzled over those questions. Dudbridge highlights the value of *XSYYZ*'s "dedication of two of its 100 chapters to a group trip to Mount Tai by women from the Shandong countryside." As the text describes, "It shows the formation of their group under female religious leadership, the financial preparations and planned coordination with local tour operators, and the physical hardships and ritual devotions along the way."[27] Such information is already rare, but the "domestic tensions" between women and their families in pursuit of the right to travel, and "the subtle colourings of class distinction" of the group under the apparently universal spirit of non-discrimination, as reflected in the text, are so fascinating that the historian, who is inclined towards social history, admits that "to the historian or sociologist of pilgrimage this must seem an inviting morsel."[28]

However, Dudbridge is also fully aware that using literary texts as a "source" for sociological research would pose certain "notorious difficulties" for researchers. He then falls back on an assessment made by his colleague Andrew H. Plaks of Princeton University, who has studied the narratives of classical Chinese novels, that the book involves both "thorough realism, like capturing all details with a camera lens," and the author's imagination, "wandering and lost outside the boundary of realistic description."[29] It is inevitably a challenging test for the researcher, who is bound to be of two minds about the text: one cannot disbelieve what is written, nor can one completely believe what is written. Dudbridge suggests two ways of dealing with this: first, to examine the fictional descriptions in relation to the actual historical material; second, to systematically perceive the "frank and lively value-judgments" used by the author in the text.[30]

We do not differ from Professor Dudbridge's proposal. Still, we want to demonstrate why there is a need to link historical research to literature and how the latter can be significantly utilized by the former.

The headwaters of Chinese historiography are inseparable from those of Chinese literature. *Zuo's Commentary on the Spring and Autumn Annals* 左传, *Strategies of the Warring States* 战国策, and *Records of the Grand Historian* 史记 are as great as historiographies as they are as literary works. It was the glamour and grace that shone from the eminence of the pre-Qin historical writings such as *The Biography of Jingke, the Assassin* that made them the targets of emulation by essay writers of the dynasties to come, especially in the Tang and Song. Good historical writings are planted with the germ of literary quality, and great historical writings must, in turn, be sustained by great literacy. The same rules apply to the Chinese historiographers' Western peers: Homer, Herodotus, and Thucydides. Similarly, their works nourished the proud tradition of both Western history and literature.

I find an analogy uttered by modern novelist Eileen Chang's 张爱玲 an appealing argument, as it bolsters that of mine previously mentioned. In her memoir recording British Hong Kong's capitulation to Japan in 1941, she induces the reader to visualize what history would look like when a historiographer is experiencing it. Instead of grasping the weight and accuracy of history, Zhang argues, a historiographer is more likely to run into a paradox as described below:

> The reality is utterly unsystematic, much like seven or eight phonographs each singing on its own, a chorus of chaos. There are, however, moments like crystals among the inextricable bedlam, cleansing one's heart and eyes and making one want to cry. . . . History, when paying too much attention to details, becomes novel.[31]

Conversely, we suggest, a novel, when boasting staggeringly rich details of the society it depicts, becomes history. Fernand Braudel, the foremost post-war French historian, in writing his *La Méditerranée et le Monde Méditerranéen a l'époque de Philippe II* [*The Mediterranean and the Mediterranean World in the Age of Philip II*],[32] sets a great example of "historical materialism." History, according to Braudel, is beyond the manipulation of its conscious actors, a corresponding term in Chinese historiography being *diwangjiangxiang* 帝王将相, or emperors, kings, generals, and ministers. The infrastructure is as vital as the superstructure; combined efforts reflect the enduring social, economic, and cultural realities. We particularly applaud Braudel's light on the ephemeral lives of the poor and the marginalized and his attention paid to food, fashion, and social customs. The Annales School believes deviating from "orthodox" historiography can remedy canonical historical narratives. If the latter's tendencies of over-emphasizing high-state affairs, clashes between cliques, struggles among the imperial consorts, and dynastic successions are to be redressed, we must not be parsimonious in feeding the reader information about the lives of the common and the ephemeral.

Liang Qichao sarcastically calls China's "Twenty-Four Histories" the "genealogy of the twenty-four surnames." Liang considers the mentality of traditional Chinese historians to be undesirable: "The country is the emperor's country alone, so his history is nothing but a narrative of how a certain dynasty gained, ruled and lost."[33] In 1920, Li Dazhao, a pioneer of the materialist school of history, attacked the old paradigm of history writing: "The old Chinese histories, which contained little more than the lives and genealogies of emperors and nobles, were quite empty of social and cultural aspects."[34] Indeed, historical scriptures have always devoted too much ink to the record of royal political affairs, party rivalries, concubine ambitions, and dynastic changes. The traditional historians' reluctance to engage with historical novels and anecdotal histories, and their refusal to refer to sketchy notes, dramas, and novels, are not so much influenced by a hereditary monarchy that gives the emperor's family absolute power as they are the result of China's long-standing philosophy of history compilation. A Ming dynasty historian would believe that the only way to ensure that his writings went down in history was to follow the *Records of the Grand Historian* and *The Book of Han*. He certainly did not intend to focus on grassroots gossip and everyday life more than the *Essay* on *Price Balancing* [Ping Zhun Shu 平准] in *Records of the Grand Historian* and *Monograph on Food and Currency* 食货 in *The Book of Han*. In the words of Ban Gu, "the reach of those trivial bits of knowledge stems from examining details" (*The Book of Han—Record of Art and Culture* 汉书·艺文志), and those of Confucius's brilliant disciple Zi Xia, "Even trivial skills must have merits, but only focusing on these will hinder one from a great career"[35] (*The Analects of Confucius—Zi Zhang* 论语·子张). Both statements refer to the content and form of historical writings not recognized by official history writers.

Is official history truly noble, dignified, and infallible? The German Rankean historiography, which emerged in the nineteenth century, significantly impacted modern Chinese historiography. Its basic approach was to attach importance to primary sources and political histories. The emphasis on political histories is consistent with the tradition of Chinese historiography and thus is nothing new, but its focus on primary sources, especially annals and archival documents, is what traditional Chinese historiography lacks. In terms of the status of historiography, this German textual research school, known as "scientific historiography," came to the fore, replacing—at least partially—the original Chinese historiographical tradition in a time of tremendous change. It can, therefore, also be regarded as a modern school of Chinese official history. After the May Fourth Movement, the "scientific history" advertised by Tsinghua University and Peking University's history departments came from Ranke. The leading figures among them were Zhang Guiyong (Zhiyuan) 张贵永 and Yao Congwu 姚从吾. After 1949 when they taught in Taiwan, they still regarded Ranke as their teaching focus. Yao always talked about Ranke and would list Ranke's German writings on the blackboards in his lectures on Western historiography. Ranke's approach to historiography was also fully endorsed by Fu Sinian 傅斯年, a leading scholar in both the mainland and Taiwan. Before the Second Sino-Japanese War, Fu told Zhang Guiyong that the Institute of History and Philology of the Academia Sinica, which Fu had founded, was based on the brilliant traditions of Sinology and the German textual research school. His ambition was to "build history to be the same as biology and geology." After the modern institutionalization and specialization of Chinese historical research, the academia produced papers and books that featured "scientific reports," assessed by their scientific qualities. Historical research became almost identical to scientific work.[36] In fact, Rankean historiography predated the birth of Ranke and originated in the eighteenth century in European historiography. Samuel Johnson, a famous English writer, made no secret of his contempt for such "mere chroniclers or compilers of official newspapers," saying that:

> True and authentic history is rare. That certain kings have ruled, or that certain wars have been fought, we may believe to be true; but all other additions,

all philosophies of history, are no more than conjectures. . . . History is but an almanac, a mere chronological string of notable events.[37]

As the ethos of scientific verification swept through European historiography in the nineteenth century, only British historiography continued to insist that history should complement literature and "adhere to an erudite academic style and an objective stance, as well as to the simplicity, clarity and elegance of style," all of which is attributable to the legacy of Edward Gibbon's style.

History cannot be what it is without the millions of threads that weave it together. Today, the philosophy of history has changed, and the trivialities that official history writers ignored are now considered necessary. Where are the things that the official history writers could not and would not write then? Such items could only be found in historical fiction, anecdotal histories, sketchy notes, dramas, and novels. It would be difficult to draw a clear distinction between the literary and historical aspects of these texts. A paradox lies here. The unofficial histories, especially gossip and sketchy notes, were mainly based on street talk and gossip and contained anecdotes and trivia about famous people of the time. As they were intended to be read by public officials for inspection, scholars for recitation, and common people for leisure, the texts might often only be partially truthful, with mixed truths and rumors and far removed from the details of everyday life.

In contrast, true literary works, which were often strong in terms of describing worldly life, recorded the social life of the time in such detail that one could read them as if one were there. If the traditional Chinese historiographical inclination is to be revised, then we need to write profusely about the lives of ordinary people and the masses. It would be too inflexible to say that the literary materials of the historical era that we want to study cannot be used or are too untrustworthy to be used because of the distinction between literature and history that we have framed in our minds.

History does not have to be boring, scripture-like books of annotations and commentaries. As to genuine history, the more details there are it carries, the more moving it is. History does not have to be a family tree of emperors and generals. Sima Qian pursued a noble cause by recording the achievements of emperors in the *Records of the Grand Historian*. However, if people today still only referred to the yellowing pages of "Biographies" 列传 and "Chronicles" 本纪, and never cared about the happiness and sorrows, and the necessities of life of the common people, then, to put it mildly, the history researching mentality would be no better than it was in medieval times. And to put it seriously, this is going against modern mentalities. In studying the lives of ordinary people in history, one cannot avoid worldly life. And among the material lives of ordinary people, clothing, food, housing, and travel are the most vital concerns.

History cannot be written without a record of its "self-conscious performers," but it must not stop there. The left-wing German playwright and poet Bertolt Brecht once questioned in his poetry, in the tone of a "worker who reads":

The young Alexander conquered India./Did he do it alone?/Caesar beat the Gauls./Did he not have even a cook with him?/Philip of Spain wept when his armada/Went down. Did he weep alone?/Frederick the Second won the Seven Year's War. Who/Else won it?[38]

Indeed, history cannot be written without recording the performances of its conscious actors, but it should not only be about them. Tang Te-kang 唐德刚, a highly regarded modern Chinese historian, adopts a metaphor to illustrate the nature of history. Suppose, as Tang remarks, we were to watch the spectacular scenery of the Qiantang Tide. Are we here as tourists of the Qiantang River, to watch the awe-inspiring tide coming with the mightiness of the open sea and its echoed billows or to amuse ourselves by watching the frolicking boys surfing up and down the waves? No doubt that the surfing boys' skills, that they can "stand still and not spill water on the red flags in their hands" 手把红旗旗不湿, are admirable. However, suppose one indulges oneself in the children's show of the surfing boys and forgets to pay attention to the real beauty of nature, that of the Qiantang Tide. In that case, the maturity of the observer is no more than that of a child.[39] Tang's analogy of the Tide to history, cogently formulated, also allegorizes the surfing boys to *diwangjiangxiang*, each of whom, be it Confucius, the Duke of Zhou, the First Emperor of Qin, or Emperor Wu of Han, is but one of a group of conscious players. "All the world's a stage; And all the men and women merely players," says Shakespeare.[40] They ride on history, marching and parading, creating spectacles, but they cannot alter the ultimate trend of that history. Therefore, the observers, "we," conscious historiographers, are responsible for noting not just the artificial spectacle displayed by those surfing boys but also the natural wonder of the mightiness of the Tide.

That is not to say, however, that we should downplay the importance of history's conscious actors by overlooking their deeds. In this introductory chapter, we would like to make it as explicit as possible that the conscious actors are of great faculty in molding the ethos of their respective societies, particularly, in the Ming's case, the founding emperor, Hongwu (1368–1398). Sometimes the measures they took checked social progress, violated economic rules, and affected the populace's lives gravely, resulting in regressions in almost every social and economic corner. In the late Ming dynasty, as we shall see, the eschatological Epicureanism had become a daring defection from the puritanical tone set by the founding emperor. On the other hand, the residues of a sumptuary economic framework remained resilient and could deform rules of economics to the degree that would have amazed Adam Smith. Hence, this project also takes an interest in investigating the wrestling of history's normal tendency with socio-economic development and the firm will of the Ming founding emperor in shaping his empire into a utopia of autarkic yeomanry. Yet the study must limit its scope so that it only inquiries into the domain of material culture, evidenced mainly by *XSYYZ*. There has not been another piece of literature, *Peach Blossom Spring* included, which extols the utopian spirit with such profond enthusiasm. The depiction of Mingshui as a paradise of yeomanry most loyally renders the vision of Emperor Hongwu's ideal rural country.

If Hongwu were to live in the era of Xizhou Sheng, he would have been as baffled and vexed as the author, discovering that his old, orderly world had been transformed into a fluid, dynamic society dominated by monetary factors. The social hierarchies were collapsing, and the social boundaries between the nobles and commoners were frequently infringed. This disorder was primarily demonstrated in the "four major concerns of the people's livelihood." That is, when it came to material comforts, commoners' secular pursuits for better clothing, food, housing, and travel had overcome the prescriptive institutions intended to subject them to pristine living conditions.

XSYYZ takes trouble in rendering such a society undergoing shocking transformations. The author vividly delineates the agony of the previously rich and noble and the elation of the formerly poor and despised in the presence of unpredictable social mobility, all on the substantial changes in their material lives. The author's passion for deciphering a Ming Ukiyoe is vast, and the attention he paid to the details is colossal. A parallel obsession with the "portrayal of things" can only be found in the near material-fetishism of *Jin Ping Mei*, which Naifei Ding rightly calls "a narrative economy of excess and luxurious consumption . . . a mania for objects insofar as they always and already are the signs of what makes them objects."[41] *XSYYZ* has been so zealously engaged in the depiction of details that sometimes it seems to be impedimental to the fluidity of the narrative. The difference between the two works is that while *Jin Ping Mei* lavishes its ink on "luxurious consumption," *XSYYZ* takes more interests in the lives of the well-to-do peasantry and urban commoners.

3. Methods and Sources

This project will be a continuation of the untarnished project once advocated, but eventually abandoned, by Hu Shih. It will strive to comb through the raw materials so afforded by *XSYYZ*. In navigating the material culture of the Ming society, it will highlight the issues of clothing, food, and travel—three of the "four major concerns of people's livelihood," *yishizhuxing* 衣食住行. Still, it will also shed significant, if not equal, light on folk customs, legal and religious practices, and women's status, among other issues. It frequents economic dimensions and probes Ming politics' impacts on the Ming ethos and social economy.

Limited by the scarcity of the available materials regarding housing in *XSYYZ*, this project does not concern itself with the study of housing, one of the people's four vital concerns. It also singles out "Luxury economics and the financial system" as an individual chapter. The subtraction and addition of these topics in the structure are of a calculated design, not the result of redundancy. Neither practically nor theoretically can a thorough survey of Ming material history be done within the length of a monograph. Therefore, in dealing with such a profound topic, we first found our footing upon what material was available, then determined the scope of the issues that both awaited and merited scholarly attention.

Although "housing" is one of the four vital concerns, we must forgo this severely under-represented area due to having limited the material to *XSYYZ*. Also, many items depicted in the Novel, mostly related to luxury goods, cannot be classified as any of the four vital concerns. Therefore, we devote a chapter to the textual research of names and descriptions of these luxury goods, the relationship between the sumptuary ethos and legislation, and how it impeded economic development. Since the financial system of the late Ming dynasty seemed prosperous but stagnated, we will discuss the issues of exchange, silver, and coinage together in this chapter.

As the variation in the published editions of *XSYYZ* hardly holds any significance to this research, and as this study intends to become the opposite of previous textological endeavors, it will limit itself to one modern edition when quoting from the original text.[42] The edition, published by Qilu Press 齐鲁书社 of Jinan, Shandong, in 1993, is primarily based on the Tongdetang 同德堂 edition of the Beijing Capital Library, the most comprehensive version known to modern researchers, and supplemented by a reprint edition of the Tongzhi reign (1862–1874) and the Yadong Library edition.[43] Its clear-cut layout, modern punctuation, and the use of simplified characters render it an ideal version for readers and researchers of a mainland Chinese background. For the sake of brevity, we will not annotate each quotation from *XSYYZ*, but only mark the chapter numbers and pages with Arabic numerals in parentheses after the text, separated by dots.

A partial translation of *XSYYZ*, Eve Alison Nyren's *The Bonds of Matrimony*,[44] renders the first 20 chapters into English. It has been a ready resource when we reference original texts within that range, but for the remainder of the chapters, the translation is rendered by this author.

While we will avoid a detailed introduction to versions and editions of *XSYYZ*, we would nevertheless like to recommend two pieces of research done by Li Guoqing 李国庆, who combed through all of the existing editions and offered valuable pointers as to where those versions can be located,[45] and Yang Chunyu 杨春宇, who conducted several field trips to a number of China's libraries to investigate the different editions.[46]

While this book intends to avoid a tedious investigation of editions, authors, and dates, it is not our intention to "skip explaining words and phrases to directly seek the meanings of the text,"[47] as a monograph on material life cannot get around the explanation of historical texts. On the contrary, we want to pursue the Qing Confucian way of "understanding the meaning of historical texts through interpreting words and phrases" and "exploring historical texts for further investigation." Behind the names and descriptions are people and systems and vibrant social material life. We in no way intend to contradict the interpretation of the names and descriptions or the search for textual meanings.

We have become aware that the scarcity of the preceding works linking the Novel to the Ming "social economy, historiography and folk culture studies" has presented this project with both new opportunities and challenges. It offers new frontiers waiting to be tamed but also warns of barren territories to be plodded through by individual effort. To specify the nature of this study, it is necessary to introduce recent academic works on related topics.

Among the Chinese works, a noticeable piece is Xia Wei's *Research on Xingshi Yinyuan Zhuan*, initially a Ph.D. dissertation supervised by Ma Ruifang, a Pu Songling specialist, of Shandong University.[48] It spends a considerable length of its chapters reinvestigating the issue of periodization, which, according to Xia, falls

16 Introduction

between the fourth year of the Yongzheng Reign (1726) and the 57th year of the Qianlong Reign (1792), a theory already amply rebutted by domestic researchers. Xia also takes great interest in analyzing the love relationship between Xue Sujie and Di Xichen, which she construes as sadomasochistic/masochistic by borrowing modern Freudian theories. Switching from a henpecking stereotype to the S/M supposition is a smart extrication from existing clichés. Still, the plethora of psychoanalysis undermines the value of the scholarship as a serious literary critique.

A study of the same name and nature is Duan Jiangli's 2003 edition of the Yuelu Press, which focuses on a literary-based analysis of *XSYYZ*'s narrative art but also addresses issues such as editions, characterization, gender relations, and the concept of karmic retribution. Both Xia and Duan's books originated from doctoral dissertations as literature majors, so a literary orientation in these cases is naturally appropriate. The most recent research, *Xingshi Yinyuan Zhuan and the Secular Life of the Ming Dynasty*, was published in 2017 by Wu Xiaolong.[49] The book is similar, to an extent, to this one in its nature. In terms of research methods, it pays more attention to the interpretation of specific folk customs, yet it lacks in-depth construction on the economic dynamics behind the social phenomena.

As for English publications, the diligent Yenna Wu of the University of California at Riverside has dedicated many of her scholastic writings to the critique of Chinese henpecking literature, of which *XSYYZ* constitutes a significant part. Her first book, *Ameliorative Satire and the Seventeenth-Century Chinese Novel, Xingshi Yinyuan Zhuan-Marriage as Retribution, Awakening the World, a Literary Critique to Xingshi Yinyuan Zhuan and the Ameliorative Style*,[50] based on her Harvard dissertation as a comparative literature major, scrutinizes the Novel from many perspectives, particularly the feature of its ameliorative satire. Although this book offers the most comprehensive English introduction to the Novel, including a chapter-by-chapter summary of its content, the methodology adopted and the ultimate research targets aimed are literary, not historical. Wu's other work, *The Chinese Virago*,[51] handles the permeability of the boundaries between literary and historical sources in an even trickier fashion. Apart from the monumental *XSYYZ*, jokes, sketch-writings, and anecdotes are all used by Wu in her psychological analysis of the cultivation of Chinese virago. Amply quoted, studied, and analyzed, the Novel nonetheless only functions to provide, to Wu's study of viragos, literary prototypes of henpecking women, among which the ferocity of Sujie, the heroine of the Novel, surpasses that of the other female figures. Her "Repetition in *Xingshi Yinyuan Zhuan*,"[52] another article published by the *Harvard Journal of Asiatic Studies (HJAS)*, exploits the Novel by highlighting repetition, a unique literary technique it has adopted. Thus, this research falls into the category of literary criticism once again. Andrew H. Plaks of Princeton University has argued in one of his articles that the novel deserves more attention from the researchers of seventeenth-century Chinese fiction.[53] Keith McMahon of the University of Kansas examines the phenomenon of Chinese polygamy by referencing the novel.[54] *Reorientation of Jinpingmei and Xingshiyinyuan*,[55] a dissertation written by Yu-chun Yang, a Princeton graduate, juxtaposes the two great pieces in a thorough comparison of their literary themes, moral didacticism, aesthetic tastes, and their contributions to Chinese literature. However, in general, these research endeavors embark from either the shore of literary critiques or gender studies, shedding light within the scopes of literary representation, maneuvers of writing, or women's social conditions. Although the literary prototypes have been abundantly studied, the material culture of the seventeenth century embedded in the composition has not.

Among the English reference books this work is to consult, the only monograph not entirely derived from a literary perspective, Daria Berg's *Carnival in China: A Reading of the Xingshi Yinyuan Zhuan*,[56] still views the Novel as a "dystopian satire." Though the work is not without its literary touch, Berg manages to lead the reader to access three realms: a topsy-turvy world of physicians, bell doctors, the clergy, and lay healers; an elite world of students, teachers, scholar-merchants, patrons of scholarship, and scholar-officials; and a world of reformers, saints, and saviors. Through the fictitious lens, Berg's work constructs, construes, and analyzes what she defines as a dystopian world by placing the three types of personalities into their respective realm. She looks beyond the fictional discourse and carefully links the Novel's objects of praise and condemnation with similar concerns in contemporary non-fictional works to achieve "glimpses of perceived reality."[57] Her approach is to "demonstrate that many types of characters developed in the Novel correspond neatly with real figures and problems discussed by other seventeenth-century writers."[58] Berg's work is the closest one could find to construe seventeenth-century Chinese social customs from *XSYYZ*, but more from a popular cultural—and not historical—footing. We deem it essential to exploit both orthodox and unorthodox historiographies. They both reflect arbitrary versions of the perceived historical reality by their narrators. Therefore, despite their differences in styles and rhetoric, they must be treated with equal mindfulness to differentiate ideological discourses from accounts of facts. The fictional narrative comes close to unorthodox historiography when contextualizing history into its composition. Both types expound on salient material and social details that might elude official records. Their attention to non-high-state affairs, vernacular cultures, and informal aspects of secular life is, at times, much more valuable than their official state counterparts.

The historical sources about the Ming period—primarily written during the regime—are much more copious than those from any other dynasty. Despite the literary inquisitions during and after the Ming, historiographies, essays, biographies, and anthologies—in significant quantities and of good quality—were being produced, published, and preserved. The shorter gap between the Ming and the present day also helps explain the large quantity of surviving sources. Take a sourcebook edited by Wolfgang Franke, *An Introduction to the Sources of Ming History*,[59] as an example. This epitome of Ming bibliographical studies lists 800 or so primary sources written during the Ming, and roughly 900 local gazetteers. Such a stunning plethora of material must preclude any dissertation-length endeavor from contemplating an egalitarian treatment of all extant Ming records.

Of the pre-modern references, this work will frequent not only the state-sanctioned Veritable Records and official histories, but also sketch notes, memoirs, iconographies, scriptures, sutras, paintings, dramas, and fiction.

In the past, Xiong Damu 熊大木 stated in the preface to *The Romance of the Song Dynasty* 大宋演义 that "historical fiction and anecdotal histories are records of what the official histories lack."⁶⁰ Xiaohua Zhuren stated in the preface to *Ancient and Modern Wonders* 今古奇观 that "historical novels complement the official history."⁶¹ Cai Yuanfang 蔡元放 stated in the foreword to *Chronicles of the Eastern Zhou Kingdoms* 东周列国志 that "historical fiction is certainly a tributary of history with more interpreted elements."⁶² Finally, Xian Zhai Lao Ren stated in the preface to *The Scholars* that "historical fictions are a tributary of history, and reading such histories can improve one's understanding of history."⁶³ The words in these four prefaces all testify to the role of historical fiction in complementing official histories. Other unofficial histories are also likely to reach heights not achieved by official histories because of their attention to non-political events, popular culture, the underlying details of material and social life, and the hidden dimensions of secular life, often blind spots of official histories. There is, however, a general unwritten rule in Ming history studies that researchers should always take extra care when it comes to writings of the late Ming period, especially works produced during the late Ming and early Qing dynasties. Due to the replacement of the Ming by the Qing and the early Qing dynasty's literary inquisition, both orthodox and unorthodox historical sources should be used with caution.

The Ming dynasty produced far more historical materials about itself than previous dynasties. Although the literary inquisition prevailed during both the Ming dynasty and the following Qing dynasty, the quality and quantity of the historical texts produced during both dynasties can be commended. In addition, the chronological proximity between the Ming and the present and the development of publishing make it less likely for written texts to be lost over time, which also explains the abundance of historical texts from the Ming dynasty. Take the German Sinologist Wolfgang Franke's *An Introduction to the Sources of Ming History*⁶⁴ as an example. This bibliographical collection of Ming studies contains over 800 entries on books written during the Ming dynasty and over 900 local chronicles. Wolfgang Franke's bibliography, however, is dwarfed by *A Study of Late Ming Historical Texts*⁶⁵ by Xie Guozhen 谢国桢, a scholar in the Republic of China. Xie Guozhen's bibliography was written when he was working in the Peiping Library and was inspired and guided by Liang Qichao. Xie recorded more than 1,140 documents from the Wanli reign of the Ming dynasty to the Kangxi reign of the Qing dynasty (1573–1722) and more than 620 unseen bibliographies. The breadth of his collection is more than a dissertation-length study could attempt to encompass.

It is often difficult to isolate the ideological meaning of the discourse from its factual parts. This period of history experienced internal and external pressures unseen in previous generations, and writers' and historians' perspectives, positions, and mindsets were susceptible to distortion under such pressure.

Therefore, we will be mindful of the extent of historical faithfulness that such works offer, as some were written to promulgate certain moralistic discourses, and some took the same political stance as the new regime, the Qing, and were designed to please the Manchu conquerors. Works borne of moral didacticism and biased political views did not offer a comprehensive survey of the moral and political worlds around them. Still, concerning material life, they were often objective. The flood of the late Ming "world-admonishing" 警世 works, harboring as they did no fondness for the debauchery of the world they criticized, never tired of depicting exactly how corrupt and debauched that world was. Ming loyalists, unable to vent their political sentiments, could escape censorial authorities by writing "perfunctory" specifics of their pre-Qing life as connoisseurs of fine food, women, or curiosities. Even the pro-Qing apostates, when releasing state-sanctioned utterances explaining what had befallen the Ming, would rely on lengthy portraits of late Ming materialism, which they thought were responsible for the dynasty's demise.

Fu Sinian, when talking about the relative value of historical materials, has proposed the research method of mutual verification of historical materials, namely direct historical materials against indirect historical materials, official records against folk records, national records against foreign records, recent records against ancient records, unintentional records against intentional records, the thing itself against related matters, plain narrative against metaphor, and oral historical materials against written historical materials.[66] Although this book may not exhaust all eight pairs and sixteen categories of historical materials, we will pay attention to using "counterpoint" historical materials wherever we can adopt a "counterpoint" perspective.

This book visits modern English works produced by Western Sinology more than it does with their Chinese counterparts. Ray Huang, Timothy Brook, Craig Clunas 柯律格, Cynthia Brokaw, Susan Naquin, and Daria Berg have pioneered the studies of Ming material history on multiple fronts. In many ways, their works represent a Sinological trend to remedy Chinese histography's plethora of moral considerations, moral justifications, and moral explanations. This author is greatly indebted to Huang's method of garnering and utilizing useful information about Ming commercialism from literary works,[67] Brook's view about economic impacts on social and cultural life, and Brokaw's approach[68] to including the Buddhist notions of karma, retribution into the examination of the Ledgers of Merit and Demerit. Likewise, Naquin[69] and Berg's[70] cultural analysis of the representative figures and characters in *XSYYZ* are of great referential value to this project. Distinctions between this undertaking and the preceding works on the Ming material history, however, are apparent. None of the academic inquiries generated from the previously mentioned works, except those of Berg, have systematically trodden the material world of *XSYYZ*; Berg's work has ventured into that world but left the material concerns of clothing, food, and travel untouched. More to the point, none has concerned itself with explaining the Ming material culture through the lens of sumptuary legislation and ethos.

Since the 1990s, English academics have witnessed an increasing interest in Chinese women's studies. With many decent works being produced that reveal Chinese women's living status in areas still relatively unknown to modern scholars, Chinese women's studies have entered into what Pao Xiaolan 鲍晓兰 calls "a phase of an advanced stage."[71] These works include scholarships on midwives, lesbians, shrews, and female students studying abroad. Among a pocket of prolific researchers, we take notice of Dorothy Ko 高彦颐, Yenna Wu, and Francesca Bray 白馥兰 because their works deal with the Late Imperial era, which overlaps with the time frame of my proposed study area, the Ming dynasty. Although this work is less concerned about women's issues than material culture, it still can benefit from Ko's historical perspective on elite women's culture, Wu's literary focus on the images of shrews, and Bray's highlighting of women's contributions concerning technology. As *XSYYZ* is primarily a literary work that deals with marital institutions, there are occasions when we address family issues, the status of slaves, and gender relationships, and we shall encapsulate them mainly in the "What Drives People to Sell their Daughters" section of Chapter 1.

4. Summary of Chapters

Chapter 1 deals with the totality of the Ming clothing institution as reflected by *XSYYZ*. By the time of the late Ming, social boundaries previously demarcated by law enforcement and social convention on apparel and accouterments were increasingly infringed, trespassed, and violated, causing anxieties among the once rich and dignified. Eunuchs who basked in imperial patronage, ministers who ascended to office through bribery, artisans who quickly amassed fortunes by selling counterfeit products, opera actors who overtly disregarded the intended denigration of their dress codes, doted-upon concubines who competed for favor with legitimate wives in domestic spheres, and deceased officials who were overdressed as City Gods—all of these constituted a kaleidoscopic world subversive to the trimly hierarchical one previously crafted by Emperor Hongwu. The pluralism of the clothing institution shattered the nerves of many, Xizhou Sheng the author included. Looking into this phenomenon, this chapter explores a society whose outlook was most perceptibly subject to fluid monetary factors. The chapter also concerns the living conditions of the extremely impoverished at the bottom of the Ming social pyramid. By asking the question "what drives people to sell their daughters?", it reveals a world where the urban destitute could not afford to buy their daughters a piece of winter clothing. To secure their children a warm winter, they had to sell them as maids to more affluent households. In the bleak world portrayed by the Novel, laborers and servants were sold in the market at appallingly low prices and petty business runners, peddlers, and artisans who had no social security to fall back on were reduced to bankruptcy at any business mishap. Therefore, this section also addresses the failure of the issue of what Mencius defines as "humane governance," which failed to meet the lowest requirement to sustain people's lives during bad years. Although Emperor Hongwu was arguably one of the most ardent adherents of Mencian doctrines, and although the Ming government had indeed strived to operate itself on such doctrines, the cases of Chunying and Little Zhenzhu, and many other cheap labor transactions, potently demonstrate that the "humane governance" creed, held dearly by the regime and its Confucianism-imbued elite souls, did not function well.

Chapter 2, "Luxury Consumption and Financial System," begins with a list of gifts prepared by Lady Tong for Di Xichen to present to his supervisors when he was about to leave for Chengdu as a prospective official. The textual studies of the enumerated names and descriptions of the luxury goods will be made. In addition to the research, this chapter discusses two broad sub-topics: a seemingly prosperous commercial society repressed by the sumptuary legislation and ethos, and the backwardness and chaos of the Ming financial system. In discussing the former, we emphasize the relationship between the decrees suppressing extravagant consumption—also known as the sumptuary legislation—and the sumptuary ethos. From the state's perspective, the series of prohibitions were designed to reserve specific clothing, accessories, food and wine vessels, carriages, and dwellings for the privileged, thus creating a hierarchical pyramid. Since farmers were nominally respected as the state's primary producers, they were placed high in the hierarchy, second to gentry scholars but above artisans and businessmen. All farmers, artisans, and businessmen were commoners who had to obey the gentry scholars, from the pool of which officials were selected to serve the central government and the emperor. It was a social order that the state desired to have. The ban on extravagance was merely a means of maintaining the needed social hierarchy. The sumptuary legislation did not necessarily reflect why the state would take legal actions to curb a luxury economy; instead, it served to stabilize the state-sponsored hierarchy.

The second half of Chapter 2 discusses the circulation of silver and coins shown in *XSYYZ* and proves that the "decuple coin" was the Tianqi Tongbao decuple coin. That silver had become the primary coin in sixteenth- to eighteenth-century China is a consensus among all scholars of Ming-Qing history. How shall we examine the circulation of silver in *XSYYZ*? It ought to be studied in comparison with gold. The monetary properties of gold and silver are endowed by nature. A series of comparisons shed light on the differences between silver and gold in their casting forms, popularity, and frequency of usage. To probe into the economic dimensions, Ming-Qing novels featuring everyday life can be used as cross-references with other historical materials of the same period. We compare the same phenomenon repeatedly against various sources and draw conclusions therefrom.

Chapter 2 also delves into a vital issue of Chinese financial history: whether there was a remote remittance system in the mid to late Ming. Regarding this question, it is essential to refer to other works of the Ming-Qing fiction. Fictitious yet based on everyday life, those works rendered the world to a warp and woof of details. The logic of the narrative dictates that the material life they recorded was more realistic than that in works of gossip and sketch notes. Saga novels, spanning 300 years from the *Water Margin* and written in the mid-Ming dynasty to the *Legend of Heroes and Heroines* 儿女英雄传, written in the late Qing dynasty, can be used to investigate what changes occurred in economic life during the period. We conclude that the way people lived financially did not alter much during these 300 years. The two phenomena, the absence of remittance and the prevalence of silver in travel, are two sides of the same coin.

As this chapter deals with the refined and prosperous civic life, the sophisticated and developed urban commerce, manufacturing industries, and the consumption of luxury goods by the wealthy citizens in both urban and rural areas, it cannot but touch upon the "budding capitalism" issue. It was a question repeatedly debated in mainland historical circles. The flow of logic in this chapter also raises the question of why, with many attributes of "early modernity" defined by Naito Konan, the late Ming failed to move further towards capitalism. While it does not intend to devote much space to the still-inconclusive discussions, the nature of this book makes it impossible to avoid the issue altogether. The two conclusions, drawn from the parallel explorations into luxury consumption and financial institution, point to the same direction. The refined and prosperous economic life and the increasing consumption of luxury goods by lower- and middle-class people in the late Ming Dynasty, seemingly in line with "early modernity" as hypothesized by Japanese Sinologist Naito Konan on Song China,[72] violated the mechanisms of capitalism.

Setting out from the famous Chinese idiom "the masses regard food as their heaven," the study of Ming food in Chapter 3 extends beyond general food consumption and supply. It sheds light on several staple foods and major crops of Shandong, the agricultural ecology of a utopian yeomanry, and the means of catering food for field laborers. As this study intends to explore various facets of Ming society, many crop issues are included in the discussion.

Salt, an inseparable element in the people's diet, had been placed under government monopoly during much of the imperial period. Though given lesser focus, the "Salt Franchise and Salt Smuggling" section adopts an anecdotal case to illustrate the problems of the Ming salt policy: rampant contraband, ineffective preventive service of the government, a foolish quota system to combat smuggling, and a forbidding salt price that spawned a saying which viewed salt as a more treasurable commodity than human lives.

The "Foods in Beijing" section scrutinizes Beijing's vibrant and comprehensive cuisine legacy beyond what one could gather from the narrative. The reader is invited to review Beijing's culinary history from the Ming capital's historical-geographic nature—one that had been traditionally receptive to the cultures of its adjacent pastoral peoples, evidence of which one can find in Macro Polo's travelogue account. Beijing witnessed an epicureanism bred in the loosened political atmosphere of the Hongzhi reign (1487–1505). Much like the clothing chapter, the food chapter also concerns itself with what is symbolized in the institution of the Ming dining code. Therefore, this segment takes great pains in going through sets of dining protocols devised by Emperor Hongwu, such as who is to use what utensil made of what material under what circumstances. Again, the Ming regulations on the entitlement to access different dining vessels in the food world were not about regulating the food material culture but were meant to mark clear demarcations of social boundaries.

We explore the trend of increased consumption by the middle and lower classes of luxury specialty foods during the Ming dynasty, ascribing it to three causes: the influence of Ming literati, the slack political atmosphere of the Hongzhi reign, and the favorable climate and geographical conditions of Beijing cuisine culture.

Chapter 4, "Traveling Cultures of the Ming," spends much of its length on Sujie's Mount Tai pilgrimage. To explore the premodern tourist culture and mechanism, we propose a concept, "Affluent Womenfolk Urban and Rural," to represent a group of women travelers in the late imperial period. The antithesis of this concept is the Ming-Qing *guixiu* 閨秀 constellation, much covered in recent-year Sinological scholarship, which has produced excellent books and articles about their travel patterns.

This chapter surveys the history, organization, leadership, and financial operation of the Mount Tai Incense Society. Semi-tourist, semi-religious, the Society enjoyed immense popularity among rural Shandong people, especially women. It functioned primarily as a tourist organization, catering to both sightseeing tourism and religious pilgrimages. Its financial operation seems rational and practical: principals were collected, entrusted in the hands of the Society's heads, and invested in construction projects three years before the journey was to take place, the philanthropic nature of the construction projects being a positive factor in absorbing investment, for attendees believed it to be generative of good karma. The high yields the investments generated attest to the remarkable organizational skills of the Society's leaders, whose positions were usually assumed by sophisticated, sociable village women of a religious background. The heads arranged the attendees' transportation, boarding, and lodging, demonstrating dexterous business maneuvers. They provided traveling gadgets, returned cash to those who used their own transportation, made personal connections with local hotel runners, and solicited new members. Year after year, the heads brought business to the innkeeper, who treated their guests in a hospitable manner and rewarded the heads with gifts. It is comparable to the tour guide/hotel commission scheme institutionalized in the modern tourist industry.

XSYYZ's vivid depiction of the bustling small restaurants, stalls, and booths, which solicited business from the pilgrims, helps reconstruct the pattern of the incense economy which took place in most of China's tourist-scenic-pilgrim cities during the middle to late imperial era. Its modern form has persisted into the present. Their ardor had spawned a vibrant local economy centered on serving Incense Guests: providing food, lodging, and entertainment; catering to the souvenir-shopping needs of visitors from the rural hinterland; and supplying goods such as candles, incense, and foil paper for pilgrims' consumption. Yet a comparison of a still-bustling Incense Economy and its less lucky, dwindling, and disappearing counterpart at the City-God Hill in present-day Hangzhou has led us to ponder the limits of the traditional cultural lure of pilgrimage sites. Disregarding a regime's preference for a particular religion, or its political antipathy to all religions in general, a pilgrimage site must have an overwhelmingly strong tradition to withstand the more vital magnetism of modern tourism or it will be soon overpowered by the latter. Of course, incense trades, religious sites, and intriguing folk customs can all be transformed into parts of the modern tourist industry, but the tradeoff would be that they are thus tinged with modern marketing.

In this chapter, to highlight the different nature of the "Affluent Womenfolk Urban and Rural" from the Ming-Qing *Guixiu* group, we provide a selective introduction to the latter first. The stark differences between the two groups draw our attention to these facts: how did the former break through the social, familial, and ethical barriers to leave the boudoir when tourist resources were scarce and Confucianism frowned upon womanly leisure? Did footbinding limit their travel? If a female traveler's husband accompanied her on her journey, what role would he play? This study thus also reviews the footbinding and seclusion traditions of Chinese women and examines certain non-leisure travel situations: family reunions, escorting the coffin of a deceased husband to his hometown for burial, and so forth, as well as exploring why elite *guixiu's* travels were eulogized and even sponsored by their male counterparts.

Guixiu adventuresses are a group of culturally privileged female elites whose traveling activities were endorsed, eulogized, or even financially sponsored by their male counterparts. Unlike them, Sujie must fight for her right to go out. Her uneventful trip to Mount Tai involves a long list of small anecdotes and adventures, from which the reader can palpably see a tourist culture on the rise, though shrouded under the cloak of religious worship and pilgrimage.

To explain Sujie's rebellious behaviors, this chapter also brings about a feminist viewpoint. All her acts condemned by Xizhou Sheng as a "lioness's roar," a metaphor for shrewlike behaviors, and are essentially the rebellion of a suppressed woman. Sujie conflicts with her natal and married families, which in combined efforts constrain her traveling freedom. The development of the Yin-Yang theory over the pre-Qin and Han periods sufficiently explains how the notion "male enjoys higher status than the female" came out.

We label the totality of opinions, thoughts, and perceptions disproving of commercial consumptions the "sumptuary ethos." Throughout all of the chapters, we ponder over the differences between sumptuary legislation and sumptuary ethos. Concerning clothing, food, and travel, three of the "four primary concerns," the Ming regime had shown an excessive obsession with forming its people into a neatly layered hierarchy. To achieve that end, sets of inclement sumptuary laws were mobilized to promulgate detailed regulations on people's clothing, dining, and traveling behaviors. By the late Ming, economic development outpaced the ossified legal codes. A kaleidoscopic world—in which the populace dressed without regard for their social roles, epicureanism swamped modes of frugality, and commoner women had access to tourist sites—surfaced, leaving the laws to exist as laws on paper. Yet the residue of the Hongwu's framework remained or, as Craig Clunas puts it, "the formal legal structures of the sumptuary laws remained in place, even if widely flouted."[73] Flouted they were indeed, but they were also ingrained in the opinions, thoughts, and perceptions of a particular segment of the Ming populace.

A strong, disapproving voice is heard towards the "chaos" and "disorderliness" brought about by the commoners' worldly pursuit of material comforts. The voice is one of sumptuary ethos. It originated from the need to maintain an autarkic and self-sufficient economic ecology featured with simplicity and crudity. Given the competitive mindsets common among domestic women, keeping them "away from the desirable and undisturbed by lust was best." Another source for the sumptuary ethos lies in Confucianism, which preferred moralization over legal punishment. It is explicitly stated in *The Analects of Confucius—For the Government* 论语 • 为政:

> When the people are governed by law and restrained by criminal law, they would only seek to avoid punishment for their crimes, but lose their sense of shame; when the people are guided by moral education and regulated by propriety, they would not only have a sense of shame but also become obedient.[74]

In terms of function, both sumptuary legislation and sumptuary ethos shared the same concern for material details, and both were repressive forces in the Ming commercial economy. They were not reflected in attire only.

Although the issues of the sumptuary ethos are dealt with at length in this chapter, the question of how sumptuary laws and ethos wrestled with Ming material life will be a query running throughout the book.

Notes

1 Shih Hu, "The Textual Research on Xingshi Yinyuan Zhuan," in *Recent Academic Writings of Hu Shih* (Shanghai: The Commercial Press, 1935), 388–89. 胡适：《<醒世姻缘传>考证》,《胡适论学近著》, 上海：商务印书馆, 1935年, 第388–89页。
2 Wanfang Data, www.wanfangdata.com.cn/. 万方数据。
3 Xun Lu, *A Brief History of Chinese Fiction*, trans. Xianyi Yang and Gladys Yang (Westport, CT: Hyperion Press, 1973).
4 Xun Lu, "To Qian Xuantong," in *Selected Works of Luxun: Letters* (Beijing: China Culture and History Press, 2002), 30. 鲁迅：《致钱玄同》,《鲁迅选集·书信》, 北京：中国文史出版社, 2002年, 第30页。
5 Dahuang Lu, *A Chronicle of Pu Songling* (Jinan: Qilu Press, 1980). 路大荒：《蒲松龄年谱》, 济南：齐鲁书社, 1980年。
6 Shouyi Wang, "The Completion Date of Xingshi Yinyuan Zhuan," *Guangming Daily*, May 28, 1961. 王守义：《<醒世姻缘传>的成书年代》,《光明日报》, 1961年5月28日。
7 Fuling Xu, "X*ingshi Yinyuan Zhuan* by Jia Fuxi, a Native of Yanzhou Prefecture," *Journal of Jining Teachers' College* 24, no. 4 (2005): 60–65; Qingji Zhang, "The Author of X*ingshi Yinyuan Zhuan* Is Ding Yaokang," *Journal of Xuzhou Normal College (Philosophy and Social Sciences Edition)*, no. 3 (1989): 46–51; Qingji Zhang, "Supplement on the Authorship of X*ingshi Yinyuan Zhuan*," *Journal of Ming-Qing Fiction Studies*, no. 1 (1995): 79–83. 徐复岭：《<醒世姻缘传>作者为兖州府人贾凫西续考》,《济宁师范专科学校学报》, 2005年第24卷第4期, 第60–65页；张清吉：《<醒世姻缘传>作者是丁耀亢》,《徐州师范学院学报（哲学社会科学版）》, 1989年第3期, 第46–51页；张清吉：《<醒世姻缘传>作者补证》,《明清小说研究》, 1995年第1期, 第79–83页。
8 Qingji Zhang, *A New Research on Xingshi Yinyuan Zhuan* (Zhengzhou: Zhongzhou Ancient Books Publishing House, 1991). 张清吉：《醒世姻缘传新考》, 郑州：中州古籍出版社, 1991年。
9 Xingyao Jin, "Dispute on the Authorship of *Xingshi Yinyuan Zhuan*," *Journal of Chinese Literature and History*, no. 4 (1980). 金性尧：《<醒世姻缘传> 作者非蒲松龄说》,《中华文史论丛》, 1980年第4期。
10 Wanzhou Tong, "Postscript," in *Xingshi Yinyuan Zhuan*, proofread and annotated by Wanzhou Tong (Zhengzhou: Zhongzhou Ancient Books Publishing House, 1982). 童万周：《后记》, 见西周生著, 童万周校注：《醒世姻缘传》, 郑州：中州古籍出版社出版, 1982年。
11 Hongqiang Liu, "Textual Research on a Zhangqiu Scholar as the Author of X*ingshi Yinyuan Zhuan*," *Journal of Jianghan University (Humanities Sciences)* 29, no. 3 (2010): 47–48. 刘洪强：《<醒世姻缘传>的作者为章丘文士考》,《江汉大学学报：人文科学版》, 2010年第29卷第3期, 第47–48页。
12 Institute of Literature, Chinese Academy of Social Sciences, comps., *A History of Chinese Literature* (Beijing: People's Literature Publishing House, 1962), 1031. 中国社会科学院文学研究所编纂：《中国文学史》, 北京：人民文学出版社, 1962年, 第1031页。
13 Pu Tian, "A New Exploration of the Author of *Xingshi Yinyuan Zhuan*," *Journal of Henan University (Social Science)*, no. 5 (1985): 77–82. 田璞：《<醒世姻缘传>作者新探》,《河南大学学报（哲学社会科学版）》, 1985年第5期, 第77–82页。

14 Sucun Wang, "A Study on the Author Xizhou Sheng of *Xingshi Yinyuan Zhuan*," *Continental Magazine* 17, no. 3 (1958). 王素存：《醒世姻缘传作者西周生考》，《（台湾）大陆杂志》，1958年第17卷第3期。

15 Jieping Liu, "Examination of Xizhou Sheng, the Author of *Xingshi Yinyuan Zhuan*," *Bibliography Quarterly* 10, no. 2 (1976). 刘阶平：《醒世姻缘传作者西周生考异》，《（台湾）书目季刊》，1976年第10卷第2期。

16 Jerome B. Grieder, "Preface," in *Hu Shih and the Chinese Renaissance: Liberalism in the Chinese Revolution, 1917–1937* (Cambridge: Harvard University Press, 1970).

17 Te-kong Tong, *The Reminiscences of Dr. Hu Shih* (Beijing: Sino-Culture Press, 1990). 唐德刚：《胡适杂忆》，北京：华文出版社，1990年。

18 Andrew H. Plaks, "After the Fall: Hsing-Shih Yin-Yuan Chuan and the Seventeenth-Century Chinese Novel," *Harvard Journal of Asiatic Studies* 45, no. 2 (1985): 555.

19 Yenna Wu, "From History to Allegory: Surviving Famine in Xingshi Yinyuan Zhuan," *Chinese Culture (Taipei)* 38, no. 4 (1997): 88.

20 Yanjing Zhu, "Research on *XSYYZ*" (master's thesis, Taiwan University, 1978). 朱燕静：《<醒世姻缘传>研究》，台湾大学1978年。

21 Bingzao Chen, "Is Pu Songling also Xizhou Sheng?" *China Newspaper Monthly* 69 (1985). 陈炳藻：《蒲松龄也是西周生吗》，《（台湾）中报月刊》，1985年第69卷。

22 Chun-shu Chang and Shelley Hsueh-lun Chang, *Redefining History: Ghosts, Spirits, and Human Society in P'u Sung-ling's World, 1640–1715* (Ann Abbor: University of Michigan Press, 1998), 209–11.

23 Glen Dudbridge, "A Pilgrimage in Seventeenth-Century Fiction: T'ai-shan and the 'Hsing-shih yin-yüan chuan'," *T'oung Pao* 77 (1991): 226–52.

24 Jiaqi Yan, "The Interest Chain Behind the 'Redology' Competition," *Huaxia Times*, December 17, 2015. 严家淇：《"红学"之争背后的利益链》，《华夏时报》，2015年12月17日。

25 Dongfang Yang, "On the Completion Date of *Xingshi Yinyuan Zhuan*—Discussion with Ms. Xia Wei," *Research on Pu Songling*, no. 2 (2008): 120. 杨东方：《也谈<醒世姻缘传>的成书年代——与夏薇女士商榷》，《蒲松龄研究》，2008年第2期，第120页。

26 Plaks, "After the Fall," 543–44.

27 Dudbridge, "A Pilgrimage in Seventeenth-Century Fiction," 229.

28 Ibid.

29 Plaks, "After the Fall," 564–66.

30 Dudbridge, "A Pilgrimage in Seventeenth-Century Fiction," 205.

31 Eileen Chang, "From the Ashes (Jin yu lu)," in *The Collection of Eileen Chang's Works* (Taiyuan: Beiyue Literature and Art Publishing House, 2004), 282. 张爱玲：《烬余录》，《张爱玲作品集》，太原：北岳文艺出版社，2004年，第282页。

32 Fernand Braudel, *The Mediterranean and the Mediterranean World in the Age of Philip II*, trans. Siân Reynolds (New York: Harper & Row, 1972).

33 Qichao Liang, "The Old History of China," in *Collection of Drinking Ice Chamber*, vol. 9 (Shanghai: Zhonghua Book Company, 1936), 3. 梁启超：《中国之旧史》，《饮冰室合集·文集第九册》，上海：中华书局，1936年，第3页。

34 Dazhao Li, "Essentials of History," in *Collection of Li Dazhao's Historical Essays* (Shijiazhuang: Hebei People's Publishing House, 1984), 200. 李大钊：《史学要论》，《李大钊史学论集》，石家庄：河北人民出版社，1984年，第200页。

35 James Legge, *Confucian Analects in the Four Books* (Hong Kong: Wanguo Publisher, 1947), 172. 理雅各：《华英对照四书·论语》，香港：万国出版社，1947年，第172页。

36 Young-tsu Wong, "Reviewing the History of Frank, the Father of Modern History," in *Nine Chapters of History* (Beijing: SDX Joint Publishing Company, 2006), 23, 28. 汪荣祖：《回顾近代史学之父兰克的史学》，《史学九章》，北京：三联书店，2006年，第23，28页。

37 Suxian Yang, "Gibbon and the *History of the Decline and Fall of the Roman Empire*," [Taiwan] *History Monthly* 202 (2004). 杨肃献：《吉朋与<罗马帝国衰亡史>》，《（台湾）历史月刊》，2004年第202卷。

38 Bertolt Brecht, "Questions from a Worker Who Reads," in *Poetry and Prose*, ed. Reinhold Grimm (New York: Continuum, 2003), 63.
39 Tong, *The Reminiscences of Dr. Hu Shih*, 145. 唐德刚：《胡适杂忆》，第145页。
40 "All the world's a stage, And all the men and women merely player." William Shakespeare, *As You Like It, Woodstock* (Ingersoll, ON: Devoted Publishing, 2016), 36.
41 Naifei Ding, *Obscene Things: Sexual Politics in Jin Ping Mei* (Durham: Duke University Press, 2002), 188–89.
42 Sheng Xizhou, *Xingshi Yinyuan Zhuan*, proofread by Bing Zhai (Jinan: Qilu Press, 1993). 西周生著，翟冰校点：《醒世姻缘传》，济南：齐鲁书社，1993年。
43 Bing Zhai, "Editor's Postscript," *Xingshi Yinyuan Zhuan*, 778. 翟冰：《校点后记》，见西周生著，翟冰校点：《醒世姻缘传》，第778页。
44 Eve Alison Nyren, *The Bonds of Matrimony* (New York: Edwin Mellen Press, 1995).
45 Guoqing Li, "A New Exploration of the Version of *Xingshi Yinyuan Zhuan* (Part I)," *Journal of Ming-Qing Fiction Studies* 76, no. 2 (2005); Guoqing Li, "A New Exploration of the Version of *Xingshi Yinyuan Zhuan* (Part II)," *Journal of Ming-Qing Fiction Studies* 81, no. 3 (2006). 李国庆：《<醒世姻缘传>版本新探（上）》，《明清小说研究》，2005年第76卷第2期；李国庆：《<醒世姻缘传>版本新探（下）》，《明清小说研究》，2006年第81卷第3期。
46 Chunyu Yang, "An Introductory Study of XSYYZ—On Edition and Periodization Issues," *Journal of Ming-Qing Fiction Studies* 68, no. 2 (2003). 杨春宇：《<醒世姻缘传>的研究序说—关于版本和成书年代问题》，《明清小说研究》，2003年第68卷第2期。
47 This statement is a general description of the study of Confucian classics in the Song dynasty by Huang Zhen, a Song scholar. 此言为宋代学者黄震对宋朝经学的概括性描述。
48 Wei Xia, *Research on Xingshi Yinyuan Zhuan* (Beijing: Zhonghua Book Company, 2007). 夏薇：《<醒世姻缘传>研究》，北京：中华书局，2007年。
49 Xiaolong Wu, *Xingshi Yinyuan Zhuan and the Secular Life of the Ming Dynasty* (Beijing: The Commercial Press, 2017). 吴晓龙：《<醒世姻缘传>与明代世俗生活》，北京：商务印书馆，2017。
50 Yenna Wu, *Ameliorative Satire and the Seventeenth-Century Chinese Novel, Xingshi Yinyuan Zhuan-Marriage as Retribution, Awakening the World* (Lewiston: E. Mellen Press, 1999).
51 Yenna Wu, *The Chinese Virago: A Literary Theme* (Cambridge, MA: Council on East Asian Studies distributed by Harvard University Press, 1995).
52 Yenna Wu, "Repetition in Xingshi Yinyuan Zhuan," *Harvard Journal of Asiatic Studies (Cambridge, MA)* 51, no. 1 (1991).
53 Plaks, "After the Fall."
54 Keith McMahon, *Misers, Shrews, and Polygamists: Sexuality and Male-Female Relations in Eighteenth-Century China* (Durham: Duke University Press, 1995).
55 Yu-chun Yang, "Reorientation of *Jinpingmei* and *Xingshiyinyuan*" (PhD diss., Princeton University, 2003).
56 Daria Berg, *Carnival in China: A Reading of the Xingshi Yinyuan Zhuan* (Leiden and Boston: Brill, 2002).
57 Robert Hegel, "Review of *Carnival in China: A Reading of the Xingshi Yinyuan Zhuan*, by Daria Berg," *Harvard Journal of Asiatic Studies* 63, no. 2 (December 2003): 450–57.
58 Ibid.
59 Wolfgang Franke, *An Introduction to the Sources of Ming History* (Kuala Lumpur: University of Malaya Press distributed by London: Oxford University Press, 1968).
60 [Ming] Damu Xiong, "Preface," in *The Romance of the Song Dynasty* (Beijing: China Culture and History Press, 2003). [明]熊大木著：《大宋中兴通俗演义》，北京：中国文史出版社，2003年，《序》。
61 Baoweng Old Man, ed., *Ancient and Modern Wonders*, proofread by Zizong Lin (Guangzhou: Guangdong People's Publishing House, 1981), 4. 抱瓮老人辑，林梓宗校点：《今古奇观》，广州：广东人民出版社，1981年，第4页。

62 [Ming] Menglong Feng, *Chronicles of the Eastern Zhou Kingdoms*, proofread and revised by [Qing] Yuanfang Cai, 5th ed. (Jinan: Qilu Press, 1996), 1. [明]冯梦龙著，[清]蔡元放校订：《东周列国志》，济南：齐鲁书社，1996年第5版，第1页。
63 Old Man in the Leisure Room, *Preface to the Commentary of the Reclining Thatched Cottage (Woxian Caotang), The Scholars*, ed. [Qing] Jingzi Wu (Changsha: Yuelu Publishing House, 2007), 1. [清]吴敬梓著，闲斋老人序：《卧闲草堂评本·儒林外史》，长沙：岳麓出版社，2007年，第1页。
64 Franke, *Ming History*.
65 Guozhen Xie, *A Study of Late Ming Historical Texts* (Shanghai: East China Normal University Press, 2011). 谢国桢：《晚明史籍考》，上海：华东师范大学出版社，2011年。
66 Sinian Fu, "Introduction to Historical Methods," in *Fu Sinian's Essays on Academic Culture*, ed. Zhenping Huang and Lingji Li (Beijing: China Youth Publishing House, 2001), 146–67. 傅斯年：《史学方法导论》，见黄振萍、李凌己编著：《傅斯年学术文化随笔》，北京：中国青年出版社，2001年，第146–67页。
67 Ray Huang, "Late Ming Merchants Viewed from the *Sanyan Stories*," in *Broden the Horizons of History* (Beijing: SDX Joint Publishing Company, 2001), 1–30. 黄仁宇：《从<三言>看晚明商人》，《放宽历史的视界》，北京：三联书店，2001年，第1–30页。
68 Cynthia Brokaw, "Supernatural Retribution and Human Destiny," in *Religions of China in Practice*, ed. Donald S. Lopez (Princeton: Princeton University Press, 1996); Cynthia Brokaw, *The Ledgers of Merit and Demerit: Social Change and Moral Order in Late Imperial China* (Princeton, NJ: Princeton University Press, 1991).
69 Susan Naquin and Chun-fang Yu, *Pilgrims and Sacred Sites in China* (Berkeley: University of California Press, 1992).
70 Berg, *Carnival in China*.
71 Xiaolan Bao, "An Analysis of the Dynamics of Chinese Women's Studies in the United States," in *Equality and Development*, ed. Xiaojiang Li, Hong Zhu, and Xiuyu Dong (Beijing: SDX Joint Publishing Company, 1997), 361–84. 鲍晓兰：《美国的中国妇女研究动态分析》，见李小江、朱虹、董秀玉编著：《平等与发展》，北京：三联书店，1997年，第361–84页。
72 Hisayuki Miyakawa, "An Outline of the Naito Hypothesis and Its Effects on Japanese Studies of China," *The Far Eastern Quarterly* 14, no. 4 (1955): 533–52.
73 Craig Clunas, *Superfluous Things: Material Culture and Social Status in Early Modern China* (Cambridge: Polity, 1991), 148.
74 Legge, *Confucian Analects*, 7. 理雅各：《华英对照四书·论语》，第7页。

1 The Clothing Culture and Clothing Choices of the Ming People

1. Historical Background: A Thorough Reverse from Chinese Antiquity and a Strict Differentiation in Hierarchy

While apparel and accouterments established by the Ming dynasty are still being seen on the stages of the Peking Opera, they are not simply the artistic projection of an intricate Ming costume institution. To err on the side of roughness, we might say that the Ming costume can be indexed by that of the Peking Opera, but not vice versa.

Enumerating the categories of the Peking Opera costume and their proper usage can be painstaking. For example, the subcategories of the ceremonial robe, or *mang* 蟒, worn mainly by emperors and nobles on formal occasions, are very broad.[1] A *mang* with a dragon opening its mouth is only reserved for emperors, while that for ministers and generals requires the dragon's mouth to be sealed. On the robes of civil ministers, the dragons are placid and quiet, but the ones on the robes of generals, mighty and belligerent. Colors are discreetly used according to the figures' social dispositions. Red belongs to the majestic and noble, green the warlike generals, white the young and handsome scholars, and black the upright and unconstrained officials. Palace eunuchs, when projected as awe-inspiring dignitaries, wear red too, but their *mang* must have tassels appended. Socially venerable figures always wear *mang* long enough to reach their feet, but bandits, even of heroic character, can only wear short, knee-length *mang*. A male figure's *mang* always goes with a jade belt. The color choices for women's *mang* are rather limited: the orthodox yellow is reserved for empresses only, imperial consorts and princesses are in red, and mourning women in white.[2]

The classification of Ming apparel and accouterments is at least ten times more complicated than described here. The nearly hundred years of Mongol rule was a period of ethnic consolidation and integration, but in the eyes of the Ming nationalists, a century that stained the purity of Han culture. Due to its inability to cope with a large mix of ethnic groups and the continuous domestic and external wars at its commencement stage, the Yuan founders did not regulate its costume code until 1321. During that year, Yuan Yingzong 元英宗 promulgated a standard. The Yuan rulers had been ambivalent towards the Song cultural legacy from the onset. On the one hand, the conquerors' superiority and the need to maintain a social

DOI: 10.4324/9781003406143-2

caste had led them to undermine Song institutions; on the other hand, they easily fell for the beauty and grandiosity of Chinese culture. The *zhisun* costume 质孙服 was the consequence of such ambivalence. The *History of the Yuan Dynasty— Records of Carriage and Clothing* 元史 • 舆服志 notes that the principle to codify the national costume was "consulting all times, ancient and present, while being ready to reduce and supplement" and "preserving the national institutions and furnishing the need of the protocols."[3] *Zhisun*, the Mongolian Grande toilette, was a widely used costume from which both the clothing needs of emperors and ministers were accommodated. This was arguably why it was called "the uniform" by the Han Chinese. The design of *zhisun*, characterized by its gauffer on the waist and large beads on the back, boasted a combination of Mongol and Han costume styles. Worn by thousands of officials uniformly in more than a dozen grand ceremonies each year, the *zhisun* costume had become so conspicuous that it was later abolished by the Ming nationalists and hence denigrated to become the uniform of Ming junior guards.[4]

Multiple reasons had goaded the Ming nationalists to reverse the majority of the institutions the Yuan had established, the costume code being one of the most drastically changed. Primarily, political and ethnic rancor towards a conquering dynasty has to be taken into consideration. China had suffered under the hooves of foreign conquerors before, notably during the havoc of the Northern Dynasties in the Age of Division, which ensued after the collapse of Western Jin, the Five Dynasties and Ten Kingdoms after the Tang, and the Jurchen Jin after Northern Song. Nevertheless, none of those foreign invasions constituted a full-blown loss of China to a nomadic regime, whether in terms of its cultural continuity or territorial completeness. Were nomads to overrun China, so long as an orthodox Chinese regime could set its footing in a fraction of the territory it previously occupied, the integrity of Chinese cultural lineage was not deemed breached. Modern scholar Lei Haizong, for example, hailed that the battle of the Fei River in 383, in which the Eastern Jin dynasty held the barbarians at bay and made possible the continuation of Chinese civilization, was a milestone victory in Chinese history. The argument, proposed in his *Chinese Culture and Chinese Soldiers*, published on the eve of the Marco Polo Bridge incident of 1937, was aimed at boosting national confidence to withstand an imminent Sino-Japanese war.[5]

For the nationalists of the newly founded Ming, the memories of the Yuan conquest, which had happened only a century before, were still too fresh to be ignored. The enormous army of Kublai Khan destroyed not only the Southern Song but also the continuity of Chinese civilization. The brutal Mongol treatment of the Han Chinese, particularly the Southerners, left scars of hatred on the Han national psyche that would last well beyond the demise of the Ming.

Second, the deep-rooted Chinese distaste for the primitivism of barbarian culture had not dissipated even after a century of Mongol rule. There was nothing more unbearable in the world, both the Romans and the Chinese knew, than having to subjugate one's highly sophisticated culture to the crude barbarianism of mere military superiority. During China's long history of being conquered by swarms of nomads from the Northern Steppes, her educated elites kept expressing aggrieved

The Clothing Culture and Clothing Choices of the Ming People 31

Figure 1.1 A man in the *Zhisun* costume. Ca. 1330–32. Silk tapestry (kesi). Overall: H. 245.5 × W. 209 cm.

Source: Courtesy of Metropolitan Museum of Art, New York.

feelings on the loss of supremacy—in equally long terms. In the Southern Song, *Ci* lyric composer Zhang Xiaoxiang 张孝祥 used the following lines to express his resentment towards the concession of North China to the Jurchens:

> Contemplating on the events of the remote past, I lament our destiny that has gone beyond human efforts; now, along the rivers of Zhu and Si [where Confucius used to lecture his disciples 洙水, 泗水], the previous prosperity is replaced by the stinky smell of mutton and beef.[6]

David Morgan, who studied the Mongol conquest between the thirteenth and fifteenth centuries as a world phenomenon, denotes that "the Chinese civilization had ample experience in taking barbarian invaders in its stride and taming them." He brings to our notice that the *History of the Yuan Dynasty*, authored by Ming historians, was written in a style that "conformed to the historiographical pattern that the Chinese had established 1200 years previously."[7] Yet what Morgan does not seem to comprehend is that the upward accommodation of a foreign dynasty into its historiography cannot be equated to forgiveness. In the deepest corner of the Han national consciousness, the Yuan was but a backward, primitive regime that overwhelmed China with its military machine through killing and massacres and whose culture was inferior to that of the Chinese and could never be blended into that of the latter. Therefore, the founding of the Ming was acclaimed not merely as the establishment of a new polity but also as an opportunity to wipe out all barbarian residues, culturally and institutionally, cosmetically, and spiritually. This attitude was reflected in even the most insignificant matters. Take the position of buttons on Confucius' clothing in an image of Confucius as an example. Emperor Yingzong had officially issued an edict ordering that the images of Confucius dressed in Mongolian style with buttons on the left [*zuoren* 左衽] be changed to the Chinese style of buttoning on the right [*youren* 右衽]. The emperor also gave orders to prohibit Mongolian dress and speech in Beijing.[8] However, even with this level of commitment, a thorough eradication of the Yuan influence did not happen. The campaign to restore the Han clothing style was only partially successful. Antonia Finnane, author of *Changing Clothes in China: Fashion, History, Nation*, identifies the garments retrieved from Ming tombs as both showing signs of restoration endeavors and providing "evidence of the sustained influence of the far north on Chinese clothing."[9]

Third, albeit Emperor Hongwu was the least likely Chinese sovereign to embrace Daoism, nor was he a personification of the syncretic Daoist-Confucian ideal of "internally a sage and externally a king," he was arguably the most ardent Chinese ruler in his patronage of Confucianism. Despite advocating shaping people into distinguished classes on the social spectrum by birth or education, Confucian theologians never explicitly instructed how to do so. However, the lack of practicability on this theoretical surface hardly intimidated the emperor. Since the most straightforward way to differentiate people was to dress them differently, this was the approach the throne adopted.

2. A Kaleidoscopic World: The Apparel of Different Classes

1) The Newly Rich and Newly Dignified: The Blurred Boundaries

In the opening chapter of *XSYYZ*, one finds the karmic origin of the retributions that drive Chao Yuan into the next life: Chao Yuan's killing of a fox spirit and his mistreatment of his wife, Née Ji.

Chao Yuan, the spoiled only son of a *nouveau riche*, estranges his wife and takes a beautiful concubine, Zheng. His association with a gang of scoundrel friends has only exacerbated his debauchery; as winter draws near and the first snow falls, a hunting plan is broached among him and his friends. A retired prostitute, Zhenge has previously escorted funerals on horseback when such business calls for her presence, making her an experienced equestrian. As a veteran opera actress, she has played roles of heroic females on stage and worn the specially tailored accouterments of female generals. Still quite attached to the glamour of her previous career, she deems the forthcoming hunt an opportunity to display her untamed beauty and fashionable apparel, especially when she is to be among Chao Yuan's friends, the majority of whom she has slept with. The couple differs over whether they should borrow the "golden quirt," the "pheasant head-dress," or the "python embroidered shoulder piece" from Zhenge's troupe, but soon concludes that borrowing is not an option. Chao Yuan decides he is to furnish all the hunting apparel for her.

> For Zhenge, he has made a new, bright red, narrow-sleeved "flying fish" shirt, a dark green shoulder-piece with a sitting-dragon embroidered onto it for 36 *taels*,[10] he buys a mink lined cap, and for seven silver coins he has a pair of wearable little riding shoes sewed in purple hemp lined with lambskin. He orders a golden-yellow braided belt and buys her a double-bladed sword. He selects a black horse and has it trained, and picks out six plump servants' wives, four robust housemaids and ten sturdy farmers' wives. He has a fox-lined cap made for each of these women, and a sky-blue padded outrider's jacket, a dull green plain cloth padded shoulder piece, and puce cloth riding shoes lined with leather. They are to have knives shoved in their belts, left and right.
> (1.6)

The mink-lined cap that costs 36 *taels* here, commonly known as the "Zhaojun-styled lying-rabbit cap" 昭君卧兔, is by function a shawl. Drawings of the westward journey of Wang Zhaojun, the Western Han imperial consort who was married to the khan of the Xiongnu under Han's conciliatory policy, had long been a source of inspiration to costume designers. In *A Dream of Red Mansions*, when Granny Liu first meets with Wang Xifeng, the latter "has on a little cap of red sable, which she wears about the house for warmth, fastened on with a pearl-studded bandeau."[11] This type of cap is called a "Zhaojun cap" 昭君帽.

Mantles, shawls, and caps named after "Zhaojun" are most characterized by the exoticism of the remote Western Regions, notably the adoption of sable as a material. They can be decorative or for practical wearing purposes and are suitable to be worn indoors or outdoors. Modern scholar Shen Congwen 沈从文 notes that Song paintings and Ming carvings that depicted Wang Zhaojun and another Han elite woman, Cai Wenji 蔡文姬, on their journeys to or from the Western Regions had fermented the "Zhaojun" fashion that prevailed in the South.[12] Cai was married to a Xiongnu leader but was later fetched back by Cao Cao 曹操.

Zhenge goes hunting in such a costume, making a big splash in the neighborhood. A group of women comes to gossip with Chao Yuan's wife, Nee Ji, in a sour tone, saying that riding a horse in military attire is not something a decent woman would do. And it so happens that, in Chen Yinque's *Unofficial Biography of Liu Rushi* 柳如是别传, which was finished in his later years, Chen cites three documents on the travel of Qian Qianyi 钱谦益 and Liu Rushi from Changshu to Nanjing in 1644.

> When Qian Qianyi was in the capital, his concubine Liu Rushi rode a horse in military attire with pheasant's tails in her crown, like those of Wang Zhaojun. It's indeed a sultry look.
> 　　　　　Wu Weiye 吴伟业, *Luqiao Chronicle* (Luqiao Jiwen 鹿樵纪闻)—Part 1

> Qian Qianyi's concubine Liu Yin [Liu Rushi], with pheasant's tails in her crown, rode into the state gate in military attire, as if she were Wang Zhaojun going beyond the frontier.
> 　　　　　Xia Wanchun 夏完淳, *Nandu Notes* [Nandu Zazhi 南都杂志], in the *Survival Records Continued* (Xu Xingcun Lu 续幸存录)

> Qian Qianyi was summoned when Hongguang usurped the throne, and Liu followed him. When coming out of Danyang, Qian either joined hands with Liu in the carriage or had Liu take the donkey, and he followed her, saying to Liu in private: "It seems like Zhaojun's way out of the fortress." It was then rumored that Qian made Liu dress up as Zhaojun to show off on the road. The public's rumor is undoubtedly fearful.
> 　　　　　Anonymous, The Legacy of Muzhai (Muzhai Yishi 牧斋遗事)

Chen, in his defense of Liu Rushi, argues that Qian and Liu may "occasionally play a joke, which was later rumored and used as a means of denigration by their enemies."[13] However, women riding a horse in military attire were considered unacceptable and not tolerated by orthodoxy. The image of a woman riding a horse in military attire made it easy to associate her with the identity of a prostitute, for, in the seventeenth century, families holding funerals often hired prostitutes to dress up as "Zhaojun going beyond the frontier" or "Meng Rihong defeating the enemies." Zhang Zhenglang 张政烺, therefore, took Chen Yinque's statement as a mistake, saying that "the rumor makers meant that Qian was to die and Liu was to attend the funeral."[14]

The "little riding shoes sewed in purple hemp lined with lambskin," in official terms called *geweng* shoes 革翰鞋, are by origin a compromised version of boots designed to be worn by commoners in the North. Emperor Hongwu resented the assumptive dressing behaviors of his commoner citizens and found it to his utmost intolerance that the general populace should wear boots with golden-braided decorations. In the 25th year of Hongwu (1392), he issued an order prohibiting commoners from wearing boots. Still, considering the rigidity of the weather in the North, he made an exception, allowing them to wear *geweng* shoes—essentially a much-shortened version of boots, covering up to the ankle's height, which could not be made of leather. During its inflexible early years, the prohibitive edict was carried out: "all commoners, civilian and military alike, as well as merchants, actors, underlings, servants and eunuchs," whom "if they are found to be bold enough to wear boots, they will be beheaded in front of the doorways of their houses, and the rest of their families be banished to Yunnan."[15]

This proclamation was due to the capture of Yan Suozhu and 37 other people by the Nanjing *Wuchengbingmasi* 五城兵马司, a bureaucratic-military institution in charge of public security, firefighting, and city administration, in the 26th year of Hongwu (1393). These people:

> have changed the original leather *geweng* shoes into half and short boots with the lining as long as the boot tube. They either wore the modified and more comfortable boots themselves or sold them. They were arrested for their drinking, whoring, and wobbly walking and sent for questioning by the military police.[16]

Zhenge starts out as a prostitute who sings opera, giving her a background in theater. Although the rest of her outfit is sumptuous, these *geweng* shoes are not outrageous. However, with the soft cyan cloth as a surface and lined with leather, such *geweng* shoes are still among the best. A song by Gao An'dao 高安道, "The Tanner Lies," is recorded in *All Verses in the Yuan Dynasty* [Quan Yuan Sanqu 全元散曲], describing the making of *weng* shoes in detail:

> [Shua Hai Er 耍孩儿] The new material is chosen in the shop, and we are instructed about the desired pattern. The stitching is done with great care and attention so that no order would be disobeyed. Thin cones and thick threads are forbidden, and the thick soles must be solid and sturdy. The line is tightened, and the tubes of the boots are even on the tops and bottoms. The toplines are wide, making the shoes easy to take off.[17]

When we look at Zhenge's choice of *geweng* shoes, we may come up with two curiously opposite conclusions. First, the enforcement of the sumptuary laws of the early Ming might well have persisted into the middle and late Ming to force a retired prostitute to obey the dress code. Second, the choice of the fancy lambskin shoes is such a brazen betrayal of the initial intention of restricting commoners from wearing modest dresses that the founding emperor's agenda can be said to have failed.

36 *The Clothing Culture and Clothing Choices of the Ming People*

Figure 1.2 Child's boot (one of a pair). 18th–19th century. Silk, costume-embroidered. H. 29.21 × W. 13.34 cm.

Source: Courtesy of Metropolitan Museum of Art, New York.

In *The Practice of Everyday Life*, Michel de Certeau, a French cultural sociologist, reveals to us the phenomenon of the unyieldingness of commoners. He devises two terms in dichotomy to describe the enforcers and the enforced: "strategy" as the binding force inflicted by an authority, and "tactic" as the individualized defiance from the receiver.[18] Products from the regime of power, such as laws, language, rituals, literature, the arts, inventions, and discourses, can equally be treated "tactically." The "non-artist" commoners, Certeau asserts, are not merely passive receivers of the dominant power, be it government city planning, company headquarters' regulation, or law enforcement. The former, obviously weaker and constantly being regulated, would infringe on the territory of the latter in their everyday lives and infringe on the rules and laws but never be wholly determined by the same. The making of the lambskin shoes constitutes a solid case of Certeau's "tactics" theory.

The Chaos are natives of Wucheng town, Shandong, where the market value for buying a maid lingers around anywhere from four to six *taels* of silver. Chao Yuan's father, Chao Sixiao, a corrupt official, in the boredom of his retirement, takes his wife's maid, Chunying, as his concubine. Chunying was purchased years prior when she was 12; she was initially offered the meager price of five *taels*. Owing to Madame Chao's mercy for her father's difficult situation, she was priced at a premium, seven *taels*. A reader astounded by Chao Yuan's squandering of the equivalent of six maids' market value on his concubine's shawl must be reminded of the yawning rich-poor gap in the late Ming so that his conscience is not troubled too much by the blasé tone as reflected from the narrative.

Née Ji, hearing the rumblings of their departure, hurries out to look. "She wraps a cloth around her head, puts on a pair of brocade boots bound in lambskin, a short-sleeved bodice and a pair of trousers, and goes out" (2.9). Unlike the parvenu of the Chaos, Née Ji has a prestigious family background. Having passed the metropolitan-level civil examination, her grandfather is known by the locals as Ji *huiyuan* 计会元, the Number One Metropolitan Candidate. Having secured social prestige through civil service examinations, the official-gentry can claim nothing akin to aristocratic birthright, though. If his family could not produce success in the series of examinations, downward social mobility would soon follow through property division and other factors. Susan Mann says, "in China, no class system offered a safety net to catch those who found wealth and power slipping away."[19] Her father and brother have not gained any official titles, so the finances of her natal family are in poor straits. Still, they are socially influential and well-respected. When the Chaos are in a desperate financial condition, she is dominant to her husband. Yet, right after Old Chao secures an official posting, Chao Yuan estranges her physically and financially. The "brocade boots" she wears might well have been the remains of her natal family's well-off past. They exemplify the local folk saying: "Rich first and poor later, one is still able to wear brocade for three years."

The Ji family remains socially influential and respected among their kin and community, as evidenced by the fact that Nee Ji's male elders respond actively after her suicide. During the Chao family's economic difficulties, Nee Ji could manage to keep her husband under control. Once Chao Yuan rises to be the son of a high official with Chao Sixiao's gain of an official position, however, he immediately distances himself from Nee Ji, leaving her to live off the dowry of her parents' family.

The *banbi* (literally half-sleeve 半臂), also known as *beizi* (背子 or 褙子), is a kind of half-sleeved jacket. Gu Yanwu's 顾炎武 *Daily Record* (Rizhi Lu 日知录) notes that:

The present *zhaojia* [coat 罩甲] is a coat that can be fastened in the front. In *Jie'an Manuscript* [Jie'an Manbi 戒庵漫笔], it is said that *zhaojia*, created in the Zhengde reign of Emperor Wuzong (1505–1521), is slightly longer than *jia* [armor 甲] and shorter than *ao* [a lined jacket 袄]. Recently, some scholar-officials wear *zhaojia*. According to *the Origin of Chinese Characters* 说文, clothes without sleeves are called *duo* 裰. Zhao Huanguang 赵宦光

said: "Half-armed clothes are called *bijia* 蔽甲 by warriors, *pi'ao* 披袄 by common people, and *beizi* by children." These descriptions are in line with *banbi*.[20]

Meanwhile, Old Chao, magistrate of Huating County, having amassed a great fortune by exploiting people, is actively seeking to advance himself. On a particular occasion, he gets acquainted with two opera actors, the female impersonator Hu and the male impersonator Liang. Both relate to dignitaries in the capital. Magistrate Chao dispatches Hu thither to secure him an office. It turns out that Hu's maternal grandfather, Commander Su, and Liang's uncle, Commander Liu, are both favorite subordinates of Wang Zhen, the paramount eunuch who was once the tutor of Emperor Yingzong and is currently lording over the court. It is the third year of the Zhengtong reign (1438), on the eve of the Tumu Fort Incident.

Hu, in Huating, is merely a socially insignificant, if not despised, opera actor. However, once back at his grandfather's, he instantly puts on "a straight-belted robe of chrysanthemum-green floating silk gauze, a black-velvet plain square cap with a purplish mink hat over it, red shoes, and white socks" (5.34). So stunning is his new appearance that the accompanying Chao servants can barely recognize him. For Hu, dressing up like the gentry could have constituted a serious breach of the Ming regulations on theater professionals' dress. As we shall find, all the Ming dress codes were compulsory—some intended to dignify and others to debase the bearers' classes. Since the Ming government commanded that theater professionals be debased, they were ordered to identify themselves openly onstage.

> An actress . . . has to dress in a horned hat of bright color and a black vest. She is not allowed to dress as a commoner's wife. An actor . . . dresses in ordinary clothing but wears a green headdress to distinguish himself from gentlemen or commoners.[21]

The practice of capping male actors with green headdresses derived from the association of the color green with that of the turtle's head, the turtle being symbolically analogized to a cuckolded husband whose wife commits adultery in a Chinese cultural context.

In Feng Yuanjun's textual research masterpieces, *On the Ancient Entertainer* (Guyou Jie 古优解) and *Additions and Corrections to On the Ancient Entertainer* 古优解补正, she tries to prove that the commonality in dressing between the Chinese and Western ancient entertainer, or theater performers for imperial courts, is that "both use green and yellow." Feng cites Leber, who writes that these two colors were often used for "rebels or other criminals."[22] She also proves that "since the Spring and Autumn Period and the Western Han dynasty, the green headdress has always been a symbol of the lowly." In the fifth year of Zhiyuan reign in the Yuan dynasty (1268), a document from the Central Secretariat 中书省 was approved, ordering the father and other male relatives of prostitutes to wear green headdresses. For this reason, people of the Yuan and Ming dynasties called the plays written by the actors in the government offices managing imperial music "Green Headdress Lyrics."[23]

However, Hu's presumptuous offense, compared with the extravagant lifestyle of Commander Su and Commander Liu, who, by origin, are theater professionals, becomes insignificant. The reverses suffered by the Ming's orthodox social hierarchy reached new heights when Wang Zhen, the head of the eunuch agency and advisor of Emperor Yingzong, became the *de facto* ruler of the empire.[24]

Wang Zhen rose from a court advisor to become the eunuch of Silijian in the reign of Emperor Yingzong, a position only next to the emperor. Wang Zhen wielded unlimited power, rivaled in history only by Wei Zhongxian 魏忠贤 at the end of the Ming dynasty. To be above the civil bureaucracy with the identity of a eunuch and the background of an opera actor indeed constituted a great offense to the former, as evidenced by the former's merciless retaliation after Wang Zhen fell from power.

As the Novel reveals, the occasion of Wang Zhen's birthday delivers a spectacle. "A whole landscape of mountains and seas of people," "the three Secretaries, six Board Presidents, nine Ministers, and twenty-four Palace Ministers" (5.36) crowd in front of the door of the paramount eunuch, waiting to pay him respect and present him with gifts. Su and Liu, long acquainted with Wang Zhen, in "red crepe official robes embroidered with Kylin designs, snow-white carved jade belts, and trailing the ribbons of their seals of office from their hands" (5.36), are ushered inside first. Wang Shizhen's 王世贞 *Special Decrees of the Ming Dynasty* (Huang Ming Yidian Shu 皇明异典述) contains an account of the clothes and colors given by the emperor. The Kylin coat, often a special gift for cabinet ministers after their performance appraisal, carried considerable weight. For example, in the reign of Jiajing, the cabinet ministers Yan, Xu, and Li were given Kylin coats because the Kylin design matched the costume of lords.[25] In this light, the "red crepe official robes embroidered with Kylin designs" of Liu and Su are undoubtedly absurd. In the sixth year of the Ming Yongle (1408), it was stipulated that all officials in the capital had to wear an ivory token to enter and leave the city gate. The token was usually made of ivory and had a ten-inch-long red or green tassel underneath. The owner's official position was engraved and was divided into several categories by the title: Gong, Hou, Bo (titles granted to meritorious officials and royal relatives 公,侯,伯) with the word *Xun* (exploits 勋), military officials with the word *Wu* (military 武), music officials with the word *Yue* (music 乐), and eunuchs with the word *Gong* (palace 宫).[26]

Their gifts are presented and delightfully accepted: a translucent jade box with a tiny, gnarled jade peach tree inside and a similar jade box with a plum tree inside. The bribery has such an immediate effect that their proposal to promote Magistrate Chao to the Tongzhou post meets with the eunuch's prompt approbation. Su and Liu use the chance to exploit a 2,000-*tael* sum from Magistrate Chao.

Chao Yuan takes Zhenge to the North. As it is inconvenient to openly bring the concubine to his father's court in Tongzhou, he temporarily arranges for her

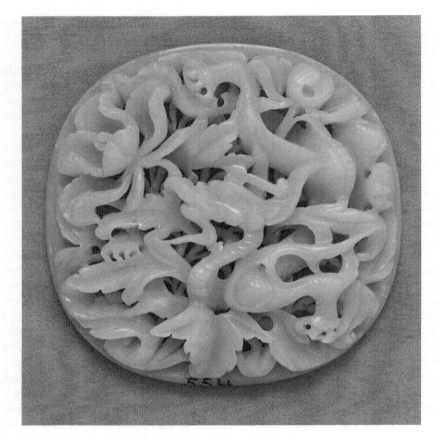

Figure 1.3 Belt plaque. 15th–16th century. Jade. H. 8.3 cm.
Source: Courtesy of Metropolitan Museum of Art, New York.

to live in a rented house in Shawo Men in Beijing. This decent house costs only three *taels* of silver (about 1,980 RMB yuan) for monthly rent, which must be the envy of today's tenants in Beijing. Ironically, his servant, Chao Zhu, soon becomes involved in an adulterous affair with his concubine, Zhenge. To find a pretext to live in Beijing, Chao Yuan then pays the Imperial Academy to study there and acquire a square cap.

Xizhou Sheng is acutely aware of the connotation of the green-colored male headdress. "He does not need to bother so much to secure another cap," comments Xizhou Sheng, on Chao Yuan's newly obtained status, "Has not he already gotten one," the author asks, rather teasingly, "in the color of green, gorgeously made, sent to him as a gift of gratitude from his servant, Chao Zhu, who is having an affair with Zhenge?" (6.41). The author's humorous remarks like this one permeate the entire composition.

The Clothing Culture and Clothing Choices of the Ming People   41

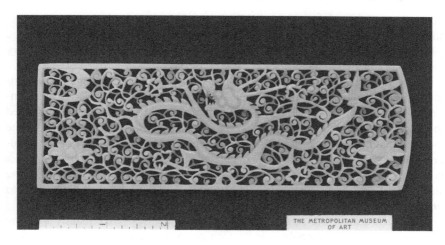

Figure 1.4 Belt plaque. 16th century. Jade. H. 5.4 × W. 13.2 × D. 0.7 cm.
Source: Courtesy of Metropolitan Museum of Art, New York.

According to *The History of the Ming Dynasty, Volume 69—Zhi 45* 明史•卷六十九•志第四十五:

> Those who enter the Imperial Academy are all called *jiansheng*, among which candidates in the imperial examinations at the provincial level are *jujian*, elected students from local academies are *gongjian*, sons of the magistrates are *yinjian*, and those who have paid the government to gain the place are *lijian*.

As for Chao Yuan, he should not be a *yinjian* but a *lijian*, the reasons for which can be analyzed here. At the beginning of the Ming Dynasty, a civil official of the first to seventh rank was allowed to choose one son to carry on his position due to the previous system of appointing officials' offspring. Later, the offer was gradually restricted, and only those above the third rank in the capital were allowed to apply for such an appointment, called *guansheng* (official students 官生). Those who came from special grace, not limited to the official rank, were called *ensheng* (grace students 恩生). They were either given a job or sent to study in the academy. *Guansheng* must be the offspring of those officials above the third rank in the capital. Given the fifth official rank of his father, Chao Sixiao, Chao Yuan is certainly not qualified.

The "Dong Jiang Mi Xiang" 东江米巷 was later to become the famous "Dong Jiao Min Xiang" 东交民巷 in Beijing's embassy district. This area was still called "Dong Jiang Mi Xiang" in the *Collection of Lanes and Hutongs in the Five Cities of Beijing* (Jingshi Wucheng Fangxiang Hutong Ji 京师五城坊巷胡同集), a Ming work, for there was a Jiang Mi Xiang main street and a "Xi Jiang Mi Xiang" to its west.[27] Due to its proximity to the imperial palace, the lane was an excellent commercial location. Xiao Jin Pu Gai 销金铺盖 was a common name for silver shops or silversmith shops. Jin Bo Hutong was one of the 75 most famous old hutongs in midtown Beijing during the Ming and was also renowned for its handicraft workshops;[28] long famous for gauze caps, it was not far from Dong Jiang Mi Xiang, which was known for the Dings' Boots. These large shops all had their subsidiary workshops attached to them.[29]

The Confucian square headdress, *fangjin* 方巾, was Ming scholars' most commonly worn cap. Legend held that Yang Weizhen 杨维桢, a prestigious Yuan Confucian who also lived to witness the founding of the Ming, was once summoned to Emperor Hongwu's audience wearing a square headdress. When the throne inquired about the strange-looking cap, he replied, "The squareness of the headdress has a special connotation: the pacification of the four squares of that which is Under Heaven." Delighted, the monarch ordered the universal adoption of the square headdress by all Confucian scholars who had not advanced themselves to *jinshi* degrees, notably the *shengyuan* and *jiansheng* candidates.[30]

But, in fact, the "four squares pacification headdresses" were mainly worn by commoners rather than scholars, as the Confucian scholars had more options. The Ming scholars could wear a wide range of hats, including various headdresses: Han, Jin, Tang, Zhuge, Chunyang, Dongpo, Yangming, Jiuhua, and Xiaoyao (Free and Unfettered 逍遥). However, commoners were limited to three types: the net headdress, four-squares pacification headdress, and the six-sides unification cap.[31] In the third year of Hongwu (1370), the scholars were ordered to wear square headdresses and, in the same year, they were also ordered to change the Sidai headdresses to square headdresses. Then, in the sixth year of Hongwu (1373), the commoners were instructed not to use gold, jade, onyx, coral, or amber for the headdress ring; were banned from fashioning the top of their hat; and were only allowed to use crystal and incense wood for the hat beads.[32]

In the second part of the Novel, the character Di Xichen, a *jiansheng* candidate, purchases the office of the Secretariat Drafter of the Legislative Bureau of the Wuying Palace (Wuying Dian Zhongshu Sheren 武英殿中书舍人) for 4,000 *taels* of silver (about 2.6 million RMB), almost the entirety of his wealth. Without realizing the capital officialdom's ephemerality, Xichen zestfully rushes to prepare his and his concubine's official accouterments.

> He has a round-neck robe made, reserves the court cap, bonnet, and black gauze cap, has a silversmith produce him a silver belt, a shoemaker a pair of leather boots, purchases the Jinling brocade ribbons, and has an umbrella-like protocol canopy made. In addition, he has a straight-sleeved Kylin robe and silver belt forged for Jijie, buys her a jade phoenix coronet with pearl decorations, and a "steady-high" embroidery vest.
>
> (83.639)

The Ming official costume was comprised of an open-foot and a round-neck bag-sleeve long robe, known as the round-neck, *yuanling* 圆领. The colors of the round-neck robe varied according to the ranks of the wearers, and so did the materials of the official belt, made of, from rank one to rank five, respectively: jade, flowery rhinoceros horn, carved gold and silver, plain gold, and carved silver. A rank-six-to-seven belt was made of plain silver, and that of rank eight or nine,

Figure 1.5 Rank badge with lion. 15th century. Silk and metallic-thread embroidery on silk gauze. Overall: H. 36.8 × W. 36.2 cm.

Source: Courtesy of Metropolitan Museum of Art, New York.

ebony.[33] The position of the Secretariat Drafter of the Legislative Bureau, securable either by passing the civil service examination or alternatively, through purchase, ranked sub-seventh in the Ming administrative system and was among the lowest strata in Beijing officialdom. Though ascending to such a position did not grant one substantial power, it allowed the officeholder to feel elated. The late Ming officialdom, over-flooded by office purchasers like Xichen, had lost its vitality.

After the Zhengtong reign, scholars of the two houses, the East and the West, of the Wenyuan Pavilion (Wenyuan Ge Zhongshu Sheren 文渊阁中书舍人) were allowed to draft imperial replies as representatives of the throne. They were directly under the Cabinet, with a significant difference in status between them and the scholars of Wenhua Palace and Wuying Palace, the so-called "two palaces." After the Xuande and before the Chenghua reigns (1435–1465), the status of the "two houses" and "two palaces" was almost the same. However, the status of both was lower than that of the scholars of Zhongshu Ke, most of whom were *jinshichushen* 进士出身, descended from graduates who ranked second class in the imperial *jinshi* exam. And of the two palaces, the Wuying Palace was always

44 *The Clothing Culture and Clothing Choices of the Ming People*

Figure 1.6 Rank badge with two phoenixes. 16th century. Silk and metal thread tapestry (kesi). Overall: H. 34.9 × W. 34.9 cm.
Source: Courtesy of Metropolitan Museum of Art, New York.

slightly more complicated. Due to the low requirements for their educational backgrounds, although they worked as close servants, making a name for themselves in an institution directly under the Ming Central Government was challenging.[34] Di Xichen's outfit reveals the reckless and serendipitous appointment of those who obtained a bureaucratic position without passing the civil service examination.

The defaulting of the legitimacy established by the civil service examination institution was thought to have become one of the fatal factors leading to the regime's final collapse.

2) The Concubine and Legitimate Wife: The Blurred Boundaries Continued

Chao Yuan, summoned from his hometown to stay with his parents in Tongzhou, does not feel ready to present his concubine to them. Therefore, he rents a house in

The Clothing Culture and Clothing Choices of the Ming People 45

Figure 1.7 Rank badge with *Qilin*. 19th century. Silk and metallic thread embroidery on silk satin. H. 25.4 × W. 25.4 cm.
Source: Courtesy of Metropolitan Museum of Art, New York.

Beijing, settles Zhenge and the servants there, and uses the residence requirement of the Imperial Academy as a pretext to sojourn to the capital.

Huang Yunmei 黄云眉, one of the "eight famous professors" in the History Department of Shandong University and a great scholar of Ming history, has noticed the habitual abuses of the "residence length" requirement of the Imperial Academy. In the Ming dynasty, the "allocation of students to government departments" was initially based on the admission year in the Yongle reign (1403–1424); that is, the principle of "entering the Academy first, graduating first" was used. Chen Jingzong 陈敬宗, Directorate of the Nanjing Imperial Academy, found that many students were staying at home on the pretext of their parents' funerals and ancestral worship. Hence, he requested that "the student's seniority must be based on their actual study length in the Academy." Chen Jingzong and Li Shimian 李时勉, Directorate of the Beijing Imperial Academy, were both highly regarded by the scholarly community and were known as the "Chen in the South and Li in the North." In the seventh year of Zhengtong, Li Shimian again requested:

> I hope that in the future, students will be assigned for government internships according to the actual length of their studies at the Academy and that all leaves taken on such grounds as parents' funerals and ancestral worship will be subtracted from the time spent studying, so that laziness will be punished, and diligence encouraged.

As for the effects of Li Shimian's request, Huang Yunmei was not optimistic.[35]

Magistrate Chao, a doting father, sends an errand boy to Beijing to fetch the couple back upon hearing the news of his son's absence. The messenger witnesses Zhenge, an energetic 20-something woman, playing shuttlecock in the courtyard. She wears "a dark green gauze jacket, a sky-blue bodice, and bright red satin trousers with no skirt over them" (7.47).

The depiction of her winter costume, especially the lack of a skirt, befits the figure of an unrestrained, dynamic young concubine in a comfortable milieu. As the result of de-Mongolization and restoration of the Han culture, the style of the Ming costume was heavily reminiscent of that of the Tang and Song. The jackets were generally right-clasped, long, and wide enough to cover the knees. Gu Yanwu records the evolution of the length of women's jackets:

> During the Hongzhi years, women's jackets only covered the waistband. During the Zhengde years, the jackets got more prominent, the dresses got more pleated, only gold-colored *buzi* [square decorative fabrics 补子] was used, and the bun got higher. During the early Jiajing years, the jackets got large enough to cover knees, and the dresses became short and less pleated.[36]

Women's jackets were made right-clasped, over-stretched, and long enough to cover knees, thus sparing the need to wear skirts on less formal occasions.

Zhenge, following her husband, comes to Tongzhou to meet her in-laws. As a concubine, she is over-dressed for the meeting. In "a bright red narrow-sleeved robe and a white damask embroidered skirt, with kingfisher pins all over her head" (7.48), she walks to the middle of the courtyard and kowtows for eight rounds, followed by the presentation of her needlework gifts. The Chaos dismiss her perfunctorily by bestowing her two *taels* of silver. They dislike her for one simple reason: she boasts a beauty that makes them uneasy. On Madame Chao's part, this uneasiness might well have been ignited by Zhenge's wearing "bright red," a color reserved only for primary wives like herself and her legitimate daughter-in-law, Née Ji.

Gu Yanwu says, "Former women did not dare to wear the *liang* crown, the red robe, and the dragging belt unless they were ordained, but now the rich are all wearing them."[37]

The default color for concubines is the less dazzling pink. In the ordinary scenery of a traditional Chinese family, the tension between the rival pair of mother-in-law/daughter-in-law is commonplace. Still, it can be curiously soothed by the intrusion of a third party, the son's concubine. The two legitimate wives, allied by the common ground of their scorn for the low-birth concubine, would team up to dispense the difficult feelings of losing their son and husband to a coquettish "fox spirit." This sentiment, not surprisingly, is to become palpable within the Chao household.

The Tumu Fort Incident soon ensued. Wang Zhen, the instigator of the military expedition, died in the Incident, and the Mongols captured Emperor Yingzong. In the turbulent aftermath, with their influential relatives gone and charged as accomplices of Wang Zhen, the opera actors Hu and Liang seek asylum under the Chaos' roof. Still, they are gulled by Chao Yuan into a penniless and hazardous situation, which drives them to tonsure their hair and become monks to evade the manhunt.

When the crisis is over, Magistrate Chao dispatches Chao Yuan and Zhenge home. In her newly found sympathy towards Née Ji, Madame Chao decides to compensate the abandoned daughter-in-law. She asks one of the servant wives to bring her some cash, jewels, and clothes: 50 *taels* of silver to supply her sewing needs, two pearls and two *taels* of gold, a bolt of raw silk gauze, one of gold cloth, one blue satin and one plain pink pongee, two skirts, and two catties of cotton (8.54). Despite Zhenge's discontent and frustration, the gifts arrive safely in Née Ji's hands when they return home. Days later, in defending her innocence against a charge that she has committed adultery with a peripatetic monk, Née Ji commits suicide. The timely arrival of the gifts from her mother-in-law paves the way for her suicide plan, for she could not have possibly created a decent shroud for herself from her meager savings.

She has the blue satin tailored into a long-sleeved robe, the plain pink pongee into a half-coat and some underwear padded by cotton. She then entrusts the rest of her belongings to her father and brother. At the dawn of the following day, she takes a bath, burns incense, combs her hair, and tightens her feet; clamping one gold stick and one silver stick into her mouth, she takes a peach-red phoenix sash and quietly hangs herself in front of Chao Yuan's door (9.64). The image of her in her death vestments afterward becomes a ghostly visitor to the Chao residence. In a pair of new cinnabar-pink silk trousers with a moon-white damask under-garment, a sky-blue short jacket with a cinnabar pink pongee jacket over it, a moon-white great robe, and the blue satin wide-sleeved robe, the ghost frequents Chao Yuan's hallucinations and, on occasion, haunts Madame Chao's dreams as well.

Née Ji is thoughtful in arranging her funeral affairs and her revenge on Chao Yuan. The way she prepares her shroud and the several measures she takes before committing suicide are in strict accordance with the known Shandong practices of burial rites. The materials of the shroud cannot be furs, lest the dead is incarnated into an animal in the next life, nor brocade, *duanzi* 缎子, out of concern that the homophone, which means "sever the sons" 断子, would cut the lineage of male descendants of the dead person's family. Cotton and satin *juan* silk are always preferred for their homophones, *mianmian* 绵绵 and *juanjuan* 绢绢, which deliver the connotation of lasting prosperity. The dead's face and body should be cleansed, preferably by the children or spouse,[38] and the feet should be tightened, regardless of gender. Jewelry, such as pearls and coins, are often placed in the mouth of the deceased.[39] Thus, Née Ji single-handedly carries out almost half of her burial preparations before she even dies.

Née Ji's funeral is but one of many depicted in the Novel. Undoubtedly, the author's familiarity with the folk customs in North China is profound, for we can easily find examples that range from the bitter sorrow of funerals to the cheerful festivities of weddings, one of which is Sujie's bridal shower. The term "bridal shower" is borrowed from the Western context but does not denote a gift-giving event delivered by the bride-to-be's friends. The ritual is called "capping the head" (*shangtou* 上头) in China, and is usually performed by a married, senior woman, sometimes by the future mother-in-law herself. It is also known as one of the variations of the "plucking the bride's face" (*kailian* 开脸), a ceremony widely practiced until late modern times. We have no difficulty locating relevant depictions in assorted modern literature, such as Lin Yutang's *Moment in Peking*[40] or Lao She's *Beneath the Red Banner* (Zheng Hongqi Xia 正红旗下).[41]

Before the formal wedding ceremony, Xichen's mother, Lady Di, comes to the Xues to cap Sujie's head:

> When the auspicious hour comes, Sujie is ushered out, wearing a scarlet bridal garment, orthodox-green brocade embroidered skirt adorned with seven-piece jewels; indeed, she is like a fairy descending into the sub-celestial world. She greets her mother-in-law and, facing the southeast direction where the happy gods dwell, sits on a barrel. Lady Di uses a thread to pluck her face up and down as if in the shape of a cross, caps her with a *diji* coiffure, and Sujie, in her newly adorned bead row jewels, kowtows to her mother-in-law in four rounds of kneeling and eight rounds of bowing.
>
> (44.337)

It is essential to add that face-plucking should be done in a place away from others. The bride should face the south or the north, avoiding the east-west direction. After the rite, the bride's family will throw the water out of the bucket, meaning "Married girl, splashed water." The "happy god" (*xishen* 喜神) is the god of good fortune for the wedding ceremony but is not a god that is commonly worshipped in Chinese folklore. The ancient custom asks the bride to sit and stand in the right direction for the god, but this direction varies according to the specific time.

On the 1st and 6th days, the direction is northeast, and the time is 3 a.m. to 5 a.m.; on the 2nd and 7th days, the direction is northwest, and the time is 7 p.m. to 9 p.m.; on the 3rd and 8th days, the direction is southwest, and the time is 3 p.m. to 5 p.m.; on the 4th and 9th days, the direction is south, and the time is 11 a.m. to 1 p.m.; on the 5th and 10th days, the direction is southeast, and the time is 7 a.m. to 9 a.m. Cao Zhengui said: "It is the mother who sees her son who makes things happy."[42]

In *Beneath the Red Banner*, Lao She also makes the point that the "fully blessed" identity of her mother, which means the health of her husband and children are good and her family complete, enabled her to act as a "bridesmaid" and "pluck face" for girls who were about to be married. However, the honor brought by this identity aroused the envy of Lao She's widowed aunt, the elder sister-in-law of his mother.[43]

The *diji* coiffure was worn by upper-class adult women in the Ming dynasty to signify their privileged identities. In the shape of a cap containing meshes, a *diji* can allow hairpins to come through it. A *diji* does not have to be made of silver or gold, but it is indicative of the wearer's affluence and dignity when it does. In specific households, only primary wives and important concubines wear *diji*, the values of which are supposed to decrease in line with the proper familial hierarchy, ranging from the first wife to the lowest concubine. In *Jin Ping Mei*, when Li Ping'er has just married Ximen Qing, upon learning that the primary wife, Wu Yueniang, does not have a gold *diji*, she dares not wear hers, which weighs nine *taels* of pure gold. Most times, Ximen Qing's least favored concubine, Sun Xue'er, is deprived of the right to wear a *diji*. In the 25th chapter, Song Huilian complains about Ximen Qing:

> you promised you were going to have a proper fret made up for my hair. How come you haven't had it made yet? If I'm not to wear it now, when am I to wear it? I suppose I'll have to keep on wearing this excuse of a hairpiece from one day to the next.[44]

In Eileen Chang's autobiographical novel *Little Reunions* 小团圆, she writes that her distant cousin was balding and "wore a thin, fake mesh cap,"[45] showing that the hair shell is also used as a *diji* wig.

The *diji* coiffure was, after all, a fashionable hair accessory, so its style followed the fashion. At the end of the Qing Dynasty, there was a boom in the popularity of *diji* coiffure fashions in Yangzhou. The full range of names indicates that *diji* coiffures were available in all forms: butterfly, full moon, flower basket, *zhexiang*, arhat, lazy combing, double flying swallows, loose pillow hairstyle, eight-faced Avalokitesvara cap, fisherwoman *lezi* [mesh fabrics 勒子], and so on.[46]

The style of the *diji* coiffure is also reflected in the policy of "dividing the good and the bad between courtesans and other people." *The History of the Ming Dynasty—Records of Carriage and Clothing* 明史・舆服志 records, "A regulation has been set in the 3rd year of Hongwu, stipulating that all women officials in charge of music and dance rituals in the palace should wear a hair-color *diji* coiffure."[47]

In the bustling material world of the late Ming, nevertheless, that one was entitled to, or prohibited from, wearing what kind of fiber, or in what format or color, was of lesser and lesser concern to those who could pay and were willing to purchase the clothes they liked. Moreover, the boundaries between legitimate wives and concubines, females of high birth and celebrated prostitutes, and elite womenfolk and parvenu wives were also blurred due to the slackened regulations on social hierarchies.

50 *The Clothing Culture and Clothing Choices of the Ming People*

Figure 1.8 Silver coronal covered with black crepe inlaid with a turquoise on the top (*Diji*). H. 13.5 cm; Diam. 12.7 cm.
Source: Courtesy of Wujin Museum, Changzhou.

More than ten years after his unhappy marriage with Sujie, Xichen takes a concubine, Jijie, in Beijing. The wedding is almost as formal as his first one; after Xichen purchases his sub-seventh official title in Beijing, the dresses he procures for Jijie are, in theory, reserved only for his legitimate wife. Yet nobody even notices this bold presumption. In the Ming, the dress of an official's wife was strictly decided by her husband's rank. In the 24th year of Hongwu (1391), it was decreed that wives of officials, after attending a court audience, were to wear their official dresses on two occasions: greeting their in-laws and attending family sacrifices. The most elaborately dressed women were the wives of the highest-ranked dignitaries. The following description, only on the design of their caps, is already of baffling complexity:

(Wives of) officials wear caps decorated with gold and silver accessories. There ought to be two birds of pearls, two strings of cherry-bay pearls in the front, six rows of half-opened pearls, twenty-four pieces of emerald jade leaves, eighteen pieces of emerald jade cherry-bay leaves, and an emerald-orifice circle, which has eight gold and silver flowers, and two birds of gilded gold and silver, each holding a pearl knot in its mouth.[48]

The rigid differentiation between legitimate wives and concubines only existed in laws by the late Ming. In practice, if a concubine was dominant, or favored, or both, she could be treated on social occasions with etiquette usually only reserved for the primary wife. The situation was, however, only when issues of legitimacy were not involved. In Jijie's case, she gains access to such glorious dresses and appears in family banquets as the hostess under her husband's and his acquaintances' acquiescence. But when a lawsuit involving her maid's death must be made known to the legal authorities, Xichen still needs to specify her as his "concubine" when he petitions the case for her.

Curiously, several years later, when the rebellious legitimate wife, Sujie, joins the family in Chengdu, she is first beaten and then intimidated by the shrewd concubine. Her lack of tactics and supporting attendants aside, Jijie's dominating her, an abnormality even in the chaotic late Ming, must be viewed through the lens of Ming martial law, which regulated that any of the seven conditions—the lack of

Figure 1.9 Crown of phoenixes set with beads.
Source: Image Unaltered.

a son, adultery, thievery, un-filial behavior to one's parents-in-law, garrulousness, jealousy, and incurable disease—could constitute a valid reason for divorcing one's wife.[49] Since one of Sujie's eyes and nose are permanently bruised by a monkey, Jijie exploits her physical defects to call her divorceable.

The blurred boundaries between wives and concubines mirrored the late Ming's disorderly social constitution.[50] Still, one is cautioned against over-construing the perversion of orthodox hierarchy, especially the concubine's superseding of a wife, for it is indeed a rarity at any moment in imperial Chinese history.

3) The Deceased Official and City God

Funerals, one coming after another, constitute significant events for the Chao family in the following years. Not long after Magistrate Chao takes Chunying as his concubine to entertain him during his retirement years, he catches a cold, and the indisposition soon develops into a disease that takes away his life. Though not a filial son, Chao Yuan insists on holding a grand funeral for his father. He has the "Happy God" of Magistrate Chao portrayed by a painter. Happy God is a likeness of a deceased senior, usually of an imperial conferred title regardless of gender, sitting in the official outfit. The portrait, created to solicit respect from mourners, can be flexibly complimentary in featuring the deceased but must be accurate in rendering the rank and the title by detailing the dress. However, Chao Yuan desires his father to be portrayed in attire that exceeds his late father's rank: dragon robe, jade belt, and gold bonnet. When the painter protests, arguing that the deceased should not be seen in a more elegant dress than he deserves to wear, Chao Yuan lies about Magistrate Chao's rank and bribes the painter to get his way. Moreover, he orders the title "Lord Chao, first in erudition and most glorious minister" (18.137) to be written on his father's posthumous tablet by the Yin-Yang functionary.

The left and right *zhuguo* (literally pillar of the country 柱国) were first ranks and were not conferred on civil officials in the early Ming dynasty. In the conferment of ranks for meritorious officials in the third year of Hongwu, "Li and Xu were conferred left *zhuguo*, Li Wenzhong and others were conferred right *zhuguo*, and no civil officials were included." It was not until after Zhengde's reign that civil officials were conferred this rank. In the Wanli reign, even for political magnates such as Zhang Juzheng 张居正 and Shen Shixing 申时行, the conferment was only done after a term of nine years.[51] And the rank of the upper *zhuguo* was even rarer. Yan Song 严嵩 and Xu Jie 徐阶 had been conferred for their merits, but they voluntarily resigned. According to Wang Shizhen, only Xia Yan 夏言 and Zhang Juzheng were granted the title[52]—he did not count Gu Bingqian 顾秉谦 in the late Ming. Xia Yan was conferred the title during his lifetime, yet he later provoked trouble and was executed publicly. Zhang Juzheng, though granted the title posthumously, was stripped of his ranks and nearly had his corpse flogged.

In the following *dianzhu* 点主 ceremony, local gentleman Chen, a *fangbo* 方伯, the invited *dianzhu* performer, is rightly exasperated. *Dianzhu* is usually performed by the most distinguished literary acquaintance of the deceased's family when the burial is prepared in advance and the writing of the wood tablet near finished, leaving only the single dot in the Chinese character *zhu* (host 主) to be filled in. The dignitary is invited to fill that blank dot with a brush in red ink or blood, often with considerable pomp; the finishing dot gives life to the tablet. The word *zhu* means "divine master." The process of making the tablet for the deceased is called *zuozhu*, while the ceremony of asking someone to add the first stroke of the word *zhu* on the tablet with a vermilion pen is called *dianzhu*.[53] The deceased's tablet is written in advance with the phrase "The *wang* place of so-and-so," and the bereaved family then invites the most prestigious local gentry to attend the ceremony and add a stroke on the word "wang" with vermilion or even blood to make it a character "zhu." This stroke needs to be written with full ink and brush, after which the "divine master" tablet will gain liveliness.

Fangbo was used in the Ming dynasty as a particular address for provincial governors and could also refer to former provincial governors. No details are given in the book as to where Chen Fangbo served. While arranging his father's funeral, Chao Yuan, with 30-*tael* invitation cards, obtains "the epitaph by Hanlin Scholar Hu, the calligraphy by Governor Chen, and the cover by Deputy Minister Jiang." Jiang, who carries out *dianzhu* at the funeral, would later become the father-in-law of Chao Yuan's half-brother Chao Liang. As Chen Fangbo is highly ranked, he is supposed to act as the chief figure among the gentry at the public ceremony and offer incense at the table. The painter was initially reluctant to raise the standard in painting the portrait of Happy God precisely because he was "afraid of being blamed by Chen Fangbo again" (18.138).

Chen Fangbo is there to attend a funeral, and it would be improper to express his anger. In this portrait, the deceased, with a white face and a long beard, wears a bonnet and a red *mang* robe. Who does it resemble other than City God in the temple?

Shrewd enough, Chen Fangbo does not publicly extricate himself from the honorable duty, but pretends to be confused by the appearance of the Happy God.

"Who is the god in this altar?" Chen Fangbo asks.
"Why, that's Old Master Chao," asserts a household servant.

"Nonsense!" Chen Fangbo berates his own servant in a fume, "I told you to take me to the Chaos. Why did you bring me to the temple of the City God instead?"

(18.138)

He thus successfully manages to extricate himself from the utterly improper ceremony. However, this hilarious incident nevertheless reveals the resemblance of the clothing between the excessively portrayed Magistrate Chao and that of the City God.

City God narratives abound in both folk literature and literary sketches. David Johnson dates the first appearance of a City God playing a karmic role in anecdotal literature to the late ninth or early tenth century. The deity's primary job is to protect people by summoning up demonic creatures to do his bidding; he also rescues people from famine, epidemics, warfare, and drought.[54] Although occasionally punishing errant civilians and officials, the City God is not expected to render justice for the sinful deeds committed by men who had died recently. His benevolent, protective nature and the exhibited resemblance to the mundane magistrate ensure that he, albeit inherently a ghostly being, is respected but not feared enough. He lacks any traces of devilry, gruesomeness, and atrocity. And these are nowhere to be found in the indigenous belief in cosmic retribution, either.

The position of a City God is typically assumed by a deified local magistrate of great moral integrity who enjoys a posthumous reputation among his people. He is believed to have supernatural powers to "stand guard over the hills and mountains of the city and control the good and bad fortune of both soldiers and civilians."[55] From today's literary portraits, we usually get the impression that he wears an embroidered robe and elaborate headdress and carries a scepter of jade, a symbol of his rank. Yet if the salient details have not escaped, we are to find that the ranking and classification of the Ming City Gods, and accordingly their dress codes, are indeed as complex as that of their earthborn counterparts, the civil officials.

Emperor Hongwu intentionally promoted the City God cult upon the dynasty's founding to leave officials and civilians awestruck. Emperor Hongwu once revealed to Song Lian, the advisor of the heir apparent, "I set up the City God institution to make people fear; when they have something to dread, they will refrain from behaving boldly."[56] Imperial edicts were issued as early as the third year of Hongwu's reign to regulate that any new local magistrate, upon arriving in the post, must first pay homage to and then pledge to work with his counterpart City God.[57] A pair of Yin-Yang magistrates were thus formed to bring peace and good governance to the district, mundanely and supernaturally.

The Ming City Gods were ranked, titled, and dressed according to their respective geographical significance. For example, the City God of Jinling, the first Ming capital, and that of the other five governmental districts (*fu* 府), respectively Kaifeng *fu*, Linhao *fu*, Taiping *fu*, Hezhou *fu*, and Chuzhou *fu*,[58] were all titled "kings" and ranked foremost in posthumous officialdom, but they were dressed differently. Only the Jinling City God wore imperial gowns and crowns with 12 *zhang*, the same as the crown of the Son of Heaven; the other five kings, though in similar robes, could only wear nine *zhang*.[59]

Zhang is the set of strings of beads attached to the formal hat, a rectangular black mortarboard worn by the sovereign. The 12 pendulous sets of beads on the front and back of the hat give the wearer a curtain-like feeling, and they function to remind him to move about decorously.[60] The matching of the Son of Heaven with the City God of the Ming capital makes sense in terms of maintaining an institutional symmetry between the centers of the secular and supernatural worlds. In the same vein, City Gods of lesser geographic significance, in the descending order of *fu*, *zhou*, and *xian*, were ranked lower, were inferior in title, and were given fewer decorated *zhang* in their official costumes. Still, even a county City God would hold a Fourth Rank Proper 正四品, outranking most middle and minor civil bureaucrats. On that ground, we argue that the excuse of Chen Fangbo, the *dianzhu* performer, bears considerable validity. His claim to have run into a City God is entirely believable, for the grandeur of a City God's costume would have

The Clothing Culture and Clothing Choices of the Ming People 55

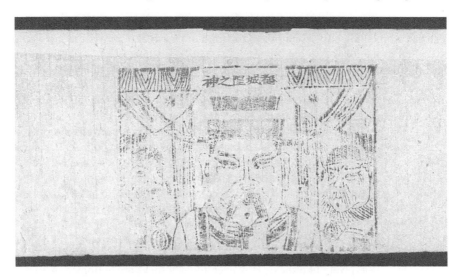

Figure 1.10 Paper God: Capital City God. Early 20th century. Woodblock print; ink on paper; with a printed inscription reading from right to left: "Du Cheng Huang Zhi Shen" ("Town God of the Capital"). H. 20.9 × W. 41.3 cm.

Source: Harvard Art Museums/Arthur M. Sackler Museum, Gift of Langdon Warner, Photo. ©President and Fellows of Harvard College, 1935.36.81

easily surpassed that of a mediocre magistrate, who, alive or deceased, can hardly have had access to the wearing of a dragon robe, jade belt, and gold bonnet, which are exaggeratedly attached to the likeness of Magistrate Chao.

4) *The Country Woman*

Having concluded the funeral and paid thanks to the mourners, Chao Yuan spends the summer on his villa farm to supervise the harvest, where he meets shoemaker Xiaoya's 小鸦 wife, Née Tang 唐氏, a rural woman who boasts a pretty face and a pair of tiny feet. A poem depicts her pristine yet stylish outfit:

> In her long-sleeved, dark robe,
> And pink gauze pantaloons,
> Her skirt kilted up,
> Hose pulled snugly.
> (19.140)

The long-sleeved dark robe is made of a particular type of cloth of an abraded quality. Though neither silk nor brocade, the *maoqing* fabric 毛青布 was popular among the Ming women mainly because it offered a low-cost option for making good-quality clothes. The making of the cloth involves no sizing, and the softness of its texture delivers a comfortable touch to its wearer. It befits slender-waisted and slim-featured women the best, giving them the kind of charm akin to what today would be called Bohemian fashion: unorthodox, anti-mainstream, anti-establishment, yet full of untamed attractions. The author must have been consciously or unconsciously inspired by the image of Pan Jinlian, the sensual female protagonist of *Jin Ping Mei*, for she is also a wearer of *maoqing* cloth. Before she kills her cake-selling husband and marries Ximen Qing, Pan Jinlian, like Née Tang, has also been a discontented wife. The commonality between the two women dwells not only in their dress but also in their restless spiritual states, in that they both seek to have affairs with rich men who can satiate both their sexual and financial needs.

The pantaloons Née Tang wears differ from women's pants or long socks. More like liners, the pantaloons covered the wearer's legs from knee to ankle, strapping them to the shanks; they are thought to have been essential for skirt wearing.

Zhao Yi's textual research is very detailed:

> According to Lü Lanyan's 吕蓝衍 *Interesting Speech* [Yan Jing 言鲭], *xiku* [leggings 膝裤] were like socks. However, today's socks are bottomed, while *xiku* were bottomless and shaped differently. According to *Zhi Gu Zi* 炙毂子, such socks had been called *jiao* socks since the Xia dynasty, consisting of two pieces, each with a central band. Ancient socks were made like today's leg warmers. In fact, the so-called socks in ancient times were the same, in terms of style, as leg warmers nowadays, but later, as someone added bottoms, the socks were divided into two types, one still called socks, and the other *xiku*.[61]

In addition, the *World Browsing Series* (Yueshi Bian 阅世编) mentions that *xiku* were available in various styles and colors, "Some are decorated with colored inlays, some with embroidery, some plain, some even with golden beads and jade. Despite different decorations, the form is the same." The styles changed over time; for example,

> After the 10th year of Chongzhen reign (1637), *xiku* were still short, only covering the shins and the lower edge hanging down to the shoes. It was common to wrap a cotton cloth around the shins in wintertime or to make the trousers longer. Research shows that the original reason for modification was to cover and hide the fat feet of some people.[62]

When used as gifts, pantaloons could either be intimate souvenirs from male lovers or lovely presents for women on social occasions.

The adultery between Chao Yuan and Née Tang, though carried out in extreme secrecy, is discovered; the enraged husband, Xiaoya, kills both of them in their bed, throwing the sonless Madame Chao into despair.

5) *The Prostitute*

Xichen, in his boyhood, is a prankish, wild boy. He excels at tricks but hates books. Old Di, aspiring to provide his son with a good education and thus elevate his son's future career prospects, finds him a good teacher, Mr. Cheng, whose private tutorship also extends to Xichen's cousin, Xiang Yuting, and the two sons of Old Xue, Xue Rubian and Xue Rujian. Years later, Cheng takes the four students to Jinan to have them take the entry-level civil service examination, where Xichen encounters his first love, a pretty prostitute named Sun Lanji. Merely 16 and a country bumpkin, Xichen hovers in front of the girl's house, not daring to call on her. Lanji learns about his presence and, despite having other business to attend to, rushes out, "uncombed hair coiled up in her hand with a hair-band, wearing a garment of raw gauze, a pair of pale-blue autumn-silk trousers, pantaloons decorated with white flowers, and high-heeled little red shoes." She falls for the shy boy, takes him to her bedroom, and develops an intimate relationship.

Their budding love affair is doomed, nonetheless, as Xichen has long been engaged with Sujie, and Lanji, a ready source of money for her procuress, is not allowed to choose a husband of her free will. Instead, she is sold to a pawnshop merchant as a concubine. Three years later, the lovers meet again in a tricky situation while Xichen engages in a business transaction with her husband. Without saying a word to him, Lanji tucks a gift set into his arms. Unwrapping it, Xichen finds the following items that stir up his emotions: a pale-blue gauze handkerchief, a three-piece golden toothpick kit, a small red damask silk wrapper with Zhao Mansion Upper-Throat Clearing Pills and Huguang jasmine tea inside, and a pair of worn red-silk sleeping shoes (50.386).

Handkerchiefs had traditionally been used by lovers as souvenirs in Chinese love scenes and thus required no more explanation; the three-piece golden toothpick kit was a personal hygiene kit invented during the Ming dynasty, popular among women because of its portability. It was a combination of two or three items: an earwax remover, a toothpick, a pair of tweezers, and a clipper. The kit sometimes did not include a toothpick or was made of silver, but it was called a "three-piece golden toothpick" anyway. The kit was often exchanged between lovers but also frequently used as a gift from a senior to a junior, especially on such social occasions as a women's gathering. For example, in chapter 14 of *Jin Ping Mei*, when Li Ping'er first meets the quick-witted Chunmei and learns that she has slept with Ximen Qing, she "expediently gives her a three-piece golden toothpick kit as a gift."

Together with the three-piece golden toothpick kit, there were often small boxes containing scented tea or sachets. The scented tea was not for people to drink but for oral cleansing, like our chewing gum today. There are exquisite examples of these objects among the unearthed Ming cultural relics. One three-piece golden toothpick kit, excavated from the tomb of Wang Shiqi at Zhangjiadu in Linhai, Zhejiang province, has a toothpick and an earpick chained together, running through a small gold tube painted with a lady holding a peach. The tools were pulled out when in use and reinserted afterward with a peach-shaped gold stopper to plug the tube—quite an exquisite design.[63]

Sleeping shoes were a pair of soft-soled slippers worn by a woman with bound feet during the night after she took off her outer shoes, leg binders, and leggings.[64] They could be made of cotton or silk, with or without embroidery, but comfortability was the primary concern. For traditional women who took footbinding as a lifelong business, their feet had to be under tender care day and night; not a moment could elapse without having their feet wrapped with proper shoes, for the loosening of the feet, even for just a short period, would have ruined all the initial efforts. Besides that, by design, texture, size, and subsequent relation to sexual intimacy and eroticism, sleeping shoes helped generate a tremendous sex appeal for men. Captured by traditional Chinese culture any time after the Southern Song and before the influx of Western notions, the appreciation of tiny feet had been blended into national aesthetics. Even the brutal Manchu invasion did not fundamentally change this lasting practice. The author, obviously one of the captives of the golden lotus culture, ardently extols the extraordinary beauty of the shoes:

> Crimson damask silk is the surface, and white satin is the upper; the softness is afforded by the cotton-padded sole, while lacework in emerald blue is embroidered on the sides. From a brief glimpse, the golden lotuses are crescent and tiny, but upon closer scrutiny, the bamboo shoots are slender and exquisite. Chang E, the immortal fairy on the moon, at night changes her shoes to a pair of those and rests them on the shoulders of Wu Gang.
>
> (52.399)

The appeal is to prove phenomenal concerning Xichen's fragile mind. Upon receiving the pair of sleeping shoes, he behaves like a lost soul. He has a small wrapper made for him by a needleman in the white damask face and pale-blue sarcenet with which he either conceals the shoes in his sleeves or under his waist, and only when no one is around would he take them out and twiddle with them, tears on his cheeks.

Because of the design, texture, size, and foot fetish associated with sleeping shoes, in the old days, a woman gave her lover a pair of sleeping shoes as a promise of physical and emotional affection from which the man could draw endless sexual associations. Between the Southern Song dynasty and the importation of Western ideas in modern times, the appreciation of tiny feet had been blended into national aesthetics. Even the ban after the Ming-Qing transition could not abolish the deep-seated foot-binding practice among Han Chinese women. The Qing rulers banned footbinding in 1636, 1638, and 1664. In her book *Cinderella's Sisters: A Revisionist History of Footbinding*, Dorothy Ko presents a "revisionist" view that these bans had the opposite effect to reenforce footbinding among Han Chinese women in the seventeenth and eighteenth centuries. According to Ko, footbinding was a means by which the Han Chinese fought against Manchu rule and maintained their national identity.[65]

Sleeping shoes and handkerchiefs, in mutual gift exchanges, were the most accessible fuel with which to kindle an affair between a man and a woman. In *Jin Ping Mei*, Pan Jinlian loses one of her "embroidered shoes of scarlet silk, figured with flowers from each of the four seasons and the symbolic representations of the 'eight treasures,' with fat, white satin soles, green heel lifts, and blue hook and eye fastenings." Chen Jingji then finds the red embroidered shoe "as curved as the

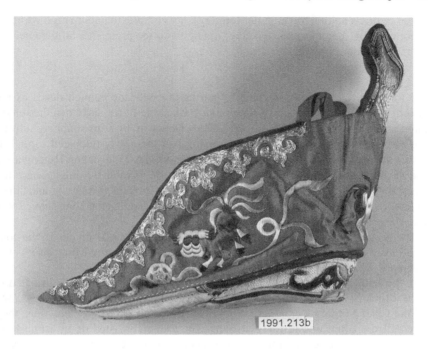

Figure 1.11 Slipper (one of a pair). Late 19th century. Silk satin embroidered with silk and metallic thread. L. 15.9 cm.

Source: Courtesy of Metropolitan Museum of Art, New York.

new moon at heaven's edge/as red as the fallen petal of a lotus blossom, exactly just three inches in the palm," which he uses to hook up with Pan Jinlian. Having developed a mutual affection for each other, Pan sends Chen a "fine, tasseled, white satin handkerchief, decorated with a drawnwork motif: Ts'ui Ying-ying Burning Evening Incense."[66] Ming scholar Feng Menglong writes in *Sleeping Shoes* in the *Folk Song* 山歌: "A personal affair is like shoes, which take a lot of effort."[67]

6) The Well-to-do Artisan Housewife

Xichen, in fulfillment of the residence requirement for his studentship at the Imperial Academy, goes to Beijing accompanied by his father, Old Di. They rent a house from Silversmith Tong, a pleasant landlord, and his wife, an amiable landlady. Lady Tong is sophisticated, warm-hearted, resourceful, and extroverted, and does not shy away from social engagements. The first time she meets with the Dis:

> She wears a gold-threaded seven-girder *diji* with a mirror-faced crow-black silk bandana covering her forehead, in her bright oil-green double-breasted lu silk coat, white mini-flower song silk skirt, black-fastener snow-white silk high-heel bow shoes, and white damask silk embossed-embroidery leggings.

Her figure is neither too high nor too short, her complexion neither too white nor too dark, her appearance neither too ugly nor too pretty, her attitude neither rustic nor philistine.

(54.413)

The Tongs have amassed a fortune by partnering with the eunuch heads of the Eastern Depot, the Ming secret police agency, Chen the Elder, and Chen the Junior. Emperor Yongle first established the Eastern Depot in 1420 to suppress subversive activities of officials and civilians in Beijing, the newly relocated capital. It was located north of the Dongan Gate in the present-day Dongchang Hutong area, with an intimidating physical layout.[68] People in the capital Beijing, "where the sovereign's imperial carriages rest, are snobbish," comments the author, and "their eyelets are shallower than the height of a saucer; knowing that the Tongs have some coins, they admire them." (70.535)

The social status of artisans remained low throughout the Ming due to the continuation of the Yuan hereditary system. The beginning of the Ming also saw a systematic conversion of prisoners and felons into artisans.

In the early Ming dynasty, all artisans in the country were under the jurisdiction of the Ministry of Works 工部, Neiguanjian (the Imperial Works Office 內官监) and the Chief Military Command of the Five Armies 五军都督府 and, thus, they were called artisans and military artisans. The group consisted of an astonishing 300,000 people. Moreover, this was also because many convicted and displaced people were converted into artisans in the early Ming.[69]

The conversion of many social outcasts effectively debased the class. However, it was still ranked number three in the gentry-farmer-artisan-merchant hierarchy and was thus theoretically lower than the farmer class. This inferior status demanded that artisans and their families wear much humbler outfits than farmers and the gentry. In this sense, although Lady Tong is befittingly dressed as a housewife from a middle-class urban family, as the wife of an artisan, she is not dressed correctly.

The "mirror-faced, crow-black silk bandana" she wears is a *baotou* (a forehead wrapper 包头), made of silk or gauze, usually black. Legend holds that during the spring and autumn period, the King of Wu, Fu Chai 夫差, took his favorite consort Xi Shi 西施 to tour a lake. Seeing a lotus-gathering village girl folding a piece of lotus leaf to make a triangular sunshade on her forehead, she emulated her; the triangular forehead wrapper looked so becoming on Xi Shi that all imperial consorts and maids of the Wu palace started to emulate the fashion by making their wrappers using silk or gauze. The practice is believed to be the origin of the *baotou* wrapper.[70]

The Dis maintain good terms with the Tongs during their tenancy. After the wicked cook of the Dis is thunder-struck to death, Lady Tong helps Old Di secure a *quanzao* 全灶 maid, Tiaogeng, to fulfill the cook's vacancy. A *quanzao* is a well-trained female chef, costing much more than a regular maid because of her cooking skill. An owner would be prone to take her as his concubine to prevent such an asset from running away. Old Di, with the intent of finding himself a potential concubine and a family chef, spends 24 *taels* of silver on Tiaogeng, a sturdy, diligent,

The Clothing Culture and Clothing Choices of the Ming People 61

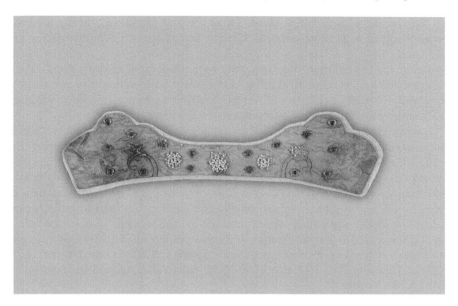

Figure 1.12 Plain satin headscarf inlaid with gems. H. 12.5 × L. 55 cm.
Source: Courtesy of Wujin Museum, Changzhou.

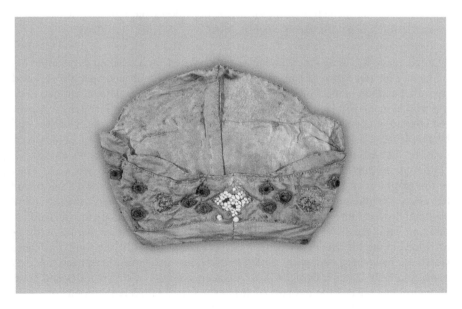

Figure 1.13 Plain satin headscarf inlaid with gems. H. 21 × W. 28 cm.
Source: Courtesy of Wujin Museum, Changzhou.

yet ugly maid who is "thick-faced, broad-cheeked, flat-nosed, beetle-browed, broad-mouthed and coarse-waisted." Clearly, beauty is not a definitive factor for Old Di at all.

Before the Dis return to Shandong, the two families exchange gifts at the departure party. The Tongs give them three *taels* of silver for traveling expenses (which they politely return), two bolts of Peking Green Cloth, ten packs of *chensu* incense, 200 corner-shaped soaps, and four pounds of Fujian soft candy.

Chensu incense (aloes wood and shuhsiang 沉速香) was commonly known as "benzoin" in the Ming dynasty and was one of the popular spices during the Ming. Of all *chensu* incense, Liu He's was the most famous, and more will be discussed later. Incense's popularity among the public was related to the Ming scholars' admiration for Wang Yangming's Philosophy of the Mind, which advocated "meditation." At one time, famous monks and Taoists competed to build "quiet rooms" in which to "meditate while immersed in incense" and "seek inner peace." Such practices led to the proliferation of incense during the Ming. Women's leisure interests also drove up incense's popularity. Shen Fu 沈复 recorded the pleasure his wife Yunniang 芸娘 took in using incense. What Yunniang used was none other than *chensu* incense:

> To burn incense in a quiet room is one of the cultivated pleasures of a leisurely life. Yun used to burn aloes wood and shuhsiang [a kind of fragrant wood from Cambodia]. She used to thoroughly steam the wood in a cauldron and then place it on a copper wire net over a stove about half an inch from the fire. Under the action of the slow fire, the wood would give out a kind of subtle fragrance without any visible smoke.[71]

The Dis leave the Tongs their unconsumed coal and food. Xichen gives Jijie, his playmate, the ten-year-old daughter of the Tongs, a pair of jade vase flowers and two silk handkerchiefs, while she reciprocates by gifting him with an antique folding trinket made of black silver. Lady Tong, in addition, gives Tiaogeng a pair of red silk leg wrappers and three inches of black vamp cloth (56.428). The "antique broken trinket" is a kind of antique-style folding hair stick made of gold, silver, jade, or just ordinary metal. Prostitute Cheng, especially mentioned in *XSYYZ*, "horizontally pins two antique folding trinkets of gold and jade" when she goes to the temple with Sujie (73.561). In *A Dream of Red Mansions*, Jia Lian opens her chest after the death of You Erjie and sees only "some broken trinkets, soiled artificial flowers and some of her half-worn silk clothes," which are the old trinkets that had belonged to You.[72] Here, the descriptions highlight that there is nothing of value among the things left behind by You. Unsurprisingly, the folded trinkets, which are placed together with "soiled artificial flowers," must have been made of the less-valuable copper or niello. The Tongs are a family of silversmiths, and Tong Qi would have been able to make niello jewelry. It is unlikely that a girl of Jijie's age would have valuable jewelry yet, so her own family would have most likely made the antique broken niello trinket she gave Di Xichen.

3. What Drives People to Sell their Daughters

1) The Case of Chunying

After Chao Yuan's death, the Chao clan—composed of the deceased's uncles, cousins, and nephews—begins maneuvering for the Chao property. Facing the pack of predators, Madame Chao finds, to her comfort, that her husband's concubine, Chunying, is pregnant. Monk Liang, the previous opera actor and beneficiary of Madame Chao, obliged by a desire to repay her incredible kindness, vows to become her son in name. He enters nirvana on Chunying's due day to be borne by her and is named Chao Liang 晁梁, nicknamed "Little Monk." The posthumous son of Magistrate Chao is now the only male heir of the Chaos. The newborn's arrival saves Madame Chao's crumbling world, for, however socially dignified she might be as a deceased official's wife, her ultimate social and economic security depends on whether or not she has a son—even one merely in name. Francesca Bray asserts that the biological term "reproduction" entails much more than simply giving birth to children perpetuating her husband's patriarchal lineage. She is also expected to function as a "social mother" or "ritual mother" to all her husband's offspring, educate them and treat them with undifferentiated kindness, whether they are biologically related to her. In case she is barren or has passed the age of childbirth, "adoption or polygamy would allow her to substitute the fertility of a lower-status woman" to fulfill her motherhood.[73]

With the succession issue of the Chao family line solved, the situation of Chunying, the 17-year-old widowed concubine, is given a unique feature in the Novel. Out of either her attachment to Madame Chao and her son or consideration of practical economic factors, she refuses her parents' proposal to get her remarried. Even at the apex of the Ming widow-chastity cult, her decision is unusual, for she is so young. During the Ming and Qing times, juridical and social sanctions discouraging widow remarriage and rewarding chastity had become a hallmark of the moral education programs sponsored by the courts. Under Ming legal code, families headed by chaste widows were exempted from the labor tax; for the first time in history, the Ming court regulated how chaste widows should be singled out from obedient grandsons, righteous men, and filial sons to be given exceptional Imperial Testimonials of Merit; Qing's concerns to female chastity seemed to be so aggravated that it became a cult. Qing rulers established aggressive and elaborate procedures for locating, verifying, and recognizing widow chastity, specifically in commoner households. Names of selected chaste widows were inscribed on arches or installed in shrines erected in every county.[74]

By the time Chao Liang is three, when the mourning period for Magistrate Chao is about to end, Madame Chao decides to reward her by having some dresses made for her: a mineral-blue crepe skirt, a twig-red arch-gauze skirt, a water-red lake-silk skirt, and a black ice-gauze skirt. She also has jewels made for her: a pearl hair band, a pair of golden bead rows, a set of seven small golden phoenixes, many little golden twigs, four golden rings, and a silver bracelet that weighs four *taels*.

She also has these made for Little Monk: a chestnut-colored *pianshan* (a kind of monk's gown draped slantingly over the left shoulder 偏衫), a tasseled *piao* hat, a pair of red monk shoes, and a yellow silk coat (36.278).

The unusual lavishing of gifts from the matriarch to the young concubine bespeaks not only the harmonious bond between the two, but also Madame Chao's approval of Chunying's choice to stay with them. All four skirts are of excellent quality in terms of color and texture. The arch gauze and ice gauze are also recorded in a Ming court clothing collection, according to Yang Yi's *Research on Regulations of the Ming Inner Court* (Ming Neiting Guizhi Kao 明内廷规制考), which also reflects the rarity of these items. The pearl hairband is decorated with beads and jade, and the aforementioned "cap of red sable" 貂覆额 can be included in this category. Because of the inlaid beads and jade, such a band is much more expensive than plain cloth or animal skin. The pearl hairband for young women is narrow, while that for older women is wide, at least in the Chongzhen fashion.[75]

Chao Liang's children's outfit is worth mentioning. The *pianshan* is a type of monk's ritual gown created in China, unlike the cut-off robe or uncut monk's *gi*, which originated in India and is still worn by monks at Toshodaiji Temple and Nishi-Daichi Temple in Nara, Japan.[76] The origin of *pianshan* is still disputed today, but it is generally elieved to have started in the Wei dynasty. The *piao* hat is one of the eight kinds of monk hats. Huang Yizheng 黄一正, in his *Records of Things*, notes that the Mahavira hat, Baogong hat, Samgha hat, Shanzi hat, Banzha hat, *piao* hat, Six Harmony scarf, and "top bag" are hats for monks.[77]

In olden times, parents who were at pains to get a son, intimidated by the mortality rate of children, would often send the boy to the temple as a foster monk or Taoist priest, adopting the monk's or Taoist's clothes as auspicious clothing. In *Jin Ping Mei*, Ximen Qing gives his only son, Guan Ge'er, a dharma name, "Wu Yingyuan," and asks for a set of Taoist gowns. The moment the wife and concubines put on the little gown for the child, even modern people who would never agree with polygamy will feel the warmth of the family. The third concubine, Meng Yulou, attracted by the exquisite stitching of the little gown, says to Wu Yueniang, the primary wife:

> Elder Sister, look at this. How clever the Taoist priests are. These little shoes have white damask soles, which have been backstitched in interlocking lozenges. This ornamental cloud pattern is also very well done. My guess is they must have wives to help them. Otherwise, they would never be able to produce such fine stitchwork themselves.[78]

Chunying's story leads one to wonder about her family background and why she was sold to the Chaos. The supplementary account tells us that she used to be the daughter of a tailor surnamed Shen, who always tried his hand at exploiting petty advantages from his customers. He never cut out a piece of cloth or silk without stealing some of his customer's clippings. Unfortunately, this time, his scissors ventured the wrong way. The county magistrate had secured from him a bolt of top-grade bifurcated silk and intended to have it made into a round-neck robe;

knowing Tailor Shen's petty habit, he watches the tailor as the piece is cut. Awed by the magistrate's presence, Tailor Shen dares not to steal clippings as usual, but he manages to cut a considerable chunk, big enough to make a pair of woman's shoes after the magistrate leaves. The round-neck robe, an over-compact sartorial work, rips instantly when the magistrate tries it on, who, rightly enraged, orders Tailor Shen to compensate him for the total price of the bolt of silk, 17 *taels* of silver.

The shrewd Tailor Shen resizes the torn robe into a more petite robe and sends it as a gift to a gnome-figured official, who happily accepts the robe and rewards him 20 *taels*. Unfortunately, on the way to Linqing to buy the replacement bolt, Tailor Shen's silver gets stolen: two thieves walking behind him on the pontoon bridge cut his cloth wrapper open and take the money away. Dumbfounded, Tailor Shen can still partially remedy the situation. He knows two young men who had recently lost their father. Yet, for the two rich boys, the bereavement is hardly as painful as the mourning protocol, which prohibits them from wearing sable hats. Tailor Shen spends 0.4 *taels* of silver buying a piece of white velvet fur and making it into two velvet hats. While the young brothers vex over not having appropriate hats to wear in the chilly early spring, Tailor Shen shows up with the two warm, white, decently needled velvet fur hats. Delighted, the brothers take the hats, each giving him five *taels*. But there remains a shortage of seven *taels*, and even the resourceful Tailor Shen has no better idea than to sell his daughter. Understanding that the fair market value for a maid in Wucheng is only four to six *taels*, the Shens are about to auction all of their family possessions, an amount of two *taels*, to make up the difference. Thankfully, Madame Chao offers seven *taels* to buy Chunying and thus saves them (36.275–278).

To what degree a modern reader can equate the price of a maid to that of a hat is only of marginal significance to this study. However, from the blasé tone of the author and the omnipresent descriptions of transactions of servants, laborers, and maids, it is not difficult to deduce that the price of labor was indeed appallingly low. More striking are the living conditions of the urban destitute: thoroughly impoverished, with no savings or social security to fall back on. As a result, any disarrangement of their lives might have driven them into absolute despair.

Chunying is 12 when she is sold to the Chaos. Madame Chao dresses her up like a typical little maid:

> Red damask dress, green damask underskirt, the homely green cloth coat, black cotton-cloth pants, blue cotton-cloth sleeveless jacket, a pair of black cotton-cloth *geweng* shoes, and green silk headgear. Indeed, she is neat!
> (36.278)

Her ensemble bears a remarkable resemblance to that of the little maids of unnamed characters in *A Dream of Red Mansions*, who usually appear in the backdrop wearing a "dress of red damask," a "black silk sleeveless jacket which has scalloped borders of some colored material" and so forth.[79] Women's costumes had not changed much from late Ming to early Qing. The Tonsure Decree 剃发令, also known as the Queue Order, issued after the Manchu conquest, pertained strictly to men, not women. Philip Kuhn concurs with Edmund Leach's on its ritual meanings, stating that "Manchu tonsure was a symbol of restraint triumphant over license."[80] The shaving of Han Chinese males' foreheads and the changes in the male costumes had to be enforced.[81] "Men surrendered; Women did not" 男降女不降; the Chinese dictum mainly refers to the asymmetric gender conformity to the Tonsure Decree. One also notices that the *geweng* shoes Chunying wears are made of black cotton cloth, unlike the lambskin shoes worn by Zhenge, though they are in the same shoe category.

2) The Case of Little Zhenzhu

Before Xichen takes the grown-up Jijie, daughter of his previous landlady Lady Tong, to be his concubine, he has bought a maid, Little Zhenzhu 小珍珠, as a gift to the bride. As the reincarnation of Née Ji, Jijie comes back to avenge herself on Xichen for his treating her miserably in her previous life. As she still holds an unexplained grudge against the good-looking Little Zhenzhu, the reincarnation of Zhenge, the sweetness of the newlywed's matrimony is soon replaced by quarrels.

The austerity of the Beijing winter drives everyone to wear cotton clothes as early as October. However, even when December arrives, Jijie still has not allowed little Zhenge to wear any cotton-padded garments, "she does not even have a cotton jacket coat; two shabby shirts and a pair of worn-out pants are all she wears." Xichen begs Lady Tong to interfere, but the petition only infuriates Jijie. She strips off her "parrot-green *lu* silk cotton coat, the oil-green damask silk vest, and the purple damask silk cotton pants," throws them into Xichen's face, and rants:

> Me wearing any cotton is indeed the only thing this family resents. Now that I have taken them off, I guess you do not have anything to complain about— look, those are what I have just removed from my body. Take them to her and let her wear them!
>
> (79.607)

She successfully has her husband petrified.

Xichen then comes up with another idea. He sneaks two *taels* of silver to the Hans, the parents of Little Zhenzhu, and asks them to purchase cotton clothes for their daughter. Han Lu, the father, goes into a tailor's shop and buys a bright-green cloth cotton singlet for four *maces* and five candareens, a pair of stippled-blue cloth pants for three *maces* and two candareens, three *jin* of cotton for four *maces* and eight candareens, a bolt of oil-green shuttle cloth for four *maces* and five candareens, and a bolt of flat white fabric for four *maces* and eight candareens. Using these, his wife, Née Dai, makes a *zhuyao* 主腰 vest, a back gallus, and, unpicking and washing the singlet and the pants, she pads them into a cotton jacket. When everything is done, Née Dai takes the items to Xichen's place, intending to furnish her daughter with a warm winter (79.608–609).

The *zhuyao* vest is like a bellyband, but made of cotton. It neatly envelops one's waist to protect the wearer from being chilled by the wind, leaving two gaps on

The Clothing Culture and Clothing Choices of the Ming People 67

the flanks to be buckled with the back gallus. A *zhuyao* vest is not cumbersome because it does not affect the movements of the arms.

Little Zhenzhu is sold for 12 *taels* of silver, twice the price of a maid in rural Shandong. Adjusted for the expensive living standard of Beijing, it is still quite a fortune. Since good-looking maids were usually purchased for more leisure-orientated purposes, owners were supposed to provide them sustenance, including clothes for all seasons. The pure cost without considering the labor factor, which her mother provides, and that of the singlet and the cloth pants, purchased second-hand for making her a set of winter accouterments has run well over one-fifth of the price her master pays her. At this point, Jijie's complaint, "Does this family still own an inch of spare cloth or one *jin* of spare cotton?" is not without a grain of truth, even considering her rage. The two *taels* of silver spent on Little Zhenzhu's winter clothing are not easy for Xichen to scrabble up.

The livelihood of the Di-Xue family in Beijing, which could well be regarded as representative of the median level of Beijing inhabitants, chiefly relies on a small pawnshop Xichen has been running. The family's finances are, at best moderate, if not strained. One might use the family's economic profile to assess the living conditions of the Ming urban bourgeoisie.

Figure 1.14 Zhuyao vest.
Source: Courtesy of Taizhou Museum, Taizhou.

68 The Clothing Culture and Clothing Choices of the Ming People

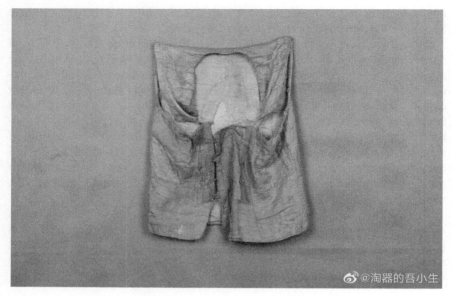

Figure 1.15 Zhuyao vest (the front).
Source: Courtesy of Bijie Museum, Bijie.

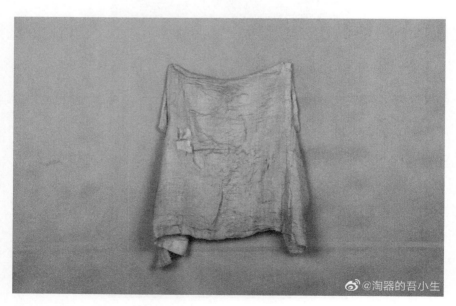

Figure 1.16 Zhuyao vest (the back).
Source: Courtesy of Bijie Museum, Bijie.

They have but one maid, Little Zhenzhu, to help with the housework, a servant boy to dispatch on errands, a cook, and an old servant couple stationed at the pawnshop. Lady Tong and Tiao Geng (after Old Di passes away, she and her baby come to live with Xichen) take care of sundry household duties, including preparing food; Jijie is occupied by her new baby full-time.

Yet compared to the Hans, they are fortunate, for they can at least dress warmly and eat their fill. Little Zhenzhu's father, Han Lu, is an underling of the Department of Military Forces. Her mother, Née Dai, is a "hair comber," whose profession is not to be confused with that of a hairdresser of the modern definition. She "serves the wives of rich families, combing their hair and grooming their feet." She also occasionally functions as a midwife's assistant, literally a "waist holder" 搂腰, who is called to use her strength to hold a woman in labor (80.615). The couple works hard day and night but can barely make a living. In the lowest social strata of Beijing, parents selling their daughters to well-off households to secure warm winters was considered a rational choice, for they could not have possibly afforded two *taels* of silver to buy a daughter a set of winter clothes. Née Dai thus pleads to Jijie:

> My family's poverty drove us to sell the child; otherwise, she would have had to live in hunger and cold. We needed the money, for sure, but another consideration was to find shelter for the girl. Look at the child in her thin shirt and pants in this severe winter! We could have retained her at home had we known she would suffer all this. Why would we want to sell her to your wealthy family? Should she do anything wrong, you are at your liberty to punish her, but please, do not intentionally freeze her to death. If she gets sick, my dear madam, she is the pound of flesh that I have already cut out of my body, but don't you regret wasting your money . . . I have my girl here in your trust. It is up to you to let her live or die. As long as she still has a single breath, I have no word to say; but if you torture her to death, does the Censorate Office not have a door or, in the Court, hanging drums? I shall have somewhere to appeal my case!
>
> (79.609)

A mother's expectation has been lowered to keeping "a single breath" of her child. It does not take long for the reader to discover that even this meager wish is not sustained, as Sujie has driven Little Zhenzhu to hang herself. The Dis compensate the Hans 30 *taels* of silver, an excessive price in the Beijing labor market for reimbursing the parents of a deceased maid, even though the death is of an atypical nature. However, the Dis' biggest problem comes from a vile neighbor, Liu, who jumps into the midst of the affair, instigates the Hans, and is unsatisfied even after being bribed 40 *taels*. To prevent them from being further blackmailed, Xichen sues Liu and the Hans in the Censorate Office and gets his ransomed money back. Two *yamen* runners, not knowing the fact that the Dis had already reimbursed the Hans, comment on the matter:

> You guys had a maid die in your care . . . now that her family comes, you guys should have dispensed several *taels* to seal their mouths, and that should

conclude the matter. Poor fellows, losing their child for nothing. Should there be a third party abetting them, why wouldn't they latch onto a lawsuit against you?

Nevertheless, upon learning that the Dis have paid 30 *taels*, their tones change instantly, for they sense that the Hans were overpaid. "This is indeed irritating!" the two runners exclaim, "even if you were to go through the lawsuit and get a verdict of 'proper burial' from our Office, it would not cost you more than ten *taels* and three *maces* of silver" (81.624–625). We can safely surmise that the price of a private settlement for the unnatural death of a maid between the owner and her family in the Beijing labor market would not have exceeded ten *taels* and three *maces*. Mencius, when defining what constitutes humane governance, utters:

> When determining what means of support the people should have, a clear-sighted ruler ensures that these are sufficient, on the one hand, for the care of parents, and, on the other, for the support of the wife and children, so that the people always have sufficient food in good years and escape starvation in bad.[82]

On multiple occasions, Ray Huang, a celebrated Ming historian, has criticized this standard as "low-standard thoughts of equalization" or the evil wellspring of "reducing the national living standard to a minimum to ensure everyone scratches a living."[83] From the Hans' case, we can hardly tell whether Mencius sets his standard too low or Ray Huang too high. In a neither-war nor famine-struck social environment, the lives of the urban destitute, represented by the Hans, miserably fall below Mencius's already very modestly defined standards.

Notes

1 Young-Suk Lee, "A Study of Stage Costume of Peking Opera," *The International Journal of Costume Culture*, no. 6 (2003).
2 Chengbei Xu, *Peking Opera* (Beijing: China Intercontinental Press, 2003), 53, 115. 徐城北：《中国京剧》，北京：五洲传播出版社，2003年，第53，115页。
3 Lian Song, ed., "Carriage and Clothing I," in *The History of the Yuan Dynasty*, vol. 78 (Beijing: Zhonghua Book Company, 1976), 1930. [明]宋濂编纂：《元史》卷七十八《舆服一》，北京：中华书局，1976年，第1930页。
4 Lisha Li, "A Study on the Zhisun—a Kind of Mongolian Grande Toilette of the Yuan Dynasty," *Journal of Inner Mongolia University (Humanities and Social Sciences)* 40, no. 2 (2008): 26–31. 李莉莎：《质孙服考略》，《内蒙古大学学报（哲学社会科学版）》，2008年第40卷第2期，第26–31页。
5 In his mind he had intended the forthcoming anti-Japanese war to be a chance of "the second rebirth" of Chinese nation. Haizong Lei, *Chinese Culture and Chinese Soldiers* (Changsha: The Commercial Press, 1940), 22–44, 125–26, 216–18. 雷海宗：《中国文化与中国的兵》，长沙：商务印书馆，1940年，第22–44，125–26，216–18页。
6 [Song] Xiaoxiang Zhang, "First Chapter of the Six States Lyrics," in *Selected Lyrics of Zhang Xiaoxiang* (Hefei: Huangshan Publishing House, 1986), 116. [宋]张孝祥：《六州歌头》，《张孝祥诗词选》，合肥：黄山出版社，1986年，第116页。
7 David Morgan, *The Mongols* (Oxford: Wiley-Blackwell, 1990), 15.

8 Ssu-yü Teng, "Ming T'ai-tsu's Destructive and Constructive Work," *Chinese Culture*, 8 (1967): 33.
9 Antonia Finnane, *Changing Clothes in China: Fashion, History, Nation* (New York: Columbia University Press, 2008), 44.
10 Tael, a unit of currency. One *tael* of silver in the Ming dynasty is equivalent to about 660.8 yuan today.
11 [Qing] Xueqin Cao and [Qing] E Gao, *A Dream of Red Mansions (Hong Lou Meng)* (Beijing: People's Literature Publishing House, 1996), 98. [清]曹雪芹，[清]高鹗：《红楼梦》，北京：人民文学出版社，1996年，第98页。
12 Congwen Shen, *Ancient Chinese Clothing Research* (Shanghai: Shanghai Bookstore Publishing House, 2002), 584. 沈从文：《中国古代服饰研究》，上海：上海书店出版社，2002年，第584页。
13 Yinque Chen, *Unofficial Biography of Liu Rushi* (Shanghai: Shanghai Classics Publishing House, 1980), 848. 陈寅恪：《柳如是别传》，上海：上海古籍出版社，1980年，第848页。
14 Zhenglang Zhang, "Twelve Widows' Expedition to the West and Related Issues—The Second Volume of Liu Rushi's Biography," in *Academic Papers in Commemoration of the Centenary of Mr. Chen Yinque's Birthday*, ed. the Research Center of Chinese Medieval History of Beijing University (Beijing: Beijing University Press, 1989). 张政烺：《十二寡妇征西及其相关问题—<柳如是别传>下册题记》，见北京大学中国中古史研究中心编著：《纪念陈寅恪先生诞辰百年学术论文集》，北京：北京大学出版社，1989年。
15 [Ming] Qiyuan Gu, "Declarations at the Commencement of the Dynasty," in *Guest Language Superfluous*, proofread by Dihua Tan and Jiahe Chen, vol. 10 (Beijing: Zhonghua Book Company, 1987), 347. [明]顾起元著，谭棣华、陈稼禾点校：《客座赘语》卷十《国初榜文》，北京：中华书局，1987年，第347页。
16 Ibid.
17 An'dao Gao, "Banshe Tune/Shaobian/Tanner's Lies," in *The Complete Works of Appreciation of Yuan Opera [2]*, ed. Sisi Chen and Xiangwan Yu (Beijing: The Chinese Overseas Publishing House, 2012), 601. 高安道：《般涉调·哨遍·皮匠说谎》，见陈思思、于湘婉编著：《元曲鉴赏大全集[下]》，北京：中国华侨出版社，2012年，第601页。
18 Michel de Certeau, *The Practice of Everyday Life*, trans. Steven Rendall (Berkeley: University of California Press, 1984).
19 Susan Mann, *Precious Records: Women in China's Long Eighteenth Century* (Stanford, CA: Stanford University Press, 1997), 14.
20 [Qing] Yanwu Gu, "Front Clothes," in *Collection and Interpretation of Daily Record (Part III)*, annotated by Rucheng Huang, proofread by Baoqun Luan and Zongli Lü, vol. 28 (Shanghai: Shanghai Classics Publishing House, 2006), 1587. [清]顾炎武著，黄汝成集释，栾保群、吕宗力点校：《日知录集释（下）》卷二十八《对襟衣》，上海：上海古籍出版社，2006年，第1587页。
21 Guangren Shen, *Elite Theatre in Ming China, 1368–1644* (New York: Routledge, 2005), 32.
22 Yuanjun Feng, "Additions and Corrections to On the Ancient Entertainer (Guyoujie)," in *Collection of Classical Literature by Feng Yuanjun*, ed. Shishuo Yuan (Jinan: Shandong People's Publishing House, 1980), 100. 冯沅君：《古优解补正》，见袁世硕主编：《冯沅君古典文学论文集》，济南：山东人民出版社，1980年，第100页。
23 Yuanjun Feng, "On the Ancient Entertainer (Guyoujie)," in *Collection of Lu Kanru and Feng Yuanjun*, ed. Shishuo Yuan and Keli Zhang, vol. 3 (Hefei: Anhui Educational Publishing House, 2011), 252. 冯沅君：《古优解》，见袁世硕、张可礼主编：《陆侃如冯君合集》第三卷，合肥：安徽教育出版社，2011年，第252页。
24 Louise Levathes, *When China Ruled the Seas: The Treasure Fleet of the Dragon Throne, 1405–1433* (New York: Oxford University Press, 1997), 176.

25 [Ming] Shizhen Wang, *A Special Collection of Yanshantang* (Beijing: Zhonghua Book Company, 1985). See the items of "granting corresponding clothes to civil and military officials" and "taking full examination of special charity" in the *Special Decrees of the Ming Dynasty*. [明]王世贞：《弇山堂别集》，北京：中华书局，1985年。见《皇明异典述》内的"赐衣文武互异""考满非常恩赐"等条目。

26 Deming Kong and Hui Chen, "The Brilliant Afterglow of Han Nationality Costumes: Clothing of Emperors and Empresses and Officials of All Ranks and Descriptions in the Age of Extreme Imperial Power," in *The Chinese Costume Modeling Appreciation Atlas* (Shanghai: Shanghai Lexicographical Publishing House, 2007), 182. 孔德明，陈卉：《汉族服饰的艳丽余晖·皇权极至时代的帝后百官服制》，《中国服饰造型鉴赏图典》，上海：上海辞书出版社，2007年，第182页。

27 Yongbin Wang, *Commercial Streets and Time-honored Brands in Beijing* (Beijing: Yanshan Publishing House, 1999), 167. 王永斌：《北京的商业街和老字号》，北京：燕山出版社，1999年，第167页。

28 Yue Wang, "Recommended Hutongs in The Ming and Qing Dynasties," in *Long-standing Hutongs: A Study on The Origin of Beijing Hutongs and the Hutong Culture* (Beijing: China Environmental Science Press, 2009), 200. 王越：《明清推崇胡同》，《源远流长话胡同：北京胡同的起源及胡同文化研究》，北京：中国环境科学出版社，2009年，第200页。

29 Beijing History Compiling Group, ed., "Economy of Beijing in the Ming Dynasty," in *History of Beijing, First Draft*, vol. 1 (Beijing: Department of History of Beijing University, 1960), 70. 北京史编写组：《明代北京的经济》，《北京史·初稿》卷一，北京：北京大学历史系，1960年，第70页。

30 Qi Wang, *Collected Illustrations of the Three Realms*, vol. 2 (Shanghai: Shanghai Classics Publishing House, 1988), 1508. [明]王圻：《三才图会》卷二，上海：上海古籍出版社，1988年，第1508页。

31 Hongtao Cao, *Local Specialties of the Ming Dynasty* (Shantou: Shantou University Press, 2008), 5–6. 曹鸿涛：《大明风物志》，汕头：汕头大学出版社，2008年，第5–6页。

32 Bingwen Nan, Xiaorong He, and Anli Chen, *Cultural Studies of the Ming Dynasty* (Beijing: People's Publishing House, 2006), 339. 南炳文，何孝荣，陈安丽：《明代文化研究》，北京：人民出版社，2006年，第339页。

33 [Qing] Tingyu Zhang, ed., "Carriage and Clothing III," in *The History of the Ming Dynasty*, vol. 67 (Beijing: Zhonghua Book Company, 1974), 1650. 张廷玉编纂：《明史》卷六十七《舆服三》，北京：中华书局，1974年，第1650页。

34 Tianyou Wang, "Forbidden Institutions of Assisting the Emperor in Handling Government Affairs," in *Research on State Institutions in the Ming Dynasty* (Beijing: Beijing University Press, 1992), 69. 王天有：《辅助皇帝处理政务的禁直机构》，《明代国家机构研究》，北京：北京大学出版社，1992年，第69页。

35 Yunmei Huang, *Textual Research on Ming History*, vol. 1 (Beijing: Zhonghua Book Company, 1979), 493. 黄云眉：《明史考证[第一册]》，北京：中华书局，1979年，第493页。

36 Gu, "Crown Costume," in *Collection and Interpretation of Daily Record (Part III)*, vol. 28 (1585). [清]顾炎武：《日知录集释（下）》卷二十八《冠服》，第1585页。

37 Ibid., 1586.

38 Liangcai Zhang, *History of Chinese Customs* (Taipei: Taiwan Commercial Press, 1993), 203. 张亮采：《中国风俗史》，台北：商务印书馆，1993年，第203页。

39 Susan Naquin, "Funerals in North China," in *Death Ritual in Late Imperial and Modern China*, ed. James L. Watson and Evelyn Sakakida Rawski (Berkeley: University of California Press, 1988), 40.

40 Yutang Lin, *Moment in Peking* (Beijing: Foreign Language Teaching and Research Press, 1999), 156.

41 She Lao, *Beneath the Red Banner* (Beijing: People's Literature Publishing House, 1980), 24. 老舍：《正红旗下》，北京：人民文学出版社，1980年，第24页。

42 [Qing] Lu Yun, "The God of Joy," in *The Book of Disciplinary Discrimination of the Imperial Concierge (Qinding Xieji Bianfangshu), vol. 7*, in *Complete Library of the Four Treasures, Photocopied Wenyuan Pavillion Edition*, vol. 811 (Taipei: Taiwan Commercial Press, 1986), 954. [清]允禄：《钦定协纪辨方书》卷七《喜神》，《影印文渊阁四库全书》第811册，台北：台湾商务印书馆，1986年，第954页。
43 Lao, *Beneath the Red Banner*, 24. 老舍：《正红旗下》，北京：人民文学出版社，1980年，第24页。
44 Hsiao-hsiao-sheng, *The Plum in the Golden Vase or, Chin P'ing Mei, vol. 2, the Rivals*, trans. David Tod Roy (Princeton, NJ and Oxford: Princeton University Press, 2001), 157–58.
45 Eileen Chang, *Little Reunions* (Beijing: Beijing October Literature and Art Publishing House, 2009), 137. 张爱玲：《小团圆》，北京：北京十月文艺出版社，2009年，第137页。
46 [Qing] Dou Li, "Records of Little Qinhuai," in *Records of Yangzhou Gaily-Painted Pleasure Boats*, proofread and annotated by Chundong Zhou, vol. 9 (Jinan: Shandong Friendship Publishing House, 2001), 231. [清]李斗著，周春东校注：《扬州画舫录》卷九《小秦淮录》，济南：山东友谊出版社，2001年，第231页。
47 [Qing] Tingyu Zhang, "Carriage and Clothing III," in *The History of the Ming Dynasty*, vol. 67 (Beijing: Zhonghua Book Company, 1653). [清]张廷玉编纂：《明史》卷六十七《舆服三》，第1653页。
48 Maotong Chen, *Chinese Clothing and Costume System Through the Ages* (Beijing: Xinhua Publishing House, 1993), 260. 陈茂同：《中国历代衣冠服饰制》，北京：新华出版社，1993年，第260页。
49 Tongzu Qu, *Law and Society in Traditional China* (Paris and The Hague: Mouton, 1961), 110–20.
50 Chia-lin Pao-Tao and Xiaoyi Liu, "'Two Beauties, One Husband'— Marriage Model Reflected from Traditional Chinese Literature," in *the 6th Volume of the Collections of the Studies of Chinese Women's History*, ed. Chia-lin Pao-Tao (Taipei: Dao Xiang Publisher, 2008), 271–310. 鲍家麟，刘晓毅：《娥英两花并蒂开》，见鲍家麟编著：《中国妇女史论集》卷六，台北：稻乡出版社，2008年，第271–310页。
51 Wang, "Zuo Zhuguo," in *A Special Collection of Yanshantang, Special Decrees of the Ming Dynasty*, vol. 1 (Beijing: Zhonghua Book Company, 1985), 113–14. [明]王世贞：《弇山堂别集·皇明异典述》卷一《左柱国》，第113–14页。
52 Ibid., 113.
53 Naquin, "Funerals in North China," 42.
54 David Johnson, "The City-God Cults of T'ang and Sung China," *Harvard Journal of Asiatic Studies* 45, no. 2 (1985): 374–446.
55 Ibid.
56 [Ming] Jideng Yu, *Collections of Anecdotes*, vol. 3 (Beijing: Zhonghua Book Company, 1981), 47. [明]余继登：《典故纪闻》卷三，北京：中华书局，1981年，第47页。
57 [Ming] Sheng Ye, "City God," in *The Diary of East Water*, vol. 30 (Beijing: Zhonghua Book Company, 1980), 296–97. [明]叶盛：《水东日记》卷三十《城隍神》，北京：中华书局，1980年，第296–97页。
58 Romeyn Taylor, "Ming T'ai-tsu and the Gods of the Walls and Moats," *Ming Studies*, no. 1 (1977): 31–50.
59 Ray Huang, *1587, a Year of No Significance: The Ming Dynasty in Decline* (New Haven: Yale University Press, 1982), 6.
60 Ibid.
61 [Qing] Yi Zhao, *Miscellaneous Research Made While Serving My Mother*, vol. 33 (Shijiazhuang: Hebei People's Publishing House, 1990), 580. [清]赵翼：《陔馀丛考》卷三十三，石家庄：河北人民出版社，1990年，第580页。
62 [Qing] Mengzhu Ye, "Internal Service," in *World Browsing Series*, vol. 8 (Beijing: Zhonghua Book Company, 2007), 206. [清]叶梦珠：《阅世编》卷八《内服》，北京：中华书局，2007年，第206页。

63 Miao Wang, "'Three Things' and 'Seven Things'," in *Splendid Luxury: A History of Chinese Jewelry* (Beijing: Gold Wall Press, 2012), 388–89. 王苗：《"三事儿"与"七事儿"》，《珠光翠影：中国首饰史话》，北京：金城出版社，2012年，第388–89页。
64 Dorothy Ko, *Cinderella's Sisters: A Revisionist History of Footbinding* (Berkeley: University of California Press, 2005), 135.
65 Ibid.
66 [Ming] Hsiao-hsiao-sheng Lanling, *Notes and Comments on Jin Ping Mei* (Beijing: People's Literature Publishing House, 1985), 337–40. [明]兰陵笑笑生：《金瓶梅词话》，北京：人民文学出版社，1985年，第337–40页。
67 [Ming] Menglong Feng and [Qing] Guangsheng Hua, *Complete Compilation of Romantic Ci Qu in Ming and Qing Dynasties* (Guangzhou: Guangzhou Publishing House, 1995), 648. [明]冯梦龙，[清]华广生：《明清艳情词曲全编》，广州：广州出版社，1995年，第648页。
68 Shih-shan Henry Tsai, *The Eunuchs in the Ming Dynasty* (Albany: State University of New York Press, 1996), 98.
69 Jian Hang and Qiuhui Guo, *Traditional Chinese Crafts* (Beijing: CITIC Press, 2006), 30. 杭间，郭秋惠：《中国传统工艺》，北京：中信出版社，2006年，第30页。
70 Xidan Lin, *Essays on Suzhou Embroidery* (Nanjing: Jiangsu People's Publishing House, 1981), 46. 林锡旦：《苏绣漫话》，南京：江苏人民出版社，1981年，第46页。
71 [Qing] Fu Shen, *Six Chapters of a Floating Life*, trans. Yutang Lin (Beijing: Foreign Language Teaching and Research Press, 1999), 102. [清]沈复：《浮生六记》，林语堂译，北京：外语教学与研究出版社，1999年，第102页。
72 Cao and Gao, *A Dream of Red Mansions*, 962. 曹雪芹，高鹗：《红楼梦》，第962页。
73 Francesca Bray, *Technology and Gender: Fabrics of Power in Late Imperial China* (Berkeley, CA and London: University of California Press, 1997), 359.
74 Susan Mann, "Widows in the Kinship, Class, and Community Structures of Qing Dynasty China," *The Journal of Asian Studies* 46, no. 1 (1987).
75 Xing Xu, *Art of Dressing and Accessories* (Beijing: China Textile and Apparel Press, 1999), 21. 许星：《服饰配件艺术》，北京：中国纺织出版社，1999年，第21页。
76 [JAP] Rei Yoshimura, "On the Clothes and Names of Ancient Tathagata and Bhikkhu Statues: Monk Zhizhi, *Youtan* Robe, *Pian* Robe, *Zhiduo*," in *2004 Longmen Grottoes International Academic Seminar*, ed. Zhengang Li (Zhengzhou: Henan People's Publishing House, 2006), 629–34. [日]吉村怜：《论古代如来像和比丘像的衣服及其名称——僧祇支·右袒衫·偏衫·直裰》，见李振刚主著：《2004年龙门石窟国际学术研讨会文集》，郑州：河南人民出版社，2006年，第629–34页。
77 [Ming] Yizheng Huang, "Taoist Interpretation of Official Hats (Dao Shi Guan Lei)," in *Records of Things*, vol. 13, included in the *Unannotated Catalog of the Complete Library in the Four Treasures Series* compiled by the Compilation Committee of the *Unannotated Catalog of the Complete Library in the Four Treasures Series* (Jinan: Qilu Press, 1995), 5. [明]黄一正：《事物绀珠》卷十三《道释冠类》，收录于四库全书存目丛书编纂委员会编：《四库全书存目丛书》，济南：齐鲁书社，1995年，第5页。
78 Hsiao-hsiao-sheng, *The Plum in the Golden Vase or, Chin P'ing Mei, vol. 2, The Rivals*, 472.
79 Cao and Gao, *A Dream of Red Mansions*, 40. 曹雪芹，高鹗：《红楼梦》，第40页。
80 Philip A. Kuhn, *Soulstealers: The Chinese Sorcery Scare of 1768* (Cambridge, MA: Harvard University Press, 1990), 58; Edmund Leach, "Magical Hair," *Journal of the Royal Anthropological Institute of Great Britain and Ireland* 88, no. 2 (1958): 147–64.
81 Ko, *Cinderella's Sisters*, 51.
82 Mencius, *Mencius*, trans. D. C. Lau (New York: Penguin Classics, 1970), 58.
83 Ray Huang, *Discussing Chinese History from the Banks of the Hudson River* (Beijing: SDX Joint Publishing Company, 1992), 4–5.

2 Luxury Consumption and the Financial System

1. Luxury Consumption

1) Enumerating Famous Luxury Goods of the Ming

Feeling good about having purchased the office of the Secretariat Drafter of the Legislative Bureau of the Wuying Palace, Di Xichen drinks too much, oversleeps the morning court, and is downgraded by one rank. He is to be demoted to a regional post in Chengdu, Sichuan. Taking his family on such a long journey from the capital to Sichuan, a remote province "no more accessible than the sky," was considered a treacherous and frightening trip at that time. Furthermore, having spent 4,000 *taels* of silver on the official position, Di Xichen is no longer wealthy. Besides, as he is newly appointed, some "thoughtful" gifts must be prepared for his superiors and colleagues. Pondering over those difficulties, Di Xichen is so worried that "his hair almost turns white overnight."

Fortunately, he has a wise mother-in-law, Lady Tong, who comes up with a clear and precise action plan "like a typesetting layout." The following is just an excerpt from the Novel, representing her ideas on gift purchasing:

> You are a man, and now you are an official wearing a black gauze cap. How can I trust you two on such a long journey if you cannot arrange things well? You are worried about having no money, but I can help you. There are still 400 to 500 *taels* of silver at home, so if you ask the Minister for 500 *taels*, you will have 1,000 *taels* in total. You have all the clothes you need, so there is no need for new clothes, but you can buy and carry 20 feet of cloth and silk. As for thoughtful gifts, buy two ivory *hu* tablets; four pairs of ivory chopsticks; four ivory combs; four ivory statuettes; *buzi* painted with crane, *xiezhi*, *qilin*, and bull, two pairs each; one rhinoceros girdle; and a few more of the Liu He family's exquisite fragrant girdles, which must meet the taste of your superiors. As for other things, like the *saxian*-embroidered tablecloth, mattress, tent, embroidered quilt, embroidered robe, embroidered skirt, embroidered vest, outer garment, Huzhou mirror, bronze stove, bronze *gu* vase, Huzhou silk, Huzhou cotton, Meigong cloth, Songjiang damask silk, Huzhou writing brush, Huizhou ink, Suzhou gold fan, Huizhou copper-nickel lock,

DOI: 10.4324/9781003406143-3

bamboo-strip case, and Nanjing crape. I now give you the list, and you can buy them in Nanjing. Shandong cocoon silk is in vogue now; buy a dozen authentic bolts of cocoon silk for central officials and those in charge of criminal justice. You should also buy four rhinoceros cups and ask the incense maker to make two packs of benzoin and two packs of yellow incense slices. That would be enough, and it would be troublesome to carry too much. You can also buy silk in the south. In Beijing, you buy gauze boots and shoes from the Temple of Heaven, and then you will have almost everything you need for both big and small gifts. When you arrive in Nanjing, buy exquisite jade hairpins, jade knots, jade buttons, soft jadeite flowers, and gold foil to include among the small gifts to win the favor of the official's wives.

(84.644)

Lady Tong's list of "thoughtful" gifts can be used to study luxury goods in the late Ming dynasty. It can also be seen from this list that, in the late Ming metropolises such as Beijing and Nanjing, the extent to which the public consumed luxury goods cannot be overestimated. Lady Tong, a middle-class housewife in Beijing, has deep insights into the comprehensive and extravagant arts of "dressing" and "using accessories" to enrich one's life.

Ivory *hu* tablets, ivory chopsticks, ivory combs, and ivory statuettes are all implements. The crane, *xiezhi*, *qilin*, and bull are all commonly used *buzi* on the robes of civil officials, with *xiezhi* 獬豸 being a rare animal used for law enforcement officials. In *Five Miscellaneous Morsels* (Wu Za Zu 五杂俎), it is stated that:

among all the animals, only *xiezhi* is obscure, and is believed by some to be a sacred sheep. However, the sacred sheep is found in *The Book of Gods and Spirits* [Shenyi Jing 神异经], but its words are absurd and not credible. There are many records of *qilin*, lion, *fuba* 扶拔, *zouyu* 驺虞, and *jiaoduan* 角端 in books on the Five Elements [metal, wood, water, fire, earth 金,木,水,火,土] and books on the Four Barbarian Tribes [*yi, man, di, rong* 夷,蛮,狄,戎], but *xiezhi* is never mentioned, so it probably does not exist in the world at all. It was Emperor Wen of Chu who started to wear a crown of *xiezhi*, and this custom was then followed as a tradition in the Han dynasty. Even now, the *xiezhi* is still used and represents law enforcement officials, but its existence is, in fact, quite ungrounded.[1]

The rhinoceros girdle is, as the name implies, made from rhinoceros horn. As it was stipulated that only officials of the second rank and higher could use rhinoceros, a rhinoceros girdle could only be worn by a reasonably high-ranking official in the Ming dynasty. According to *The History of the Ming Dynasty—Biography of Zhang Juzheng* 明史 • 张居正传, when Zhang succeeded in the provincial examination, Governor Gu Lin untied his rhinoceros girdle and gave it to Zhang. He said that one day Zhang would wear a jade girdle; therefore, even the rhinoceros one would be unworthy of him. The prophecy implied that Zhang Juzheng would later become a paramount councilor and that the second-rank girdle would be a waste of his competence. The girdles of Ming officials were just for decoration, with thin cords tied at the ribs under the armpits. Because of that, the quality of the girdles became indicative of the wearer's status.

In one section of *Jin Ping Mei*, Ximen Qing has official robes made after gaining an official position. For girdles alone, he orders seven or eight; all are of a width of four fingers. They are fragrant ones made from exquisite mica, rhinoceros horn, crane crest, tortoiseshell, and fishbone. While he is most satisfied with a rhinoceros girdle from the fallen family of Wang Zhaoxuan, Ximen Qing is only a fifth-ranking official who is not allowed to wear a rhinoceros girdle at all. However, he buys it for 70 *taels* of silver, driven by his vanity and lust for power and wealth. As soon as Ying Bojue, his friend who is good at flattery, sees the girdle, Ying praises it:

> Who else but you, Brother, would know where to find the like? Each of them is a finer girdle than the last. They are rarely to be seen as wide and capacious as this. Regarding the rest of them, enough said; but as for this girdle with its decorative plaque of rhinoceros horn, and this one of "crane's crest red," you couldn't find the like in the entire metropolis, though you had the money in hand. I am not flattering you to your face. They say that Chu Mien, the defender-in-chief of the Embroidered Uniform Guard in the Eastern Capital, though he may possess girdles of jade and girdles of gold, does not have anything to compare to this rhinoceros horn girdle. This is the horn of the water rhinoceros, not the horn of the dry land rhinoceros. The latter is not worth anything. The horn of the water rhinoceros is called "Heaven penetrating rhinoceros horn." If you don't believe me, bring a bowl of water, put the rhinoceros horn in it, and it will divide the water in two. This is a priceless treasure. Moreover, if you ignite it at night, it will illuminate an area of a thousand *li*, and the flame will not be extinguished all night.[2]

The rhinoceros cups Lady Tong mentions are made from rhinoceros horns. The cups are always bought in pairs for both gifts and personal use, so one purchases four at one time.

Liu He's was the leading private incense maker in Beijing during the Ming dynasty. At that time, the incense made by the Lius had a good reputation and was highly sought after by out-of-towners. Some of the products were even comparable to the imperial ones made in the palace workshops. *Playthings Collection of a Hermit* (Kao Pan Yu Shi 考槃馀事) records:

> There are several types of benzoin incense in the capital, collectively called "benzoin." The best benzoin incense is made by Liu He. The three varieties of flower fragrance, namely, *yuelin* 月麟, *juxian* 聚仙, and *aloes-wood and shuhsiang*, are the crown jewels of all varieties. There are two kinds of *longgui* incense, yellow and black, and the latter is more expensive. The best *longgui* incense is made in the palace, but Liu He's is also fine. As for cotton rose incense and warm pavilion incense, Liu He's are better. As for dragon house [*longlou* 龙楼] incense and eternal spring [*wanchun* 万春] incense, the

palace prevails. As for black incense slices, the kind that weighs one *tael* and two *maces*, made by Liu He, reigns supreme.[3]

Lady Tong's subsequent mention of "benzoin incense" probably refers to this kind. As for the "yellow incense slice," there is a recipe that has been passed down:

six *taels* of aloes-wood and shuhsiang incense, three *taels* of sandalwood, one *tael* of clove, one *tael* of wood incense, two *taels* of frankincense, one *tael* of jinyan incense, three *taels* of anba incense, five *maces* of moss, two *taels* of Storesin, three *maces* of musk, one *mace* of dragon brains [*longnao* 龙脑] eight *taels* of hyacinth powder, and four *taels* of refined honey.[4]

The "*saxian* tablecloth, mattress, tent, embroidered quilt, embroidered robe, embroidered skirt, and embroidered vest" are all embroideries, of which *saxian* 洒线 is a unique embroidery technique that will be described in more detail when we come to Gu embroidery.

The "outer" garment, also known as the *chang* garment 敞衣, can refer to either a cloak or official robes, the latter being the case here. The bronze stove is self-evident. *Gu* 觚 was a drinking vessel in the Shang and Western Zhou periods initially. The bronze *gu* vase, modeled on the bronze vessel, was used to decorate a hall. The Huzhou mirror, Huzhou silk, and Huzhou cotton were all made in Huzhou, Zhejiang province. The Huzhou mirror made by the Xues is best known, and there also were the Suns and the Xus, who were less famous than the Xues. The square poetry mirror, which could be decorated with poetry, was the most outstanding among the Xue mirrors. The Huzhou gazetteer in the Chenghua reign of the Ming dynasty records: "The Huzhou workers are the best at casting mirrors, and the mirrors are known as Huzhou mirrors."[5] Xue Huigong was a leading figure in making Huzhou mirrors, although he lived in the Qing. There is still a "Huzhou mirror painted with a group of children" made by Xue Huigong on display in the Forbidden City.

Meigong cloth, also known as Mei woven cloth, was produced in Songjiang and enjoyed equal popularity with two other types of fabric, *feihua* 飞花 and *longdun* 龙墩, in the region. Meigong is the literary name of Chen Jiru 陈继儒, a calligrapher, painter, and literary scholar in the Ming dynasty, and one of the "Four Great Ming Masters," along with Shen Zhou, Wen Zhengming, and Dong Qichang 董其昌.

During the reigns of Tianqi and Chongzhen (1621–1644), Meigong was well-known, even among women and children. Many types of utensils, especially food and drink containers, were named after Meigong, who was comparable to Su Shih 苏轼, one of the most accomplished Song dynasty scholar-officials. Meigong's closest friend was Dong Sibai. Their friendship was on par with that between Shen Shitian and Wang Ao. A contemporary writer and calligrapher, Wang Zhideng (1535–1612) was famous for his excellent writings, and he had extensive friendships with various officials like Meigong. However, Meigong was better off because Wang didn't become a scholar-official. Instead, Wang retreated from society and lived in obscurity.[6]

Chen Jiru was a native of Huating, part of the Songjiang prefecture of the Southern Zhili province in the Ming. So naturally, his inventions, named after "Meigong," were well-known in Songjiang. Meigong cloth was certainly a representative product of the Songjiang cotton textile industry. Still, in a district where "cotton was available anywhere" and "looms were found everywhere," other cotton fabric also boasted no less fame.

In addition to cotton weaving, silk and satin making in Songjiang were also unparalleled in China. Among the types of satin were such precious varieties as *zhusi* damask, medicine damask, official damask, window-pasting damask, silk damask, silk brocade, *zhisunjiayi* 只孫駕衣, red woven gold crane, lion chest and back, woven cassock, and *boluo* velvet-embroidered satin. The county of Wu used to offer a square pattern damask, commonly known as Wu damask, as a tribute. During the Zhengde reign, Songjiang silk and satin fabrics were mainly produced by the government. However, local production in Dongmen was massive, whose "exquisite craft ranks first in China, even putting Wu to shame."[7] The wide and long variety offered to the court yearly was called the official damask. A dense and light type was called window-pasting damask. The Songjiang Provincial Weaving and Dyeing Bureau produced both kinds.

Among the Songjiang silk damasks, some varieties have a long history, such as the *zhusi* 紵丝 damask, also known as thread damask, which dates to the Tianbao reign of the Tang dynasty (742–756).[8] In *XSYYZ*, *zhusi* is mentioned twice as a precious clothing material. The first is when Di Xichen takes Jijie as a concubine in an equal position with his wife:

> Di Xichen rides a horse in his official robe, with flower hairpins on his head and red silk draped slantingly over his shoulder. Tong Jijie wears a scarlet *zhusi qilin* long-sleeved wedding garment and a white silver girdle and is covered with a brocade bundle painted with Emperor Wen's one hundred sons. Four people lift the sedan chair, and twelve drummers play. Welcome home, Jijie worships Heaven and Earth with Di Xichen, who leads her with a strip of red cloth, drinks the cross-cupped wine, and the new couple sits on the edge of the bed together, with some elderly women scattering money and colored fruits.
> (76.582)

Here the *zhusi* is used as the bride's wedding garment. As for the second mention of *zhusi*, on his way to the appointed post by ship, Di Xichen buys a piece of red *liuyun zhusi* in Nanjing, one kind of the "Nanjing crape" that Lady Tong recommends he "buy in Nanjing." Di Xichen "buys this piece of *zhusi* with nine *taels* of silver as a gift to his superior." However, Jijie, bored from being on the boat, cuts up the precious piece to make herself a dress, causing Di to become outraged. A massive fight breaks out between the couple (87.667–669). Fundamentally, *zhusi* is so valuable that even a henpecked man like Di Xichen disobeys the orders of his wife in distress because of it.

The Huzhou writing brush was produced in Shanlian town of Huzhou, Zhejiang province. There is a unique technique in the production of the brushes called "end alignment," which means that the ends of the brushes must be aligned. In his *Posthumous Collections of Pinluo An* 频罗庵遗集, Liang Tongshu 梁同书, of the Qing dynasty, cites *Ni Gu Lu* 妮古录: "the brushes have four virtues: sharpness, good alignment, resilience, and roundness"; cites *Playthings Collection of a Hermit*: "the method of making brushes emphasizes the four virtues of being pointed, aligned, round and resilient"; cites Liu Gongquan's 柳公权 copybook: "The brush tip must be long . . . and the switching of strokes must be neat"; and cites Wei Shuo's *Stroke Diagram* 笔阵图: "The strokes should be neat, and the middle should be resilient."[9] There is a formula in the first chapter of *Instruction to the Scholar's Four Jewels* 文房四谱: "hard penholder, thin covering hair, sharp like a cone, and neat like a chisel."[10] The brush end, in all literature, is required to be neat and sharp. The "end alignment" requirement makes the Huzhou brush superior to other brands.

Huizhou ink was produced in Huizhou, Anhui Province. As it goes, "The ancient people used pine soot to make ink, which was taken from Fufeng in the Han, from Lushan in the Jin, and from Yizhou and Shangdang in the Tang Dynasty." Legend had it that Li Chao, of the Southern Tang dynasty, migrated to She and began to make ink with his son Tingbang. Their later generations inherited the trade; thus, Huizhou ink emerged and continues to this day.[11] After the Jiajing reign, Huizhou ink workshops included "Luo Xiaohua's, Cheng Junfang's, Fang Yulu's, and Wu Quchen's, all of which were famous for a time."[12]

The Suzhou gold fan was the "Ebony-bone gilded fan" in the system of Su fans (also known as the Wu fans). The gold foil base was painted. The golden fan surface conveyed a sense of luxury and wealth, and the ingenuity lay in that it could be wielded with ease and be unfolded and closed at will. According to *Five Miscellaneous Morsels*,

> The Wu fan, initially valued for its gold-foil-decorated surface, is now considered extremely well-made for its fan bones. Liu Yutai uses white bamboo for the bones of his fans, whose thickness and weight are all weighed and measured without a hairsbreadth difference and whose surfaces are particularly smooth. Each fan he made, worth half a tael of white gold, is also an ingenious artifact of little practical use.[13]

The Huizhou copper-nickel lock was a novelty combination lock, often necessary for weddings. A famous saying goes, "a gold-painted chest with a copper-nickel lock." The lock, engraved with characters or pictures that constitute the code, has three to seven rings and can only be opened by turning the rings to the set combination. The three-ring lock, for example, has three rings, each with four Chinese characters, which can be combined at random, but the number of combinations that can be made from it is not enough.

The bamboo-strip case was a case woven with thin wisps of split bamboo strips used to hold invitations, gift envelopes, and other objects when visiting guests and sending gifts. It was mostly made in rectangular structures, sometimes with small locks. Wood was more common. While using bamboo strips here was not necessarily more expensive, it was quite a novelty. Bamboo strips could be used to make lanterns, but some scholars believed "they still look shabby, despite being made elaborately."[14] In addition, bamboo strips were also used as the rough equivalent of today's carrying cases. In the famous story *Jiang Xingge Reunites with His Pearl Shirt* 蒋兴哥重会珍珠衫 in *Instruction Words to Enlighten the World*, Xuepo, a woman selling headwear, "carries a bamboo-strip case" with her.[15]

The popularity of Shandong cocoon silk in the late Ming dynasty is evidenced by the record of Ye Mengzhu 叶梦珠 in the early Qing dynasty:

> Shandong cocoon silk was produced with collected cocoons, the best from pepper trees in Shandong. The silk was pale black with a peppery aroma. Any dust gathered would easily shake off after a year, making the silk clean without washing it. In the Ming dynasty, both the price and purpose of Shandong cocoon silk were like those of velvet. In recent years, as it has become much cheaper, Shandong cocoon silk has almost become extinct. Nowadays, the best ones cost only a few *maces* for a *chi* [approx. one foot], and some can be sold at a price of as little as 0.3 or 0.4 *maces* per *chi*. As a result, Shandong cocoon silk has become more commonplace than bourette. It was commonly woven in Jiangsu, Huzhou, Jiaxing, and Songjiang and became increasingly cheaper as more people used it.[16]

The records of Ye Mengzhu reflect in detail the changes in price and popularity of silk fabrics from the Ming to the Qing dynasties. Shandong cocoon silk was a rare commodity in the Ming dynasty, whose price was equal to that of velvet. At that time, quality velvet, especially a kind of *da* velvet called "*gu* velvet," was quite pricey and "cost hundreds of *taels* of gold for each ten-*chi*-long piece." Good velvet was used for robes that could be worn for decades and sometimes even be passed on to posterity. When Hu Dan takes two servants of the Chaos to visit his uncle Su Jinyi, Su, "in a square headdress and *gu* velvet Taoist robe," is "dressed so solemnly" that the servants cannot help but feel weak in the knees and "kneel under the hall platform and kowtow four times" (5.35). *Da* velvet was a generic term for velvet fabrics; its production was concentrated in Nanjing at the time. According to *Gazetteer of the Capital* (Shoudu Zhi 首都志), "Nanjing was capable of producing three kinds of velvet: *Zhang*, *Jian*, and colored velvet."[17] *Zhang* velvet, named after its origin in Zhangzhou, Fujian, was the modern-day velvet. As previously mentioned, the fur hats for the bereaved brothers made by Tailor Shen for four taels of silver are made of velvet.

However, in the Qing dynasty, velvet lost much of its value, primarily due to the rise of the fashion of "wintering in fur even in the South since the Shunzhi reign." In this way, as it is recorded:

> Today's finest *gu* velvet is worth no more than 10 to 20 *taels* of gold for each ten-*chi*-long piece. Those inferior ones cost 0.8 or 0.9 *maces* for each *chi*, and those of poorer quality only cost 0.5 or 0.6 *maces*. In recent years, there have been few sellers and customers, leading to increasingly lower prices and poorer quality.[18]

The devaluation of cocoon silk was due to the expansion of production, as more and more people tended to wear it.

Lady Tong's reference to buying shoes at the Temple of Heaven is evidence that the Temple was already a commercial paradise for ordinary people in the late Ming dynasty. In *A Compilation of Histories in the Wanli Reign* (Wanli Ye Huo Bian 万历野获编) by Shen Defu 沈德符, it is recorded that "In the capital, the Temple of Heaven is the most crowded, where people gallop on horses. Not only the nobles and merchants but also the officials on leave, all ride, and shoot for fun."[19] Besides, in *Textual Research on Past Events Under the Imperial Edict* (Qinding Rixia Jiuwen Kao 钦定日下旧闻考), a record of the Dragon Boat Festival by *Records of Four Seasons in Beijing* (Beijing Suihua Ji 北京岁华记), a festival folklore ethnography of Beijing in the Ming dynasty, is quoted: "At the Dragon Boat Festival, people give each other *zongzi* and apricots, and bring wine to visit the Gaoliang Bridge or the Temple of Heaven, where people ride and shoot weeping willows, and compete to demonstrate their archery skills."[20] Thus, the Temple of Heaven has become a popular tourist attraction for scholars and commoners in Beijing, as has the Gaoliang Bridge. The Temple of Heaven was originally the only place where the national rituals for worshiping Heaven and Earth were held in the Ming dynasty. Emperor Jiajing later built the Temple of Earth, the Temple of the Sun, and the Temple of the Moon to perform rituals outside the city according to the specific direction. Therefore, the status of the Temple of Heaven declined and ceremonies there were less frequent. After Emperor Jiajing moved to Xiyuan Palace, he did not participate in the rituals for many years. Only officials were appointed for the significant ceremonies at the Temple of Heaven, leading to an increasingly deserted management. The shoe shop mentioned here is suspected to be the "Song's Boots" shop on Dashilan Street, a commercial center not far from the Temple of Heaven.

2) On Sumptuary Legislation and Sumptuary Ethos

Scholars often debate how to interpret the highly developed commodity economy of the Ming dynasty. Still, they mostly agree on the fact that the series of sumptuary laws enacted in the early Ming dynasty was almost obsolete in its middle and late period when materialism became widespread. The decline of the sumptuary legislation was reflected in the open defiance of the ban by the wealthy, who had the purchasing power to purchase goods far beyond the limits of their status under the law, and in the blatant disregard of the state's dress code by actors, pimps, procuresses, and prostitutes, who were explicitly required to be dressed in a derogatory manner in terms of style, texture, and color of clothing and headgear, but only dressed according to their economic capacity. The law had no control over them, and this was particularly true of wealthy concubines and eunuchs. The early Ming sumptuary legislation was reduced to a mere piece of paper that few commoners followed, and there were a thousand ways in which it was violated. Moreover, some of its weaknesses—being too costly to enforce, cumbersome, overly detailed, etc.—prevented it from being implemented for long. Taiwanese scholar Wu Jen-shu 巫仁恕 is an expert on the Ming consumer culture. He notes that there were approximately 119 bans on extravagance consumption during the Ming, of which only 11 were issued before the Chenghua reign of Emperor Xianzong (1465–1487), with the rest issued afterward. Wu points out that, indeed, there were voices endorsing luxury consumption, represented by scholar-literati such as Jiang Yingke 江盈科, Lu Ji 陆楫, and Wang Shixing 王士性. However, the voices opposing luxury consumption were much louder.[21]

In corners beyond the reach of the law, there was still a sumptuary impetus heavy enough to assume a weighing-down force on the upward trend of the booming consumerist economy of the late Ming dynasty, which was a catalyst that widened the already gaping divide between the northern and southern economies, and urban and rural consumption. The sum of these sumptuary ideas, concepts, customs, and practices is the "sumptuary ethos." Without it, even if we take into account such factors as the anti-business policy, the inconvenience of transport, the income gap between urban and rural areas, and regional disparities in economic development, we still cannot explain why the consumerist economy failed to spread throughout the country, and why there were significant differences between urban and rural areas and between the North and South in terms of material consumption in the Ming dynasty. We are not suggesting, of course, that all the factors and forces of anti-consumerist culture that did not fall within the sumptuary legal framework should be attributed to the sumptuary ethos, nor are we suggesting that the sumptuary ethos was unique to the Ming dynasty.

But we believe this ethos had the most potent and most obvious symbiosis with the Ming among all Chinese dynasties: its roots were deep and wide, and its breadth was diffuse. The reason is that the Ming government—at least initially—worked tirelessly to lay down a complex and sophisticated sumptuary legal framework to support the class stratification it favored. The sumptuary ethos was protected, encouraged, and given moral legitimacy by the sumptuary legislation. Still, the former was much more moderate, acceptable to the people, and free of cruel punishment and imprisonment. The representatives of the sumptuary ethos would frown at the intention of extravagant consumption and painstakingly advise consumers to avoid material pleasures that were not in keeping with their status. However, as the ethos would not punish or discipline consumers, it could do nothing about the extravagant consumption that had already taken place. Of course, a stern moralist can always threaten that the state's decree is here and that transgressors will be punished, but the threat is always far from being implemented.

2. Silver the King

1) *Was there Remote Remittance in the Ming Financial Institutions?*

From *Jin Ping Mei*, a novel written around the time of the reigns of Jiajing to Wanli (1522–1620) in the Ming dynasty, it is clear that by the middle to late Ming, silver was already in widespread circulation in China's economic life. In *XSYYZ*, silver is exchanged in numerous social and economic situations, from ones involving large amounts, such as official position purchases, bribes, house purchases, and human trafficking, to ones involving small amounts, such as daily consumption and social gifts. Given the ubiquity of silver, the use of copper coins was secondary, and bartering was not common, even in the countryside. Gold, a precious metal, was rarely seen in circulation unless used for bribes or high-class gifts.

In *XSYYZ* and other Ming-Qing literary works, descriptions of traveling with large quantities of silver are commonplace. Why was silver, not the best hard currency in terms of portability, more widely used for long-distance transfers and transactions than gold? Did remittance between different areas ever appear in mid-Ming to enable people to avoid unsafe travel with silver? Or did it ever exist? Whether or not there was a remote remittance mechanism in the mid- and late-Ming society has been of interest to historians working on the economic history of the Ming dynasty and the financial history of China. These questions, in a way, resemble a small-scale discourse on the "budding capitalism of the late Ming."

The silver circulation issue can be analogized to the inside of a pagoda if we treat the Ming-Qing economic life as a park. Again, the remote remittance issue can be likened to an arguable feature of the pagoda, say, the leaning of its spire. This feature, however, must be observed under the condition that we cannot enter the park and cannot see the pagoda in person. We have, in our hands, some historical and literary records and photographs taken outside the park, on the pagoda or its spire. There are very few close-up shots of the spire, but quite a few of the pagoda itself. While A sees a straight pagoda spire in the photographs, and B sees a sloping one, the issue now comes down to whose judgment we should follow. Should we compare those few close-up shots of the spire with those of the pagoda? Before freezing our frame on the spire, let us first give the pagoda an overall look.

The initial recognition of silver taxation by the Ming state was revealed by the approval of *Banjiang* Silver 班匠银, issued in the 21st year of the Chenghua reign (1485), which allowed artisans to pay silver in lieu of servitude. In the early years of the Zhengtong reign, Emperor Yingzong converted the rice and wheat tax of the southern provinces into a silver toll, known as *Jinhua* Silver 金花银. The order "converting rice and wheat into silver" established the status of silver as a recognized means of payment by the state. In the 21st year of the Jiajing reign (1542), *Banjiang* Silver was officially decreed, replacing all craftsmen's services with a silver levy while prohibiting them from working in the capital. The tax and service system implemented during the Wanli reign established silver as the only fully functional currency.[22]

The emergence of silver as the dominant coin in the Chinese market in the sixteenth to eighteenth centuries is a phenomenon noted by all scholars of Ming and Qing history. According to Peng Xinwei 彭信威, a researcher on Chinese monetary history, the use of silver was already prevalent in the late Hongwu reign. Still, it was not until after Emperor Yingzong relaxed the ban on silver that silver acquired its two essential monetary functions: as a measure of value and a means of circulation.[23]

Silver imported into China during the Ming was mainly from Mexico and Peru in Spanish America. In large quantities, it totals more than ten times China's production. The importation source was complex, with various routes through the Philippines, Macau, and Japan, and the importers included Portuguese, Spanish, Japanese, and Chinese merchants. The silver importation phenomenon has aroused the interest of East Asian economic historians worldwide. More than 20 leading scholars from home and abroad have participated in the ongoing debate since the 1930s. Due to the different years and units of statistics, the conclusions reached by each scholar vary greatly. The imported amount has been surmised by Fu Jingbing 傅镜冰, who began his research in 1933; Quan Hansheng 全汉升, an elder authority on economic history; Zhuang Guotu 庄国土 of Xiamen University; Richard Von Glahn 万志英 of UCLA; Japanese American scholars Kozo Yamamura 山村耕造 and Tetsuo Kamiki 神木哲男; and Taiwanese scholar Li Longsheng 李隆生. Those researchers came to varying conclusions due to statistical age and unit differences. If we take the average, the total would be around 300 million *taels*.[24]

Noticing the importance of silver to the Chinese economy, and, indeed, to the world economy after mid-Ming, German scholar Gunder Frank wrote *Reorient: The Global Economy in the Asian Age*, whose core argument was that China was the center of the pre-modern world economy. This book shocked the pre-millennium Western history academic world, winning the 1999 Book Prize of the World History Association for breaking the established Eurocentrism. The book has often been cited to support the rebellious propositions of two earlier European historians:

> There is no history but universal history as it really was.
> Leopold von Ranke, German Language Positivist historian.

> Il n'y a pas d'histoire de l'Europe, il y a une histoire du monde! [There is no history of Europe, only history of the world!]
> Marc Bloch, French Annalist Comparative historian.[25]

Such a large importation of silver could explain silver's dominance in financial systems during Ming and Qing. We would like to propose further that "Silver the King" also stands in circulation. The lack of remote remittance can reversely demonstrate the prevalence of silver in travel.

We shall call the side that believes in the existence of remote remittance "the affirmative" 有派 and the side that denies its existence "the negative" 无派. For historical textual research, it is always "easy to prove that something exists, but hard to prove that it does not." We cannot deduce from *XSYYZ* and other sources that there must have been no remote remittance activities, but we can at least prove that the sources cited by "the affirmative" are not credible enough.

Both "the affirmative" and "the negative" have noticed *hui piao* 会票, a late Ming financial bill mentioned by Huang Zongxi 黄宗羲 and Gu Yanwu, who lived through the Ming-Qing transition. *Hui piao* was thought to be similar to the Tang dynasty's *fei qian* (flying money 飞钱). *Hui piao* has the same pronunciation as our modern "bill of exchange" 汇票. Huang states, "The paper money originated from the Tang dynasty as *fei qian*, which was similar to the present *hui piao*, and was produced and issued by the government from the Song dynasty onwards."[26] Gu states:

> The paper currency institution was devised based on the previous dynasties. Silver was not adopted as coinage standard for it's too heavy. Therefore, the Paper Money Law [Decree on the Issuance, Circulation and Exchange of Paper Money 钞法] was issued. The *fei qian* rising in the Xianzong reign of the Tang (805–820) is now known as *hui piao*.[27]

He Liancheng 何炼成 sees Huang Zongxi's theory of the *hui piao* as an elaboration of the *Chengti* Paper Money Law in the Southern Song, a method of issuing and managing paper money, but doesn't link it to remittance.[28] Gu Jiguang, an older-generation economic historian, is more neutral in his attitude, acknowledging on the one hand that the exchange shop was created for money transfers and, on the other hand, trying to push back the time of the creation of the Shanxi exchange shop. Gu argues that *Records of Shanxi* 晋录, a book by Shen Sixiao 沈思孝 in the Wanli reign, details the economic life of Shanxi without any mention of the exchange shop. Therefore, the Shanxi exchange shop could not have been created earlier than Shen Sixiao; it had to be at least in the late Ming and early Qing dynasties.[29]

Ye Shichang's 叶世昌 attitude towards the *hui piao* referred to by Huang and Gu varies in several monographs on the economic history of the Ming and Qing dynasties. Sometimes he only affirms its nature as an exchange ticket.[30] In the context of the Qing dynasty, he would say with certainty that "*hui piao* is the bill of exchange."[31] *History of Chinese Monetary Theory*, co-authored by Ye Shichang and two others, acknowledges that in the Ming context, "*hui piao* is the same as the bill of exchange." Still, we cannot confirm that this is necessarily Ye's own opinion.[32]

The representative of the "affirmative side" is Sun Qiang 孙强, a young scholar studying the financial history of the late Ming dynasty in recent years. After exploring the meaning of the term *hui piao* in the context of the Ming economy, he concludes that there was indeed a considerable scale of private remote remittance in the late Ming dynasty, and *hui piao* had the same function as "bills of exchange" in the modern sense.[33] Sun Qiang argues that remote remittance activities in late Ming civil society can be proven by the discussion of the monetary law triggered by the severe money shortages in the late Ming and early Qing dynasties. He cites the example of Ming scholars Lu Shiyi 陆世仪 and Chen Zilong 陈子龙. According to Lu Shiyi:

> Nowadays, many people need to carry huge sums of silver to the capital. Because of the inconvenience of traveling, they will entrust their silver to rich merchants in the capital and get a bill, with which they can get their silver back when they arrive. The bill is called *hui piao*, much similar to the *fei qian* of the previous dynasties.

Lu Shiyi advocated the issuance of silver coupons in place of silver:

> A silver bill department should be established in each Provincial Administration Commission [Buzhengsi 布政司] or significant prefecture. The

government can issue bills so that merchants could exchange the silver for bills, by which they can get the silver back, with interest levied in between.[34]

Chen Zilong was one of the few literary figures in the late Ming dynasty with literary talent, economic vision, and organizational skills. He said:

> Nowadays, people who lend money for interest mostly use bills, while merchants and businessmen use *hui* for travels with little need to carry silver. Both bills and *hui* align with the original intention of the paper money. Why can't they be used officially, given the widespread private application?[35]

In our view, the reference to "rich merchants in the capital" in Lu's text clearly points to the private sector. In Chen's text, the *hui* corresponds to "travels with little need to carry silver." Given the contrasting contexts, the "bill" would not be intended for the same purpose and thus would have little to do with remote places or travels. The "bill" is a savings certificate for local savings with interest. The *hui* in Chen's text was a small-scale business partnership between merchants and traders to exchange funds for working capital, which is still common today. As merchants traveled around, capital could flow across regions. The characteristic of the *hui* was that it did not serve the public to make profits. In our view, elements of financial credit could indeed be found in the transactions of the *hui piao* and through the *hui* in the mid- and late-Ming period. Here there are three cases: first, long-distance traders or retailers who purchased goods from a dealer's shop and, for lack of funds, drew up bills as evidence that payment would be made at another time and place; second, the act of lending money and funds; and third, pledging physical assets for cash, where the pledger could obtain money from the merchant either locally or from the merchant's business in a different place. The last of these, along with the aforementioned remote money transfers within the *hui*, is most likely mistaken for remote remittances. It is likely that Lu and Chen, based on sporadic private currency transfers, propose that the Ming government introduce a remote remittance system dominated by a central or national bank. However, given their birth time, such a proposal was pie in the sky. Lu was only 33 years old when the Qing dynasty replaced the Ming, and even his high-minded arguments were included in He Changling's 贺长龄 *Imperial Classic Selection of the Qing* 皇朝经世文编 in the late Qing. Chen Zilong, moreover, died a martyr's death after the establishment of the Qing, making it even less likely for him to implement this financial vision. The private financial activities cited in Lu's and Chen's texts, along with a Xu Guangqi's family letter and a story from *Idle Talk Under the Bean Arbor* 豆棚闲话, which are cited later in Sun Qiang's book, are all money transfers among individuals or small groups. They were fundamentally different from a remittance business operated for the general public. In fact, even in the mid-Ming period, a remote remittance mechanism did not emerge in China's economy. It was not until the late Ming that we can vaguely see from a hypothesis that the mechanism sprouted in the Shanxi merchant group only as a byproduct of Shanxi merchants' silk business at that time. In the book *Talking about the Past* (Tan Wang 谈往) by an adherent of the Ming with the pseudonym "Huacun Kanxing Shizhe,"

88 *Luxury Consumption and the Financial System*

it is written that in the 15th year of Chongzhen reign (1642), the Ministry of Revenue issued a loan to "the silk shop merchants in Jiangmi Lane" and ordered the merchants to "exchange their bills for silver at the official treasury of the state and county." According to that, Wang Shouyi speculates that "the government used the internal fund circulation of the silk merchants to transfer the treasury silver from local governments to Beijing." Based on the historical fact that there were many Shanxi silk merchants in and around the front gate of Beijing who had close ties with the southeastern textile base, Wang deduces that "the adoption of bills of exchange in the allocation of funds is possible." With less than a coherent argument and hardly credible historical material, this daring hypothesis on the "remittance origin" barely pushes back the emergence of remittance to the Chongzhen reign.[36]

Europe, by contrast, was indeed a long way ahead of China. In the late thirteenth and early fourteenth centuries, before the Ming dynasty was established, the great Italian family-based commercial companies had already opened branches in Barcelona, Marseille, and Tunisia on the Mediterranean coast, in the ports of the Near East, and the metropolises of Western Europe, such as London and Paris. The Peruzzi family had 16 branches and employed 150 agents, while the Acciaioli family had 12 offices and 41 proprietors.[37] Their handling of capital and bookkeeping and the various forms of credit thus spread throughout Europe. Larry Neal, in his *A Concise History of International Finance: From Babylon to Bernanke*, describes the leading innovations in the financial system of the Italian city-states and of family banks, such as the Medici. In addition, Larry gives a detailed account of how Italian banks remitted parish taxes collected from Western Europe for the popes in Rome or Avignon, France.[38] The "Papal Remittance" is considered a demand that significantly contributed to the development of European finance in the early Renaissance. Another economic study on the financial activities in the early Renaissance places a great emphasis on the leading role of Bruges, a northwestern Belgian city, in remittance and other financial operations. Hence, the author refers to Bruges as the "cradle of capitalism."[39]

By the mid-fourteenth century, as the Ming dynasty was just established, well-capitalized Italian banks and major merchants had opened permanent branches in all the major economic centers of Europe. At the same time, a wave of credit innovation swept across Europe like the passing of a torch, with the adoption of new systems originating in Italy for the associations, agents, communications, insurance, methods of payment, remittance, credit, and so on. The widespread use of bills of exchange made commercial activities more secure, and this means of credit soon developed into bond certificates. The lowering of interest rates contributed to the development of budding European capitalism.[40]

Many scholars of ancient Chinese financial history regret that the start of financial credit in China was behind that of Europe. With a compensatory attitude, they always work to find an "originator of the exchange system" for Chinese financial history, and the earlier it may be, the better. After much effort, they discovered that Xu Jie, the "Huating Prime Minister" of the late Jiajing reign, was worthy of the title. In one of his notes, Yu Shenxing 于慎行 mentions that when Xu Jie was in the prime ministerial position, relying on the established manufacturing industry in Songjiang, he:

> concentrated the weavers . . . and allocated local taxes directly to the private residences of major bureaucrats. Then officials brought empty "certificates [*die* 牒]" into the capital and exchanged them for silver at the prime minister's residence, where the prime minister summoned workers to lay out the silver, and every seven *zhu* was recognized as one *tael*. Even the officials who managed the state's agricultural taxes could not notice the loophole.[41]

Scholars of economic history like to cite a story from Fan Lian's 范濂 *Yunjian Authentic Records* (Yunjian Jumu Chao 云间据目抄), to prove that Xu Jie had opened a private remittance enterprise. The story was about a merchant surnamed Ma who was cheated in Beijing during the Jiajing and Longqing reigns (1522–1572). Merchant Ma was about to return to Songjiang from Beijing, and a swindler, Su Kewen, says to him:

> I heard you would return on a certain day, but as you travel thousands of miles alone, are you not afraid of encountering thieves? I will send your money to Xu's shop and take a *hui piao*. It's like a promissory note. When you bring the *hui piao* back to Xu's shop, they will pay you back. This way, you can take the money with you without carrying the silver physically. You can feel more reassured on such a long journey. Merchant Ma feels very grateful to Kewen and gives him 150 *taels* of silver without hesitation. Su Kewen pretends to go into Xu's shop and act on Ma's behalf, then presents Ma with a forged *hui piao* and says: "Your money is here." Ma later returns and presents the *hui piao* at Xu's shop, which considers it a forgery and rejects it. Ma then returns to the capital and asks Su Kewen: "Your scam bankrupted me. What should I do?" Su Kewen, having anticipated Ma's return, makes another forged *hui piao*, and pretends to ask for a letter from Xu, making it seem real in every way. Ma immediately returns with the new *hui piao*.[42]

As mentioned previously, the practices of the tax collectors in Songjiang, namely transferring local tax money directly to the Xu family in Songjiang and sending officials to the prime minister's residence in Beijing to get silver with "certificates" used as a promissory note, are recorded in Yu Shenxing's note. We believe that neither Yu's account, nor Fan Lian's record of the so-called "Xu's official shop" which "stores funds" in Beijing to be retrieved in Songjiang, can constitute proof of the existence of remote remittance in the Ming dynasty. Both stories scream "exceptions" and "privileges." Yu Shenxing's story illustrates how Xu Jie abused his power to line his pockets. Xu Jie made a fortune as he siphoned off money at every opportunity and forced unfair exchanges with local governments. Yu Shenxing records this as a moral expression of his anger at the fact that the "Huating Prime Minister" had become a "minister of corruption": "How can we possibly credit him with ministerial righteousness?"[43] Yu disagrees with the time saying, "It is thought that the Prime Minister's wealth is not scavenged, but merely saved up, as he is good at saving a fortune."[44] That is, he did not think that Xu Jie's fortune was amassed in line with the principle of fairness in accruing wealth through business.

The story that Su Kewen defrauds Ma of 150 *taels* of silver is mentioned in almost every monograph on the history of Chinese finance and credit, which Fan Lian believes reflects at least two things: first, the Xu family's financial credit enterprise has been privatized (serving the mass); and second, the enterprise has been specialized; that is, "the *hui piao* is considered a forgery" because the Xu family could twice identify fake bills. In fact, in this story, we can neither infer that the Xu Family's remittance business—if it indeed existed—went private, nor can we conclude that it has been professionalized simply because of the identification of a forged bill. To understand this story of Fan Lian, we should first learn about the nature of the book *Yunjian Authentic Records*. This book, like the *Gushan Notes* (Gushan Bizhu 谷山笔塵), is also a literary sketch. As it censures the misdeeds of local officials and gentry in Wuzhong, the book is highly acclaimed, with a saying that "Confucius wrote the *Spring and Autumn Annals* that frightened rebellious officials, while Fan Lian wrote the *Yunjian Authentic Records* that frightened corrupt officials."[45] Su Kewen was a minor figure not recorded in Ming history, except for a name listed in the inscription on a bronze tablet composed by Ye Xun 叶巽 and written by Li Zhen 李镇 at the rebuilding of the pagoda spire of the White Pagoda in the Guangyou Temple in the fifth year of the Longqing reign (1571). At that time, Su Kewen was the assistant judge of the Jinan Prefecture in Shandong who was stationed at Xiuyan, Liaodong,[46] a member of the Judicial Office (Duanshisi 断事司) under the Dusi 都司 and a seventh-rank official. Su Kewen, in history, was still struggling at the outermost edge of the Ming bureaucracy even in the fifth year of the Longqing reign; hence, his situation was wretched. If we accept Fan Lian's identification of Su Kewen, would he, as a follower of Xu Jie and a son of Xu's old friend in his heyday, commit financial fraud against his fellow countryman for a mere 150 *taels* of silver, twice falsifying bills and testing the limits of the business of the proprietor's silver shop? When forging a letter from Xu, would he not be afraid of being exposed at Xu's? Such a disgraceful act is unlikely the work of a prime minister's follower with a great future ahead of him. The fact that Xu's shop can identify forged bills does not necessarily mean that the shop is specialized, as the parameters and degree of the forgery are not given. Logically speaking, it is already very implausible that Merchant Ma would make a long journey from Songjiang in Shanghai to Beijing to claim the 150 *taels* of silver—even the travel expenses were more than that. And why doesn't he exchange the bill at Xu's shop in Beijing after getting the counterfeit bill for the second time, or at least check whether it could be cashed first, but instead "immediately returns" and then goes to Xu's shop in Songjiang to take a chance on it? It can be seen, therefore, that Fan Lian's intention in this article is mainly to denigrate Xu Jie and his followers, which makes it no more plausible than the words of a novelist. But this doesn't necessarily mean that *Yunjian Authentic Records* fails to document social customs and economic life. Instead, some descriptions are pretty detailed, but mainly devoted to the local affairs of Yunjian (the alias of Songjiang), especially the silk-weaving industry. As for how Xu's shop operates the remote remittance business, Fan Lian only presents a partial picture. Citing such a private note, which lacks specific operational details and has a politically aggressive purpose, to prove that China's remittance business began with Xujie is far from rigorous.[47]

All the these discussions of remote remittance have been for one detail in *XSYYZ*. That detail just proves in reverse that there was no remittance business in Songjiang in the middle to late Ming dynasty, at least not one that was available for ordinary officials and citizens. But, of course, no matter whether it is for novels on human relationships or unofficial historical notes, a reference to, and comparison with, other contemporary sources is necessary.

In the fifth chapter of *XSYYZ*, the county magistrate bribes a eunuch for a governorship; powerful actors stir up the ministry of civil affairs 明府行贿典方州, 戏子恃权驱吏部; and Chao Sixiao, in his official position in Huating County, Southern Zhili, wants to seek the post of governor of Northern Tongzhou. To bribe the Imperial Eunuch Wang Zhen, whose power is secondary only to that of the emperor, he first needs to bribe imperial guards Su and Liu. He sends two close family members to the capital with 1,000 *taels* of silver, together with Hu Dan, the actor. The three travel by donkey on the overland route for a total of 28 days, costing an additional 200 *taels* for the journey. If the remittance business existed, why would Chao Sixiao, in his current position as county governor, not have employed this convenient means of money transfer? Even if he does need to send his servants and family members to the capital to pay bribes, taking the silver on the road would incur various risks on the journey. In *Water Margin*, the batch birthday gifts for Master Cai, escorted by the martial arts master Yang Zhi, can still be taken by Chao Gai. Who can guarantee that the silver for Wang Zhen will arrive safely? Even after entering the capital and staying there temporarily, Hu Dan and the two servants suffer apparent anxiety because of the importance of the silver they are carrying:

> The journey took twenty-eight days. On the 14th day of the first month, they entered the Shuncheng Gate and stayed in a small nunnery by the river canal. After settling the luggage . . . Hu Dan (after going to his grandfather Su Jinyi's) decided to leave for the nunnery to stay with Chao Shu and Chao Feng as the 1,000 *taels* of silver mattered a lot to all three of them. Su Jinyi said, "It would not make sense for my grandson to go to the nunnery instead of resting at his grandfather's. Send someone to help the two servants move in with us." After finishing his meal, Hu Dan took two attendants to the nunnery just before dark to move the luggage. Chao Shu and Chao Feng said, "This nunnery is clean, and the stove is convenient. It's alright to stay here. You can stay with your relatives, and we will stay here. It may be more convenient." The two attendants would not let them stay, though. While packing, they called for two horses to carry the luggage and left first. As the 1,000 *taels* of silver were in the luggage, Chao Shu and Chao Feng had to pursue them.

(5.33–34)

The book *Jin Ping Mei* has substantial descriptions of the travels of Ximen Qing and his attendants in business with large sums of silver, such as Han Daoguo's trip to Hangzhou with 4,000 *taels*. The subsequent literary works do not differ much in the way they depict travel with silver. Here we will not delve into details. These works, such as *Collections of Short Stories and Two Collections of Surprising Stories*, *The Scholars*, and *The Lamp on the Forked Road* 歧路灯, are from the late Ming, early Qing, or even mid-Qing.

The great prosperity of the remittance bank was actually after the Daoguang reign in the Qing Dynasty (1821–1850). Before then, the long-distance transfer of large amounts of silver was mainly protected by escort agencies. Wen Kang's 文康 *Legend of Heroes and Heroines*, set in the background of the late Kangxi (1662–1722) and early Yongzheng (1723–1735) reigns, was written in the middle of the Daoguang reign and its social depiction reflects the latter. The novel begins with the story of Elder An, who is in exile in Huai'an awaiting conviction for his failure in the duty to control the river and is in urgent need of 5,000 *taels* of silver to compensate for the loss. When Junior An learns of this in the capital, he tries to redeem some of the silver and:

> hires four long-travel mules: he and his two servants ride three, and one carries the luggage and silver. In addition to the money given by friends and relatives for the journey, a sum of 2,400 or 2,500 *taels* is raised. Junior An does not have time to take leave of relatives and friends, nor does he wait for an auspicious day. Hurriedly having the luggage arranged, the three set off from the manor house, followed by two mule drivers, and go along the main road to the southwest, heading for Chang Xin Dian.[48]

The abundant texts in Ming-Qing fiction that record people traveling with large amounts of silver for business or pleasure only show one thing: from the mid-Ming to the mid-Qing period, before remittance services flourished, the use of silver was still the most common means of moving large amounts of funds from place to place. In a span of 300 years, people's financial lifestyles had not changed much! Of course, taking gold on long journeys was one of the options. In *Legend of Heroes and Heroines*, He Yufeng wants to lend Junior An 3,000 *taels* of silver, so she asks Deng Jiugong for a temporary loan. Deng, thinking that "bulky and heavy luggage must attract attention on the journey," gives "200 *taels* of gold with the vermilion seal of the Tong Tai." It is noteworthy that Deng prefaces his giving of the gold with a comment, "Is it for local use, or use in distant places? For local use, there are ready-made bills in the county shops; for distant use, there is ready-made gold. Would gold be easier to carry?"[49] The "bills in the county shops" were bank notes for local use and clearly could not be used for remittance when traveling far away. This story also proves that the former so-called *hui piao* was not a "bill of exchange." Deng Jiugong himself had initially worked as an armed escort transporting large sums of money, so he would have lost that job if the remote remittance industry had developed.

Let's turn to *The Travels of Lao Can*, written in the late Qing dynasty. It has an unambiguous depiction of the bills of exchange. The third chapter, "From Golden

Thread Eastward Seeking a Black Tiger, a Cloth Sail Goes West in Search of a Gray Falcon" (金线东来寻黑虎,布帆西去访苍鹰), begins with the following story: When Lao Can arrives in Jinan, he carries with him the 1,000 *taels* of silver he has received for the treatment of Huang Dahu in Guqianxian (Bo'xing, Shandong 山东博兴).

> The next day Lao Can felt some misgivings over his one thousand taels of silver in the hotel, so he went to the main road, where he found a bank called Sunrise and sent eight hundred *taels* through the bank to his family in Xuzhou, keeping a hundred odd *taels* of silver for himself.[50]

Later, in the 14th chapter, "Big County Half Floats Like a Frog on the Water Surface, Small Boat Like Ant Distributing Steamed Bread" (大县若蛙半浮水面, 小船如蚁分送馒头), discussing with Huang Renrui at the Qihe Hotel about how to ransom prostitute Cuihuan, Lao Can says that he still has 400 *taels* of silver stored in the Yourong Tang in Jinan, which he can take out and use.[51] We believe that the nature of the silver remittance at Sunrise Bank is remote remittance, whereas the nature of the silver deposit at Yourong Tang is savings.

2) A Comparison of Gold and Silver Circulation

Gold, after all, had to be exchanged for silver before its purchasing power was brought into play on the commodity market. Therefore, it was rarely seen in everyday life, except for bribes, high-class favors, and religious donations, such as the gilding of Buddha statues. However, the occasions when gold is used as a gift are everywhere in Ming-Qing fiction. In the seventh chapter of *A Dream of Red Mansions*, "Madam You Invites Xifeng Alone at a Feast in the Ning Mansion; In the Ning Mansion, Baoyu First Meets Qin Zhong," when Wang Xifeng first meets with Qingzhong:

> Ping'er, knowing how intimate her mistress was with Qin Keqing, decides that she would want to give the boy something handsome. So, she hands him a length of silk and two small gold medallions inscribed with the wish that the owner would win first place in the Palace Examination.[52]

In the 53rd chapter, "Ancestral Sacrifice Is Carried Out on New Year's Eve in the Ning Mansion; An Evening Banquet Is Held on the Feast of Lanterns in the Rong Mansion," the Ning Mansion uses "a packet of loose gold of mixed quality" which "amounts to a hundred and fifty-three *taels* and sixty-seven cents."[53] The "New Year's *yasui* ingots" each weigh 0.6922 *taels*. *Yasui* is a Chinese New Year's custom, and *yasui* ingots are the same as today's "lucky money," whose presentable appearance is the priority. In the eighth chapter of *XSYYZ*, Madame Chao, who works in Tongzhou, asks her maid to bring home some gifts for her daughter-in-law, Nee Ji, which include, in addition to silver, "two *taels* of leaf gold" (8.54).

The leaf gold, as a thoughtful and intimate gift between mother-in-law and daughter-in-law, is a high-class favor along with others, like jewelry and silk. It goes without saying that it comes from the bribes taken during Chao Sixiao's tenure. After Nee Ji's suicide, the Jis become involved in a lawsuit when the magistrate of Wucheng county secretly extorts them by writing in vermilion on a folded invitation paper: "Prepare another sixty taels of leaf gold to repair the holy statue and send the gold in the amount requested as soon as possible" (11.82). The Chaos do comply with the order and send their servant Chao Zhu to "look for gold all over the city." It cannot be found easily. The leaf gold is said to be the gold leaf used to decorate Buddha statues and religious objects. It is also believed to be a kind of highly refined gold shaped like a leaf, with the largest share of production taking place in Yunnan. It was already used as hard currency in the Southern Song Dynasty.[54] Regardless of the type of leaf gold in *XSYYZ*, its inaccessibility and lack of market circulation are obvious.

Silver was cast into ingots to make carrying and value calculation easier. Silver ingots of 50 taels were called *yuanbao* (shoe-shaped silver ingot 元宝). Small ingots were referred to using a number of terms, including *yinke* (small silver ingots 银锞), *xiaoke* (small ingots 小锞), and *ke'er* (ingots 锞儿). Fragmented silver was called *suiyin* (silver fragments 碎银).[55] However, during the Ming dynasty, silver was not cast into coins that could circulate as a measuring currency rather than a weighing currency. In other words, although silver was the dominant currency, it did not have a standard of value and needed to be weighed before it could be exchanged for value. *Yuanbao* was almost the most accurate measurement form, but there were still disputes about its purity and weight in practice. In the sixth chapter of *XSYYZ*, "Zhenge Keeps Servants at Home for Use, and Chao Yuan Offers Money for a position in the Imperial Academy," Chao Yuan goes to the market to buy jewelry for his concubine Zhenge and takes a fancy to a sacred cat that is said to be able to "chant scriptures" and "ward off fox spirits." Even though Chao takes out "an ingot of silver," the seller is skeptical: "Although it is an ingot of silver, I wonder if it is enough for 50 *taels*. Let's find a place to exchange it" (6.43). In the 34th chapter, "Old Di Returns the Dug Silver to the Owner, but the Greedy Country Stewards Go After the Money," Old Di helps Yang Chun deal with the greedy country stewards, asking him to take out 30 *taels* of silver to eliminate his misfortune. When Yang Chun brings the silver, "Old Di takes a look at it, then takes it to the back and weighs it himself, making sure that it weighs enough" (34.264) before he dares to offer it. There are many descriptions of silver in *XSYYZ*, each of which reflects the psychological anxiety of the user caused by the inaccurate weighing of silver.

In addition to the uncertainty of its weighing standard, another problem with silver was that it was easily adulterated with lead, tin, and copper. In the 64th chapter, when Xue Sujie is to confess her sins to the nuns, she pays Nun Bai "ten snow-white silver ingots." Lady Di, Sujie's mother-in-law, had given 500 *taels* of silver to Di Xichen one year before her death in ten portions. Di Xichen, having begged Deng Pufeng to restore harmony between him and his wife through the *huibei* method 回背法, had secretly paid 150 *taels*. Afraid that Sujie would find out, Di Xichen mixed the silver with tin ingots to make the new silver ingots appear similar to the original ones and then put them back in place. However, when Sujie pays the silver, the fraud is revealed by the knowledgeable Nun Bai, who "nibbles it and finds it soft, saying, 'It's not silver, but more like pewter'" (64.493). The pewter counterfeit *yuanbao* has a soft texture, and one can leave a mark on it by scratching its surface with a fingernail, making it easy to identify. Copper-tin alloy, known as *baitong* (White Copper 白铜), has a hard texture, and one must rely on visually inspecting the ingot one by one for its greyish-white color—as opposed to silvery white; and listening to the sound of the coins, striking the coins one-by-one—as they will emit a "copper" tone—to recognize it. As to the appraisal of other semi-counterfeit silver products—such as one-third silver, one-half copper, and one-sixth tin—the "stuffed" silver produced by putting copper and iron into the silver liquid during the smelting process, and the "lead-filled" silver produced by filling drilled holes in the finished silver *yuanbao* with liquid lead, these cannot be identified by visual inspection or weighing. Even connoisseurs must employ specific chemical means to test them.[56]

Silver had many different names depending on its composition. Among the standard types of silver, there were such varieties as fine silver, snowflake silver, sycee silver, *songwen* silver, and *zuwen* silver. As for the lower-quality ones, there were *yaosi* (shaken filament 摇丝), *shuisi* (watered 水丝), *qiansi* (complicated filament 千丝), *huasi* (painted filament 画丝), *chuisi* (blown filament 吹丝), and *xisi* (sucked filament 吸丝). In the first chapter of *XSYYZ*, when Chao Sixiao gets appointed to a lucrative post in Huating:

> those who lend usurious money to the newly appointed officials keep pestering him every day, expecting him to borrow silver at a monthly interest rate of just one percent. The silver is high quality and will weigh on reliable large scales.
>
> (1.3)

In the 13th chapter, "Confess and Commit to Trial in the Department of Criminal Justice, and Approve the Crime Details Before the Judicial Inspector," Chao Yuan and his concubine Zhenge are brought to trial for the suicide of his official wife, Nee Ji. A neighboring woman, Gao Sisao, accompanies them as a witness to their trial in Linqing, where the Dongchang Provincial Court is located. Although Gao receives money from the Chaos before coming because she is asked to testify in court, she doesn't have the patience to travel a long way to "spend time on this trivia." Therefore, Gao complains loudly, causing Chao Yuan to scold her:

> I'm relying on you because you're my neighbor, and someone has identified you as a witness. I've begged you, and given you 30 taels of glistening sycee silver, ten bolts of large native cloth (about 132 meters), two bolts of ghatpot-loom silks (about 26.4 meters), and six strings of yellow-fringed coins. No one dares to take advantage of you for fear of your venom! I send you almost fifty *taels* of silver, expecting you to say a good word to the official, but you have, on the contrary, testified to my guilt. Would you be a little cleverer!
>
> (13.100)

When silver was used as a gift for everyday favors, ingots were better. However, as small favors were more frequent in real life, giving silver directly in a gift box or pouch was sufficient. In the 44th chapter, when Lady Di goes to Xue's house for Sujie's "capping the head" ceremony, she also meets her soon-to-be son-in-law, Xue Rujian. All mothers-in-law are happy to see their sons-in-law, and Lady Di is no exception:

> Lady Di is pleased and gives Xue Rujian a white silk handkerchief and a *saxian* pouch with five coins in it as gifts, which have been placed in a case. Xue's mother says, "You often see your mother-in-law and she always give you gifts. Don't take it this time." As a courtesy, Xue Rujian does not decline the gift, but accepts it solemnly as if it were heavy, puts it in his sleeve, then bows twice to his mother-in-law.
>
> (44.338)

How much would a handkerchief, a pouch, and five coins of silver weigh? Naturally, "as if it were heavy" is a figure of speech, suggesting that five coins of silver are valuable as a gift. But why does Chao Yuan present Gao with "six strings of Yellow-Fringed Coin" in addition to the "glistening sycee silver"? What was Yellow-Fringed Coin? Why was it valuable as a gift? This brings us to the topic of the Ming coinage.

3. The Ming Coinage

1) Yellow-Fringed Coin and Inferior Coins

Although the Ming had already opened the Baoyuan Bureau to cast coins before the establishment of the state, when Zhu Yuanzhang was still called the Duke of Wu, the use of banknotes at the beginning of the Ming dynasty led to the decline of copper coins, and even to a period during which they were forbidden from the 27th year of Hongwu reign to the tenth year of Xuande reign (1394–1435). During the 41 years of exclusive paper currency circulation, the issuing of copper coins was not abolished altogether for diplomatic and foreign trade purposes. Copper coins were still cast during the Yongle and Xuande reigns (1402–1435), with quite neat castings and designs, but the coins produced were used to reward foreign envoys in the tribute trades. Zheng He 郑和 also took a large amount of Yongle coins in his voyages to the West. There was still a lack of stable currency at home, while the private casting of counterfeit coins became rampant. Copper coins were permitted in some areas, yet with inconsistent laws.[57]

The failure of the Da Ming Banknotes gradually became irreversible, and during the Chenghua law, they collapsed completely. On the 23rd day of the first month in the 13th year of the Chenghua reign (1477), Zhou Guang, the commander of the Daxing Left Defense, said:

> In recent years, the banknote law has failed, and every banknote with a face value of a thousand *guan* [one 贯 is usually a string of a thousand copper coins, equivalent to one *tael* of silver], is only worth only about half a *tael*.[58]

Lu Rong, a *jinshi* in the Chenghua reign, said, "The government is the only one who is using banknotes, but one piece is only worth two *li* of silver or two coins."[59] At the beginning of the Jiajing reign, "the banknotes have long been discarded, the copper coin circulation is blocked, which has increasingly led to the exclusive use of silver."[60] This situation is best seen in the *Water Margin*, written during the Jiajing reign. There is no mention of paper money at all, and copper coins are rare, with occasional transactions denominated in *guan*, while most small purchases and sales, even those as small as a pot of wine in a restaurant or a plate of cooked beef, are always in silver. Efforts were made to reverse the situation of silver being the only transaction medium during the Jiajing reign, with a visible change made; from the Longqing reign (1567–1572) onwards, the Ming government gradually formed a monetary system based on silver, with the coin as a supplement. This pattern of silver and coin circulation was maintained until the end of the Qing dynasty, despite the various changes in the silver and coinage laws that followed.

The "coin circulation blockage" in the early years of Jiajing reign was not the same as a "money shortage." There was no shortage of money but a shortage of good coins and fine coins among the people, and users lacked essential faith in the hard currency.[61] In the third year of the Jiajing reign (1524), 70 official coins were equal to one *mace* of silver, while 140 old coins were equal to one *mace* of silver.[62] *The History of the Ming Dynasty—Record of Agriculture and Commerce* 明史·食货志, in discussing the sinister coinage law of the Jiajing reign, states:

> In the old days, the market was flooded with bad coins, with thirty or forty as one candareen [*fen* 分] of silver. Later, coins were mixed with more lead and tin, becoming thin and inferior and of irregular shape. Sixty or seventy coins came to equal one fen of silver. It was also difficult to distinguish the good ones from the counterfeits. Then the propositions of Li Yongjing, Jishizhong [an imperial censor in the Jiajing reign 给事中], were adopted using both the official and miscellaneous coins of previous generations. Every seven fine coins equaled one fen of silver, and the rest were divided into three levels depending on the composition, with 21 coins of the lowest quality equaling one fen of silver. Private manufacture of money was prohibited, and offenders would be brought to justice according to the law.[63]

In this context, there was a need to reform the coinage law and gain people's trust in the early years of the Jiajing reign. The most significant change regarding the coins cast in the sixth year of the Jiajing reign (1527) was the introduction of the copper-zinc alloy as a casting material, replacing the long-used tin bronze. The zinc was derived from calamine that contained zinc carbonate (ZnCO3) and was then known as "Japanese lead" or "water tin." According to Song Yingxing's *Exploitation of the Works of Nature* (Tian Gong Kai Wu 天工开物), written in the Wanli reign and first published in the tenth year of Chongzhen reign:

> Red copper accounted for sixty to seventy percent of every ten *jin* (about 5,968 grams) of the cast coins, and Japanese lead (called "water tin" in Beijing) accounted for thirty to forty percent. This is the approximate ratio.

Japanese lead will vanish by a quarter in a raging fire. Among the current daily-use coins, only the Yellow-Fringed Coin of Beijing Baoyuan Bureau and the Luqing Coin of Gaozhou, Guangdong, are of fine composition, one of which could be equivalent to two coins in Jiangsu and Zhejiang, Southern Zhili. The Yellow-Fringed Coin was divided into two kinds, the gold-backed [*jinbei* 金背] coin that was smelted and cast from brass four times and the fire paint [*huoqi* 火漆] coin, which was cast two times.[64]

The Yellow-Fringed Coin was a fine and unrivaled coin produced at this watershed in the history of coinage. The *jinbei* coin, which was cast by smelting the best brass four times, was golden and was among the first-class coins in the Ming dynasty; due to the molding, small granular protrusions often occurred on the back of copper coins, which would cause an illusion of gold coating coupled with the golden color.[65] The color of the *jinbei* coin was so pleasing that there were even rumors like "the back side is plated with gold" among the people. The fondness for it among civilians made it a good gift. According to the official price, ten copper coins equaled one *mace* of silver, but in actual circulation, the value of the *jinbei* coin was much higher. In the Wanli reign, only four Jiajing *jinbei* coins matched the value of one *mace* of silver. Although the later Longqing *jinbei* and Wanli *jinbei* were strong, they never caught up with the Jiajing *jinbei*.[66]

The *huoqi* coin, whose brass was smelted only twice, was iron black and slightly lower in quality. In addition, there was a *xuanbian* coin, which was smelted and ground by *xuanche* (a rotating cutting machine 镟车) and thus had a smooth and shiny edge.[67] Both *huoqi* and *xuanbian* coins can be regarded as official coins of the second class in the Ming. However, due to the high cost, the *tanglü* (an elaborate metal polishing and filing tool) polishing employed for the *xuanbian* coins in the late Jiajing reign did not continue. Therefore, we believe that the Yellow-Fringed Coin repeatedly referred to in *XSYYZ* is, in a broad sense, an umbrella term for the *jinbei* coins, *huoqi* coins, and high-quality *xuanbian* coins before the *tanglü* polishing process was adopted; and, in a narrower sense, it is limited to the *jinbei* coins.

Jinbei, huoqi, and *xuanbian* coins all belonged to high-quality "fine coins": beautiful, sufficient in weight, and high in copper. The "fine coins" recorded by Song Yingxing contained 90 percent brass and ten percent lead, and sounded like gold when thrown to the ground. The emergence of the Yellow-Fringed Coin played an excellent role in stabilizing the people's belief in the coinage law and preventing private casting. *Huoqi* coins and *xuanbian* coins were produced during the Longqing and Wanli reigns (1567–1620). Because of the minor differences among the three types of yellow-fringed coins, it is difficult to distinguish them from each other with only the historical data and the excavated objects. Still, most experts in coin collection believe that the people at that time knew the distinctions well.[68]

In the 55th chapter of *XSYYZ*, "Old Di Eats at the Restaurant All Day, and Lady Tong Instigates the Cook," Old Di buys Tiaogeng, a maid who is good at cooking, from the Ran family in the capital for 24 *taels* of silver. After the seller and the matchmaker sign and the transaction is over:

> Old Di takes out one tael of silver and asks Di Zhou to count out the number of yellow-fringed coins equaling four coins of silver for the two matchmakers. The steward who serves the tea falls to the ground and kowtows to Old Di. Knowing that the gesture was begging for a reward, Old Di then asks Di Zhou to count out the number of yellow-fringed coins equaling two coins of silver and give them to the steward to buy liquor.

The one *tael* paid to the matchmakers here is the commission they had initially agreed upon. The extra two *maces* of silver given to each matchmaker after the transaction is also according to Old Di's prior promise. Before that, to bring Tiaogeng to the Tong family for a view, "Lady Tong gives twenty yellow-fringed coins to urge her (the matchmaker, Lady Zhou) to go quickly, and ride a donkey on the journey" (55.424). This shows that it had become the custom in the capital to use silver for formal wages or transactions and the Yellow-Fringed Coin for additional rewards and small favors, errands, and transportation expenses. Because of its preciousness and the beauty of the Yellow-Fringed Coin, giving it in addition to silver as a large gift added as much grace as silk or specialties.

However, the biggest problem of the Ming coinage policy was the lack of uniformity. The uncertainty of constant promulgation and abolition added to the confusion of the coinage law, as can be seen in Table 2.1:

Table 2.1 Table of Ming coinage policies

Table of Ming Coinage Policies[69]

Year	Contents
Hongwu Reign: the Founding Year (1368)	Promulgated Coinage standard; issued Hongwu Coin.
Hongwu Reign: the 8th year (1375)	Stopped Coinage of Baoyuan Bureau.
Hongwu Reign: the 9th year (1376)	Stopped Coinage of All Provenances.
Hongwu Reign: the 10th year (1377)	Restored Coinage of All Provenances.
Hongwu Reign: the 22nd year (1389)	Restored Coinage of Baoyuan Bureau.
Hongwu Reign: the 23rd year (1390)	Renovated Coinage Standard.
Hongwu Reign: the 26th year (1393)	Stopped Coinage of All Provenances Again.
Hongwu Reign: the 27th year (1394)	Copper Coin Forbidden in Circulation.
Hongwu Reign: the 30th year (1397)	Stopped Coinage of Baoyuan Bureau Again.
Jianwen Reign: the Founding Year (1399)	Restored Coinage under Renovated Coinage Standard.
Hongwu Reign: the 2nd year (1400)	Renovated Coinage Standard Again.
Yongle Reign: the 6th year (1408)	Issued Yongle Coin.
Xuande Reign: the 8th year (1433)	Issued Xuande Coin.
Zhengtong Reign: the 13th year (1448)	Copper Coin Forbidden in Circulation.

(*Continued*)

100 *Luxury Consumption and the Financial System*

Table 2.1 (Continued)

Table of Ming Coinage Policies[69]

Year	Contents
Tianshun Reign: the 14th year (1460)	Copper Coin Restored in Circulation.
Hongzhi Reign: the 16th year (1503)	Issued Hongzhi Coin.
Jiajing Reign: the 6th year (1527)	Issued Jiajing Coin; Stopped Coinage of Jiajing Coin.
	Tax Collected in Silver instead of Coins.
Longqing Reign: the 4th year (1570)	Issued Longqing Coin; Tax Collected in Coin again.
Wanli Reign: the 4th year (1576)	Issued Wanli Coin.
Tianqi Reign: the founding year (1621)	Issued Tanchang Coin; Stopped Coinage of Big Coin.
Chongzhen Reign: the founding year (1628)	Issued Chongzhen Coin.
Chongzhen Reign: the 15th year (1642)	Issued Chongzhen Decuple Coin.

The discontinuity of the coinage policy was often because, even for the state, the cost of coinage had to be accounted for. Unlike paper money, copper coins have an inherent metal value, and the difference between the actual cost value and the issue value is called coinage interest. Gu Yanwu credited the coin of the early Jiajing reign as "the most refined" since the Hongwu reign. The quality, however, came at the cost of low or negative national coinage interests. Xu Jie refers to the crisis in his *Request for Ceasing the Coin Casting of the Baoyuan Bureau*:

> Among the official coins cast in Nanjing, some seem to be coated with gold on the back side and thus are called *jinbei* by commoners; and some, called *huoqi*, are baked with fire and have a black back side. The coins made in Yunnan or cast by the Baoyuan Bureau in previous years are of pure copper and tin, but no lead. The coin, whose edge is processed by a rotating cutting machine, is priced at one *wen* each but weighs 1.2 *maces*. Due to their beautiful yellow color, hard texture, and round and neat edge, such coins are commonly called *xuanbian* coins. Following the officials' suggestions, the recently cast coins no longer involve rotary cutting, but only casting and filing. The craftsmen, however, always steal the copper materials. In this way, as the coin is mixed in composition, light in weight, and has a rough edge caused by rough filing, Commoners often call it *yitiaogun* [bare stick 一条棍]. The so-called *xuanbian*, with its exorbitant cost and complex process, is difficult for the treacherous to counterfeit. But the *yitiaogun*, which costs less, is commonly cast privately. What's more, it is challenging to distinguish *yitiaogun* coins from privately-cast ones. If one accidentally gets a counterfeit *yitiaogun* coin from A, he cannot pass it on to B at once, so people are reluctant to use such coins. And other types, such as the *jinbei* coin, do not circulate well either.[70]

The high cost of coinage often made it impossible to meet the quotas. After the 40th year of the Jiajing reign (1561), even the quality of the official coins of the

Beijing Baoyuan Bureau could not be guaranteed. From the deputy supervisor to the foremen, furnace heads, and craftsmen, the Baoyuan Bureau skimped on work and stinted materials. Cracking down on cheating turned out to be a futile effort. As the quality of state coins declined, private casting became rampant. Initially a mild issue in the Jiajing reign, it quickly spiraled out of control in the Tianqi (1621–1627) and Chongzhen reigns.[71]

In the 33rd chapter of *Jin Ping Mei*, Chen Jingji is punished by Pan Jinlian for losing a key, and he sings a song called "Sheep on the Mountain Slope," which puns on many of the names and production processes of silver coins of the time.

I sent that little nugget, Lion-head, with a yellow chit to summon you;
But you were in Ministry of War Hollow, having a merry night of it at the Silver Ingot.
I'm willing to put up with your brass, verdigris and all, to avoid abandonment;
You're imprinted on my heart like stamped silver;
there's no way I can do without you . . . .

Sister! When you were at K'ai-yüan's place, the two of us burned incense and swore oaths together.
I spent jingling cash and shiny-edged coins in order to be one of those who danced attendance on you.
But you claimed your furnace was out of order, and I couldn't take the goose-eyes of your madam.
It may be said of you that "elm-pod cash are lightweight, and brush-handles are hollow."
Sister! Like an antique cash; your body's shrunk and your hole's too big, no longer of any use;
Unless you let some bare stick, with a worn legend, play up to you with his oily mouth.
Baring your shiny tail, milled rim, and baked lacquer hue, he'd debase you into utter compliance,
And then leave you so topsy-turvy you wouldn't be worth so much as a single black sand-plate.
"Sister!" I call out. "You two-faced androgynous mule!
Just you try and listen to what I say.
It would be a pity if this shiny gold-back were paired with such a wrinkle-faced, mis-struck ingot.[72]

We have already described the terms associated with the Yellow-Fringed Coin in this song. The "Lion-head" was a silver ingot in the shape of a lion, the "yellow chit" was a kind of "Da Ming Banknote" made from mulberry bark, and "goose-eyes," "elm-pod," "brush-handles," "antique cash," "bare stick," "black sand-plate," and "two-faced androgynous mule" were all popular nicknames for the various kinds of inferior copper coins and privately cast coins on the market at that time. The words "one of those who danced attendance on you" and "topsy-turvy" referred to the ratio of good coins to poor-quality coins.[73] Of the many kinds alluded to in the ballad, all are inferior except for Yellow-Fringed Coin. The ballad is a testimony to the prevalent private casting and mass disgustful sentiment towards bad coins at the end of the Ming dynasty.

2) Textual Research on the Decuple Coin

The difference between silvers of different relative purities can be significant in the actual exchange. In the 50th chapter, "Gongshi Di Meets an Acquaintance While Exchanging Money, and Secretary Zang Deceives Him with Nonsense," Di Xichen, out of the need to purchase an official position, goes to Jinan, the provincial capital, with his father to exchange their silver for "decuple coins." One *tael* of standard silver could be exchanged for 78 decuple coins (a kind of large denomination coin), and the high-quality silver could be exchanged for 80.

Much ink was devoted to the decuple coin exchange, which takes up a whole chapter in *XSYYZ*, along with the meeting of old friends, Di Xichen and Sun Lanji. Unfortunately, the historical value of the "exchange of money" has been ignored in all previous textual studies of *XSYYZ*. Therefore, we would like to take the opportunity to shed a little light on some of the financial phenomena of the late Ming dynasty through the exchange of decuple coins.

It is at the Provincial Administration Commission of the province that Di Xichen offers the silver for the position of *jiansheng*. He enjoys government food subsidies because he is already a *xiucai*. Huang Guiwu, the head of the education department, says to Di Xichen and his father:

"Now the decuple coin hardly circulates and will be withdrawn by imperial ordinance. Generally speaking, we exchange ninety coins for one *tael* of silver in common practice. When you offer, eighty coins will be exchanged for one *tael* of silver." Di Binliang asks, "Where can we exchange these coins?" Huang Guiwu answers, "There are a lot in Qin Jingyu's pawnshop at the east gate. If it is the glistening sycee silver in good quality, it can be exchanged for ninety-two or ninety-three coins."

(50.384)

When the Dis go to Qin's pawnshop (owned by Qin Jingyu, the merchant from Yiwu, Zhejiang province, who married Sun Lanji as a concubine in an equal position with his wife) to make inquiries, they are told:

I'm confident there are still 300 *taels* left, but if it's not enough, I'll find more for you. But these days, decuple coins are expensive. Previously, the government used to collect decuple coins, so all cases of promotion and acceptance were paid for with those coins. Upon hearing this news, the people who had decuple coins wanted to get rid of *zhezi* all at once as they were afraid that such coins would not be used again. At that time, one tael of silver could be exchanged for ninety coins, and even ninety-one or ninety-two if the amount was large and the silver was fine. Now the decuple coin is about to run out.

Still, the government is too rigid to accept silver, making it hardly possible for one tael of silver to be exchanged for seventy-seven or seventy-eight decuple coins.

(50.384)

These two texts reveal a phenomenon: when the circulation of the decuple coins encountered obstacles, the government had to mandate the use of decuple coins in the cases of promotion and acceptance to take them back. Regarding the circulation blockage of large denomination coins, Song Yingxing gives some advice after reflection:

The disadvantage of large denomination coins, which are equivalent to five or ten coins each, is that it is easy to cast them privately, to the detriment of the people. For this reason, such coins have stopped circulating in the capital and the provinces after a short time.[74]

In fact, the ease with which they can be cast privately is only one of the disadvantages. Poor circulation can also be attributed to political reasons and even the psychology of the people.

The means of taking back decuple coins was somewhat like the means used to support the Da Ming Banknotes in the early Ming dynasty. The government worked hard to maintain the banknotes that continued to depreciate. During the Xuande and Zhengtong reigns (1426–1449), the production of new banknotes was stopped, more taxes and punitive fines were paid in banknotes, and the payment of banknotes for official salaries or other expenditures was reduced. However, the banknotes nevertheless suffered from hyperinflation and were eventually withdrawn from circulation.[75]

Among the Tongbao, that is, standard coins issued in reigns from the middle to late Ming dynasty, only three types, namely Jiajing Tongbao, Tianqi Tongbao, and Chongzhen Tongbao, had decuple coins. The Jiajing Tongbao, imitating the standards of Hongwu Tongbao, was cast by the Baoyuan Bureau of the Ministry of Works. Its large denomination coins, equivalent to two, three, five, or ten coins in one, each had only 30,000 pieces cast, and none were put into circulation. On the decuple coins, in addition to "one *tael*," "ten" was also cast to record value, which is rare nowadays.[76] Both Tianqi and Chongzhen coins were inferior because the economy had collapsed amid domestic troubles and foreign incursions, and coins were cast to cope with financial difficulties. The Chongzhen Tongbao was cast in the first year of the Chongzhen reign when the coinage law was highly chaotic. All areas capable of casting, including the capital, the provinces, the border towns, the military posts, and warehouse courtyards, were ordered to open furnaces and start casting. The size, weight, thickness, and workmanship of coins thus varied, making Chongzhen Tongbao one of the most complex Chinese coins.[77] Because of the nonuniform coinage standards, the increasing frequency of unlawful private casting, and the overflow of counterfeit coins in the market, the situation was said to be a sign of the state's downfall. The government, however, was not in a position to overhaul, let alone systematically and massively take back the old coins that were poorly circulated.

The father of Emperor Xizong of the Tianqi reign, Emperor Guang Zong, was a short-lived monarch who died suddenly after only 29 days on the throne due to the "Red Pill Case." His Taichang reign (1620) was too short to even start a coinage, and Emperor Xizong later made up the Taichang Tongbao. According to the *Records of Agriculture and Commerce of The History of the Ming Dynasty*:

> Taichang coins were cast in the first year of Tianqi reign. Wang Xiangqian, Minister of War, requested that three large denomination coins be cast of decuple, centuple, and thousandfold, engraved with the dragon pattern and slightly imitating the dragon, horse, and turtle patterns of the "Bai Jin San Pin" of the Western Han dynasty. As a result, large-denomination coins were cast in Beijing and Nanjing. Later, as the disadvantages of large denomination coins were pointed out, the emperor issued a proclamation to stop the casting of large denomination coins in Beijing and Nanjing and recalled large denomination coins for recasting in coin bureaus. At that time, such bureaus were opened all over the state, and large-denomination coins were re-collected.[78]

Tianqi people boycotted its large- and small-denomination coins as "the society during the Tianqi reign is dark, and people quit using Tianqi coins."[79] The Small and Flat Coin (*xiaoping qian* 小平钱) issued late in the Tianqi reign was brittle and fragile, and 5,000–6,000 could be exchanged for one *tael* of silver.[80] But the quality of the coins issued in its early period was not categorically corrupt. *Jinling Trifles* (Jin Ling Suo Shi 金陵琐事) by Zhou Hui in the Ming dynasty records:

> In the early Tianqi reign, the treasury had Japanese lead, Japanese tin, and impure copper with which to cast coins, which were white and with fine print, called *baisha* [white sand 白沙] coins. The coppersmiths could cast a small teaspoon worth ten ordinary copper coins out of two *baisha* coins. Therefore, *baisha* coins were the least in number in circulation and could not be cast by private casters.[81]

This story can support the view of Li Jiannong 李剑农, an economist. According to Li, since the theory of Kong Ji 孔觊 during the Northern and Southern dynasties that "coins should not be minted with excessive frugality in terms of copper and workmanship" was followed too closely by the Jiajing coinage law, the copper content of fine coins was so high that private casters would smelt them in secret to obtain the metal, while the fine coins that were not destroyed and cast would remain hidden among the people.[82] In his comments on Li Jiannong's view, Ray Huang believes that Li has stated Gresham's Law that bad money drives out good, which has some merit but is not entirely satisfactory because Li ignores the quantitative element and government administration of official coinage in the sixteenth century.[83]

The Tianqi decuple coin, also of white brass, was indeed of good quality. Its casting began in the second year of Tianqi reign (1622) and stopped in the fifth year (1625). There were several types of official decuple coins: the front side bore the inscription "Tianqi Tongbao," while the back patterns varied, with one of the following: a *shi* (ten 十) at the top, a *shi* at the top with a star at the bottom, a *shi* at the top with a "one *tael*" on the left, a *fu* at the top, a *zhen* (town 镇) at the top with a *shi* at the bottom, and a *shi* at the top with a "one *tael*" on the left and a *mi* (secret 密) on the right. It is no wonder that contemporary coin collectors give strong backing to it, believing that the Tianqi decuple coin is not inferior to that of any dynasty in terms of the copper quality, weight, shape, and writing on the surface.[84]

It is not fair to attribute the failure of the Tianqi decuple coin to the people's political discontent with the Tianqi governance. The boycott of the Tianqi coin was actually because Zhou Shunchang 周顺昌 of Wu County was arrested and killed by Wei Zhongxian's henchmen for his association with and his giving asylum to the Donglin clique, which later provoked a mass uprising in Suzhou. The rebellion was the "Wu People's Revolt" during which "the five died out of righteous anger when Zhou Shunchang was arrested," as Zhang Pu recorded in his famous *On the Tombstone of the Five* (Wuren Mubei Ji 五人墓碑记).[85] This ancient text, which all Chinese high school students are familiar with, requires no elaboration here. As the Wu people boycotted the Tianqi coin because of Zhou, "the districts, the prefectures, and the counties thus acquiesced and accumulated numerous Tianqi coins. Only after provinces issued initiatives was the coin put back into circulation. The private ban lasted for over ten months."[86]

However, since the mass uprising in Suzhou occurred in the sixth year of the Tianqi reign (1626), it is insufficient to explain the poor circulation of the Tianqi coins. In our view, the interpretation of the everyday economic behaviors of the people should be based on a perspective of the intertwined nature of economics and politics.

The value of Ming coins manifested a unique trend: the reigning emperor's Tongbao coin was always valued higher than the ones of the previous emperors of the dynasty. Emperor Shizong set this precedent in the 32nd year of the Jiajing reign (1553) when he made 70 Jiajing coins equal to one *fen* of silver, double the original value.[87]

In this context, if, in the reign of an emperor, with stable governance and abundant resources, as people were well off, and the emperor himself was in his prime, people would naturally be happy to use the reign's Tongbao, for its was currently solid and would remain strong solid in the foreseeable future. However, if the opposite were true, the people would resist using the reign's Tongbao because of their low confidence in the current relentless government.

Emperor Xizong was dim-witted. Although the Tianqi reign only lasted seven years, it was overshadowed by the people's grievances throughout. In its first year, Nurhaci had already led his army to capture Shenyang, after which the Ming lost troops almost every year; in its third year, Wei Zhongxian came in charge of the Eastern Depot, for whom temples were built everywhere, and Wei was worshiped as "Nine-Thousand-Years" (second only to the emperor); later, the Donglin Six Noble Men, including Yang Lian, Zuo Guangdou, and Wei Dazhong, died in vain successively. Meng Sen, a great Ming historian, sighs that "after the middle of the Ming dynasty, the successes and failures of the important endeavors of the government depended on the support or rejection of the eunuchs." What's more, nee Qie, the wet nurse of Emperor Xizong, committed adultery in the imperial harem and conspired with Wei Zhongxian to force the killing of Wang An, a good eunuch who "in the Wanli reign, assisted the education of, coached, and protected the eldest son of the emperor from targeting and fault-finding by Zheng, the highest-ranking imperial concubine."[88] In Chen Zilong's *Classic Selections of the Ming* (Huangming Jingshi Wenbian 皇明经世文编) and Hou Zhenyang's 侯震旸 *Impeachment of Qie* (He Qieshi Shu 劾客氏疏) of the late Ming, it was already recorded that "It is known that anyone who speaks of Qie is shocked speechless."[89]

Liu Ruoyu 刘若愚, a eunuch who experienced the four reigns of Wanli, Taichang, Tianqi, and Chongzhen during the late Ming, wrote *A Weighted and Unbiased Record* (Zhuo Zhong Zhi 酌中志), saying that Qie was jealous of Empress Yi'an Zhang. He noted:

> In the 3rd year of the Tianqi reign, Empress Zhang Niangniang was pregnant. Qie and Wei, removing the maids that did not plead allegiance to them in Zhang's palace, deliberately assigned some know-nothing eunuchs and maids. One day, Zhang had occasional back pain and thus suffered excessive pounding, resulting in her firstborn child's loss.[90]

Such harem rumors spread most easily among the people, so the people concluded that the emperor was spineless and doomed. In addition, Emperor Tianqi was childless and lacked an heir to the throne; his father, Emperor Taichang, died on the 29th day of his reign, making the harbinger of the emperor's short life pretty clear. In the fifth year of the Tianqi reign, the Houjin army captured Lüshun. In the grip of this sign of demise, the people naturally boycotted the Tianqi coin, just as the speculators expect a particular stock so that they'd refuse to invest in to plunge. The same is true of the decline of the Chongzhen Tongbao.

In summary, since both the decuple Jiajing Tongbao and Chongzhen Tongbao coins were excluded from circulation, and those of Tianqi did not circulate well, considering the later "recall of large-denomination coins for recasting in coin bureaus," there is no doubt that the decuple coin in *XSYYZ* is the decuple Tianqi Tongbao. Therefore, the withdrawal of this high-quality coin from circulation cannot be fully explained by economic reasoning but must be seen in the context of the politics of the Tianqi reign.

We believe that financial development in the Ming dynasty failed to reach sufficient depth and breadth. After the failure of the issuance of Da Ming Banknotes, only silver was king in the field of financial circulation for a long time. However, the situation was eased by the minting of coins after the Jiajing reign, though the state kept changing rules and had no coordinated plan regarding coinage, leading to the minting of coins of different quality even within a single reign. In this way, good coins were either taken to be melted or hidden among the people. The phenomenon that "Bad money drives out good" is related to the economy and politics. From the Jiajing reign onwards, a norm was established in which the reigning emperor used executive orders to impose a higher price on the current Tongbao than the previous ones. This practice, which violated the laws of economics, was often at odds with the political situation and sometimes drove good currencies out of circulation. In the late Ming dynasty, the market was flooded with all kinds of private and official bad coins, so much so that the people could make up songs to circulate and sing about the situation. Given the distrust of the people in the national financial system and the inaccuracy and instability of the measurement of silver and coins, the leading media of economic exchange, how could the late Ming gather enough momentum for capitalism to emerge?

The issue of the amount of silver imported into China from abroad in the Ming dynasty, as mentioned earlier, has attracted the interest of experts in the economic history of East Asia worldwide. In fact, how silver was imported from abroad has also attracted the attention of experts in East Asian economic history. As a precious metal, silver had been an instrument of preserving value and a means of payment since ancient times. Still, silver coins were not minted and issued as a unified national currency in ancient China. Before the mid-Ming period, silver did not have a full monetary function recognized by the state. But why did silver rise to prominence at this point, in this reign, and this dynasty alone? Even Peng Xinwei, the author of *A Monetary History of China* (Zhongguo Huobi Shi 中国货币史), cannot offer a definitive explanation for this phenomenon, and he does not believe that there was a leap in production at the beginning of the Ming dynasty that necessitated more money. Instead, he emphasizes the Ming government's reluctance to relax the silver ban.[91] On the mechanism of the importation of silver from abroad, four main theories have emerged, each with a different meaning. The mainstream view of Chinese scholars can be referred to as "the productivity recovery theory" or "the commercial revolution theory," and is represented by Tang Wenji 唐文基. It argues that the importation of silver resulted from the rise of merchant power, the development of overseas trade, the growth of domestic long-distance trade, and the deepening of urbanization and commercialization—and that it had a positive impact.[92] Another school, "the taxation system theory," argues that the growth of silver was brought about by changes in the national taxation system between the sixteenth and eighteenth centuries. This theory is represented by Liang Fangzhong 梁方仲, Chen Chunsheng 陈春声, and Liu Zhiwei 刘志伟. The last two focused more on Qing Dynasty studies.[93] Liang Fangzhong famously concludes that "under the Single Whip Law, a Ming rule of taxation reform that combined all miscellaneous duties into one, collected in silver coins instead of real goods, silver was mainly circulated in the realm of the taxation economy."[94] The third school is "the theory of the joint role of the national taxation system and the private market" proposed by Wan Ming 万明 and others, who suggest that silver originated in the private market, which was reinforced by the shortcomings of copper coins and banknotes. Compounded by the state taxation system, silver was extensively circulated.[95] The last is Liu Guanglin's 刘光临 theory of "the need for a stable currency." Liu rejects "the theory of silver indicating progress," arguing that "silver's replacement of copper coins" in the Ming dynasty was not a sign of financial progress but a choice forced on the market by the proliferation of bad money and privately-cast money.[96] In our view, Liu's "theory of the need for a stable currency" is the most realistic explanation for the rise of silver in the sixteenth century.

After the failure of paper money in the Ming dynasty, the coinage laws were also in disarray. Although the state minted fine coins occasionally, the minting policy was by no means farsighted, but rather tended to interfere with economic laws. Under these circumstances, the masses turned to believe in silver as a stable currency, as it was the only option left. It must be stressed, however, that silver's effectiveness as a stable currency was also limited. The state never minted coins in this precious metal, which was a genuine currency of public trust, and it was never possible to obtain an accurate measure of the weight and fineness of silver. In silver-based transactions, there were likewise problems of credit, forgery, exchange, and scope of circulation, all of which significantly increased transaction costs and constrained the development of the national market in the Ming dynasty. Travels with silver, troubled by the bulky and inconvenient silver and the high possibility of suffering loss by theft, had not been improved by the bill of exchange in three hundred years. Therefore, the dominance of silver should not be interpreted as a symptom of a mature commodity economy.

Notes

1 [Ming] Zhaozhe Xie, "Part I, Things," in *Five Miscellaneous Morsels*, vol. 9 (Shanghai: Shanghai Bookstore Publishing House, 2001), 168. [明]谢肇淛：《五杂俎》卷九《物部一》，上海：上海书店出版社，2001年，第168页。
2 Hsiao-hsiao-sheng, *The Plum in the Golden Vase or, Chin P'ing Mei, vol. 2, The Rivals*, trans. David Tod Roy (Princeton, NJ and Oxford: Princeton University Press, 2001), 276.
3 [Ming] Long Tu, *Playthings Collection of a Hermit [Colorful Graphic Edition of the History of Ancient Material Civilization in China]*, ed. Jing Zhao, vol. 3 (Beijing: Gold Wall Press, 2012), 193–94. [明]屠隆著，赵菁编：《考槃馀事（中国古代物质文明史彩色图文版）》卷三，北京：金城出版社，2012年，第193–94页。
4 [Ming] Jiazhou Zhou, "Book of Incense," in *Complete Library of the Four Treasures, Photocopied Wenyuan Pavillion Edition, vol. 25, Subministry. Genealogy. Genus of Utensils* (Taipei: Taiwan Commercial Press, 1986). [明]周嘉胄：《香乘》，《影印文渊阁四库全书》卷二十五《子部·谱录类·器物之属》，台北：台湾商务印书馆，1986年。第844册。
5 [Ming] Qi Chen and [Ming] Cheng Lao, "The Prefecture Records of Chenghua Huzhou, vol. 8," in *Series of Rare Local Chronicles of China in Japanese Collection* (Beijing: National Library of China Publishing House, 1991). [明]陈顼，[明]劳铖：《成化湖州府志》卷八，《日本藏中国罕见地方志丛刊》，北京：书目文献出版社，1991年。
6 [Qing] Liuqi Ji, *Northern Strategy in the Ming Dynasty*, vol. 15 (Beijing: Zhonghua Book Company, 1981), 265–66. [清]计六奇：《明季北略》卷十五，北京：中华书局，1981年，第265–66页。
7 Shanghai Municipal Cultural Relics Preservation Committee, ed., *Collection of Materials of Shanghai Local Records and Properties* (Beijing: Zhonghua Book Company, 1961), 123. 上海市文物保管委员会编辑：《上海地方志物产资料汇辑》，北京：中华书局，1961年，第123页。
8 Xi Wang, "Preliminary Study of the Fashion of Songjiang Prefecture in the Ming Dynasty," *Local Records of China*, no. 2 (2007): 45–53. 王熹：《明代松江府服饰风尚初探》，《中国地方志》，2007年第2期，第45–53页。
9 [Qing] Tongshu Liang, "History of Pens," in *Posthumous Collections of Pinluo An*, vol. 16 (Beijing: Beijing University Library), 226. [清]梁同书：《频罗庵遗集》卷十六《笔史》，北京：北京大学图书馆，第226页。

10 [Song] Yijian Su, "History of Pens," in *Instruction to the Scholar's Four Jewels, vol. 1, Life and Museum Series Collection of Treasures* (Shanghai: Shanghai Classics Publishing House, 1993), 247. [宋]苏易简：《文房四谱》卷一《笔史》，《生活与博物丛书·器物珍玩编》，上海：上海古籍出版社，1993年，第247页。
11 [Qing] Yizun Zhu, "Fang Yulu," in *Jingzhiju Poetry*, ed. Zu'en Yao, vol. 18 (Beijing: People's Literature Publishing House, 1990), 542. [清]朱彝尊著，姚祖恩编：《静志居诗话》卷十八《方于鲁》，北京：人民文学出版社，1990年，第542页。
12 Chengyao Xu, "A Study of Xi Custom and Etiquette," in *Ramblings on Things in Shezhou*, vol. 18 (Hefei: Huangshan Publishing House, 2001), 605. 许承尧：《歙事闲谭》卷十八《歙风俗礼教考》，合肥：黄山书社，2001年，第605页。
13 [Ming] Zhaozhe Xie, "Part IV, Things," in *Five Miscellaneous Morsels*, vol. 12 (Shanghai: Shanghai Bookstore Publishing House, 2001), 241. [明]谢肇淛：《五杂俎》卷十二《物部四》，第241页。
14 [Ming] Zhenheng Wen, *Treatise on Superfluous Things*, proofread and annotated by Zhi Chen (Nanjing: Phoenix Science Press, 1984), 272. [明]文震亨著，陈植校注：《长物志校注》，南京：江苏科学技术出版社，1984年，第272页。
15 [Ming] Menglong Feng, *Three Collections of Short Stories: Instruction Words to Enlighten the World, Ordinary Words to Warn the World, and Lasting Words to Awaken the World*, vol. 1 (Jinan: Qilu Press, 1993), 6–7. [明]冯梦龙：《三言：喻世明言、警世通言、醒世恒言》卷一，济南：齐鲁书社，1993年，第6–7页。
16 [Qing] Mengzhu Ye, "Agriculture and Commerce VI," in *World Browsing Series*, vol. 7 (Beijing: Zhonghua Book Company, 2007), 184. [清]叶梦珠：《阅世编》卷七《食货六》，第184页。
17 Baofeng Zhang, *Draft History of Chinese Silk* (Shanghai: Xuelin Publishing House, 1989), 170–71. 张保丰：《中国丝绸史稿》，上海：学林出版社，1989年，第170–71页。
18 Ye, "Agriculture and Commerce VI," 184. [清]叶梦珠：《阅世编》卷七《食货六》，第184页。
19 [Ming] Defu Shen, "Stay in the Government, the Dragon Boat Festival," in *A Compilation of Histories in the Wanli Reign*, vol. 2 (Beijing: Zhonghua Book Company, 1997), 67. [明]沈德符：《万历野获编》卷二，章奏留中，端阳，北京：中华书局，1997年，第67页。
20 [Qing] Lian Ying, *Textual Research on Past Events Under the Imperial Edict*, vol. 4 (Beijing: Beijing Classics Publishing House, 1985), 2356. [清]英廉：《钦定日下旧闻考》（第四册），北京：北京古籍出版社，1985年，第2356页。
21 Jen-shu Wu, *Taste of Luxury: Consumer Society and the Scholar-Literati Circle in the Late Ming Dynasty* (Beijing: Zhonghua Book Company, 2008), 35–38. 巫仁恕：《品味奢华：晚明的消费社会与士大夫》，北京：中华书局，2008年，第35–38页。
22 Shuguo Wu, "The Monetisation of Silver in the Ming Dynasty," in *The Currency of the People: The Flow of Money Through the Ages* (Changchun: Changchun Publishing House, 2005), 201–2. 吴树国：《明代白银的货币化》，《民之通货：历代货币流变》，长春：长春出版社，2005年，第201–02页。
23 Xinwei Peng, *A Monetary History of China* (Shanghai: Shanghai People's Publishing House, 1958), 452–53. 彭信威：《中国货币史》，上海：上海人民出版社，1958年，第452–53页。
24 Longsheng Li, "Estimates of Silver Stocks at the End of the Ming Dynasty," *China Numismatics*, no. 1 (2005). See also Yongzhi Qiu, "Silverization of Currency in the Ming Dynasty and the Formation of the Parallel Pattern of Silver and Coins" (PhD diss., Department of History of Tsinghua University, 2016), chart 1.1, chapter 1, "Various Estimates of the Inflow of Overseas Silver in the Ming Dynasty," 21. 李隆生：《明末白银存量的估计》，《中国钱币》，2005年第1期。又可参见邱永志：《明代货币白银化与钱并行格局的形成》第一章图表1.1，"各家关于明代海外白银流入数量估算表"，清华大学历史系博士论文，2016年，第21页。
25 Gunder Frank, *ReOrient: Global Economy in the Asian Age* (Berkeley and Los Angeles, California: University of California Press, 1998).

26 Zongxi Huang, "Finance and Accounting," in *Introduction to Waiting for the Dawn: A Plan for the Prince*, ed. Xueyuan Ji and Xingyuan Gui (Beijing: China International Radio Press, 2011), 161. 黄宗羲：《财计二》，见季学源、桂兴沅编：《明夷待访录》，北京：中国国际广播出版社，2011年，第161页。
27 Yanwu Gu, *Collected Explanations of Daily Record II* (New York: Columbia University Press, 2017), 684. [清]顾炎武：《日知录集释（中）》，第684页。
28 Liancheng He, "Money Management Ideas," in *History of Chinese Economic Management Thought* (Xi'an: Northwest University Press, 1988), 410–11. 何炼成：《货币管理思想》，《中国经济管理思想史》，西安：西北大学出版社，1988年，第410–11页。
29 Jiguang Gu, "Shanxi and Shanxi Exchange Shop in the Ming and Qing Dynastie," in *A Collection of Essays on the Economic History of Ancient China* (Nanchang: Jiangxi People's Publishing House, 1980), 306–7. 谷霁光：《明清时代之山西与山西票号》，《中国古代经济史论文集》，南昌：江西人民出版社，1980年，第306–07页。
30 Shichang Ye, "The Use of Hui Piao, Yin Piao and Qian Piao," in *Ancient and Modern Chinese Financial History* (Shanghai: Fudan University Press, 2001), 119. 叶世昌：《会票、银票和钱票的使用》，《中国古近代金融史》，上海：复旦大学出版社，2001年，第119页。
31 Shichang Ye, "Hui Piao and the Circulation of Banknotes Among the People," in *A General History of Chinese Finance: Pre-Qin to Qing Opium War Period*, vol. 1 (Beijing: China Financial Publishing House, 2002), 599. 叶世昌：《会票和民间的纸币流通》，《中国金融通史：先秦至清鸦片战争时期（第一卷）》，北京：中国金融出版社，2002年，第599页。
32 Shichang Ye, Baojin Li, and Xiangcai Zhong, "Monetary Theory in the Chongzhen Reign," in *History of Chinese Monetary Theory* (Xiamen: Xiamen University Press, 2003), 174. 叶世昌、李宝金、钟祥财：《崇祯年间的货币理论》，《中国货币理论史》，厦门：厦门大学出版社，2003年，第174页。
33 Qiang Sun, *A Study of the Raising, Management and Credit Relationship of Commercial Capital During the Late Ming Period* (Changchun: Jilin University Press, 2007), 246–51. 孙强：《晚明商业资本的筹集方式、经营机制及信用关系研究》，长春：吉林大学出版社，2007年，第246–51页。
34 [Ming] Shiyi Lu, "On Coinage," in *Imperial Classic Selection of the Qing*, vol. 52, Household Policies 27, Coins (I), ed. [Qing] Changling He (Beijing: Zhonghua Book Company, 1980), 4. 陆世仪：《论钱币》，见[清]贺长龄辑：《皇朝经世文编》卷五二《户政二十七·钱币上》，北京：中华书局，1980年，第4页。
35 [Ming] Zilong Chen, "Banknote Theory," in *On Coins*, ed. Liu Wang (Shanghai: Shanghai Classics Publishing House, 2002), 615. Qing Xiao also noticed Chen Zilong's thought when studying ancient Chinese currency thought. Qing Xiao, *History of Ancient Chinese Monetary Thoughts* (Beijing: People's Publishing House, 1987), 276. [明]陈子龙：《钞币论》，见王鎏编著：《钱币刍言》，上海：上海古籍出版社，2002年，第615页。陈子龙的思想，萧清在研究中国古代货币思想时也已注意到。萧清：《中国古代货币思想史》，北京：人民出版社，1987年，第276页。
36 Shouyi Wang, "The Relationship Between the Ming Hui Piao (Bill of Exchange) System and Shanxi Exchange Shop," in *Studies in Local History of Shanxi [Second series]*, ed. the Ancient Chinese History Teaching and Research Group of Shanxi University (Taiyuan: Shanxi People's Publishing House, 1962), 103. 王守义：《明代会（汇）票制度和山西票号的关系》，见山西大学中国古代史教研组编著：《山西地方史研究（第二辑）》，太原：山西人民出版社，1962年，第103页。
37 H. M. Robertson and M. Weber, *Aspects of the Rise of Economic Individualism: A Criticism of Max Weber and His School* (Cambridge: Cambridge University Press, 1933), 40.
38 Larry Neal, *A Concise History of International Finance: From Babylon to Bernanke* (Cambridge: Cambridge University Press, 2015), 28–50.
39 James Murray, *Bruges, Cradle of Capitalism, 1280–1390* (Cambridge: Cambridge University Press, 2005), 144–46.

40 James Thompson, *Economic and Social History of Europe in the Late Middle Ages*, trans. Jialing Xu (Beijing: The Commercial Press, 1992), 567. 詹姆斯·汤普森：《中世纪晚期欧洲经济社会史》，徐家玲译，北京：商务印书馆，1992年，第567页。
41 [Ming] Shenxing Yu, "Lessons for Grand Councilors," in *Yuan and Ming Historical Notes Series: Gushan Notes*, vol. 4 (Beijing: Zhonghua Book Company, 1984), 39. [明]于慎行：《元明史料笔记丛刊：谷山笔麈》卷四《相鉴》，北京：中华书局，1984年，第39页。
42 [Ming] Lian Fan, "Records of Auspicious and Evil Events," in *Yunjian Authentic Records*, vol. 3 (Fengxian: Version Reprinted by Chu in Fengxian in the Seventeenth Year of the Republic of China, 1928), 12. 范濂：《云间据目抄》卷三《记祥异》，民国十七年奉贤褚氏重刊，卷三第12页。
43 Yu, "Lessons for Grand Councilors," 39. 于慎行：《谷山笔麈》卷四《相鉴》，第39页。
44 Ibid.
45 Ibid.
46 Liaoning Provincial Local Chronicles Compilation Committee, ed., "Stele for Restoration of Guangyou Temple Pagoda," in *Liaoning Provincial Records—Religious Records* (Shenyang: Liaoning People's Publishing House, 2002), 353. 辽宁省地方志编纂委员会：《重修广佑寺宝塔题名记》，《辽宁省志·宗教志》，沈阳：辽宁人民出版社，2002年，第353页。
47 Anecdotal histories and notes of the Ming dynasty are famous for their political prejudice. Any comment on political figures should be used in conjunction with other historical materials. 明人野史笔记以富政治偏见著称。凡涉及评述政治性人物的，都应与其他史料互参使用。
48 [Qing] Kang Wen, *Legend of Heroes and Heroines*, proofread and annotated by Run Ze (Nanjing: Phoenix Publishing House, 2008), 34. [清]文康著，泽润校注：《儿女英雄传》，南京：凤凰出版社，2008年，第34页。
49 Ibid., 103. 同上，第103页。
50 [Qing] E. Liu, *The Travels of Lao Can*, trans. Xianyi Yang and Gladys Yang (Beijing: Foreign Languages Press, 2005), 25.
51 Ibid., 162. 同上，第162页。
52 [Qing] Xueqin Cao and [Qing] E Gao, *A Dream of Red Mansions (Hong Lou Meng)* (Beijing: People's Literature Publishing House, 1996), 146. [清]曹雪芹，[清]高鹗：《红楼梦》，北京：人民文学出版社，1996年，第146页。
53 Ibid., 1074.
54 Yanzhi Tu, "Textual Research on the Gold Leaf of the Southern Song Dynasty—And the Monetary Nature of Gold in the Southern Song Dynasty," *General Review of Coins*, no. 1 (2002): 16–22. 屠燕治：《南宋金叶子考述——兼论南宋黄金的货币性》，《钱币博览》，2002年第1期，第16–22页。
55 Guanghui Sun, "Finance in Yuan and Ming," in *A Brief History of Chinese Finance* (Lanzhou: Gansu Science and Technology Press, 2010), 56. 孙光慧：《元明的金融》，《中国金融简史》，兰州：甘肃科学技术出版社，2010年，第56页。
56 Wenchao Dong, *A General Overview of Contemporary Gold and Silver Management in China* (Beijing: China Financial Publishing House, 1994), 230. 董文超：《中国当代金银管理通览》，北京：中国金融出版社，1994年，第230页。
57 Yuxun Wang, "Textual Research on the Changes in Money Law During the Ming Dynasty," *Journal of Chinese Humanities*, no. 1 (1996): 78–82. 王裕巽：《明代钱法变迁考》，《文史哲》，1996年第1期，第78–82页。
58 Institute of History and Philology, Academia Sinica, ed., "The First Month of the 13th Year of Chenghua Reign," in *Veritable Records of Emperor Xianzong*, vol. 161 (Taipei: Institute of History and Language, Academia Sinica, 1963), 2951. 中国台湾"中央研究院"历史语言研究所校印：《明宪宗实录》卷一六一，"成化十三年正月壬戌"，台北：中国台湾"中央研究院"历史语言研究所，1963年，第2951页。

59 [Ming] Rong Lu, *Miscellaneous Notes at Shuyuan [1–2]* (Shanghai: The Commercial Press, 1936), 111. [明]陆容：《菽园杂记（1–2）》，上海：商务印书馆，1936年，第111页。
60 [Qing] Tingyu Zhang, "Records of Agriculture and Commerce V," in *The History of the Ming Dynasty*, vol. 81 (Beijing: Zhonghua Book Company, 1968). 张廷玉编著：《明史》卷八一《食货五》，第1965页。
61 Houpei Hou, *History of Chinese Currency* (Shanghai: Shanghai Book Company, 1930), 100. 侯厚培：《中国货币沿革史》，上海：上海书局，1930年，第100页。
62 Ibid.
63 [Qing] Tingyu Zhang, "Records of Agriculture and Commerce V," in *The History of the Ming Dynasty*, vol. 81 (Beijing: Zhonghua Book Company, 1965). [清]张廷玉编纂，《明史》卷八十一《食货五》，第1965页。
64 Yingxing Song, *The Exploitation of the Works of Nature*, proofread and annotated by Qiaoling Guan (Changsha: Yuelu Press, 2002), 207. [明]宋应星著，管巧灵校注：《天工开物》，长沙：岳麓书社，2002年，第207页。
65 Dong Zhang, "A Brief Description of the Jiajing Coinage," *Guoxue Wang*, February 21, 2010, http://www.guoxue.com/?p=465. 张东："嘉靖铸钱述略"，2010年2月21日，国学网，www.guoxue.com/?p=465
66 [Qing] Yuan Wang, "Coins, in Collection of Xue An—Ming, Records of Agriculture and Commerce," in *Records of Ancient Money Notes*, ed. Zhongge Zhao (Beijing: Taihai Publishing House, 1998), 292. [清]王原：《学庵类稿·明·食货志·钱钞》，见赵忠格编著：《古钱钞文存》，北京：台海出版社，第292页。
67 Shuguo Wu, "Miscellaneous Use of Standard Coins and Old Coins," in *The Currency of the People: The Flow of Money Through the Ages* (Changchun: Changchun Publishing House, 2005), 196. 吴树国：《制钱与旧钱的杂用》，《民之通货：历代货币流变》，长春：长春出版社，2005年，第196页。
68 Youmin Wang, "A Preliminary Study of Jinbei, Huoqi, and Xuanbian Coins of the Wanli Reign," *West China Finance*, no. 12 (2000): 63–65. 汪有民：《万历金背、火漆、镟边钱初探》，《西部金融》，2000年第12期，第63–65页。
69 Peng, *A Monetary History of China*, 433–46. 内容来自彭信威：《中国货币史》，第433–46页。
70 [Ming] Jie Xu, "Request for Ceasing the Coin Casting of the Baoyuan Bureau, vol. 244," in *Classic Selections of Ming*, ed. [Ming] Zilong Chen (Beijing: Zhonghua Book Company, 1962), 2551. [明]徐阶：《请停止宝源局铸钱疏》卷二四四，见[明]陈子龙编著：《皇明经世文编》，北京：中华书局，1962年，第2551页。
71 Zhang, "A Brief Description of the Jiajing Coinage."
72 Hsiao-hsiao-sheng, *The Plum in the Golden Vase or, Chin P'ing Mei*, vol. 2, *The Rivals*, 327–30.
73 Ying Wang, "Four Questions on the Period When Jin Ping Mei Was Written," in *Linqing And Jin Ping Mei*, ed. Linqing Jin Ping Mei Society (Linqing: Shandong Liaocheng Publishing House, 1992), 97. 王莹：《<金瓶梅>本事时代考四题》，见临清金瓶梅学会编著：《临清与金瓶梅》，临清：山东聊城出版社，1992年，第97页。
74 Song, *The Exploitation of the Works of Nature*, 207. [明]宋应星：《天工开物》，第207页。
75 Bincun Zhang, "Reasons for the Collapse of Paper Money in the Ming Dynasty," *Journal of Chinese Social and Economic History*, no. 3 (2015): 28–40. 张彬村：《明朝纸币崩溃的原因》，《中国社会经济史研究》，2015年第3期，第28–40页。
76 Jianye Han, Hao Wang, and Yaoting Zhu, "Ming and Qing Coins," in *Ancient Chinese Coins* (Beijing: Peking University Press, 2007), 207. 韩建业，王浩，朱耀廷：《明清钱币》，《中国古代钱币》，北京：北京大学出版社，2007年，第207页。
77 Ibid., 211. 同上，第211页。
78 Zhang, "Records of Agriculture and Commerce V."
79 Zhilu Sun, *Ershen Yelu*, vol. 7, a publication of Forty Sixth Year of Qianlong in the Qing Dynasty. 孙之騄：《二申野录》卷七，清乾隆四十六年刊本。

80 Jingcheng Liu and Zude Li, "Circulation of Copper Coins in the Mid to Late Ming Dynasty," in *The History of Money* (Beijing: Social Sciences Academic Press, 2012), 148–49. 刘精诚，李祖德：《明中后期铜钱的流通》，《货币史话》，北京：社会科学文献出版社，2012年，第148–49页。
81 Peng, *A Monetary History of China*, 490. 彭信威：《中国货币史》，第490页。
82 Jiannong Li, *Manuscripts of Ancient Chinese Economic History: Song, Yuan and Ming Sections* (Wuhan: Wuhan University Press, 2011), 854. 李剑农：《中国古代经济史稿：宋元明部分》，武汉：武汉大学出版社，2011年，第854页。
83 Ray Huang, *Taxation and Governmental Finance in Sixteenth-Century Ming China* (Beijing: SDX Joint Publishing Company, 2001), 90. 黄仁宇：《十六世纪明代中国之财政与税收》，北京：三联书店，2001年，第90页。
84 Shuinan Nie, "Textual Research on the 'Tianqi Tongbao' Decuple Coin," in *Coin Research and Collection* (Beijing: China Economic Press, 2013), 31–33. 聂水南：《明"天启通宝"折十大钱考述》，《钱币研究与收藏》，北京：中国经济出版社，2013年，第31–33页。
85 [Ming] Pu Zhang, "On the Tombstone of the Five," in *Selected Ancient Chinese Texts Through the Ages*, ed. Guangcai Sun and Yan Sun (Nanjing: Southeast University Press, 2017), 224. [明]张溥：《五人墓碑记》，见孙广才、孙燕编著：《中国历代古文选读》，南京：东南大学出版社，2017年，第224页。
86 Sun, *Ershen Yelu*, vol. 7, 16. 孙之騄：《二申野录》卷七，第16页。
87 Sun, "Finance in Yuan and Ming," 57. 孙光慧：《元明的金融》，第57页。
88 Sen Meng, "The Scourge of the Eunuchs of Tianqi Reign," in *Meng Sen's Lecture Notes on Ming History* (Changchun: Jilin People's Publishing House, 2013), 286. 孟森：《天启朝之阉祸》，《孟森明史讲义》，长春：吉林人民出版社，2013年，第286页。
89 [Ming] Zhenyang Hou, "Impeachment of Qie," in *Classic Selections of Ming*, ed. [Ming] Zilong Chen, vol. 49 (Beijing: Zhonghua Book Company, 1962), 5508. [明]侯震旸：《劾客氏疏》，见[明]陈子龙编著：《皇明经世文编》卷四十九《侯杨二公集》，第5508页。
90 [Ming] Ruoyu Liu, "A Brief History of the Plight of the Imperial Consorts of the Two Dynasties," in *A Weighted and Unbiased Record*, vol. 8 (Beijing: Beijing Classics Publishing House, 1994), 44. [明]刘若愚：《酌中志》卷八《两朝椒难纪略》，北京：北京古籍出版社，1994年，第44页。
91 Peng, *A Monetary History of China*, 452–53. 彭信威：《中国货币史》，第452–53页。
92 Wenji Tang, *The Commercial Revolution in China in 16th-18th Century* (Beijing: Social Sciences Academic Press, 2008). 唐文基：《16–18世纪中国商业革命》，北京：社会科学文献出版社，2008年。
93 Chunsheng Chen and Zhiwei Liu, "Taxation, Market and Material Life: The Inflow of American Silver and the Socia Transformation in the Eighteenth Century China," *Journal of Tsinghua University (Philosophy and Social Sciences)* 25, no. 5 (2010): 65–81, 158–59. 陈春声，刘志伟：《贡赋、市场与物质生活—试论十八世纪美洲白银输入与中国社会变迁之关系》，《清华大学学报（哲学社会科学版）》，2010年第25卷第5期，第65–81页、第158–59页。
94 Fangzhong Liang, *The Taxation System in the Ming Dynasty* (Beijing: Zhonghua Book Company, 2008), 4. 梁方仲：《明代赋役制度》，北京中华书局，2008年，第4页。
95 Ming Wan, "A Preliminary Research on Silver Monetization in the Ming Dynasty," *Research In Chinese Economic History*, no. 2 (2003): 39–51. 万明：《明代白银货币化的初步考察》，《中国经济史研究》，2003年第2期，第39–51页。
96 Guanglin Liu, "Counterfeiting and the Circulation of Money in the Ming Dynasty," *Journal of Hebei University (Philosophy and Social Science)* 36, no. 2 (2011): 24–32. 刘光临：《银进钱出与明代货币流通体制》，《河北大学学报(哲学社会科学版)》，2011年第36卷第2期，第24–32页。

3 Food Cultures of the Ming

1. The Masses Regard Food as Their Heaven

1) *The Notion of Food Culture and its Extendibility*

Fernand Braudel proposes a rather interesting, if not groundbreaking, hypothesis in the first volume of his *Civilization and Capitalism, 15th-18th Century* trilogy. He says, "The early settlement and then the spectacular increase in population in the Far East were only possible because of the small amount of meat eaten." Therefore, one way or another, an agricultural civilization on a given surface can feed ten to 20 as many people as its stock-rising counterpart because of the preponderance of the calories it provides.[1] The accuracy of Braudel's hypothesis aside, his emphasis on how food production is closely associated with the rise of cultures and civilizations cannot be exaggerated. According to Braudel, only economic, geo-historical, and social changes over long periods matter. Since food production constitutes one of the most vital activities of the material life of human beings, it is inseparable from economic changes through all times and with all forms of civilizations; modes of food production, thus, occupy great importance in Braudel's purview.

The new trend in cultural history studies, however, tends to downplay the bond between the studied objects—be they food, clothing, housing, or other consumptive articles—and their economic significances. Even when the bond is indeed being addressed, historians tend to shift from a concern with production to one of consumption, "which makes it increasingly difficult to separate economic from social and cultural history."[2]

Owing to the comprehensiveness of *XSYYZ*, the varieties of the Ming social norms, from that of the paramount Eunuch Wang Zhen to that of the famine-struck peasants who sell their children, are presented from both a macroscopic and microscopic view. Evidenced by historical materials, its rich depictions of the Ming people's livelihoods can be sampled to study the Ming food culture and its derivatives: crop species, farming technologies, culinary skills, the criteria to select cooks, general attitudes towards food-wasting, natural disasters, cannibalism, and relief actions taken by the government and public. The embracing of the latter categories as peripheries to food culture is not as far-fetched as it seems to be due to the extendibility of the definition of "food culture."

DOI: 10.4324/9781003406143-4

In a Chinese context, the idiom "the masses regard food as their heaven" contains multi-layered implications. First, since dining occupies such an important role in people's daily lives, all families, including commoners on meager incomes, would strive to sate the needs of their mouths and stomachs by preparing the best food they can afford.[3] Second, the issue of food supply occupies an unparalleled significance. Third, when the food supply falls short for the general populace, it is nothing less than the collapse of Heaven because calamities, in the forms of famine, flood, drought, poor harvest, and cannibalism, would soon make their presence known. Fourth, a severe famine was usually followed by governmental relief actions, but these were often ineffective; public and private charities would weigh in, but not all worked successfully. Fifth, when all measures failed to sustain the famine-devastated populace, the desperate masses would likely become mobs and rebels, precipitating the collapse of the existent dynasty—analogical of the fall of Heaven.

This chain of causality shows a cohesive logic centered on the unparalleled significance of food, which sends us back to the initial statement: "the masses regard food as their Heaven." The expansive nature of Chinese food culture in the imperial socio-historical context thus raises a need to study the process of food consumption and the production and supply, or lack thereof. The latter case highlights the need to research famine relief efforts. Therefore, this study of food will not only shed light on facets of Ming economic and material culture, but also touch upon the boundaries of natural disaster, famine relief, communal charity, and so on.

2) Typical Northern Chinese Food

Food culture is one of the most ingrained behaviors among human beings' cultural and productive activities. Particularly during ancient times when transportation was cumbersome, the food culture of a given region would have to be molded by the availability of its grain cultivation and breed stock. As the geographical latitudes traversed by the protagonists of the Novel are generally confined to northern and eastern China, and, most frequently, within the counties of Wucheng and Xiujiang,[4] of Shandong province, the food culture depicted can be seen as typically northern Chinese.

From antiquity, the north China Plain has been a land that produces wheat, sorghum, millet, and foxtail millet. Crops like corn, sweet potatoes, and potatoes are commonly regarded as being introduced into China after the discovery of the Americas, at a time overlapping the transition from the late Ming to early Qing— roughly the third quarter of the sixteenth century. Their influence on the subsistence of the Ming people's dining tables was limited. However, with steady production growth, they eventually became essential additions to the Chinese diet in the early to middle Qing.[5]

Grains and other staple foods make up 70 percent or more calories in the daily Chinese meal.[6] Divided by the Yangzi River, the northerners' staple foods are wheat, and the southerners', rice. This division also constitutes one of the most important regional differences between the North and South. Northern Chinese cuisine is that of Peking and the provinces of Shandong, Hebei, Shanxi, Shan'xi, and Henan.[7] In terms of staple foods, *momo* 馍馍, the steamed bread (also known as *mantou* 馒头 or *bobo* 饽饽), occupies their daily dining table, but *bianshi* 扁食 dumpling (modern name *jiaozi* 饺子, known to the Manchus as *zhubobo* 煮饽饽) are the most inseparable for the Spring Festival. The process of making *bianshi*, like that of making *jiaozi* today, has been vividly described in a lyric of Yuan Drama:

> White wrapper and soft stomach, the touch of them pleases your hands. At first, the wrappers are empty, and then you add some onions. In boiled water, they swim like mandarin ducks, pair by pair. Their reunion is temporary though, for the boiling only takes a while. Oh! You *bianshi*! When uncooked, I tweak you; when done, I chew you, your delicious flavor only known to my stomach.[8]

Bianshi is a must-have at the tables of Shandong households during New Year's Eve. Even a family in a stringent situation would manage to borrow money to buy white flour and meat and ensure the symbolic *bianshi* shows up at its dinner table. Its absence bespeaks the utter failure of the family's finances and the householder's negligence regarding the welfare of the folks living under the same roof. If he were negligent in this responsibility, maids, servants, and young housewives would have complained and grumbled for the rest of the year until they were fed *bianshi* on the next New Year's Eve.

The first marital strife depicted in *XSYYZ* is caused by the lack of *bianshi*. After taking Zhenge as his concubine, Chao Yuan treats his wife apathetically. While the alienated Née Ji lives in the backcourt of the residence with several of her maids, Chao Yuan and Zhenge, along with their servants of the forecourt, enjoy holiday food like gourmets. Since Née Ji would not deign to ask Chao Yuan for sustenance, and he would not send her any, the holiday atmosphere of her residence quarter is bleak. Seeing that Chao Yuan's quarter is stuffed with leftovers, her maids sigh and grumble, tears sliding down their long, sullen faces.

> This is what we get from devoting our lives to serving her. Even beggars get a steamed bun and a coin at the end of the year, but with this limp thing as our mistress, we have even less hope of a happy life than an eighty-year-old woman going to be a bride would!
>
> (3.19)

Née Ji, the youngest daughter of her father, is married out generously; worrying that the motherless girl is not sufficiently looked after, her father, Old Ji, endows her with 100 *mu* of land, though his financial situation is in poor straits. However, by then, the Chaos are in even worse shape. Old Chao, a senior licentiate Tribute Student 贡生, needs money to travel to the capital to take the metropolitan examination. The trip is made possible by selling 20 *mu* of his daughter-in-law's dowry land for two *taels* each *mu* and being subsidized by Old Ji, who, though no longer well-off, still manages to sell his mother's pearl cap to scrape together 38 *taels* in cash. After the Chaos become rich, Chao Yuan soon stops financially supporting Née Ji, who is thus forced to scratch out her living from the proceeds of her 80 *mu* dowry land (9.67).

A glimpse into the crop yields and the production methods of the land produces many insights into the farming circumstances in north China during the Ming.[9] Finally, a verdict is issued by the local magistrate that the Chaos must return the dowry land to the Jis, who have filed a lawsuit against the former after Née Ji's tragic suicide.

In revenge against the Jis, Chao Yuan intentionally delays the handover by claiming that:

> The Magistrate told me to cede the land, but not what is growing on it. Right now, there are black and yellow beans waiting to be harvested on that land. I'll hand it over in October, which is early enough.
>
> (11.81)

The Chao-Ji lawsuit ends on July 9, when the harvest of millet and wheat should have been done. The replanting of black and yellow beans after the autumn harvest evidences the popularity of crop rotation in the late Ming. When referring to the planting of green beans, the author uses the word *dai* 带, literarily "to bring," to indicate that the green beans are merely a byproduct of the cotton planted.

Besides regular crop rotation, the Ming farmers also adopted a method called "cotton-bean coverage-inserting crop rotation," still considered an advanced intercrop mode today. Widely applicable to cotton plants in both South and North, it optimizes the usage of the sunshine, heat, and water in limited acres of land. In the narrative, a trivial argument occurs between Old Di and his servant Di Zhou regarding how to garner the green beans intercropped in Old Di's cotton field. Although Old Di orders Di Zhou to gather only the matured beans, the latter does not follow the instructions and cuts the raw and grown plants altogether (29.223). The matter, though insignificant, exasperates Old Di, who by nature is a man of frugality.

The main reason for employing crop rotation and intercropping in agricultural production is to maintain soil fertility. Having discovered the law of combining the use and maintenance of land at an early stage, the ancient Chinese had a long tradition of intensive and meticulous farming. As early as the fourth century B.C., Li Kui, Minister of Wei, had already started to advocate "making full use of the advantages of each piece of land."

2. A Utopia of Yeomanry: Spring Ploughing, Summer Operation, Autumn Harvest and Winter Leisure

As we explore deeper into the background of the frugality that the rich peasant Old Di displays, we stumble onto a lengthy portrayal of the seasonal living patterns of his village folks and that of a peasant utopia. Though Chinese literature is by no means devoid of depictions of self-sufficient farmers on picturesque pastoral lands,[10] scarcely any composition has elaborated so much as to render the entirety of scenes on "spring plough, summer operation, autumn harvest and winter leisure" in a yearly chronology, and still rarer are the eulogistic sentiments embedded within. Xizhou Sheng, in the novel's 24th chapter, depicts a rural land where harvests are abundant, levies light-handed, and people unsophisticated, peaceful, and content. Although society is differentiated by hierarchy, under the unsophisticated spirit of the utopia society, both the rich and poor engage in work, with peasants toiling on their lands and landlords "laboring their minds." In a concerted effort, they work through the three "busy seasons:" spring, summer, and autumn:

> After planting cotton, corn, millet, and grains, it is already late April; they then hasten to build the grass storehouse, make strings, and get ready for reaping wheat. Women are prepared to raise silkworms. After the wheat reaping, rice must be planted in the paddy fields and beans in the dry lands. The planted crops during the Spring need to be attended to by hoeing the grass, cutting the vegetables, or garnering the garlic shoots. During the three summer months, it goes without saying that the petty men are busy and engaged, always having their hands full; even the gentlemen who do not need to labor in fields need to get up early and go to bed late, attending matters . . . . When July comes, people reap corn, millet, cotton, thrash vale, plow the autumn lands, plant wheat, reap black beans and yellow beans, reap all kinds of crops, buttress straw, and process paddy rice; day and night, they take no rest. The three seasons are periods of drudgery and toil for the peasants, though they are not pained by hardship because of the peace, tranquility, and abundance bestowed on them.
>
> (24.184)

After the three busy seasons and having kowtowed to thank the Earth God and bid goodbye to the farmland,[11] as it enters mid-October, the pleasant life of the peasantry, much as that of the immortals, commences.

> There are giant storehouses of amassed grains, giant urns of homebrew wine, big stockades of pigs, herds of sheep, and hundreds of geese and ducks—who do not need to be fed as long as you unleash them to the lake in the morning. When night comes, you just walk to the lakeside and call them, and your familiar voice will summon the wagging little creatures back home. You then count the heads of them, none missing. You drive them to their roost, close the door, wait until the female ones finish laying eggs, and then unleash them. Every household makes their own preserved ham, salted chickens, salted fish, crabs, and dried shrimps; chestnuts, walnuts, red dates, dried persimmons, dried peaches, and soft dates are plenty for each family grows them in their mountain land. Eggplants, pumpkins, gourds, Chinese watermelons, haricot beans, toona sinensis, fern vegetables, and needle mushrooms will be processed and dried to make it through the winter. You pick up the useless wood, cut them, and burn them into charcoal, which you store in one of your

empty rooms. You sleep through the night until the sun rises, get up, wash and dress, and then drink a cup of warmed wine if you are a morning drinker. The millet and green bean congee made of the creek-bailed sweet water is then presented in front of you, warm, fragrant, and yellowish, along with which you also eat some snow-white jellied bean curd. Now that you have your stomach full, you wear a thick cotton jacket, go out, sunbathe with your friends and neighbors and chitchat some "Monkey King Making Havoc in Heaven," "Li Kui the Rebel Making Havoc in Shishi's Mansion," and "The King of Tang Traveling to the Underworld" stories. You dissipate your time until noon and then go back home for lunch. Before it is dark, your sons or grandsons return home from school. You lairage your cattle and sheep, close your front and back doors, have a few drinks and go to bed early. Your son is in your arms, and your wife is at the back of your feet, one quilt covering the whole family.

(24.184–185)

The yellowish millet congee mentioned here still occupies today's breakfast tables of the soup-eating northern Chinese, rich and poor alike. The warmth and fragrance of the soup replenishes one's energy, soothes the stomach, and brings about a fresh start for the day. The fineness of the Chinese millet congee soup had so impressed an eighteenth-century Jesuit that he remarked:

with all our progress in the sciences of curiosity, vanity and uselessness, our peasants in Gascony and Bordelais Landes are as little advanced as they were three centuries ago in methods of making their millet into a less uncivilized and less unhealthy food.[12]

Of all the crops noted, we cannot locate most of the significant imports from the Americas during the Ming-Qing dynastic transition. For example, throughout the narrative, one finds no mention of sweet potatoes, Irish potatoes, peanuts, helianthus, tomatoes, kidney beans, and tobacco. Only corn, introduced to China during middle to late Ming, definitely no earlier than the mid-sixteenth century, is cited as *shushu* 蜀秫 in the Novel, yet we cannot ascertain whether *shushu* is not an alternative name for grain sorghum.[13]

Corn was introduced to China in the middle to late Ming dynasty in three ways: by land from Persia and Central Asia in the northwest to Gansu in China, and then to the Yellow River Basin; by land from India and Burma in the southwest to Yunnan, and then to Sichuan and Guizhou; and by sea from Southeast Asia in the southeast to the coastal provinces of Fujian and Guangdong, and then to the interior. Corn was promoted rapidly, with its high yield contributing to China's rapid population growth after the eighteenth century. Moreover, as its growing season intersperses with winter wheat, it can be rotated with the latter in the northern areas near the Yellow River with a long frost-free period to achieve two crops a year.[14] Yet it was only after the establishment of the Qing dynasty that corn was cultivated on a large scale.

Most scholars believe that the sweet potato, indigenous to the Americas, had already been introduced to Polynesia before Columbus discovered America. "Polynesia" means "the archipelago of many islands," referring to the Central Pacific Islands, including the Hawaiian Islands, the Samoa Islands, the Tonga Islands, and the Society Islands. However, another school believes that the spread into Polynesia must have been after Columbus; it was not until the mid-sixteenth century that it entered China via Fujian by sea and via Yunnan by land from India.[15]

Xizhou Sheng's identity has long been a focus of academic controversy over *XSYYZ*, and we suggest that, rather than rushing to identify the author, it is better first to clarify the main period in which the author lived and when the main body of the novel was written. Although *XSYYZ* was published in the early Qing dynasty, we are not inclined to say that *XSYYZ* was mainly completed in early Qing, still less that Xizhou Sheng was Pu Songling. That there is no mention—or even a hint—of the historical replacement of the Ming by the Qing can be seen as a piece of evidence. The lack of American crops constitutes another. Those crops were not grown in large quantities until the Qing dynasty. Since they are even lightly enumerated, can we deduce that the author had not witnessed the Ming-Qing transition when completing this book?

3. Catering Food for Field Laborers

The Dis have been peasant proprietors for generations. The early Ming policy espousing small-land husbandry in a yeomanry economy must have contributed to the accumulation of wealth for the family, for the Dis have no other engagement than farming until Old Di opens his small inn. The fact that Old Di can bequest, aside from his lands and estates, 4,000 *taels* of silver to his son must be explained through a favorable environment for yeomanry and the Dis' lifelong frugality and diligence. Old Di gets up early the following day after his son's wedding and, without waiting for the tea to be served by his new daughter-in-law, hastens to supervise his hired hands furrowing his lands (45.345). The "inner-chamber business," such as "ruling the roost, dispatching errands, entertaining guests, taking care of the hired hands, and masterminding family matters" (56.431), are overseen by Lady Di, whose energy, diligence, and capability ensure the thriving of the family.

The Yu Mingwu family, who lives next to Chao Yuan's mansion, is wealthy, but Mrs. Yu has to "go to the farm to watch the harvest of the millet" during the summer harvest. This is typical of small and medium-sized landowners, who did not attend to crops but supervised the work of the tenant farmers or short-term farm hands during the harvesting season. As mentioned by Hu Shih in his *Autobiography at Forty*, he went out with his concubine-grandmother (concubine of his grandfather) to "supervise the harvesting" as a child. The term refers to the situation that "the best fields with no worries about drought and flooding would have the best harvests, and then the tenant would ask the landowner to supervise harvesting and divide the grain equally."[16]

Big landlords like the Chaos, who own over thirty some *qing* (a Chinese unit of acreage, 100 *mu*=1 *qing* 顷) of land and employ supervisors to oversee farming during the regular seasons and attend harvest seasons. In the case of Chao Yuan, he leaves his primary residence right after wrapping up his father's funeral, relocates to his villa farm in Yongshan 雍山, and dedicates the entire summer to supervising wheat reaping. The Yongshan farm employs both long-term and short-term farm hands and rents out empty rooms to tenants; the insufficiency of field laborers calls for the help of the male tenants during the harvest season, while their wives are dispatched to be "helpers in the kitchen." When the shoemaker Xiaoya, along with his wife Née Tang, comes to the farm to find a place to live, the farm supervisor waives his rent but requires that: "You will work as our watchman during nights. As for your wife, we ask her to be a helper in the kitchen during the busy seasons."

> Catering food for field laborers is an imperative and formidable task; the short-term farm hands, reckoning on the seasonal market demand and the scarcity of labor supply, play whimsically on their employers. If the food is not on time, they will stop working and whine. For rice soup, they demand that only the finest hard rice be used, and the soup shall be so rich that when two bowls are invertedly put together, there must be no water left in between. They also require the rice bucket to be filled with plenty of leftovers when they are done eating. If not, even full, they will tell the food caterers that they are still hungry, forcing them to re-cook some new rice, which they do not have the stomach space to digest.
>
> (26.201)

Fu Yiling 傅衣凌, a Ming historian known for his studies on the relationship between economic composition, class composition, and class struggles, has also noticed the prior literary description. He quotes it in his historiographical paper *My Re-conception of Wage Labor after the Mid-Ming Dynasty*. Fu Yiling's explanation of *qi le hang* 齐了行 is that the short-term farm hands "established an organization of hired peasants to protect their own interests" rather than "the short-term farm hands were freer."[17] On this point, we think that Mr. Fu has over-interpreted. The earliest known example of *qi hang* (consistent actions 齐行) is in *Han Fei Zi—Outer Congeries of Sayings, the Upper Right Series* 韩非子・外储说右上:

> All such practices as giving up the use of power to restrain and punish officials who are kind and benevolent but trying to win the people with generous favors and of the ordinary people are like throwing away the emperor's carriages and the convenient horses to run on the ground.[18]

The word *qi hang* indeed has the very narrow meaning of "unified actions of a guild," but in this context, it simply means "consistent actions." Even if there is a temporary organization of short-term and long-term farm hands, it is still far from being as tightly organized as a "guild." Therefore, we should not understand it in the same way as we do in the phrases *qi hang xie ye* (the whole industry is closed 齐行歇业) and *qi hang ba shi* (the entire industry is going on strike 齐行罢市).

In the 16th year of the Wanli reign (1588), according to the proposal of Wu Shilai, Left Censor-in-chief, a new rule was promulgated:

> In the future, when the government and private households hire workers, if there is a documentary contract and a negotiated period, the workers should be regarded as hired workers; if the period is short and the wages are low, the workers should not be regarded as ordinary workers.

This makes it clear from the law that the status and is not subordinate to the employer. The employer can only "persuade" them to work for him. According to *Shen's Book on Agriculture* 沈氏农书, "Workers cannot be persuaded into employment without wine and food, which is much different from the situation in the last century." In Zhang Lüxiang's 张履祥 *Supplementary Agricultural Book* (Bu Nong Shu 补农书), it is recorded that "The 'three goods' can unite the workers, and the 'three earlies' help in persuading them to work hard." A similar description is also seen in *Pang's Family Discipline* (Pangshi Jiaxun 庞氏家训) by Pang Shangpeng:

> For the hired workers and servants, except for dismissing those who are cunning and stubborn, it is necessary to treat those who are qualified well, making sure that they are well fed when needed, caring for them lest they suffer from hunger and cold, and balancing their work and leisure.... If you want someone to work hard, you must win his heart. If there is a worker who is faithful and trustworthy, you should pay special attention to him to motivate him.[19]

The late Ming landlord-tenant relationship is characterized by a "commercial and contractual" flexibility,[20] or, as some Chinese historians put it, a "slackening of feudal relations." The whimsical, demanding attitudes of the hired hands indicate that some tenant peasants were enjoying the benefit of a wage-laborer system under the supervision of managerial landlords and becoming accustomed to a price mechanism.[21]

Née Tang makes good friends with the Chaos' maidservants, who reciprocate her with "a huge number of pancakes, *momo*, and steamed rolls," which she and her husband cannot consume at once, so they make soy sauce out of the sun-baked leftovers. One day, one of her girlfriends brings her "a wicker basket, inside which there are twenty-some big snow-white *momo*, and a huge bowl of boiled pork slices" (19.141); the couple eats the dainties in public, making quite a scene, their gluttony drawing a herd of piggish village women wandering about the courtyard and leaving them drooling. Still, Née Tang is not full. She goes to the kitchen and eats "three more bowls of soup, with pickled cucumber dressed with garlic shoots and sesame oil" (19.142). The vulgarism displayed by Née Tang does not make a reader loathe her; on the contrary, one is very impressed by her boorish vitality. Amateur researcher Ning Zhi 宁致 goes so far as to use this vignette to rule out the possibility of Pu Songling's authorship. She argues that the vibrant image of the philistine woman could not have possibly been penned by Pu Songling, who, by his propensity to write delicate and refined women in abstruse literary language, is incapable of rendering such earthy vitality.[22]

Landlord-tenant relations in late Ming society were known for their "commercial and contractual flexibility"[23] or, according to some orthodox historians, the "relaxation of feudal personal relations." This is reflected in *XSYYZ*'s description of how the field laborers demand prices arbitrarily and overconfidently during the busy season.

4. The Salt Franchise and Salt Smuggling

Owing to its inseparability from people's daily diet, salt has always been under a national monopoly throughout China's imperial history.[24] Nevertheless, it was not until the Ming that legal codes regulating the salt franchise were consolidated into the corpus juris.[25]

Of course, salt was not the only monopolized commodity in ancient China. Other monopoly goods included wine, yeast, vinegar, tea, incense, alum, cinnabar, tin, and iron.[26]

"Smuggling was an inevitable but deadly phenomenon that had to be rooted out," laments Madeleine Zelin, who studies the salt merchants of Zigong in early modern times. She acknowledges that counter-smuggling was not easy to achieve given the limited means imperial Chinese states could command. "Almost every stage in the process of moving salt from producer to consumer held opportunities to evade the salt-tallying officials working for the state, and all opportunities were widely exploited."[27] The problems perplexing the Zigong salt administrators in the Qing and early Republican times had also been faced by the Shandong salt officials hundreds of years before.

For the Ming, the profits and taxes derived from the salt trade constituted a vital part of the imperial revenue. According to *The Veritable Records of Emperor Taizu* 太祖实录 in MSL, *The Veritable Records of the Ming Dynasty* 明实录, a Salt Bureau had been established by the then civil-war-engaged Zhu Yuanzhang to levy a 1/20 tax on salt merchants to replenish his army as early as 1361,[28] seven years before the founding of the dynasty, though the various distractions of military and political affairs had made it impossible for him to institutionalize salt trading.[29] In the same year, copper, cash, and tea laws were also enacted. By 1368, when the founding emperor promulgated *The Great Ming Code* 大明律—the fundamental Ming legal code—12 articles were set up under *The Salt Rules* 盐法.[30] The spirit of the Ming salt legislation was to put all salt production, conveyance, and reselling activities under strict control. All 12 articles were devised to weaken the illegal salt trade.[31] The code regulated that: "Those who secretly distill seawater to produce salt for sale ought to be hung to death," "In any place outside the salt production base, anyone who carries over 30 *jin* of salt will be dispelled," and "Salt smugglers and those who harbor them are to be sentenced to death, their families exiled to frontiers, and those who carry salt across the boundary deported."[32] The rigidity of laws, however, did not deter smugglers from chasing the lucrative profits of salt production, conveyance, and resale.

Theoretically, all the salt agencies in the Ming dynasty were subordinate to the Provincial Administration Commission. However, in actual operation, the commission had little power to manipulate the tax levied on salt. As early as the Hongwu reign, the founding emperor set up the Huaibei-Huainan Salt Transportation Department, the Zhedong-Zhexi Salt Transportation Department, the Changlu-Hedong Salt Transportation Department, the Guangdong-Haibei Salt Tax Administration Department, the Shandong-Fujian Salt Transportation Department, the Lingzhou Salt Tax Administration Department, the Sichuan Tea and Salt Transportation Department, and the Yunnan Salt Tax Administration Department. In September of the fifth year of Yongle reign, Emperor Chengzu of the Ming set up a Salt Tax Administration Department in Jiaozhi, but it was removed after the fall of Jiaozhi.[33] At the same time, the Ming government implemented the Kai Zhong Law 开中法 to incentivize private merchants to hand in supplies needed by the government in exchange for salt sales and transportation licenses. In addition to providing military pay for the border guards, the Kai Zhong Law was also intended to facilitate retrieving old banknotes (merchants exchanged banknotes for salt), transporting grain (merchants who transported grain to the border were permitted to transport and sell salt), and providing famine relief.[34]

Having been a center of salt production and marketing since the Tang dynasty, Shandong brought into the empire its most significant profits;[35] on the other hand, its production method was one of the most uneconomical. Ray Huang is among the Chinese historians who have thoroughly studied the mechanism of the Ming salt monopoly. His work, *Taxation and Governmental Finance in Sixteenth-Century Ming China*, painstakingly renders various methods of salt production in different regions. In many places in Shandong, he notes, brine was obtained in the first place by washing salt-saturated soil and then carrying it over 20 miles inland to be boiled due to the lack of fuel.[36] This cumbersome means of production naturally led to the high price of salt, as well as rampant smuggling.

Even worse, salt patrols frequently conspired with the producers in manufacturing contraband salt and sharing the profits. As a result, by the time of the late Ming, a quota system had to be introduced to counteract the illegal trading of salt, which meant underlings and patrol officers of the salt production provinces were ordered to turn in a fixed amount of smuggled salt and, at times, a fixed number of arrested smugglers. This irrational regulation, as Ray Huang sees it, only reveals the ineffectiveness of the salt patrol.[37]

One of the hired hands of the Dis, Li Jiuqiang, having been gulled by his friend, salt-smuggler Chen Liu, becomes vengeful. He reports the smuggling crime to the local authority, the District Jailor (*dianshi* 典史) of Xiujiang county, Mr. Xia, who the Salt Administrator has just beaten for not turning in enough salt smugglers, per the quota request. While it was uncommon in the Ming for a District Jailor to receive physical punishment for the inefficiency of his work, Mr. Ma's case underscores the severity of salt smuggling. When Li Jiuqiang reports him, he observes:

> Our Xiujiang County might be short of other things, but certainly not salt-smugglers. To say nothing of cracking four cases of salt smuggling per month, even if you want forty cases monthly, you can still get them. Your hunt knows no bounds just in the Mingshui vicinity.

Ma eagerly follows the lead and raids Chen Liu's house, wherein "two gigantic urns, two straw baskets, two hop-pockets, and big and small vats, all full of illegal salt" are found (48.368–369).

We learn from the colloquial conversations in the narrative that salt is such a high-priced commodity that in a certain rhetorical context, one's life can be analogized to, but valued more cheaply than, salt. For example, when Sujie tortures Xichen until he bursts into a lasting moan that his mother cannot bear hearing, the heart-struck Lady Di tells her husband: "Am I to keep my life in exchange for edible salt? Let me trade my life for hers!" (52.400)

The Novel does not elaborate much on the Ming salt economy, but we can identify the following facts from the above short anecdote: 1) The hunt for salt smuggling is so severe that a quota for identified smugglers has to be met at the county level, or else the clerical officials will be punished; 2) despite the relentless governmental strikes, salt smuggling is still prevalent; and 3) for commoners, salt is hard to obtain and remains expensive.

Though brief, the account of the Li Jiuqiang incident in *XSYYZ* is in accord with the historical facts under the Ming salt monopoly: widespread smuggling, prohibitive pricing, and an ineffective quota system to seize contraband.

5. A Study of Ming Rare Local Specialties and Cuisines

When Xichen's concubine Jijie is pregnant, the morning sickness drives her to crave a long list of curious foods most people have never heard of:

Honey crucian carp of Sichuan, tadpole soup of Fujian, whole scorpion of Pingyin, qi snake of Huguang, bamboo raccoon of Huoshan, balloonfish of Suzhou, yellow mouse of Datong, goose of Gushi, chicken of Laiyang, crab of Tianjin, duck egg of Gaoyou, elephant trunk of Yunnan, lion leg of Jiaozhi, phoenix meat of Baoji, psychedelic fish of Dengzhou.

(79.611)

Though containing a tinge of exaggeration, the food list reveals the comprehensiveness of Beijing's food culture.

"Honey Chirp" is the rat pup eaten alive. According to *The Records about the Government and Society* (Chao Ye Qian Zai 朝野金载) by Zhang Zhuo 张鷟:

Lingnan barbarians like to make Honey Chirp, that is, newborn and wriggling rat pups. They feed such rat pups with honey and serve them as a dish in banquets as they move with soft sounds. When picked up with chopsticks and put in the mouth, they'd chirp, so the dish is called Honey Chirp.[38]

In the entry of "rat" in *Compendium of Materia Medica* by Li Shizhen 李时珍, there is also a relevant record: "Huizhou barbarians take the newborn rat pups with closed eyes and no hair to feed with honey and prepare with fine materials. When picked to be eaten, it cries like chirping, so it is called Honey Chirp."[39]

When Su Shih was exiled to Danzhou, his brother Su Zhe 苏辙 was also relegated to Leizhou, where he got skinny because of the lack of food and clothing and the climate to which he was unaccustomed. Learning of the situation, Su Shih wrote a poem, *Hearing That Ziyu Gets Thin*, and especially noted the misery of Danzhou's lack of meat:

> Pork is seen once every five days, and yellow chicken porridge every ten days. The locals all eat potatoes and yams, while they recommend me smoked rats and roasted bats.
> I used to vomit at the smell of Honey Chirp, but now I have gone native to bear toads.[40]

In this poem, Su Shih complained that at first, he would vomit every time he heard the word "Honey Chirp," not to mention eating it, but later the dish became his daily food for a living. Therefore, in *Welcome Cousin Zhengfu with a Poem*, his other poem, there is already a line, "Honey Chirp is prepared in the morning, and owls are heard at night."[41] It is said that a special dish of raw rats is now popular in Guangxi and Guangdong, and it is eaten in the following way: pick it up with chopsticks—the rat chirps for the first time, dip it in the sauce—the rat chirps again, and bite it in the mouth—the rat chirps for the third time. As the rat chirps three times, this dish is called "three chirps." Evidently, it is "Honey Chirp."[42]

Tadpoles, as the larva of frogs and toads, can clear away heat and toxic material and can be used to treat heat and carbuncle toxins. Li Shizhen's *Compendium of Materia Medica* states, "Tadpoles are mainly used to treat fever sores and scabies caused by heat toxins, and they can be mashed up and applied to the affected areas."

> According to local custom, on the third day of the third lunar month, people take tadpoles and scent them with water, saying that tadpoles can prevent sores, which also refers to the function of tadpoles in detoxifying and curing sores.[43]

As for boiling tadpole soup for food, it seems more common among the Miao people in Guangxi and the Dong people in Guizhou.

The Deep-Fried Whole Scorpion 油炸全蝎 is a famous dish in Pingyin. To make the dish, first, soak the fresh scorpions in water for an hour to clean off mud and sand, and then take them out; next, fry the prepared scorpions in a frying pan until they are crispy and slightly yellow.

The *qi* snake is native to Qichun County in southeastern Hubei Province and is one of the "world-famous" "Four Treasures of Qichun," together with *qi* bamboo, *qi* moxa, and *qi* turtle. This kind of snake has a high medicinal value, and the snake wine made from it can treat tendon pain and relieve convulsions.

The bamboo raccoon, also known as the bamboo rat, likes to eat the underground stems of bamboo and bamboo shoots, but also eats grass and other plant seeds and fruits. Its meat is quite tasty, with several cooking methods, such as stewing, smothering, braising, and serving with scallion oil. The bamboo rat was well known as "bamboo *liu* 竹䶉" in the Tang dynasty. A record in *Wang's Witnesses* (Wangshi Jianwen 王氏见闻) is quoted in *Records of the Taiping Era*:

> The bamboo *liu*, a kind of bamboo-eating rat, lives in uninhabited valleys and bamboo forests in deep mountains, eats nothing but bamboo and is as huge as the wild beaver. Its meat is fleshy and crisp, which the local people enjoy but take an effort in fetching.[44]

A poem by Yuan Zhen 元稹 refers to "roast *liu* coated with *su* 䶉炙漫涂苏." Wang Saishi 王赛时, a researcher at the Shandong Academy of Social Sciences and editor-in-chief of *Dietetic Culture Research*, an international academic journal, confirms that roasted bamboo rat with purple perilla as sauce was a delicacy in the Tang.[45]

The globefish, living in the shallow sea, is swept into Zhejiang by the Qiantang tide and into Suzhou by the Songjiang tide. According to Ye Mengde 叶梦得:

> The globefish becomes available to Zhenjiang residents before the Lantern Festival, first in Changzhou and Jiangyin. When the earliest batch of globefish goes on the market, each would cost nearly a thousand *taels* of silver and is a scarce commodity, so only rich people may have access to the delicacy by reserving the purchase from the fisherman. After the second lunar month, there are more and more, and each only costs dozens of *taels*. When the willow is fluttering, no one eats globefish anymore.[46]

For people in Jiangsu and Zhejiang, "risking one's life by eating globefish" was commonplace, as stated in a poem:

> The neighboring man advises me to know the truth early,
> as the poison of the globefish kills people like the hypertoxic *zhen* 鸩 bird.
> Everything in the world may be a trap,
> And getting hurt is not at all surprising.[47]

In the *Compendium of Materia Medica*, Li Shizhen records that:

> The yellow mouse, native to Taiyuan and Datong and also found in Yan, Sui, and the deserts, is particularly cherished by the Liao people. The yellow mouse resembles the rat, yellow all over, with short feet, good at walking, looking roly-poly, and living in caves. . . . The villagers use water to fill caves to catch yellow mice, whose meat is succulent, like pork, but crispy. Their skin can be made into the collar of a fur coat. During the Liao, Jin, and Yuan dynasties, yellow mice were raised on sheep's milk for the royal family to enjoy as a rare and delicious food.[48]

In a poem, *Yun Zhong Ji Shi* 云中即事, by Yu Qian 于谦, a senior official in the Ming dynasty, a line reads, "Burning charcoal by the bed to roast yellow mice, bending the bow on the horse to shoot white wolves."[49]

Nowadays, in advertising its specialties, Gushi County propagates that, as early as the Sui dynasty, the goose of Gushi was a famous dish on par with the ham of Jinhua. They also quote from the classics to prove this statement, saying that the *History of the Sui Dynasty* (Sui Shu 隋书) contains the following descriptions: In A.D. 582, Emperor Yang came to Jiangdu, playing Bai Opera and feasting all the concubines on a red ship. Nearly a thousand delicacies were prepared, but only Jinhua's ham and Gushi's goose were eaten up. Most of the anecdotes about the goose of Gushi on the internet are also based on this and then circulated, even mistaking the goose-eating imperial concubine for Zhang Lihua, the favorite consort of Chen Shubao, the last emperor of the Chen of the Southern dynasties. In fact, the *History of the Sui Dynasty* does not have such a paragraph. Yet the Gushi goose, as a meat goose raised with unique methods, certainly deserves its reputation. Qing scholar Li Yu 李渔 puts it:

> Goose meat has no other advantages but is fat and sweet. Fat meat must be sweet while eating lean meat is like chewing wax. The best goose can be found in Gushi. If you ask the local people, they will reply, "Raising geese is almost the same as raising people. Geese eat what people eat, so goose meat is as fatty as people."[50]

Li's statement has revealed the secret of raising geese in Gushi. In the third year of the Yongzheng reign in the Qing dynasty, Tian Wenjing 田文镜, a capable minister, in issuing *Rectifying Matters of Temporary Action: Officials in Charge of Various Seals of the Zhili Prefecture Are Not Allowed to Blackmail Subordinates*, expressly stated that "even if one uses cash to buy local products, he should beware of being framed and wronged." The Gushi goose was one of the four local products he cited.[51]

Chicken of Laiyang, however, has enjoyed equal popularity with chicken of Taihe and Tongzhou since the Tang dynasty and was mentioned by Yuan Zhen in *The Changqing Collection* (Changqing Ji 长庆集).[52] As for the crabs of Tianjin, there are two kinds, both famous. One is the sea crab in the spring, as "crabs are eaten in Tianjin as early as the third lunar month, and the piled sea crabs are extremely enjoyable."[53] Another is the river crab from suburban Junliangcheng, Lutai, Gegu, Xiaozhan, Xianshigu, and so forth. Despite the small size, it has rich meat and roe, and is exceptionally delicious.[54]

The technique of pickling duck eggs was already contained in Jia Sixie's 贾思勰 *Important Arts for the People's Welfare*, written 1,500 years ago. The duck breeding industry has been developed since ancient times in Gaoyou and the nearby areas, including Baoying and Xinghua, located in the water township of Lixiahe in northern Jiangsu, a place with many lakes. The duck eggs in Gaoyou are large and heavy, weighing about 30 grams on average heavier than ordinary duck eggs elsewhere, and, surprisingly, they are primarily double-yolked eggs. In the fourth volume of *The Prefecture Annals of Gaoyou* [Gaoyou Zhouzhi 高邮州志], it is recorded:

> Pickled duck eggs. The ducks are stocked in the paddy fields in Gaoyou. When the ducks lay eggs, they would be pickled and then put into a barrel,

called salted eggs. The eggs have such a perfect combination of color, taste, and appearance that people from other places come to buy them.

The salted duck eggs of Gaoyou have the characteristics of being "appetizing, fine, tender, loose, mushy, and oily," without any part hard in the core. Besides, the egg yolk is so red that it has earned the reputation of "duck eggs of Gaoyou rival vermilion."[55]

"Roast elephant trunk" is one of the eight special dishes in the Tang dynasty. According to Liu Xun's 刘恂 *Records of Unusual Things in Lingbiao* (Lingbiao Lu Yi 岭表录异):

> There are many wild elephants in Chaozhou and Xunzhou, two counties under Guangzhou. Their small and red teeth are best suited for making chopsticks. When the people of Chaozhou and Zunzhou catch an elephant, they will compete to eat the elephant trunk, saying: "It is fat and crispy, especially suitable for roasting."[56]

Duan Gonglu 段公路 of the Tang dynasty, in writing *The Beihu Record* (Beihu Lu 北户录), copied the above exactly and added: "The taste is similar to that of pork, but is more like *hanxiao* 含消."[57] *Hanxiao* originally refers to a kind of delicious pear, but here it refers to the delicate taste of roast pork. It can be inferred that the elephant trunk parallels the roast pork in taste.

"Phoenix meat of Baoji" is likely to be the cured donkey meat produced in Fengxiang, Baoji. The general explanation of "phoenix meat" is the meat made by air-drying. Because "wind" and "phoenix" are homophonic in Chinese and interchangeable, "phoenix meat" is also called "wind meat." If limiting the place of production to Baoji, then only Fengxiang donkey meat corresponds most appropriately. The cured donkey meat is made from the legs of the donkeys in Guanzhong, which are fat and succulent. In addition, the process is complex, including a step of hanging the meat in the sun during the day to dry, so it is reasonable to call it "wind meat."

The psychedelic fish, or giant salamander, is a carnivorous amphibian whose cry resembles that of a baby; hence the name baby fish. It is now a Grade II protected species. In the *Compendium of Materia Medica*, Li Shizhen quotes an explanation from Kou Zongshi 寇宗奭, a pharmacologist in the Song dynasty, saying, "The fish is slightly like an otter, four-legged, with a heavy belly like a capsule. It has a light purple body, without scales, like catfish. When I dissected it, there were several small crabs, small fish, and small stones." Li Shizhen also mentions, "Nowadays, when a fisherman catches a baby fish in his net, he thinks it is a bad omen and immediately discards it in astonishment. Probably he does not know that the baby fish can be eaten."[58] Obviously, in the Jiajing reign, when Li Shizhen was alive, the public was still unaware that the psychedelic fish was edible, much less made into a delicacy. Psychedelic fish of Dengzhou might be considered quite a niche food in the late Ming dynasty.

On Jijie's "list of exotic foods for pregnant women," the only item that cannot be found is the "lion leg of Jiaozhi." *The Travels of Marco Polo* mentions a "Jiaozhi State," but the place has been verified by Feng Chengjun 冯承钧, a modern scholar of transportation history, as Cheli 彻里, which is around modern-day

Xishuangbanna.[59] According to historical records, the Yongle, Hongxi, and Xuande reigns were the "period when Annam was under the Ming." In Vietnamese history, that is "the fourth vassal period subordinating to the north." The Chengxuan Chief Secretary Department of Jiaozhi was established in the fifth year of the Yongle reign (1407) and abolished in the third year of the Xuande reign (1428). Although the department did not last a long time, the Ming people were used to using the term "Jiaozhi" to refer to "Annam." Since the reign of Zhao Tuo 赵佗 (219 B.C. to 137 B.C.), founder of the Nanyue Kingdom, Annam had been involved with the Chinese heartland during all the dynasties. As a vassal state, it had paid tribute with abundant varieties of products to the central government for many generations, but there was no mention of lions, let alone the dish of "lion leg." Elephants and rhinoceros were the only two kinds of large animals paid as tributes by Annam. As for the lions imported to the Ming as tributes, they were all from countries in West Asia and Central Asia.[60] *Ode to Lions* (Shizi Fu 狮子赋) by Chen Cheng 陈诚, the Ming ambassador and a traveler on par with Zheng He, was quite famous. Chen Cheng had been sent as an envoy to Annam by imperial decree in the 30th year of Hongwu reign, and a letter from the King of Annam, Chen Rikun 陈日焜, dated the first day of the fourth month of that year still exists in Chen's collection.[61] It was already on the eve of the usurpation of the Chen dynasty. If Chen Cheng did see lions in Annam, would he not have written an Annam version of *Ode to Lions*? The "lion leg" could have originated in Jiaozhi.

Although the "list of exotic foods for pregnant women" is written to satirize Jijie's unreasonable demands, thus containing a tinge of exaggeration, it reflects in another way the abundance of famous food specialties in the late Ming dynasty.

The above enumeration of food specialties is not the only occurrence in the Novel. Due to the proximity, many food specialties in Beijing could also be found in Jinan, the capital of Shandong province. In the brief reunion of Di Xichen and Sun Lanji, she prepares a feast for him, the food list of which is comparable to the one previously mentioned:

> Sun Lanji brings out duck egg from Gaoyou, ham from Jinhua, pickled fish from Huguang, mussels from Ningbo, crab from Tianjin, dragon louse from Fujian, drunk shrimp from Hangzhou, suosuo grape from Shanxi, sweetmeat and sweetball from Qingzhou, bamboo terrapin from Tianmushan, dried shrimps from Dengzhou, crisp flower from Datong, salty devilwood from Hangzhou, horse betelnut from Yunnan, and amber candy from Beijing. She also arranges a fine collecting box with fifteen separate cells. Then she puts on her table four dishes of dry fruits: one of lichee, one of dried chestnut, one of fried ginkgo, and one of sheep tail bamboo shoot walnut. And again, there are four small dishes: vinegar-soaked ginger shoot, ten-spiced lobster sauce, a piece of lettuce, and a toon sprout. Knowing that Xichen does not drink heavily, she opens a semi-finished wine syrup, hoping the early arrival of Xichen and the late return of her husband Qin Jingyu might create a chance for their reunion.

(50.386)

Most of the listed local products in these two occasions remain signature foods in their regions nowadays. That a slightly well-off Beijing family can cater to those strange cravings of a pregnant concubine might be inconceivable to a modern reader. Still, considering the pervasive epicurean culture of late Ming Beijing, it is not that far-fetched. Moreover, on closer inspection, we might even say that there is considerable overlap between the rare and exotic food specialties available to the uppermost high society and the slightly well-off urban families of the late Ming.

In Ming-Qing icftion, there is a paragraph comparable to the exhaustive enumeration of specialties in *XSYYZ* from the 22nd chapter of *Criticism at Taowu* (Taowu Xian Ping 梼杌闲评), "The Concubines Visit the Spring Scenery in the Imperial Garden, and the Nannies Fall in love at the Yilan Hall":

> The doors are draped with colored embroidery, the floor is covered with brocade carpets. In the middle is a pearl lid; all around are curtains of tortoiseshell. The dense fragrance is exquisite; the exotic products are fresh. The dragon-motif incense burner diffuses aroma; the peacock-tail screen boasts novel flowers. The amber cups and glass jars are coated with gold and jade; the golden plates and white jade bowls are decorated with brocades and flowers. The plates are of artful designs and vivid colors; the seats are arranged neatly around the excellent dishes. Dried shrimp and dried lamb represent flavors of the East and the West; cauliflowers and termitophiles typify the North and South products. The ape's lips and bear's paws are prepared among the terrestrial treasures; the yellow clams and silver whitebait are lined up in the aquatic products. The deer antlers are fried with beef; the salted sturgeon is with dried conches. The pincers of crabs are full of meat like white jade; the duck eggs have yolks like red agate. The bird's nest is stewed with antlers; the seaweed is mixed with asparagus. The chicken of Laiyang and the duck of Gushi are as oily as rouge and powder; the perch of Songjiang and the triangular bream of Hanshui are even more delicious than crispy cookies. Gold-like tangerines of Fuzhou and mandarins of Dongting are served together; jade-like water chestnuts of Taihu Lake and lotus roots of Gaoyou are in dishes. The ginkgo nuts are from regions south of the Yangtze River, the pears resemble the shape of a rabbit's head, and the Chinese chestnuts are selected from Xuanzhou and the jujubes from Yaofang. Sugar apples are placed with olives; crabapples are with pimpons. Hazelnuts, lotus seeds, and grapes are large; torreya seeds, melon seeds, and candied dates are complete in variety. Walnuts and persimmon cakes are offered; longan and lychee are ready. The wine in the golden pot is fragrant; the soup in the jade dish is brimming. There are a hundred delicacies, as exotic as a banquet set in the fairy world; there are a thousand cups of wine, as fragrant as a gift from the immortal palace.[62]

Criticism at Taowu is a late Ming novel exposing the political corruption of the eunuch Wei Zhongxian, also known as *Story of the Pearl* (Ming Zhu Yuan 明珠缘). The paragraph depicts the royal life from the view of Wei Zhongxian. In this case, a feast in the imperial garden held by the empress for the imperial concubines and wives of crown princes, and is, therefore, very detailed and exaggerated. However, when it comes to specific foods, we find that the listed specialties are not beyond the reach of commoners.

6. The Downward Trend of Luxury Food Consumption in the Ming

1) The Ming Literati's Promotion of the Cuisine Culture

The food books of the Ming dynasty, based on those of the Song and Yuan dynasties, have developed culinary and food theories to a new height. *Capable of Doing All Sorts of Vulgar Things* (Duo Neng Bi Shi 多能鄙事), *Mo'e Records* (Mo'e Xiao Lu 墨娥小录), *Complete Collection of Essential Things at Home* (Jujia Biyong Shilei Quanji 居家必用事类全集), and *Compilation of Convenience Atlas* (Bianmin Tuzuan 便民图纂) are all food books designed for "serving the people." Other books, such as *Reminiscences in Dreams of Tao An* (Tao An Meng Yi 陶庵梦忆) and *Lang Collections* (Lang Wenji 琅文集) by Zhang Dai 张岱, *Book of Siyouzhai* (Siyouzhai Congshuo 四友斋丛说) by He Liangjun 何良俊, *Essays of Wangxiangtang* (Wangxiangtang Xiaopin 晚香堂小品) by Chen Jiru, *Memories of Yingmei An* (Yingmei An Yiyu 影梅庵忆语) by Mao Pijiang, *Treatise on Superfluous Things* (Changwu Zhi 长物志) by Wen Zhenheng 文震亨, and *Occasional Notes with Leisure Motions* (Xianqing Ou Ji 闲情偶寄), though not specifically works on food and drink, devote a considerable amount of ink to foods and specialties and show the "art of dining" has been a proud tradition of Chinese literati, and is still carried on by modern scholars. Liang Shiqiu's 梁实秋 delightful *Talking about Food in Elegant House* (Yashe Tan Chi 雅舍谈吃) is such a case.

Epicureanism had become such a popular topic that one's knowledge of cuisine was reckoned as a character of erudition and nobility.

Late Ming literatus Zhang Dai styled himself *qingchan* 清馋, or "high-hearted glutton," as he was an elite glutton of signature regional foods. In his *Reminiscences in Dreams of Tao An*, he notes down a list of foods that he had savored, the comprehensiveness of which exceeded that of the lists of Jijie and Sun Lanji combined in the Novel, and the origins of which covered almost every province.[63]

> No "high-hearted glutton" is more qualified in Zhejiang than I, Zhang Dai. I especially like specialties from all areas. For example, specialties from Beijing include pimpons, yellow weasels, and horse tooth pine; those from Shandong include morels, qiubai pears, shiny-leaved yellowhorns, and sweet seeds; those from Fujian include citrus tangerines, citrus tangerine cakes, sticky candies, and red fermented bean curds; those from Jiangxi include glorybower roots, and Fengcheng dried meat; those from Shanxi include cauliflowers; those from Suzhou include souffle in the shape of a snail, haw cubes, haw jelly, pine nut sugar, *baiyuan* [steamed pork leg lean meat 白圆], and dried olive; those from Jiaxing include dried Spanish mackerel and siskins of

Taozhuang; those from Nanjing include cherries, Taomen dates, water chestnut dumplings, nest bamboo dumplings, and hawthorn candies; those from Hangzhou include watermelons, chick peas, lotus roots, leek buds, bamboo shoots, and Tangqi honey tangerines; those from Xiaoshan include plums, water shields, turtledoves, green carps, and persimmons; those from Zhuji include civets, cherries, and *hu* chestnuts; those from Sheng include fern flour, fine torreya, and Longyou sugar; those from Linhai include "pillow" pumpkins; those from Taizhou include blood cockles and dried scallops; those from Pujiang include ham meat; those from Dongyang include dried jujubes; those from Shanyin include bamboo shoots of Potang, *xie* tangerines, water chestnuts of Dushan, river crabs, and razor clams of Sanjiangtun, white clams, northern anchovy, reeves shads, and *zi* fish of Lihe. If the place of origin is far away, then the specialties are accessible once a year; if not, then the specialties are accessible monthly and even daily.[64]

"The art of dining" diffused from top to bottom, from the capital to the provinces, from the cities to the countryside, and from the wealthy to the well-to-do. One of the most common phenomena was the transmission of cooking methods. Beijing's cooking method was unique and the object of learning by other counties and provinces. Tiaogeng, a native of Beijing, is bought by the Di family and follows Old Di back to Shandong. She is good at cooking Beijing-style stir-fried crab, so delicious that Old Di's brother-in-law, Uncle Xiang, is unstinting in his praise:

> The second dish is stir-fried crab. Xiang Dongyu says: "We always eat boiled crab, but this is the first time we have eaten such a delicious fried one. I've told my maid to cook the same way, but she failed." Old Di says, "Only people in Beijing can make perfect stir-fried crab. I heard that they even peel off the outer shell of the crab, leaving the complete crab meat with all the little legs to make soup. Two crabs make one bowl of soup." Xiang Dongyu replies: "How is the crab peeled exactly? Does Liu know how to peel?" Old Di says: "I'm afraid she cannot, either. Tell someone to check if there are any crabs left in the kitchen and if there are, tell her to make two." The maid responds: "There are no more crabs. She just said there wasn't enough to fry." Old Di then reminds her: "Remember to buy some crabs and ask her to make the soup for Uncle Xiang."
>
> (58.444)

If we compare this paragraph with *Jin Ping Mei*, it is easy to find that this is a rehash of Uncle Wu's praise of crabs. When Ximen Qing sponsors Chang Zhiijie to purchase a house, Chang's wife makes:

> forty large crabs, the shells of which had been scoured out and stuffed with crab meat, coated with a mixture of pepper, ginger, minced garlic, and starch, deep-fried in sesame oil, and flavored with soy sauce and vinegar, which rendered them fragrant and delectable.

When this dish is served:

> Ying Po-chüeh offered a crab to Wu K'ai (Uncle Wu), and Hsieh Hsi-ta remarked, "I don't know how these were ever done to make them so flavorful, crisp, and delicious."
>
> "They were sent over here from Brother Ch'ang the Second's place," explained Hsi-men Ch'ing.
>
> "I have led a futile existence for fifty-one years," said Wu K'ai, "without knowing that crabs could be prepared in such a way. They really are delicious."
>
> "Have our sisters-in-law in the rear compound had a chance to taste them?" asked Ying Po-chüeh.
>
> "They've all had some," said Hsi-men Ch'ing.
>
> "It's really put Sister-in-law Ch'ang to the test," remarked Ying Po-chüeh, "to demonstrate such culinary skill." Ch'ang Shih-chieh laughed at this, saying, "My humble wife was only afraid that she had not made things tasty enough, and that you gentlemen would laugh at her."[65]

XSYYZ is influenced in more ways than this by *Jin Ping Mei*. When imperial guards Su and Liu go to celebrate the birthday of Wang Zhen, who is second only to the emperor, it is also an imitation of "Ximen Qing's Birthday Celebration for Cai Jing in Dongjing." However, *XSYYZ*, a masterpiece not inferior to *Jin Ping Mei*, is much more down-to-earth in its description of food. Basically, the reason is that *Jin Ping Mei* focuses on wealthy merchants like Ximen Qing while *XSYYZ* focuses on well-to-do families like Old Di. The fact that the diet of the well-to-do gradually caught up with that of wealthy merchants indicates the tendency in the earthly life of the late Ming that the citizens' culture was learning from the top.

Yasushi Oki of the Institute of Oriental Culture, University of Tokyo, Japan, calls the writings of Wen Zhenheng, Chen Jiru, Li Yu, and others "Textbooks on the aesthetic life in late Ming China." In a study of the same name, he explores the interesting phenomenon that people followed these fashionable literati to learn the elegant style in the late Ming dynasty.[66] In Yasushi's view, the closing of the imperial examinations for intellectuals during part of the Yuan dynasty led to the emergence of pure literati who devoted their interests entirely to their private spaces for the first time in Chinese history. These interests included writing poetry and painting, eating and drinking, and having fun. They were different from literati like Su Shih of the previous dynasties. Su Shih also devoted himself to literature and art in his private space, and even to cooking tea and food. However, he still had a public identity as a "scholar" and an "official," after all. This lineage of purely literary aspirations inherited from the Yuan dynasty was carried forward in the late Ming dynasty. Why? Because the market existed. The conclusion of Yasushi Oki is that:

> In the Tokugawa period (1603–1867) of Japan, social status was fixed. Even rich merchants could never become samurai, the governors of the time. Therefore, merchants could do nothing but create their own culture, a culture

for commoners. In China, on the contrary, "literati" did not denote a rigid social class of its own. Common folk could become literati through passing the state examinations. And in the prosperous times of late Ming Jiangnan society, commoners gained economic power. They longed for high status more eagerly than before, but because there was no genuine common folk culture, they could only aspire to literati culture. Thus, they needed manuals. This, I believe, is the reason for the increase in production of literati aesthetic lifestyle manuals in the late Ming.[67]

Yasushi's generalization of the two social forms of Tokugawa and late Ming periods, we suggest, might be a bit too linear. It is well known that Chinese and foreign scholars have thoroughly studied the economic and social patterns of the Tokugawa period; conclusions are quite diverse, breaking away from the monolithic assertion that "the social hierarchy confined the development of merchants." At this point, we cannot simply agree that the unreleased internal pressure of "upward social mobility" of Japanese merchants gave rise to its unique civic culture. Yasushi's conclusion seems to imply that as commoners could imitate the literati, Chinese civic culture remained an uninspired replication of its literati counterpart. Channels of "upward social mobility" in pre-modern East Asian countries should not be so coarsely defined.

In fact, were Ming commoners to imitate the refined lifestyle of the literati, they also faced a series of confinement. The attempts to break through the social hierarchy, expressed in the excessive food, clothing, and other material comforts, were by no means permitted by the Ming sumptuary legislation.

Emperor Hongwu had a set of regulations on dining protocols devised, with particular emphasis on the classifications of dining vessels and their corresponding usage. Rank entitlement was a primary consideration when deciding the eligibility to access a specific vessel. For example, dukes, marquises, and officials of the first and second ranks were entitled to use golden wine bottles, wine cups, and silver utensils. Officials ranked from the third to the fifth were allowed to use wine bottles in silver and cups in gold; for those sixth to the ninth, both bottles and cups needed to be in silver; for the rest, in porcelain or lacquer. Commoners were only allowed to use wine bottles in tin and cups in silver.[68] Much like clothing, the system constituted yet another critical institution in which distinctions in social hierarchies had to be addressed.

Those regulations were reinforced over time through imperial edicts, circular orders, rescripts, and laws. The 35th year of Hongwu (1402) saw the promulgation of a law banning the usage of golden wine vessels by officials and civilians. In the 16th year of Zhengde (1521), the throne granted a memorial petitioning to outlaw the use of silver vessels by artisans and merchants.[69] The two sumptuary laws in the 35th year of Hongwu reign and the 16th year of Zhengde reign were more or less the same, except that the former was inventive and the latter repetitive.

On April 20, 1521 (the 16th year of Zhengde reign), Emperor Zhengde, Zhu Houzhao, died in the Leopard Hall (Baofang, a place of pleasure 豹房) at 30. Zhengde, being young and playful, deviated from the traditions and rebelled against orthodoxy. The civil officials of the Ming dynasty had never seen such a bold and out-of-the-ordinary emperor, so they simply could not do anything with him. Indeed,

136   *Food Cultures of the Ming*

the emperor did not seem to be one who would take the trouble to interfere with the people's use of drinking vessels, tables, and chairs. In August 1520, the 15th year of his reign, Emperor Zhengde fell into the water in Qingjiangpu, Zhenjiang, on his trip to the South. He came down from the shock, became seriously ill when he returned to Beijing in the following January, and laid on his deathbed in March. The sumptuary law, issued in the 16th year of Zhengde reign, was entirely the work of the civil bureaucracy, no matter whether it came out while Emperor Zhengde was still alive or after he had died. Several sumptuary laws were also issued in the reigns of Chenghua, Zhengtong, Jingtai (1450–1457), Hongzhi, Wanli, and Tianshun (1457–1464), but none were as draconian as Hongwu's initial one.

Loaded with trivial details, those laws and regulations were hard to follow from the beginning, still harder when economic progress nearly upturned the "simple and plain" early Ming social structure. However, to treat these legal proscriptions as having dissolved in a highly fluid, boundary-crossing society would be to err towards oversimplification. Hierarchical social protocols are devised to rivet individuals to their inherent social positions. Those laws and rescripts, when enforced upon people, gained momentum. They would persist long after they were disregarded, ignored, or even abolished.[70]

The effectiveness of the sumptuary legislation in attempting to confine each citizen to his original social position—a position determined from his birth and, in the unlikely event, elevated by the imperial examinations, military exploits, official position purchases, or marriage—clearly had some inertia. Nevertheless, behind the neglect of the early decrees, we should not deny that the laws and rescripts still had a deterrent effect on mid- to late-Ming society, as the government never repealed them.

A multitude of late Ming literati, perplexed by the collapse of hierarchical and moral orders, and vexed by the blurred boundaries of class and gender, vented their dissatisfactions through the writing of "morality books, family instructions, conduct books, and vernacular fictions;"[71] *XSYYZ* was one of those undertakings. In a strict sense, even the "obscene book" *Jin Ping Mei* was also a cautionary work. Moralist outcries were uttered by the figureheads of the scholar-gentry, yet paradoxically, it was also the same class that shepherded Ming society into a materialist carnival.

A considerable amount of food books were done during the Ming dynasty; literati took it as a refined activity to write about food. As a result, specialty recipes and cooking methods were abundantly seen in literary sketches, and commoners' standard forms of food and drink were often found in local chronicles.

2) The Contributing Factors of Beijing's Cuisine Culture

Perching on the northeast corner of the China domain, Beijing became the Ming capital after the third Ming Emperor, Yongle, seized the throne by wielding a civil war against his nephew, Emperor Jianwen. Even before the founding of the Ming, Beijing's geographic position had brought in a rich assemblage of food plants, spices, and flavorings. The pastoral peoples it faced in the north, particularly the Mongols, who were to become China's rulers in the fourteenth century, made substantial contributions to its culinary culture. Following the Yuan conquest, the swarming of middle-Asian collaborators whose populations penetrated northern China left some heavy Islamic marks on regional cuisines. If Marco Polo's travelogue account is to be believed, among the "Khan-balik" (Dadu of Yuan 汗八里) inhabitants, there was a sizable population of "Christians, Saracens, and Cathayans, about 5000 astrologers and soothsayers."[72] The conglomeration of varieties of foreign and domestic cultures would inevitably bestow upon the metropolis a vibrant and comprehensive cuisine legacy.

As mentioned, Beijing's geographic and political significance had rendered it a conflux of food cultures from different regions. As a result, present-day Beijing cuisine owes most of its debts to culinary imports from Shandong and that of its most recent conquerors, the Manchus. Back in the Ming, it was more of a mix of northern ethnic Chinese, Mongolian, and Islamic food styles and the gamut of Chinese fare from different regions.

The reason why Beijing could take the lead in the urban cuisine culture of the Ming dynasty, in addition to its central location, was also the ethos of the times.

To trace the origins of Beijing epicureanism, two critical periods, the Chenhua and Hongzhi reigns, must be addressed.

The founding Emperor Hongwu was a man of austerity and frugality. To prevent his descendants from indulging in gastronomy, he set up an exemplary dining pattern. He demanded the palace foods be prepared in Regular Supply (*changgong* 常供), a family-style cuisine, and to show that he had not forgotten his grass-root origins, he made tofu a requirement for his breakfast and dinner menus. Empress Ma frequently presented herself in the palace kitchen to supervise the cooking.[73]

The Chenghua reign saw the social trend of pursuing material comforts everywhere on the rise, in which the imperial palace played a leading role. For example, although tofu remained a must-have dish on the court menu, its courtly version was made not from bean curd from yellow beans, but rather from the brains of nearly a thousand birds, which was dressed to resemble the humble dish.

Born and raised in adversity, Emperor Hongzhi had grown up to be a tolerant, forgiving, self-disciplined man. He was identified as the only monogamous emperor in the entire Chinese imperial history.[74] As a result, Hongzhi received unanimous praise from the bureaucracy and people. His ministers depicted him as the one-of-the-kind model sovereign: quick in mind, diligent in attending court audiences, devoted to Confucian teachings, and adamant about principles.

The Hongzhi reign, loosening the government's grip on the civil officials in terms of material enjoyment that had been in place since the early Ming dynasty, was characterized by a relaxed political atmosphere. Chen Baoliang compares the scale of urban banquets, dishes, and wine vessels in the early Ming and after the middle of the Ming, arguing that "since the Chenghua reign, urban food life has become increasingly luxurious" and that "urban food life gradually shifted from frugality to sumptuousness."[75] Nevertheless, we argue that the starting point of such a shift occurred during the early Hongzhi reign.

Emperor Hongzhi was quite entertained by the idea that his ministers should enjoy a leisurely life of wine and banquets after withdrawing to private quarters.

Considering official parties were usually held at night, and his ministers may have been drunk on their way home, he ordered all the avenue-abutted shops and inns in Beijing and Nanjing to have their lights lit to illuminate the streets. From the Hongzhi reign onwards, the writings of the Ming scholar-officials were flooded with records of parties, menus, and cuisines.

Emperor Hongzhi lived pristinely. Judging from the available historical sources, he was not overly extravagant in his daily expenditures but did leave a record of eating tofu of "brains of a hundred birds." Tofu remained a regular meal in the palace, yet it was no longer made from soybeans but from hundreds of bird brains. There is an anecdote about this hundred-bird tofu. This delicacy was unique to the royal family; even the officials with high ranks and salaries had never heard of it. As society was in a long-term peace at that time, among all the ministers, only the Hanlin (members of the Imperial Academy 翰林) held a prominent position and essential duties but were not burdened with complicated affairs. After the official parties, only the Hanlin could ask for leftovers from the Court of Imperial Entertainments (the institution in charge of the official feasts and foods 光禄寺). One time, a young Hanlin was late for the imperial meal at the Court of Imperial Entertainments and only got tofu, which he thought was a slight on him and thus threw away in anger. An old Hanlin passed by his apartment, asked for wine, and ate all the tofu but did not reveal why. The young man was surprised when he learned later that it was not actual tofu but a delicacy from the brains of a hundred birds; he bitterly repented his folly.[76]

According to the *Codes of the Great Ming Dynasty* (Daing Huidian 大明会典), the only time that the emperor "attended a banquet at the Imperial Academy" was in the first year of Hongzhi reign. Emperor Hongzhi's visit to the Imperial Academy at the beginning of his reign released a political signal to promote Confucianism and education. The banquet was not extravagant, but abundant enough. Through menus at this banquet, we see the delightful feast Emperor Hongzhi's enjoyed with the tutors and students at the Imperial Academy.

> Superior banquet: five dishes go with wine, five kinds of fruit, a large oil pastry in the shape of a silver ingot, a variety of ducks, small dim sum, pork bones, three types of soup, four types of vegetables, large steamed buns, sheep sacrum, and five cups of wine. Medium banquet: five dishes go with wine, five types of fruit, five types of tea cakes, grilled fish, small dim sum, three types of soup, four types of vegetables, large steamed buns, rice with sheep's hooves, and five types of wine.[77]

And the *Codes of the Great Ming Dynasty* records three "special imperial banquets given by the emperor in honor of new *jinshi*," which we take the trouble to list here for comparison:

> The thirteenth year of the Yongle reign. Superior banquet: four fried dishes go with wine, a variety of tea cakes, five kinds of fruit, five boiled dishes go with wine, four types of vegetables, three types of soup, two large steamed buns, mutton rice, and five cups of wine. Upper medium banquet: four fried dishes go with wine, a variety of tea cakes, four types of fruit, five boiled

dishes go with wine, four types of vegetables, three types of soup, two large steamed buns, mutton rice, and five cups of wine.

The first year of the Tianshun reign (1457). All banquets have: fried fish, a sizeable glutinous rice cake in the shape of a silver ingot, two pieces of pork bones, a variety of deep-fried dim sum, nectar [*ganlu* 甘露] cakes, large deep-fried dough cakes, chicken, braised pork, braised lamb, a small molasses cake in the shape of a silver ingot, pork with pepper and vinegar, beef and horse meat with pepper, chicken, and fish with pepper and vinegar, three types of soup, five types of fruit, small steamed buns, two large steamed buns, beef and mutton rice, and five cups of wine.

The third year of the Hongzhi reign. Superior banquet: five dishes go with wine, five types of fruit, five dishes of various tea cakes, a tufted duck, a bowl of small steamed buns, two bowls of small molasses cakes in the shape of silver ingots, two pieces of pork bones, a piece of sheep sacrum, two *huatou* [flower-head 花头] cakes, five types of soup, four types of vegetables, a large steamed bun, a dish of refillable lamb, and seven cups of wine. Upper medium banquet: five dishes go with wine, five types of fruit, five dishes of various tea cakes, a tufted duck, a bowl of small steamed buns, two bowls of small molasses cakes in the shape of silver ingots, two bowls of fried fish, two bowls of rice with sheep's hooves, two *huatou* cakes, five types of soup, four kinds of vegetables, two large steamed buns, a dish of replaceable lamb, and seven types of wine. Medium banquet: five dishes go with wine, five types of fruits, five dishes of tea cakes, a bowl of *ganlu* cakes, a bowl of small steamed buns, two bowls of small molasses cakes in the shape of silver ingots, two pieces of fried fish, two bowls of beef rice, two *huatou* cakes, three types of soup, four types of vegetables, two large steamed buns, a dish of refillable lamb, and seven cups of wine.[78]

These lists show that Emperor Hongzhi's banquets offered to the *jinshi* were far more generous than those during the Yongle and the Tianshun reigns. Such a difference suggests a respect Emperor Hongzhi had for his scholars. Emperor Hongzhi was indeed much more generous in terms of material offerings than his antecedents. *Emperor Hongzhi's Speeches and Edicts* (Mingxiaozong Baoxun 明孝宗宝训), in *Ming Emperors' Speeches and Edicts* (Huangming Baoxun 皇明宝训), was particularly detailed in its entries on "giving generously to scholars," "promoting learning," and "honoring Confucianism." The most direct result of Emperor Hongzhi's generosity was the praise he won from historiographers of later generations. Zhu Guozhen 朱国桢, Grand Secretary in the Wanli reign, commented: "After the three reigns of Yao, Shun, and Yu, only Emperor Wendi of the Han, Emperor Hongzhi of the Song, and Emperor Hongzhi of our Ming dynasty can be described as wise emperors." Deng Yuanxi 邓元锡, an orthodox Confucian scholar during the Ming dynasty, commented:

> I have heard older people say that the reign of Emperor Hongzhi boasted signs of peace. The relationship between the emperor and ministers was modest and gentle, and the country was stable. People lived in increasing

affluence, and scholars enjoyed perusing texts from the times of Yao, Shun, and Yu and the two Han dynasties.[79]

Zeng Guofan 曾国藩 also called Emperor Hongzhi "a ruler of extraordinary talent and insight," and compared him to "Emperor Wu of the Han, Emperor Wen of the Tang, Emperor Ren of the Song, and Emperor Shizu of the Yuan."[80]

Emperor Hongzhi, who did not expand the territory or conquer foreign states, had harmonious governance on the one hand and a vast reserve of wise officials on the other hand as characteristics of his reign. The prosperity of the Hongzhi reign was domestically oriented and relaxed. However, there are always two sides to the same coin. Material abundance inevitably brought the prevailing custom of pleasure-seeking. Emperor Hongzhi was also criticized by Zha Jizuo 查继佐, Master Jingxiu of Haining, as "treating royal relatives on the distaff side too generously, rewarding officials too indiscriminately, having too much redundant staff, and favoring too many close ministers."[81] A historian living through the Ming-Qing transition, Zha Jizuo had a clear insight into the complex nature of history. He was implicated in the case of Zhuang Tinglong 庄廷鑨 of Nanxun in the early years of the Kangxi for his private compilation of Ming history; he almost died in prison. After Hongzhi, the ethos of luxury and pleasure continued to ferment, manifested in the refined diets enjoyed by all levels of classes, from the high officials to commoners.

On a trip home to attend his father's funeral, Zhang Juzheng, the prime minister to the young Wanli Emperor, complained that he had "nowhere to settle chopsticks" when over 100 dishes were laid in front of him by the local supplying office.

Qian Pu 钱普, the prefecture chief of Zhending, was a native of Wuxi. He created for Zhang Juzheng an "aircraft carrier-level" sedan chairman that took "thirty-two servants as carriers" and "with a small room on each side and a page boy standing on each side." He also supplied fabulous Wu food for Zhang. In addition, he recruited all capable chefs in the Wu County to cater to Zhang's culinary needs. As a result, Zhang was quite satisfied, saying, "Until now, I finally have a full stomach."[82]

Sujie, unable to find her husband in Beijing, sojourns at the home of Xichen's cousin, Xiang Yuting, who has recently acquired a *jinshi* degree. Before leaving for Shandong, she takes a chance to stop over at servant Lu Haoshan's home, intending to tour Beijing during the last few days of her trip. Upon learning the news, Xiang gets furious and interrogates his servant personally. Lu Haoshan, full of grievances, kneels and kowtows to the ground, explaining how the brief sojourn of Sujie at his home has cost him dearly:

> The rice is priced at one tael per *picul*, and pork, eight candareens per *jin*; a chicken costs one *mace* and a half; wines are expensive, you know.

When Xiang Yuting asks how much he had spent on Sujie's boarding over her three or four days of sojourn, Lu replies: "At least five or six *taels* of silver" (78.603)— that is roughly the equivalence of the price of a maid in rural Shandong. Lu Haoshan's statement might be somewhat of an exaggeration, given his attempted elicitation of his master's sympathy and reimbursement. Xiang Yuting understands the situation and does not give him further punishment.

The family-styled everyday food for commoners did not cost very much. When Xichen goes to Beijing the second time, his old landlady Lady Tong prepares a welcome dinner. Items she purchases include "pig feet from the Jins, pig head from the Huas, *yi* wine, tofu, fresh lettuce, and pancakes with sesame dressing," costing only several hundred coins. Along with the self-prepared "green bean and rice soup," she has sufficiently entertained Xichen and his three servants (75.575).

In Beijing, Di Xichen lives with his mother-in-law Lady Tong, his stepmother Tiaogeng, and his half-brother Little Wing. To make a living, he opens a small pawnshop. As the revenue is limited, the family must be frugal about everything, and only one maid, Little Pearl, is employed. Lady Tong and Tiaogeng are always busy together when it comes to cooking. Although not wealthy, the family always has good food. Once, Tiaogeng and Little Pearl work on "pancakes of leek and mutton" 青韭羊肉合子 together in the kitchen beside a wood-fired pot, the fragrant smell spreading all over the front and back of the house. The servant of the Xiang family, Xiang Wang, who happens to be passing by the Di family, gulps and salivates. This servant, who has "gentlemen compete for manners, but servants compete for their mouths" as his philosophy, vows to take revenge for not being invited to eat the mutton pancakes. Therefore, he takes the opportunity of going back to Shandong to reveal to Sujie about Di Xichen's remarriage in Beijing.

On another occasion, when Di Xichen is in a good mood after he purchases the official position of the Secretariat Drafter, he is taught the government's rules by Captain Luo, brother of Lady Tong and uncle of Jijie. Xichen teases Luo by telling a joke:

> A man eats Sichuan fried chicken, praising it as a delicacy. A young waiter says, "If the chicken is fried with dozens of chestnuts, it will be even better." So, the man asks him: "Have you ever eaten it?" The waiter replies: "I heard it from my brother." The man asks: "Has your brother ever eaten it?" The waiter replies: "My brother heard it from an official without a fixed position." The man asks: "Has the official ever eaten it?" The waiter replies: "He heard it from his supervisor."
>
> (83.640)

Upon hearing the joke, Luo's cheeks flush red. The joke itself is a testimony to the food culture in Beijing. It tells how culinary fashion permeates from top to bottom: when the upper class has a good dish, the lower class, although unable to reach it, aspires to it.

"Chuan fried chicken" means "Sichuan fried chicken," the preparation method of which was like today's fried chicken with chili in Sichuan cuisine. The dish became popular as early as the Yuan dynasty and had the following process recorded in a note written by someone from the Yuan:

> Wash the chicken and chop it into small pieces. Add three *taels* of sesame oil to the pan and stir-fry the chicken when the oil is hot. Add the shredded

spring onions and half a *tael* of salt, and stir-fry until the chicken is medium done. Prepare a spoonful of thick sauce, some ground pepper, some ground Sichuan pepper, and some ground fennel; add water to make a large bowl of sauce and pour it into the pan to cook thoroughly. It would be better to add some good wine.[83]

This recipe, however, omits chestnuts, a vital ingredient in the present dish. According to *Records of Things—Brief Introduction of Meat in Imperial Diet of the State* (Shiwu Ganzhu—Guochao Yushan Roushi Lue 事物绀珠・国朝御膳肉食略) by Huang Yizheng in the Ming dynasty, "Chuan fried chicken" was also one of the typical meat dishes of the Ming imperial cuisine. There were several other chicken dishes: brocade-wrapped chicken, steamed chicken, deeply pickled chicken, and simple fried chicken.[84] Chuan fried chicken could be ranked as one of the five imperial chicken dishes, so it naturally did not have an undeserved reputation. The process by which this dish was passed from the palace to the official banquets, and then from the official banquets to the people's homes, illustrates the downward trend of luxury food consumption in the Ming dynasty.

Raw food materials became cheaper after the country had been at peace for a long time. This factor contributed to consumption of luxury food in the lower to middle classes. In *Anecdotes from the Political Turmoil* (Luanli Jianwen Lu 乱离见闻录), Chen Shunxi 陈舜系, an adherent of the Ming, recalls the first half of his life, with a detailed recollection of the price of commodities during the Wanli reign:

I was born around 5 a.m. to 7 a.m. on the 26th day of the 8th lunar month in the 46th year of the Wanli reign when my parents were both 23 years old. It was a time of peace, and the people in all areas were happy. My family lived by the sea, in the land of fish and rice. A *dou* of rice costs less than twenty coins, a *jin* of fish only one or two coins, ten betel nuts two coins, a *jin* of meat or a duck six or seven coins, and a *dou* of salt three coins. The prices remained low. Even the poor were fortunate enough to live in peace, and the burden of corvee and taxation was very light. The land yielded two crops a year, so those who farmed were well-fed. Scholars roamed in poetry and writings, and artisans of all industries and businessmen enjoyed life. People were comfortable and at ease. What a happiness it was![85]

Of course, as Chen Shunxi was from Wuchuan in Guangdong, the prices he recorded should have been lower than those in Beijing.

There are valuable records of the folk life of Beijing during the Ming dynasty in books such as *Miscellaneous Records of Wanping* (Wan Shu Zaji 宛署杂记), *The Diary of East Water* (Shuidong Riji 水东日记), *The Prefectural Records of Shuntian* (Shuntian Fuzhi 顺天府志) of the Wanli reign, *A Brief Record of the Scenery of the Imperial Capital* (Dijing Jingwu Lue 帝京景物略), *A Weighted and Unbiased Record*, and *Records of Four seasons in Beijing*. Shen Bang 沈榜, the author of *Miscellaneous Records of Wanping*, was the governor of Wanping county, Shuntian

Prefecture, in the 18th year of the Wanli reign. During his tenure, he kept an eye on current affairs and searched for old rules and regulations. In his own words:

> in my spare time, I gathered a variety of things and evidence-based matters in the county government offices and recorded them together with accounts of things that happened, without setting out examples of argumentation or arranging the order of chapters.[86]

His records are almost as detailed as an archive. The 17th volume of *Miscellaneous Records of Wanping* records the general appearance of the festive folklore of the four seasons in the general Beijing area (near Wanping). According to a tradition set by the founding emperor, on the first day of each month, the Palace Secretariat shall entreat the emperor to issue a *Xuanyu* (Imperial Proclamation 宣谕), teaching the people what they should do that month. The Shuntian Prefecture issued the *Xuanyu* to reach the whole country. Shen Bang recorded the monthly *Xuanyu* issued over 16 years, namely the 12th, 14th, and 15th years of the Zhengde reign; the 3rd, 7th, 17th, 22nd, 23rd, 28th, and 33rd years of the Jiajing reign; the 2nd year of the Longqing reign; and the 4th, 5th, 18th, and 19th years of the Wanli reign.[87] "The contents of all months are complete, except for the first and twelfth months, as farming has not yet begun."[88]

Shen Bang also recorded the expenses of various government offices on different occasions in detail, such as "monthly offerings of seasonal food," the "annual first-day offerings," and the "offerings in the first month of the fall" at the Imperial Ancestral Temple. He left us the most valuable records of the breathing material lives. The following is a record of the costs of the items required for the "monthly offerings of seasonal food" in the first and second months of the year:

> For the first month, the total cost was 2.2 *taels* of silver. Four *jin* of shepherd's purse cost 1.2 *taels*; two *jin* of lettuce cost 0.5 *taels*; two *jin* of leeks cost 0.5 *taels*. For the second month, the total cost was 0.9995 *taels* of silver. Two *jin* and eight *taels* of dried sea grass cost 0.5 *taels*; one *jin* and eight *taels* of celery cost 0.4995 *taels*.[89]

In short, multiple mechanisms gave rise to the "art of eating, drinking, and playing." Cuisine culture, transmitted from the palace to the homes of ordinary people, was a rare occurrence in Chinese history. In terms of the intellectual history of the mid-Ming, Wang Yangming's School of Mind broke the monopoly of Cheng-Zhu neo-Confucianism by consolidating Confucianism, Buddhism, and Taoism. With its conscience theory, the school provided momentum to break through the confinement of sumptuary laws and the insurmountable boundary between superiors and inferiors.

Regarding historical causes, a generous political climate starting from the reign of Hongzhi must be considered. In terms of geographical and ethnic factors, Beijing, having been the capital of the Jin and Yuan dynasties, had an exceptional contribution. Boasting a dense population, inhabitants of ethnic diversity, and numerous good chefs, it was more open to culinary culture. When the whole country imitated the cuisines of the capital, and when the rare and the specialized became more securable, the downward trend of luxury food consumption commenced.

Notes

1 Fernand Braudel, *Civilization and Capitalism, 15th-18th Century: The Structure of Everyday Life*, 3 vols., trans. Siân Reynolds (Berkeley: University of California Press, 1992), 104.
2 Peter Burke, *New Perspectives on Historical Writing*, 2nd ed. (University Park, PA: Pennsylvania State University Press, 2001), 1.
3 Take Robert Fortune, a Scottish botanist and traveler best known for introducing tea plants from China to India, for example. Fortune, after his 1850s' trip to China, commented on the food of his Chinese laborers: "The food of these people is of the simplest kind—namely, rice, vegetables, and a small portion of animal food, such as fish or pork. But the poorest classes in China seem to understand the art of preparing their food much better than the same classes at home. With the simple substances I have named the Chinese laborer contrives to make a number of very savoury dishes, upon which he breakfasts or dines most sumptuously." Robert Fortune, *A Residence Among the Chinese: Inland, on the Coast, and at Sea—Being a Narrative of Scenes and Adventures During a Third Visit to China, from 1853 to 1856* (London: J. Murray, 1857), 42.
4 Xiujiang (Embroider River) is a bogus county name the author creates to camouflage the real site of the backdrop of the Xichen-Jijie story. However, the Mingshui town being a realistic geographic existence, we have no problem identifying the location of the fictitious Xiujiang County to the vicinity of Jinan, the capital of Shandong.
5 Frederick W. Mote, *Imperial China, 900–1800* (Cambridge, MA: Harvard University Press, 1999), 750.
6 Jacqueline Newman, *Food Culture in China, Food Culture Around the World* (Westport, CT: Greenwood Press, 2004), 90.
7 Frederick J. Simoons, *Food in China: A Cultural and Historical Inquiry* (Boca Raton: CRC Press, 1991), 45.
8 Xianglin Li, "Bianshi in Yuan Drama," *Journal of Sichuan Tourism University*, no. 4 (2002): 5–6. 李祥林：《元曲当中说"匾食"》，《四川烹饪高等专科学校学报》，2002年第4期，第5–6页。
9 For example, Song Yingxing, a great naturalist in the Ming, detailed four systems for the rotation of grain and leguminous plants in his *Exploitation of the Works of Nature (Tian Gong Kai Wu)*; *Complete Works of Agronomy*, by noted Ming scholar and agronomist Xu Guangqi, also illustrated the techniques of intercropping wheat and broad bean. See Hui-lian Xu, J. F. Parr, and Hiroshi Umemura, *Nature Farming and Microbial Applications* (New York: Food Products Press, 2000), 16–17. 明代科学家宋应星在所著《天工开物》中，曾详细记录了谷物和豆类的四种轮作之法。另外一位明代科学家徐光启则在《农政全书》中记录了轮作小麦和蚕豆的技术。见。
10 Much of the pastoral poetry was composed by what Stephen Owen sees as a stereotyped "misanthropic recluse." He may be "obsessively defensive of his values and acts," or hiding in mountains and farms, still "in hopes of being recruited for service," but the real agricultural life is certain not of his concern. See Stephen Owen, *Traditional Chinese Poetry and Poetics: Omen of the World* (Madison, WI: University of Wisconsin Press, 1985), 30.
11 Here it refers to alters or temples of She Ji 社稷, an agricultural cult of making sacrifices to Earth God (She) and God of Grain (Ji). The cult can be dated back to the very beginning of the Chinese civilization. See Jonathan D. Spence and John E. Wills, *From Ming to Ch'ing: Conquest, Region, and Continuity in Seventeenth-Century China* (New Haven: Yale University Press, 1979), 79.

12 Braudel, *Civilization and Capitalism*, 109–10.
13 As stated in the Introduction chapter, I take Xizhou Sheng as a "thorough Ming author" on the ground of the absence of even the slightest hint of the Ming-Qing transition; the absence of the imported crops further supports my assumption.
14 Ling Cao, "Influence of the Introduction of American Cereal Crops on Agricultural Production and Social Economy of China," *Ancient and Modern Agriculture*, no. 3 (2005): 79–88. 曹玲：《美洲粮食作物的传入对我国农业生产和社会经济的影响》，《古今农业》，2005年第3期，第79–88页。
15 Simoons, *Food in China*, 102.
16 Shih Hu, *Collected Works of Shih Hu*, vol. 18 (Hefei: Anhui Educational Publishing House, 2003), 35. 胡适：《胡适全集第18卷》，合肥：安徽教育出版社，2003年，第35页。
17 Yiling Fu, "My Re-conception of Wage Labour After the Mid-Ming Dynasty," in *Collected Papers on the Economic History of China*, ed. Research Office of Chinese Economic History, Institute of History, Xiamen University (Fuzhou: Fujian People's Publishing House, 1981), 278. 傅衣凌：《我对于明代中叶以后雇佣劳动的再认识》，见厦门大学历史研究所中国经济史研究室编著：《中国经济史论文集》，福州：福建人民出版社，1981年，第278页。
18 Fei Han, *Han Fei Zi*, annotated and trans. Huaping Gao, Qizhou Wang, and Sanxi Zhang (Beijing: Zhonghua Book Company, 2010), 466. 韩非著，高华平、王齐州、张三夕译注：《韩非子》，北京：中华书局，2010年，第466页。
19 Xuewen Chen, "Selections from the Textual Research and Interpretation of Contractual Instruments of the Ming Dynasty," in *Ming History Series*, ed. Chunyu Wang (Beijing: China Social Sciences Press, 1997), 219. 陈学文：《明代契约文书考释选辑》，见王春瑜编著：《明史论丛》，北京：中国社会科学出版社，1997年，第219页。
20 Harriet T. Zurndorfer, *Change and Continuity in Chinese Local History: The Development of Hui-Chou Prefecture, 800 to 1800* (Leiden and New York: E. J. Brill, 1989), 118.
21 Keiji Adachi, "Min-Shin Jidai No Sho Keiei to Jinushisei Ni Kansuru Oboegaki," *Atarashii Rekishigaku no tame ni* 143 (1976): 10–18. 足立啓二：《明清時代の小経営と地主制に関する覚書》，《新しい歴史学のために》，1976年第143卷，第10–18页。
22 Zhi Ning, "Research on Xingshi Yinyuan," *Oliver Tree Literature Society* 57, no. 11 (1999). 宁致：《初谈醒世姻缘》，《橄榄树文学月刊》，1999年第57卷第11期。
23 Zurndorfer, *Change and Continuity in Chinese Local History*, 118.
24 Salt was not the only monopolized commodity. Other monopoly goods included wine, yeast, vinegar, tea, incense, alum, cinnabar, tin, and iron. John King Fairbank and Denis Crispin Twitchett, *The Cambridge History of China*, vol. 6, *Alien Regimes and Border States, 907–1368* (Cambridge and New York: Cambridge University Press, 1994), 294.
25 Fairbank and Twitchett, *Alien Regimes*, 294.
26 Ibid.
27 Madeleine Zelin, *The Merchants of Zigong: Industrial Entrepreneurship in Early Modern China* (New York: Columbia University Press, 2005).
28 "The Veritable Records of Emperor Taizu," in *MSL*, ed. [Ming] Zhang Juzheng (Taipei: Academia Sinica, Institute of History and Philology, 1963), 111–12. 《明实录·太祖实录》卷九《辛丑春正月甲申》，台北：中国台湾"中央研究院"历史语言研究所，1963年，第111–12页。
29 Fangzhong Liang, *Supplement on A Collection of Essays on the Economic History of Liang Fangzhong* (Zhengzhou: Zhongzhou Ancient Books Publishing House, 1984), 109. 梁方仲：《梁方仲经济史论文集补编》，郑州：中州古籍出版社，1984年，第109页。
30 Yonglin Jiang, trans. and intro., *The Great Ming Code: Da Ming Lü* (Seattle: University of Washington Press, 2005), 100.
31 Yuquan Wang, ed., *General History of Chinese Economy: Economy of Ming Dynasty* (Beijing: Economic Daily, 2000), 1008–9. 王毓铨主编：《中国经济通史：明代经济卷》，北京：经济日报出版社，2000年，第1008–9页。

32 Jiang, *The Great Ming Code*, 100–49.
33 Jiaguo Zhang, Yaode Yin, and Hongwei Li, "A Pilot Analysis of the Changing Trajectory of Salt Law in the Ming Dynasty," *Law Review*, no. 5 (1997): 69–75. 张家国，殷耀德，李红卫：《试析明代盐法变迁之轨迹》，《法学评论》，1997年第5期，第69–75页。
34 [Japan] Nakayama Hachiro, "Kai Zhong Law and Zhanwo," in *Dr. Hiroshi Ikenouchi Memorial Lecture on the Oriental History* (Tokyo: Zoupo Publishing Company, 1940); [Japan] Fujii Hiroshi, "The Meaning of Kaizhong and Its Origins," in *A Collection of Translations of Studies on the Social and Economic History of Huizhou*, ed. Miao Liu, trans. Miao Liu (Hefei: Huangshan Publishing House, 1988). [日]中山八郎：《开中法与占窝》，《池内宏博士换历纪念东洋史讲座》，东京：座右宝刊刊行社，1940年；[日]藤井宏：《开中的意义及其起源》，刘淼译，收录于刘淼编，《徽州社会经济史研究译文集》，合肥：黄山书社，1988年。
35 Fairbank and Twitchett, *Alien Regimes*, 2.
36 Ray Huang, *Taxation and Governmental Finance in Sixteenth-Century Ming China* (Beijing: SDX Joint Publishing Company, 2001), 190.
37 Ibid., 198.
38 Zhuo Zhang, *The Records About the Government and Society*, proofread by Runhua Hao and Qiong Mo, vol. 2 (Jinan: Shandong People's Publishing House, 2018), 43. 张鷟著，郝润华、莫琼辑校：《朝野佥载辑校》卷二，济南：山东人民出版社，2018年，第43页。
39 [Ming] Shizhen Li, "Animals, Part 3," in *A Detailed Translation of Compendium of Materia Medica (Second)*, ed. Chaochen Qian and Lianrong Dong, vol. 51 (Taiyuan: Shanxi Science and Technology Publishing House, 1999), 2149. [明]李时珍著，钱超尘、董连荣编：《<本草纲目>详译 [下册]》卷五十一《兽部兽之三》，太原：山西科学技术出版社，1999年，第2149页。
40 [Song] Shih Su, "Hearing That Ziyu Gets Thin," in *Notes on the Collection of Poems by Su Shih*, annotated and proofread by Huaichun Zhu, vol. 41 (Shanghai: Shanghai Classics Publishing House, 2001), 2123. [宋]苏轼：《苏轼诗集合注》卷四十一《闻子由瘦》，朱怀春校注，上海：上海古籍出版社，2001年，第2123页。
41 Ibid., vol. 39, "Welcome Cousin Zhengfu with a Poem," 2009. 同上，《卷三十九，闻正辅表兄将至以诗迎之》，第2009页。
42 Qinghe Wang, "Famous Local Food in Classical Novels," *Mei Wen*, no. 12 (2012): 88–96. 王清和：《古典小说里的地方名吃》，《美文》，2012年第12期，第88–96页。
43 Li, vol. 42, "Insects, Part 4," 1801–02. [明]李时珍：《<本草纲目>详译 [上册]》卷四十二《虫部虫之四》，第1801–02页。
44 [Song] Fang Li, ed., "Bamboo Liu," in *Records of the Taiping Era*, vol. 163 (Beijing: Zhonghua Book Company, 1961), 1187. [宋]李昉编纂：《太平广记》卷一百六十三《竹䍦》，北京：中华书局，1961年，第1187页。
45 Saishi Wang, *Cuisine in the Tang Dynasty* (Jinan: Qilu Press, 2003), 69–70. 王赛时：《唐代饮食》，济南：齐鲁书社，2003年，第69–70页。
46 [Song] Mengde Ye, "Shilin Poetry Critique," in *Poetry Critique Through the Ages*, ed. [Qing] Wenhuan He (Beijing: Zhonghua Book Company, 1981), 404. [宋]叶梦得：《石林诗话》，收录于[清]何文焕编，《历代诗话》，北京：中华书局，1981年，第404页。
47 [Song] Chengxun Zhou, "Eating Globefish," in *Gleanings from Small Collections of Former Sages*, ed. Qi Chen, vol. 1, 3. [宋]周承勋：《食河豚》，见陈起编著：《前贤小集拾遗》卷一，第3页。
48 Li, vol. 51, "Insects, Part 2," 2156. [明]李时珍：《<本草纲目>详译 [下册]》卷五十一《兽部兽之二》，第2156页。
49 [Ming] Qian Yu, *Selected Poems of Yu Qian*, annotated and proofread by Han Lin (Hangzhou: Zhejiang People's Publishing House, 1982), 67–68. 于谦著，林寒校注：《于谦诗选》，杭州：浙江人民出版社，1982年，第67–68页。

50 [Qing] Yu Li, "Foods and Drinks, Meat III," in *Occasional Notes with Leisure Motions*, trans. Shulin Li (Chongqing: Chongqing Publishing House, 2008), 383. [清]李渔：《闲情偶寄·饮馔部·肉食第三》，李树林译，重庆：重庆出版社，2008年，第383页。

51 [Qing] Wenjing Tian, *Political Activities During My Tenure as Governor of Xuanhua, Henan* (Zhengzhou: Zhongzhou Ancient Books Publishing House, 1995), 99. [清]田文镜：《抚豫宣化录》，郑州：中州古籍出版社，1995年，第99页。

52 Zongdian Min, "Historic Chinese Chicken," in *Studies in Agricultural History [7th Series]*, ed. Agricultural Historical Heritage Research Office of South China Agricultural University (Beijing: China Agriculture Press, 1988), 131. 闵宗殿：《中国历史名鸡》，见华南农业大学农业历史遗产研究室编著：《农史研究[第七辑]》，北京：农业出版社，1988年，第131页。

53 [Qing] Chengdong Mei, *Collected Poems of Tianjin*, annotated and proofread by Senghui Bian and Wenqi Pu (Tianjin: Tianjin Classics Publishing House, 1993), 986. [清]梅成栋著，卞僧慧、濮文起校注：《津门诗钞》，天津：天津古籍出版社，1993年，第986页。

54 Lin Yang, "Tianjin Folklore," in *Knowledge of Chinese Folklore*, ed. Gansu Ancient Books and Documents Sorting and Compiling Center (Lanzhou: Gansu People's Publishing House, 2008), 75. 杨琳：《天津民俗》，见甘肃省古籍文献整理编纂中心编著：《中国民俗知识》，兰州：甘肃人民出版社，2008年，第75页。

55 Peng Zhou, Yi Zhong, and Yue Wu, *Jiangsu Specialties* (Nanjing: Phoenix Science Press, 1982), 51–53. 周彭、钟益、吴越：《江苏特产》，南京：江苏科学技术出版社，1982年，第51–53页。

56 [Tang] Xun Liu, *Records of Unusual Things in Lingbiao*, proofread by Xun Lu (Guangzhou: Guangdong People's Publishing House, 1983), 10. [唐]刘恂著，鲁迅校勘：《岭表录异》，广州：广东人民出版社，1983年，第10页。

57 [Tang] Gonglu Duan, "The Beihu Record, vol. 2," in *Books Series in the Hundred-Thousand-Volume Building*, ed. Xinyuan Lu (edition of the 6th year of Guangxu reign), 8. [唐]段公路：《北户录》卷二，收录于陆心源编，《十万卷楼丛书》光绪六年版，第8页。

58 Li, "Scaly Animals, Part 4," vol. 44 (1884). [明]李时珍：《<本草纲目>详译 [下册]》卷四十四《鳞部鳞之四》，第1884页。

59 [Italy] Marco Polo, *The Travels of Marco Polo*, trans. Chengjun Feng (Shanghai: Shanghai Bookstore Publishing House, 2006), 342–43. [意]马可波罗：《马可波罗行纪》，冯承钧译，上海：上海书店出版社，2006年，第342–43页。

60 Ting Wang and Guangyan Qu, "The Roar of the Beasts in Lulin—the Lion as a 'Contribution' to the Encounter Between Cilicia and Ming," *Journal of Northwestern Ethnic Studies*, no. 1 (2004): 136–47. 王颋、屈广燕：《芦林兽吼—以狮子为"贡献"之中西亚与明的交往》，《西北民族研究》，2004年第1期，第136–47页。

61 Cheng Chen, *Chen Cheng's Notes on the Western Region*, annotated and proofread by Jiguang Wang (Wulumuqi: Xinjiang People's Publishing House, 2012), 20–22. 陈诚著，王继光校注：《陈诚西域资料校注》，乌鲁木齐：新疆人民出版社，2012年，第20–22页。

62 [Ming] Anonymous, *Criticism at Taowu*, proofread by Hong Li (Xi'an: Taibai Literature and Art Publishing House, 2000), 267–68. [明]无名氏著，李虹校点：《梼杌闲评》，西安：太白文艺出版社，2000年，第267–68页。

63 Baoliang Chen, *The Urban Life of the Ming Dynasty* (Changsha: Hunan Publishing House, 1996), 69–71. 陈宝良：《飘摇的传统：明代城市生活长卷》，长沙：湖南出版社，1996年，第69–71页。

64 Dai Zhang, "Local Product," in *A Collection of Essays of Zhang Dai: Reminiscences in Dreams of Tao An*, annotated and proofread by Xianchun Xia and Weirong Cheng, vol. 4 (Shanghai: Shanghai Classics Publishing House, 2001), 71–72. 张岱著，夏咸淳、程维荣校注：《陶庵梦忆；西湖梦寻》卷四《方物》，上海：上海古籍出版社，2001年，第71–72页。

65 Hsiao-hsiao-sheng, *The Plum in the Golden Vase or, Chin P'ing Mei*, vol. 4, *The Climax* (Princeton: Princeton University Press, 2011), 104–9.
66 Yasushi Ōki, "Textbooks on an Aesthetic Life in late Ming China," in *Quest for Gentility in China: Negotiations Beyond Gender and Class*, ed. Daria Berg and Chloe Starr (Hoboken: Taylor & Francis, 2007), 179–87.
67 Ibid., 186.
68 [Qing] Tingyu Zhang, "Records of Vehicle and Costume IV," in *The History of the Ming Dynasty*, vol. 68 (Beijing: Zhonghua Book Company, 1672). [清]张廷玉编纂：《明史》卷六十八《舆服四》，第1672页。
69 Ibid.
70 [Ming] Dongyang Li, [Ming] Shixing Shen, and [Ming] Yongxian Zhao, "Codes of Great Ming Dynasty [Photocopied Imperial Printed Version in Wanli Reign of the Ming Dynasty], History, Political Regulations, vol. 62, Housing and Equipment," in *Renewed Complete Library of the Four Treasuries* (Shanghai: Shanghai Classics Publishing House, 2002). [明]李东阳，[明]申时行，[明]赵用贤：《大明会典·史部·政书类[影印明万历内府刻本]》卷六十二《房屋器用等第》，《续修四库全书》，上海：上海古籍出版社，2002年。
71 Yenna Wu, "From History to Allegory: Surviving Famine in Xingshi Yinyuan Zhuan," *Chinese Culture (Taipei)* 38, no. 4 (1997): 91.
72 Marco Polo, *The Travels of Marco Polo* (Harmondsworth, Middlesex: Penguin Books, 1958), 158.
73 Chen, *The Urban Life of the Ming Dynasty*, 60. 陈宝良：《飘摇的传统：明代城市生活长卷》，第60页。
74 Mote, *Imperial China*, 634.
75 Chen, *The Urban Life of the Ming Dynasty*, 61. 陈宝良：《飘摇的传统：明代城市生活长卷》，第61页。
76 [Qing] Qian Wu, *Poetry Critique of Baijinglou*, vol. 4 (Shanghai: Shanghai Boguzhai, 1922). [清]吴骞：《拜经楼诗话》卷四，《拜经楼丛书三十种》，上海：上海博古斋，1922年。
77 [Ming] Dongyang Li, [Ming] Shixing Shen, and [Ming] Yongxian Zhao, "Feasts I, The Emperor Attended a Banquet at the Imperial Academy," in *Codes of the Great Ming Dynasty*, vol. 114 (Shanghai: Shanghai Classics Publishing House, 2002), 1083. [明]李东阳，[明]申时行，[明]赵用贤：《大明会典[影印明万历内府刻本]》卷一百十四《膳羞一·驾兴太学筵宴》，第1083页。
78 Ibid., Special Imperial Banquets Given by the Emperor in Honor of New *Jinshi*, 1083. 同上，卷一百十四《膳羞一·进士恩荣宴》，第1083页。
79 [Ming] Qian Tan, "The 18th Year of Hongzhi Reign of Emperor Hongzhi," in *National Debates*, annotated and proofread by Zongxiang Zhang, vol. 45 (Beijing: Zhonghua Book Company, 1958), 2832. [明]谈迁著，张宗祥校注：《国榷》卷四十五《孝宗弘治十八年》，北京：中华书局，1958年，第2832页。
80 [Qing] Guofan Zeng, "Collected Works of Zeng Wenzheng Gong, vol. 4," in *Collected Works of Zeng Wenzheng Gong Engraved by Chuanzhong Shuju* (the 13rd year of Tongzhi reign), 661. [清]曾国藩：《曾文正公文集》卷四，《传忠书局刻本曾文正公全集》（同治十三年），第661页。
81 [Qing] Jizuo Zha, "The Chronicles of Emperor Xiaozong," in *A Convict's Compilation of History, Chronicles of Emperors*, vol. 10 (Hangzhou: Zhejiang Classics Publishing House, 1986), 181. [清]查继佐：《罪惟录（第一册）》帝纪卷之十《孝宗纪》，杭州：浙江古籍出版社，1986年，第181页。
82 [Ming] Hong Jiao, "Yutang Series, Vol. 8, Pride and Extravagance," in *Yuan and Ming Historical Notes Series* (Beijing: Zhonghua Book Company, 1981), 276. [明]焦竑：《玉堂丛语》卷八《汰侈》，《元明史料笔记丛刊》，北京：中华书局，1981年，第276页。

83 [Yuan] Anonymous, "Complete Collection of Essential Things at Home—G. Food and Drink," in *Ancient Chinese Culinary Books Series*, annotated by Pangtong Qiu (Beijing: China Commercial Publishing House, 1986), 100. [元]无名氏，邱庞同（注）：《居家必用事类全集·庚集饮食类》，《中国烹饪古籍丛刊》，北京：中国商业出版社，1986年，第100页。
84 [Ming] Huang, "Brief Introduction of Meat in Imperial Diet of the State," in *Records of Things*, vol. 14, 21. [明]黄一正：《事物绀珠》卷十四《国朝御膳肉食略》，第21页。
85 [Ming] Shunxi Chen, "Anecdotes from the Political Turmoil, vol. 1," in *The Third Series of the Ming History Sourcebook*, ed. Research Office of Ming History, Institute for Ancient History of China, Chinese Academy of Social Sciences (Nanjing: Jiangsu People's Publishing House, 1983), 232. [明]陈舜系：《乱离见闻录[卷上]》，见中国社会科学院历史研究所明史室编：《明史资料丛刊第三辑》，南京：江苏人民出版社，1983年，第232页。
86 [Ming] Bang Shen, *Miscellaneous Records of Wanping* (Beijing: Beijing Classics Publishing House, 1983), 3–4. [明]沈榜：《宛署杂记》，北京：北京古籍出版社，1983年，第3–4页。
87 Bo Zhang, "A Study of New Year's Folklore in Miscellaneous Records of Wanping," in *Festive Studies [2nd Series]*, ed. Song Li and Shishan Zhang (Jinan: Shandong University Press, 2010), 129–30. 张勃：《<宛署杂记>中的岁时民俗记述研究》，见李松、张士闪编著：《节日研究[第2辑]》，济南：山东大学出版社，2010年，第129–30页。
88 Shen, *Miscellaneous Records of Wanping*, 1. [明]沈榜：《宛署杂记》，第1页。
89 Ibid., 122. 同上，第122页。

4 Traveling Cultures of the Ming

1. Women and Traveling: When Bound Feet Venture Out of the Confined Domain

1) Guixiu, Cloistering, and Travel

Thanks to the recent studies of Timothy Brook, Susan Naquin, and Chun-fang Yu,[1] we now know that by the sixteenth century, leisure travel had become a culturally sanctioned activity for China's educated elite. Two of Yu's important works, *The Renewal of Buddhism in China*[2] and *In search of the Dharma*,[3] examine how the renewed zeal for Buddhist pursuits had led to a boom in travel-intensive pilgrimages to sacred mountains during the late Imperial era. Her work *Kuan-yin, the Chinese Transformation of Avalokitesvara*,[4] addresses the issue of the domestication process of the foreign, male bodhisattva and why the transgendered feminine Guanyin was able to wield such a great influence on the spiritual world of traditional women.

Culturally prestigious female elite, *guixiu*, as a cluster of works by Dorothy Ko, Susan Mann, Daria Berg, and Chloe Starr[5] has demonstrated, also eagerly espoused the newfound pleasure of tourism. Susan Mann's study on the relationship of Chinese women and travel gives valuable insights into the nature of the late Imperial traveling *guixiu*, who, much like the Victorian English "adventuresses," also sought out travel for "the freedom both to contrast an identity and to embrace anonymity, to scrutinize and to retreat from self."[6]

Susan Mann, in her study of the traveling patterns of late imperial Chinese women, divides women tourists into the following categories:

a) Ladylike visits by the leisure-minded *guixiu* in joining their *guixiu* friends in poetry clubs or casual tea parties;
b) Religious quests or spiritual development;
c) Married women traveling back to their natal families, or *guining* 归宁, usually accompanied by husbands or sons;
d) Married women accompanying their husbands to their new posts;
e) Bereaved wives taking back their deceased husbands' coffins to bury in their ancestral homes.[7]

DOI: 10.4324/9781003406143-5

Until now, very few scholarly works have touched on women's travel as a means of "religious quest or spiritual development." Nevertheless, with sufficient awareness that "in the Confucian value system of late imperial China, travel was a man's world," Mann also points out the de facto invasion of this world by elite women.[8] Her work emphasizes the last category, using the diary of a Qing *guixiu* Zhang Wanying 张婉英 to analyze women's own feelings about traveling. The diary, on Zhang's trip to Taicang 太仓 to bury her late husband, presents an image of a woman who, even in bereavement, radiates the high culture of her breeding as a fine daughter, wife, and mother.

Like most pre-modern societies, traditional China desired women to commit themselves to what Bray calls "demure behavior."[9] The female talents, usually of high birth, must curtail any showing of strong affection or emotion, whether in life or writing. Yet there are more expectations for women in traditional Chinese aesthetics. When it comes to a traveling theme, ennui and nostalgia, two prominent sentiments approbated by the tradition of Chinese Poetics, usually occupy women writers. The plethora of self-portrayed images of exquisite, unhappy beauties significantly undermines the value of the *guixiu* tourist literature, leading one to wonder if a genuine woman who enjoyed the pleasure of tourism ever existed. Given this premise, researchers and readers often hope to unearth material that reflects the joy of women's travel, even if the traveler does not come from a noble and educated background.

Travel is an immense topic in *XSYYZ*, yet barely any depicted trips fall into the two previously mentioned categories. In the Novel, male protagonists travel for various reasons, but primarily for job relocation; female protagonists travel with their husbands to go to designated office posts or, accompanied by family and servants, set out for family reunions. Those journeys, driven by practical needs, can hardly be deemed leisure-oriented. Only Sujie, the rebellious heroine who has absolute authority over her husband, has exercised her self-determination in choosing where she wants to go and with whom she would like to travel. Given the sturdiness of her personality and the obedience of her husband, she is probably the most disengaged housewife among her fictional peers in Ming-Qing literature. Therefore, only this trip, the Mount Tai pilgrimage, boasts some tinge of free-willed tourism.

Yet Sujie should not be treated as another *guixiu* adventuress who takes sojourning at scenic spots as part of self-cultivation. Although she is born and raised in, and later married into, a wealthy family, her upbringing and education are not akin to those of the topmost educated elite women.

Sujie's father is an old tribute student who has served as an instructor of Confucianism at various levels, including *xundao* 训导, *jiaoyu* 教谕, *jiaoshou* 教授, and *jishan* 纪善 in several counties in Henan and Shandong for many years. With some accumulated savings, he settles in Mingshui, Shandong, and opens a cloth store to make a living. At 52, he has no choice but to take a concubine, Nee Long, to have an heir, as his wife has not had any children. Sujie, as the eldest and only daughter of the concubine, has three younger brothers and thus is in both a unique and awkward position in the family. Being the first daughter of a long-time childless family, she is undoubtedly valued by her father, birth mother, and her legal mother, Lady Xue, who has truly loved her. The night before her wedding, Sujie has a nightmare of her heart being replaced:

> The family has not yet gone to bed and are all busy when they see Sujie screaming out loud from her sleep. Lady Xue is so frightened that she runs in quickly. Sujie jumps up and burrows into her mother's arms, saying, "I'm scared to death!" She keeps crying strangely. Lady Xue says, "My dear, what's wrong with you? You are dreaming. Wake up, and you will be fine." She cannot speak for quite a while after waking up.
>
> (44.340)

Sujie's embarrassment is caused by her birth mother, who has neither status nor ability. Old Xue has a good relationship with his wife, Lady Xue; the two share the same old-fashioned moral values. For Old Xue, taking the concubine Nee Long is just a kind of surrogacy. Nee Long, simply a tool of fertility, has given birth to one daughter and three sons for the Xue family, but spends her days working with the cooks and her status is no better than that of an ordinary servant. Old Xue hits and kicks Nee Long several times over how to discipline Sujie. If Sujie were the only child in the family, she might have been able to read and write, but with three younger brothers, she is destined to be deprived of an education. As for the sons, Old Xue only pays for the training of his eldest and second eldest sons to gain the status of *xiucai*, but does not provide a decent education for his youngest son for the sake of economy and practicality. In this way, although she is born into a Confucian family, Sujie grows up to be a woman who cannot read a single word. Her looks are undoubtedly attractive, but her upbringing is somewhat course due to her birth mother's vulgarity; the ideas of being a good daughter-in-law that Old Xue and Lady Xue have attempted to instill in her are simply disregarded by Sujie, and it is the restraints that her parents place on her freedom that she detests most. Her two *xiucai* younger brothers, who are no different from Old Xue, try desperately to discourage Sujie from traveling or going out whenever she wants the slightest right to do so. Failing to prevent her, they show moral contempt. Nevertheless, Sujie's freedom of movement increases considerably after the death of her father and legal mother. The two *xiucai* younger brothers are still often cynical, but thanks to the fact that she is the eldest sister, they cannot overly discipline her according to the order of precedence. The youngest brother, Xue Zaidong, is closer to her, but as a man without an education or rank, he is oppressed at every turn by the two *xiucai* brothers.

Sujie has only one firm ally in her natal home, her birth mother, Nee Long. Unfortunately, in her lowly position, Nee Long must take orders from her husband, then from the hostess when her husband dies, and finally from her sons when the hostess dies. On one occasion, she cries after being reprimanded by her eldest son:

> Oh my God! Why can't I have a trace of dignity? When I had a husband, he oversaw me. When he died, his first wife watched me so closely. At last, after

the death of his first wife, I am in the hands of my sons, and I am not granted a shred of freedom! Oh, my God!

(68.527)

When Sujie quarrels with her in-laws due to her obsession with travel, or when she is insulted by rogue bachelors, and even when she loses her way on a trip, her brothers seldom care about her. Except once, when Sujie learns that Di Xichen has taken a concubine who has given birth to a son, and that the new family has left for Chengdu, she is so furious that she lodges a false accusation against her husband, saying he is a rebel. The local magistrate then accuses her of being unruly, punishing her corporally. Her youngest brother, Zaidong, follows her to the county *yamen* but is also beaten with wooden staves and shackled. With a sister and a brother in prison, the two *xiucai*, Xue Rujian and Xue Rubian, have no choice but to go to the magistrate to plead for mercy. As mentioned in the previous chapter, in the Ming and Qing dynasties, *shengyuan* with the lowest academic rank were exempted from corporal punishment if they went to court for litigation, but this did not mean they were free to enter and leave the court and interfere with a lawsuit. To qualify, the default requirement was that one must at least hold a *juren* degree. Philip Kuhn mentions "a privilege (for those with high academic degrees) of visiting the local magistrate on terms of social equality" and a long list of other benefits such as "virtual exemption from corporal punishment, exemption from labor service." Precisely because the degree is "the surest road to fame and fortune," the lower strata of the scholar-gentry "committed themselves to the constant grind of the examination system."[10]

The magistrate eventually releases Sujie and Zaidong for the sake of the two *xiucai*, but he scolds them before the release:

As *xiucai* and local scholars, managing the household is your primary duty. How can you allow them to act so boldly and not even try to persuade her? As for Sujie, you can still say she is your elder sister and is already married. As for Xue Zaidong, he is your youngest brother and could have been controlled, so how can you let him act so recklessly?

(89.686)

The magistrate stresses that the Xue brothers should discipline their youngest brother, Xue Zaidong, but he acknowledges the right of the eldest sister, who is already married, to be free from her brothers' restraints. In short, although Sujie's family background has elements of Confucianism, she does not personally possess the typical qualities of "Ming and Qing *Guixiu*."

She belongs to a less-known, less-studied group, largely comprised of undereducated or illiterate womenfolk. Due to their relative wealth and not needing to attend to crops or household affairs, they tended to show a passion for participating in social activities outside the boudoir. They were often seen joining religious associations, making charitable donations, going out to incense-related activities, partaking in managerial work, and so forth. They also quested for independence and self-identification through traveling but were not adequately recorded, for they lacked literary resources to represent or to be represented. Having left hardly any literary legacy behind, as the *guixiu* had done through their diaries and travelogues, they were even less remembered than the witty courtesans.

As a group of writers, not only did Ming and Qing *Guixiu* leave behind a large number of diaries, poems, and travelogues, but their male literati contemporaries also recorded their existence. Male literati were most delighted in compiling anthologies or writing prefaces and postscripts for the *guixiu*. Should talented women die tragically early, they would be most heartsick and would indeed pen down passionate memoirs and eulogies. Yuan Mei 袁枚, an elegant man of letters, left many romantic anecdotes of accepting *guixiu* disciples. In this way, Ming and Qing *Guixiu* gained their "immortal" position in history. According to Susan Mann's statistics, based on Hu Wenkai's 胡文楷 *Textual Research on Women's Works of Past Dynasties*, there were 3,684 women writers in the Qing dynasty, of whom 3,181 are traceable to their place of origin, far exceeding the scale of the previous dynasties. More than 70 percent of them were from the lower reaches of the Yangtze River, and the prefectures of Suzhou, Songjiang, Changzhou, Hangzhou, Jiaxing, Huzhou, and the surrounding areas were home to many talented women.[11]

Similar to Ming-Qing *Guixiu* was the group of Ming-Qing Courtesans, represented by the constellation of the Eight Beauties of Qinhuai 秦淮八大名妓. They frequently appeared in the anecdotal essays penned by foremost Ming-Qing literati, their travels having enlivened the *jiangnan* porno-literary culture. Relevant works include memoirs of the sentimental love life like Mao Pijiang's *Memories of Yingmei An*, responsories like that of Liu Rushi with Chen Zilong and Qian Qianyi, poems in the old style like that of Wu Meicun 吴梅村 for Chen Yuanyuan 陈圆圆, and the romantic-political entanglements between famous prostitutes and Donglin scholars are reflected in dramas by Kong Shangren 孔尚任. In the late Qing dynasty, the relevance of the life of prostitutes to the political dynamics of the state faded away. Still, mature prose and novels on prostitute life, as a literary genre, continued to emerge, some of which achieved considerable success, such as *Records of Winds and Rains in Qingxi* (Qingxi Fengyu Lu 青溪风雨录) by Xueqiao Jushi 雪樵居士 and *Flowers on the Sea* (Hai Shang Hua 海上花) written in pure Wu dialect by Han Bangqing 韩邦庆 (Hua Ye Lian Nong 花也怜侬).

Until the 1980s, Western Sinological studies of traditional Chinese women, especially aristocratic women, emphasized the cloistered nature of their living spaces. In recent years, Dorothy Ko, Ellen Widmer 魏爱莲, Kang-i Sun Chang 孙康宜, Maureen Robertson 茂林·罗伯森, Paul Ropp 罗溥洛, and Grace Fong 方秀洁, among others, have demonstrated in many studies that since the late Ming dynasty, the activities of Ming and Qing *Guixiu* broke far beyond the physical confines of Confucian norms of etiquette.[12] In regions south of the Yangtze, the "hotbeds of humanities" 人文渊薮, it was seen as an attitude of elegance and a privilege that the rich and powerful should manage to have their wives and daughters to go out of their boudoirs, composing poetry, scenic sightseeing spots, and making friends with peers.[13] The flourishing high culture in the Yangtze and the networks formed by intermarriages among aristocratic families made it impossible for talented women to remain anonymous. With very few exceptions, such as He Shuangqing 贺双卿, elite literary women generally came from families of great learning, and they were sure to have a father, brother, or uncle who was a famous literatus and who would praise them for their literary work. Moreover, such families often produced talented women in bunches, so their poems were frequently read and replied to by their mothers, sisters, and aunts, who were equally gifted. This phenomenon was most representative in the family of Ye Xiaoluan 叶小鸾 of the late Ming dynasty.

Ming-Qing talented women fascinated researchers, contemporary and present. For example, He Shuangqing, held in esteem as the "Li Qingzhao of the Qing" in later times, became known because of Shi Zhenlin 史震林, a Qing scholar who rendered her life and recorded her writings in his *Notes in Xiqing* (Xiqing Sanji 西青散记). He Shuangqing has also attracted the attention of some modern scholars, such as Xu Zhimo, Shu Wu, and Yu Dafu. American Sinologist Paul Ropp penned a monograph for her, *Banished Immortal: Searching for Shuangqing, China's Peasant Woman Poet*.[14] In a rather humorous tone, Paul Ropp laughs at himself, saying that his role is "a literary man of the last days, following the example of Shi Zhenlin and his literary friends, diligently searching through the piles of old papers of the eighteenth century, only to be fascinated by the beautiful peasant woman poet." Ropp also writes that people often tease him, saying, "Professor Ropp, you are the American version of Shi Zhenlin!"[15]

However, we must acknowledge that non-*guixiu* women in traditional China have been seriously under-researched. A stereotyped view of them is that constrained by rituals and customs, non-*guixiu* women only lived a sedate and cloistered domestic life.

We should not be deluded by this stereotypical assumption that all non-*guixiu* women were sedated and cloistered. Since *guixiu* was a small, prestigious clique, and their traveling a rare, restricted circumstance, a researcher might want to probe into the world of the underrepresented, understudied womenfolk, which preponderated *guixiu* in population.

In the uneventful and prosperous years of the late empire, among the non-*guixiu* women, we believe that there was a group of affluent but illiterate urban and rural women whom we might call "Affluent Womenfolk Urban and Rural." Of course, peasant women, female servants, and women from impoverished urban families who worked all day to live from hand to mouth did not belong to this group. Affluent Womenfolk Urban and Rural were mainstay consumers of narrative Buddhist sutras and narrative literature, foremost purchasers of all the novel and expensive items of material life of the time, and leading participants in urban and rural festivals and religious events.

Taiwanese scholar Wu Jen-shu, in his research on women's consumption culture during the Ming-Qing period, not only surveys an overall picture of luxury consumption, but also devotes an entire chapter to discussing the luxury consumption of commoner women and another chapter to discussing that of prostitutes, aided by another chapter on critical male perspectives. Wu asserts that women's luxury consumption in clothing, food, and travel was of great importance to the development of the Ming-Qing economy and therefore awaits further studies.[16]

If the *guixiu* are likened to the elite petty bourgeoisie of modern society who culturally led the way, the Affluent Womenfolk Urban and Rural were the me-too petty bourgeoisie with considerable purchasing power; they desired to consume but lacked originality. It is reasonable to deduce that these women would have had a strong desire to participate in secular life and enjoy material pleasures. Since they were not burdened with making a living, they would have had plenty of time and energy to spend outside their homes. Their desire to break free from social and family constraints and to go out into the outer world was also bound to be strong. Their status within their marriages and families dictates their economic and social status and, ultimately, the latitude of freedom they could enjoy. Even Sujie, aggressive and bellicose, can only gain the right to travel after fighting hard for it again and again.

It stands to reason that these women must have been extroverted, vibrant, and even belligerent to breach the social and familial confinements imposed upon them. But how exactly did they fight for the right to travel? Under what pretext would they have been allowed to depart from domesticity? In what religious form did they appeal to as a congregation? How did they raise money to sponsor their planned trips? In addition, when they did travel, who was to accompany them and what measures were taken to ensure the desired gender segregation? The study of Sujie's travel to Mount Tai provides a feasible approach to these questions. I propose that by tracing the tracks of Sujie's bound feet, one not only delves into the landscape of the late imperial tourism—scenic spots, Buddhist temples, and magnificent mountains—but also into the dynamics that made such extraordinary tourism possible.

2) Footbinding and Travel

Despite being a "Roaring Lioness of the East of the River" 河东狮, Sujie nonetheless boasts a pretty face and a pair of delicate "golden lotus." Back on their wedding night, the author compliments her appearance:

> She has two curved willow brows and a pair of gleaming almond eyes, with a medium height and a perfect figure. Under her colored robe, a hibiscus rises in mist; by her embroidered skirt, two lotus petals appear on the ground. If she does not reveal her majestic presence, she would be comparable to the Ming Consort of Luopu; if hiding her heroic spirit, she would be praised as a lady by the river.
>
> (44.341)

She is married to Xichen at 16 and, having gained dominance over her husband and in-laws, fights her way through to secure the privilege to attend local religious festivals or sojourn to her natal family of her free will. By chapter 68, when the Mount Tai pilgrimage is proposed, she is over 20, her mother-in-law is dead, and the voices of her husband and father-in-law, which represent patriarchal authority, are half-muzzled.

Had the pair of Sujie's bound feet, the symbol of good birth and an icon of women's physical shackles, impeded her traveling capability? In the view of Juan Gonzalez de Mendoza, who has never set foot in China, they naturally were. The Spanish Sinologist suggests that Chinese women were always kept at home due to "the lameness of their feet," for "their going is very ill, and with great travail."[17]

Many contemporary scholars also hold the "theory of painful footbinding." For example, in his famous paper *The Seeds of Change: Reflections on the Condition of Women in the Early and Mid Ch'ing*, published in the mid-1970s, Paul Ropp argues that "footbinding was the most painful symbol of women's humble subordination to male sexual interests."[18]

This view, aligned with the general perception of footbinding, has been seriously challenged by a small group of feminist Ming-Qing historians in recent years. Dorothy Ko, for one, identifies footbinding not as a measure of heightened oppression towards women but as a symbol of "cultural prestige and erotic appeal"[19] when it reached its historical climax, the High Qing. That is, after the Manchus conquered the Ming and established a new dynasty, footbinding had become a need to reemphasize the difference between "we," the pure Han civilized Chinese, and "they," the barbarian Manchus.[20] Even before the Manchu invasion, to emphasize and create new forms of sexual distinction and making an erotic appeal, footbinding had already become a cherished tradition.[21]

As her revisionist theory develops, Ko assures the reader that seclusion or cloistering, at least on the part of gentry women, and partially caused by footbinding, contributed to its practitioners' freedom and dignity, helping to identify them as good mothers and housewives. However, the theory that gentry women did not feel the need to "challenge the age-old ideology prescribing the functional separation between sexes" and that they were "oblivious" to the hierarchical dimension of this doctrine, is not accepted by Francesca Bray, who points out that the women were "conscious" of it, but "accept(ed) it as a natural fact.[22]

The "revisionist theory" constructed by Ko on the tradition of footbinding, which emphasizes that footbinding is a "body aesthetic," something women did willingly, and that "footbinding was not a burden but a privilege," is not acceptable to us. Ko's theoretical construction is in line with the current trend in Western academia to reinterpret existing propositions in postmodernist terms, using the so-called feminist theory of the "body" to make shocking statements under the banner of an in-depth reflection on the pursuit of progressive "modernity." Moreover, she deliberately reduces the progressive view of women's history represented by the abolition of footbinding in the May Fourth period to the dichotomies of "barbarism-civilization" and "oppression-emancipation."

However, while a non-Chinese mind might have been impressed by the novelty of Ko's hypotheses, a Chinese soul adequately exposed to the spirit of May Fourth would have difficulty accepting the thesis that the practice of footbinding elevated late Imperial women's status rather than abating it. Neither would a profound China historian easily entertain the idea that gender segregation/cloistering had been positive for women, making their status more privileged. The May Fourth generalization on footbinding, though not without its pitfalls of oversimplification, is more of a historically truthful stand. The issue can be summarized as follows:

> The ordeal of footbinding crippled women's bodies; besides the physical sufferings, it also caused women to 1) Lose their freedom of mobility and disable them from escaping catastrophes in times of emergencies; 2) Lose the potential to be financially independent by working outside the domestic sphere, and 3) Have their minds shackled to triviality.

Those conclusions are perhaps reminiscent of the male feminists' arguments in the late Qing anti-footbinding movement, whose rationalism or practicality has been under severe criticism by recent feminist scholarship. Researchers of Chinese feminist movements of the late nineteenth and early twentieth century, no matter how differently they might have looked upon other issues, would largely agree that the Chinese feminist movement was primarily a movement initiated by male intellectuals, and served for the propose of nationalism. It was a process other third-world feminist movements had likewise undergone. Wendy Larson quoted from Peter Zarrow: "until 1907 virtually all Chinese feminism was nationalistic."[23]

That women had to rely on men's financial support burdened both men and women, fundamentally deteriorating the status of women. Francesca Bray, an Oxford-trained China historian, has done much work on technology, gender, and the state. Also an anthropologist of science, technology, and medicine, she is particularly interested in how politics are expressed and enacted through everyday technologies. She presents a rather interesting interpretation of Chinese women's status deterioration. Instead of blaming it on the rise of Neo-Confucianism, Bray argues that in the eleventh century, with the Song dynasty's enforcement of its new tax policy, cash, instead of concrete production, was being collected for tax payments by the government, and textile production had since then been largely taken over by workshops full of male workers. Bray perceived this change as having "deskilled" women in history, causing them to be devalued and marginalized. She hypothesizes that women's status started to decline from the Song and onward because their economic importance to the family economy declined.[24]

Regardless of how scholars differed over the issue of footbinding, in the case of Sujie, a Roaring Lioness of the East of the River, the reason she cannot travel is not because of her bound feet. Instead, the burden of footbinding on Sujie is less physical than spiritual. A healthy, vigorous woman who moves about ably on her pair of bound feet, her vexation springs more from a societal tether than a familial one. There is a place for Sujie in Wu Yenna's *The Chinese Virago: A Literary Theme*, a comprehensive study of the literary and historical portrayal of the "virago." However, in a closer look at Sujie, the arguably most intimidating shrewd in all literary representations, we find that that, seven or eight out of ten times, Sujie's conflicts with her husband, her in-laws, and her natal family, which also represents patriarchal authority, are due to their interference with her freedom of movement.

With the Ming adopting Neo-Confucianism as its official ideology, stricter regulations based on Confucian doctrines were codified into laws to limit women's physical freedom.

This phenomenon was particularly prevalent during the High Qing period of Emperor Kangxi, Emperor Yongzheng, and Emperor Qianlong. Susan Mann notes that "several local officials, Yin Huiyi 尹会一 (1691–1748), Wang Huizu 汪辉祖 (1730–1807), Chen Hongmou 陈宏谋 (1696–1771), Lan Dingyuan 蓝鼎元 (1680–1733), and Huang Liuhong 黄六鸿 (1633–1693), who were known for their frequent writings on state policy, each wrote articles that explicitly instructed women on their behavior and moral character." Huang Liuhong's *Complete Collection of the Benevolence* (Fuhui Quanshu 福惠全书), written based on Huang's personal experiences as well as his experience with local administration, acts as a set of maxims for future officials to master the government's institutions and gain a thorough understanding of local affairs. The book contains a passage with a robust reprimanding tone:

> "Three Gu and Six Po," lower-class women of various liberal professions, cannot enter people's homes to entice others and sell their goods. Young women are forbidden to enter temples to burn incense or to go for a walk. If girls in this locality should be involved in prostitution, *Jia* should strictly expel them. If any juniors act frivolously, the local police may instruct them to behave in the same way their brothers and fathers behave. In this way, there will be no more immodest things happening. Rites and rituals will thrive, but lewdness will not exist. Is this not the effect of establishing edification? For the wealthy, evil desires burst with indulgence in pleasure; for the poor, their integrity is lost for lack of food and clothing. A fierce man always becomes lustful when he sees a beautiful woman, and a frivolous man may soon forget his honor, position, and status when he is pleased with a beautiful face.[25]

Such ordinances, although they had the underlying intention of maintaining local security by reducing women's travels and were often repealed when magistrates were transferred to another post, certainly did much to discourage women from leaving the house. But, of course, decrees that were not issued by the central government and were subject to changes at any time were too costly to enforce from the government's perspective and were thus not fully enforceable.

Yet, out of the reach of the law, patriarchal authority does not always prevail, for, as shown, too much insistence on female subordination also brings about psychological frustration in women and incites rebellious behaviors among the less compliant.[26] The domestic strife enkindled by the cloistering laws would sometimes end with the triumph of the more powerful instead of the more orthodox, and this is to prove true in Sujie's case.

2. The Mount Tai Pilgrimage

1) The Mount Tai Incense Society

Despite traditional China's lagging tourism infrastructure and lack of a broad conception of tourism, pilgrims' unabated zeal for visiting famous mountains for religious purposes gave birth to the earliest Chinese "theme-based" tourism.

Theming is a modern tourist technology for building and operating an environment for the sake of consumption. It is commonly applied to theme parks, shopping malls, festival markets, themed restaurants, and planned communities.[27] China has many sacred mountains, some Taoist and some Buddhist, but only five are eligible to be called *yue* 岳, each of which enjoys an unparalleled reputation and prestige. They are collectively the Eastern Peak of Mount Tai, the Western Peak of Mount Hua, the Southern Peak of Mount Heng, the Northern Peak of Mount Heng, and the Middle Peak of Mount Song. Mount Tai, being hailed as "the first mountain under Heaven," takes precedence over the other four peaks, not because of its loftiness—1,532 meters above sea level (the height of the peak of Mount Tai, Yuhuang Ding 玉皇顶, is lower than that of Mount Hua and Mount Huan)—but owing to its historical and political prestige as the very mountain where ancient emperors offered *fengshan* 封禅 sacrifices.

Religious worship of Mount Tai has a tradition 3,000 years old and has been practiced from the time of the Shang to that of the Qing Dynasty. Over time, this worship evolved into an official imperial rite so that Mount Tai functioned as the principal place where emperors paid homage to Heaven (on the summit) and Earth (at the foot of the mountain) in *fengshan* sacrifices. Orthodox historiography recognizes ten *fengshan* rituals done by six emperors, ranging from the First Emperor of the Qin to Emperor Zhen of the Song 宋真宗. Still, if the legendary figures enumerated in *Records of the Grand Historian* were to be,[28] 12 more pre-imperial kings should be added to the list.

The "sensational effect" brought to Mount Tai by the humanistic tradition of *fengshan* sacrifices made Mount Tai famous everywhere. Yi Junzuo 易君左, a literary figure of the Republic of China, wrote *On Making Mount Tai a National Mountain* (Taishan Guoshan Yi 泰山国山议), in which he proposed to establish Mount Tai as a "national mountain." Yi Junzuo notes that since the Song and Yuan dynasties, Mount Tai sacrifices have undergone a significant transformation in that the state monopoly, which previously excluded the commoners, has been broken, and sacrifices made by commoners have become the norm.[29]

In the Novel, the prestige Mount Tai enjoys has less to do with its state-sanctioned sacred stature than the religious ardor it arouses in believers of the Cult of the Mother of Mount Tai, a female patron saint worthy of being venerated within the inner chambers. The cult is believed to be closely related to an ancient all-purpose Taoist goddess, Bixia Yuanjun, from whom people sought a good harvest, profit in trade, general safety, and above all, children and good health.

Bixia Yuanjun Worship 碧霞元君信仰, commonly known as the Cult of the Mother of Mount Tai, is Taoist mountain-god worship centered in northern China, and its importance in Han Chinese folk religion is reflected in the phrase "Yuanjun in the North, Mazu in the South" 北元君，南妈祖. This worship has been practiced for thousands of years. During the Ming and Qing dynasties, it became prevalent and greatly influenced the culture of northern China, especially on the domestic activities of women. After the Cultural Revolution, the Cult of the Mother of Mount Tai has flourished again in northern China. Keeping watch over Mount Tai, Bixia Yuanjun is also known in Taoist classics as "Tianxian Yunü Bixia Hushi

Hongji Zhenren" 天仙玉女碧霞护世弘济真人 and "Tianxian Yunü Baosheng Zhenren Hongde Bixia Yuanjun" 天仙玉女保生真人弘德, and has other popular names, including "Niangniang of Mount Tai" 泰山娘娘, "Granny of Mount Tai" 泰山奶奶, "Old Mother of Mount Tai" 泰山老母, and "Mother of All Mounts" 万山奶奶, apart from "Mother of Mount Tai." This female deity, powerful and compassionate, can bless the harvest of grains, the safety of travels, and health, but her most important and famous power is to bring a woman to give birth to a child. According to *The Monument to Bixia of Mount Tai* (Dongyue Bixia Gongbei 东岳碧霞宫碑) by Wang Xijue 王锡爵, a Grand Secretary in the Ming dynasty:

> Yuanjun can benefit all sentient beings and fulfill people's wishes. The poor wish to be rich, the sick wish to be healthy, the farmers wish for a good harvest, business people wish for fortune, the old wish to live longer, and the childless wish to have children. The sons make wishes for their parents, and the younger brothers make wishes for their elder brothers. The relatives are so close with each other that their wishes always overlap, but the goddess always fulfills them.[30]

It can be said that from the mid-Ming dynasty onwards, the function of Bixia Yuanjun has transformed from a single fertility goddess to an omnipotent deity, universally adapting to the needs of the faith of different classes and genders. In fact, before the rise of the Bixia Yuanjun faith, the mountain worship at Mount Tai was dominated by the Dongyue Emperor. However, this vital mountain worship, which had prospered since the Northern Song dynasty, could still resist the power of folk beliefs. The transformation was so great that the scholars and the officials in the Ming dynasty had a sense of putting the cart before the horse, denouncing the fact that "Mount Tai cannot have its god, but has an official female lord with a different surname. Those people coming from all directions also put the cart before the horse."[31]

Recent scholarship on the *baojuan* 宝卷 religious literature reveals that despite the cult's occasional connection with sectarian movements and rebellions, its espousal of the state's status quo had earned it reciprocal patronage from the latter.[32]

During the late Imperial era, when no commercialized tourist organizations were yet instituted, group participants of pilgrimages usually submitted their tourist plans to folk societies. In light of the cult's immense popularity among Shandong natives, particularly women, a semi-tourist, semi-religious folk organization, the Mount Tai Incense Society, had come into being as early as the Tang.[33] It gained more momentum in the Song,[34] prospered during the Ming and Qing, and has persisted into the present day. The word "incense" here stands for food, clothes, cash, and a variety of material goods offered to the Mother of Mount Tai, but it can also denote the meaning of "incense" in the strict context of "burning incense." Zhou Jiazhou 周嘉胄, who has studied "incense," explains incense money: "every year, on the birthday of Emperor Taizong of the Song dynasty, money was collected, rice was given to monks, and incense was offered, to celebrate his birthday. The money is called incense money."[35]

Figure 4.1 Sovereign of the Clouds of Dawn [Bixia Yuanjun 碧霞元君]. 1375–1450. Bronze with traces of pigment. H. 98 × W. 57 × D. 32.5 cm.

Source: Courtesy of The Art Institute of Chicago, Chicago.

It is worth mentioning that the Bixia Yuanjun Worship and its incense-offering activities did not necessarily have to take place on Mount Tai. There were more than 20 Bixia temples in and around the capital at the end of the Ming dynasty,[36] of which the "Five Top Temples" in the east, west, north, south, and center attracted many pilgrims, and the most prosperous ones were in Zhuozhou and Tongzhou. According to *A Weighted and Unbiased Record* by Liu Ruoyu, a eunuch in the late Ming dynasty:

> In the early to late afternoon, people can go to Xishan, Xiangshan, Biyun Temple, etc., and go to Zhuozhou Niangniang Temple, Majuqiao Niangniang Temple, and Xiding Niangniang Temple outside the Xizhimen Gate to offer incense. People go to the Yaowang Temple on the twenty-eighth day to offer incense.[37]

Moreover, "Zhuozhou is more than 50 kilometers from the capital. The imperial palace respects the Niangniang Temple here. There is a constant stream of incense-goers in the imperial harem."[38] Majuqiao was in Tongzhou and Xiding (the West Top 西顶) in Landianchang. *A Brief Record of the Scenery of the Imperial Capital*, written by Liu Dong 刘侗 and Yu Yizheng 于奕正, two literary figures of the Chongzhen reign, represents the elegant and refined literary style of the Jingling School of the late Ming, and also records the scenic beauty of Beijing and the customs of its citizens extensively. The entry "Hongren Bridge" records the bustle of men, women, and children from Beijing who traveled 20 kilometers from the Zuo'an Gate to offer incense on the 18th day of the fourth month of every year—the birthday of Yuanjun—as well as the locations of the "five top temples":

> On the 18th day of the fourth lunar month of every year, the birthday of Yuanjun, the people in the capital would come to offer incense. Before this day, the Head of Incense beats a gong and orders the congregation to follow. The head and the congregation's relationship is as obedient and close as that between teachers and students, officials and citizens, fathers and sons, and brothers and sisters. From the 1st to the 18th day of the fourth month, people travel 20 kilometers to offer incense. An endless stream of people travels by carriage, on horseback, on foot, on their knees, holding banners, and beating gongs and drums. Those in carriages are from families of the high and mighty or the rich and powerful. Those on horseback are wanderers and women from small families. Those on foot are the poor, who come to redeem a vow to the goddess and pray. Those who walk on their knees, topped with the statue of Yuanjun and carrying paper ingots, kneel at every step and spend three days to arrive. Their garments are short in the back, and they wear silk pants and no socks. For those who kneel every five, ten, or twenty steps, it takes them one day to get to the temple. Many people sing and play while walking to have fun. Among the people holding banners and beating drums, ten percent each hold embroidered banners and red banners, ten percent each hold green, yellow, and black embroidered veils, and those who ride and beat drums and gongs are in about the same proportion. The people's heads are topped with small signs with the word "jin [gold 金]," small shoulder banners with the word "ling [order 令]," and carry small wooden palaces in their hands, saying that Yuanjun is coming. People's clothes and utensils are all in

gold and silver to match. Behind are black flags measuring two *zhang* [about 6.67 meters 二丈], dotted with seven stars, and in the front are embroidered pennants measuring three *zhang* [about 10 meters 三丈], decorated with the title Yuanjun. There are also acrobats doing tricks or modeling performances on poles. The poles are several *zhang* in length, twisting and turning, decorated with the shape of pavilions, cliffs, water, clouds, and smoke. Four or five children perform underneath. The principle behind the show is that the children's waist is girded with an iron ring, and the children's buttocks hold up a platform. Clothes cover the ring, and the pole can stick out from the jumble of clothes. Below the shape of clouds and the smoke, a child sits in the void or straddles a horse floating in the air. The people on the roadside are surprised, and the performing children are exhausted. People would pick up pancakes with long poles to feed the children. The road is long, and the spring breeze is warm, so the children soon fall asleep.

Moreover, some youngsters dress up as monks, beggars, fools, scoundrels, and other theatrical characters for entertainment. In the restaurants near the bridge, there is a kind of noodle dish called *Mahu* 麻胡 in children's speech.

The soup and fried rice dumplings are called *Huanxituan* [joyful dumplings 欢喜团]. The straw-woven helmets and crowns are called *Caomao* [straw hat 草帽]. The paper and clay masks are called *Guilian* or *Guibi* [ghosts' faces and noses 鬼脸 鬼鼻]. The long-dyed hairs of horses are called *Guixu* [ghosts' beards 鬼须]. On the way home, the pilgrims have some dust on their clothes, straw hats on their heads, ghosts' faces, noses, and beards on their faces, and *Mahu* and *Huanxituan* in their sleeves. People are pleased when they enter the city gate, as are the people on the road. Entering the gate, husbands take their wives, sons, and daughters, whirling around them merrily. However, some people get drunk and make a lot of noise, jostling other people as they vie for space, and even fighting with each other. No one could tell whether they were men or women, and they will have to go to a court hearing for a lawsuit the next day.[39]

But after the mid-Qing dynasty, the Bixia Yuanjun Worship in Zhuozhou, Tongzhou, and Landianchang (known as Xiding) was overshadowed by Mount Miaofeng in Mentougou in western Beijing. Taking away the worshippers from many of the other temples in Beijing, Mount Miaofeng became a popular choice for pilgrimages to worship Bixia Yuanjun in the capital and was also known as Jinding (the "Golden Top Temple" 金顶). In 1925 and 1929, Gu Jiegang and other scholars from Beijing made two field investigations at Mount Miaofeng. Gu Jiegang published his research in 1925 in *The Peking Press Supplement*, and later collected it into a book, *Mount Miaofeng*. Two days before Gu Jiegang's investigation in 1925, Li Jinghan 李景汉 and his team from the Department of Sociology at Yanjing University also visited Mount Miaofeng. Still, Li Jinghan's paper came out later and quoted extensively from Gu Jiegang's materials and arguments. Therefore, it is generally accepted that Gu's investigation was a pioneering trip in fieldwork in Chinese folklore.[40] Fu Yanchang 傅彦长 even argues that Gu Jiegang's survey at

Mount Miaofeng is more meritorious than his "Ancient History Debate," a work that has shocked the historical community.[41]

In his study, Gu Jiegang expresses a very high opinion of the tightness of the organization of the Mount Miaofeng Incense Society: "How well organized they were! They had commissioners for finance, ceremonies, police, transportation, payroll ... and a leader to direct everything, so they had the makings of a state."[42] The significant difference between the Mount Miaofeng Incense Society and the Mount Tai Incense Society is that the former prevented women not only from being the "Head of Society" but also from holding the following positions: the Head of *Yinshan* (the head and the deputy head of the incense society 引善都管), the Head of *Cuixian* (the person who collected fees 催线都管), the Head of *Qingsheng* (the person in charge of rituals 清声都管), the Head of Money and Food (the person who purchased the offerings 钱粮都管), the Head of the Treasury (the person who managed the money 司库都管), the Head of the Army (the manager of the guards 中军哨子), the Head of the Vehicles (the manager of the vehicles 车把都管), and the Head of the Kitchen (the manager of the food 厨房查房). The Incense Society has a separate section called "Lady of the Faith" for female members of the congregation.[43]

In Mingshui, the hometown of Sujie, two Daoist practitioners, Sister Zhang and Sister Hou, function as the heads of the society. The two Taoist Nuns travel from house to house, reaching out to women and inducing them to participate in Buddhist activities by donating to the temples under the pretext of accumulating merit for reincarnation. It is worth noting that although Hou and Zhang are known as "Taoist Nuns," and the Bixia Yuanjun Worship is a folk religion under the Taoist system, in practice, the two Taoist Nuns worship both Buddhism and Taoism as one. To amass more money, the two would take advantage of the anniversaries of Buddhist or Taoist immortal saints and would not miss any opportunity to receive alms from the women of the congregation nor miss any chance to make money for themselves. The author of *XSYYZ*, out of his distaste for these gossipy and sophisticated town women, refers to Hou and Zhang in a derogatory manner. As readers and researchers, though, we should be careful to consider the actual behavior of the characters and try not to be influenced by the moral judgments of the author. The actions of Hou and Zhang are described in the following accounts:

> The two mention the building of a temple at the village in the east and the casting of a bell at the village in the west, the establishment of a golden bodhisattva here, and the holding of solemn rituals at the birthday of a Taoist Immortal Saint there. They claim that those who are willing to give will enjoy glory, splendor, wealth, and rank in not only this life but also the next, but those who are stingy and refuse to give will not only be inferior to others in the next life but will also be transformed from noble to poor and from rich to poor in this life.... They would follow to places where statues and bells are cast, temples are built, and Taoist priests perform rites and look for their names on the monuments and in the account books of alms. The two women only dare to withhold 60 or 70 percent of the money, leaving 30 or

40 percent. However, should concubines, keeping the donations back from their in-laws and husbands, contribute hundreds and thousands of things, the two would not even utter a "thank you" when they accept the gifts. The money given by women is saved up for Hou and Zhang's lands and houses. Rice, grain, wheat, and beans donated are all carried to their homes in big sacks and devoured by their families. Clothes donated are either given to their husbands and sons or put on themselves.

(68.521)

Hou and Zhang have long heard that Sujie is a big spender and have thought about coming to make acquaintance with Sujie several times. They, however, "ponder over it for a long time but have nowhere to start." In Sujie's husband's family, Lady Di has "such an irascible character that no one would dare to offend her" (68.521); and after the death of Lady Di, the two Taoist Nuns make several trips to Di's house but are always dismissed by the shrewd and loyal Old Di with small amounts of money for their requests for donations, rather than being allowed to see Sujie. With Sujie's parents' family, the two Taoist Nuns are still at their wits' end, as Sujie's father is "Old Xue, who teaches Taoism," and her legal mother, Lady Xue, is too formal and old-fashioned to handle. Only when Lady Xue dies of old age and illness do Hou and Zhang dare to try their luck. Sujie's two maiden brothers are certainly "conservatively decent," but this heaven-sent opportunity provides Hou and Zhang a pretext for mourning for Lady Xue. "We claim to burn paper money for his mother; could they refuse us?" Then the Xue brothers, as expected, "take them to the coffin and ask the mourning women and daughters to bow in thanks" (68.522). It is only then that Hou and Zhang come into contact with Sujie.

All of this story can represent the multiple barriers that protected the female members of a family from being exposed to unorthodox influences in a patriarchal society. The pressure for patriarchal and marital power did not necessarily have to come from the father and husband, but could also come from the mother-in-law, mother, and brothers who agreed with patriarchal and marital power. The best way for the unorthodox to get around the barriers was to raise the banner of tradition (mourning for Xue's legal mother) to block traditionalists' eyes.

Hou and Zhang belong to the group of Taoist nuns among these gossipy and sophisticated town women (three *gu* and six *po* 三姑六婆). The term "three *gu* and six *po*" originated in the Yuan dynasty. In the secular world, the "three *gu*," namely *nigu* (nuns 尼姑), *daogu* (Taoist nuns 道姑), and *guagu* (female fortune-tellers 卦姑), were used in conjunction with the "six po," namely *yapo* (procuresses 牙婆), *meipo* (matchmakers 媒婆), *shipo* (witches 师婆), *qianpo* (women pimps 虔婆), *yaopo* (medicine women 药婆), and *wenpo* (midwives 稳婆). From the beginning, orthodox society showed a strong sense of precaution against them. In general literature, these women were already portrayed in a negative light as plausible liars, annoying troublemakers, venal villains, and disgusting pimps. Family instructions and warning books used for preaching even regarded them as evil beasts. Tao Zongyi 陶宗仪 of the end of the Yuan dynasty says: "It is rare that a family with such a person does not commit adultery and theft."[44] In the book *The Three Gu and*

Six Po (San Gu Liu Po 三姑六婆) by Yi Ruolan衣若兰, a Taiwanese scholar of women's history, a chapter is devoted to discussing the causes of the "Apologists' uneasiness." The conclusion is that the ethical and moral values of the intellectual class had continuously attached importance to the "distinction between inside and outside" and the "social distance between men and women." Still, the disruption of the ritual order caused by the free access of the "three *gu* and six *po*" to people's inner rooms made the scholars feel anxious about the increasingly blurred social divisions.[45] Dudbridge believes that Xizhou Sheng's reference to Hou and Zhang as "Taoist Nuns" has some moral preaching in mind, as these two words are synonymous with "thieves" in Chinese. In addition to praising this fantastic idea of a pun, he coins the term "temple thieves" because there is no equivalent in English.[46] In response, we think he is overplaying it a bit. What Hou and Zhang do, after all, is not the same as stealing; if we remove the filter of moral judgment, we may even find that they make a significant contribution to the enrichment of the domestic life of traditional society, which is not just reflected in the organization of the Mount Tai Incense Society. Even in the case of the Mount Tai Incense Society, it would have been unthinkable for a group of 70 to 80 people to make such a trip without the availability, flexibility, and efficiency of Hou and Zhang.

Hou and Zhang have multiple duties in the Incense Society. Respectively Head and Deputy-Head (the equivalent of the Head of *Yinshan* of the Mount Miaofeng Incense Society), they are in charge of transportation (the Head of *Cuiliang*), securing mules and donkeys (the Head of the Vehicles), providing traveling gadgets such as eye-patches and handkerchiefs (the Head of Money and Food), and managing the Society's finances (the Head of Treasury).

Although they take profits from organizing the pilgrimage and tend to coax gullible women into joining the society, the leadership they have demonstrated is quite impressive. The entire pilgrimage is divided into three stages. The first phase involves enrolling participants, collecting funds, and rehearsing the journey; the second is the journey to the mountain; and the third is the returning journey and the ensuing rituals of receiving. The first preparation stage can take as long as three years to accomplish.

For the Mount Tai pilgrimage, transportation was the main problem, while the Incense Society showed considerable flexibility in handling transport. Sedan chairs, the best means of transport, were not used since the society had to cater to the needs of members who wanted to travel and visit. "When one goes to burn incense, it is partly to accumulate blessings, and partly to see the scenery leisurely. It would be too vulgar to sit rigidly in a sedan chair, and we all ride mules and horses" (68.524).

According to Hou and Zhang, if a woman joins the society three years in advance, the three *taels* of silver she initially deposits as principal will have grown to 10 *taels* when the pilgrimage sets out. Most wonderfully, the principal will only be invested in philanthropic enterprises—such as building bridges, mending roads, helping the elderly, and relieving the poor—thus ensuring an accumulation of positive karma for the investor. As the compound brings in huge returns over the three years, and as only five *taels* of silver are needed for the journey, the early-bird attendee may still use the other five *taels* to purchase *renshi* gifts for her family. Yet for a latecomer who does not invest in advance, the society will have to charge her ten *taels* in full unless she can supply her transportation, in which case the society can reimburse her eight *maces* as the rent for a traveling donkey (68.524).

Yet the Mount Tai Incense Society's goal of generating profits, which would have been difficult to achieve with modern financial management, was not a pipe dream at the time. Arthur H. Smith, a Sinologist who was a missionary of the American Congregational Church, had already taken a sociological interest in the Mount Tai Incense Society phenomenon in his monograph *Village Life in China*, published at the end of the nineteenth century. Smith came to China in 1872 and was trapped at the embassy in Dongjiaominxiang Alley during the Yihetuan Movement. Having lived in China for nearly half a century and knowing much about the countryside owing to his missionary career, Smith had an in-depth analysis of rural social phenomena. According to him, the Incense Society arose in response to the needs of incense travelers. His detailed account of the financial operations of the Mount Tai Incense Society is recorded in the following:

> To surmount this difficulty, Incense societies levy a fee of each member, of one hundred cash a month. If there are fifty members, this will result in collecting 5,000 cash as a first payment. The managers who have organized the Society proceed to loan this amount to someone with an interest of two or three percent a month. . . . When the time has expired, and principal and interest are collected, it is again loaned out, thus securing a very rapid capital accumulation. Generally, for three years, successive loans at a high rate of interest for short periods are repeatedly affected.[47]

Hou and Zhang are good at waging psychological warfare to elicit women to join the society. The first time they meet with Sujie, they do not immediately mention burning incense on Mount Tai. Instead, they first talk about something else, such as how Old Di prevented them from entering the house to meet with Sujie and how they felt wronged that their good intentions to pray for Sujie had been wasted. When they have won the favor of Sujie, who wants them to stay for dinner and sit for a while, they pretend to get up again. They impress her by talking about the grand feast to come, the birthday of the Mother on the Fifteenth of April, and mention that they are busy arranging a pilgrimage to Mount Tai. As Sujie's interest is sufficiently intrigued, they entice her by expounding on the wonderfulness of the pilgrimage:

1. The travel is entertaining.

> People say there are 290 *li*. This fare is easy, not quite as much of a 200-*li* journey elsewhere. We'd browse scenes of magnificent temples along the road and spectacles everywhere: bustling travelers, aromatic carriages and precious horses, handsome ladies and gentlemen—all countless and great. Endless spectacles, indeed. You'd hate that the journey is not long enough.

2. The view of Mount Tai is terrific.

> My Good sister-in-law, do you think there are two Mount Tais in the world? When you get to the top, you can survey the whole world at a glance: all the kingdoms, the Dragon Palace, the Sea Palace, and the Buddha Palace. Why do you think the men and women of Yunnan, Guizhou, Sichuan, Hunan and Hubei, Guangxi and Guangdong come from thousands of miles away to offer incense here?

3. Attending pilgrimage amasses credits for the attendees, enabling them, once their piety reaches to a certain level, to see the true face of the Mother, whose magic power would then, in turn, increase their fortunes and relieve their sins. "There are numerous sights on the mountain, such as the Facing-the-Sun Cave (Chaoyang Cave 朝阳洞), the Southern Heavenly Gate, the Yellow Flower Island, the Life-sacrificing Cliff, Sutra Rock Valley, the Wordless Stele, the Qin Pine, the Han Cypress, the Golden Slip, and the Jade Book, all of which are places where the gods live. Can a mortal with a shallow destiny reach there?"

4. Offering incense works in praying for blessings.

> And it is the Mother of Mount Tai who is in charge of the life, death, happiness, and richness of all people in the world. Therefore, if people offer incense piously, a red cloud will be hung from the sky and draped on their bodies, and the music of the pipes and strings will be played; if people are not pious, Immortal Official Wang will bind and trap them at once.

5. Joining the Incense Society is a great way to strengthen one's ties with Buddhism.

> It depends on who the person is. If it is someone we know well, we will ask her to pay the same as other people, principal and interests included, and she is allowed in. If it is someone we don't know, we won't take her with us without reason.

6. A women's tour without any men is safe. "There will be no men but all women, almost eighty."

7. The Incense Society congregation is of high social status.

> If they are not respectable, would they dare to come to our society? There are five or six women in the family of Minister Yang, Madam Meng on the north street, Madam Hong, Madam Wang, and Madam Geng on the east street, Madam Zhang on the main street, Madam Wang on the south street, Mother Liu on the back street, all of whom are from big families. Does one from a low-income family even fit in?

7. It is also a convenient shopping trip.

> The temple fair brings together the people of the twenty official offices and the goods of the world. Clothes, jewelry, agates, and pearls are sold. What is not available? The rich women all go to the temple and choose what they would like to buy.
>
> (68.523–524)

As outlined, the benefits of joining the Mount Tai Incense Society are beyond the reach of the "wealthy women from urban and rural areas" who travel on their own. It is important to note that although conservative social attitudes discouraged women from traveling, it was not impossible for women who had the means to do so to travel on their own. It was not uncommon to see "wealthy women from urban and rural areas" traveling on their own as long as they had enough money to pay for the travels, had livestock to ride or could afford to hire a sedan chair, and were accompanied by male relatives or servants. In *Jin Ping Mei*, Wu Yueniang sets up an incense burner to pray for her husband Ximen Qing, during his grave illness, wishing that if Ximen Qing recovers, she will go up to Mount Tai to offer incense and robes for the Mother of Mount Tai for three years. After Ximen Qing's death, she decides to go to Tai'an Prefecture 泰安州 to redeem her vow. Wu arranges for her brother, Uncle Wu, to accompany her, buys incense, candles, paper horses, and other offerings, and has two menservants, Dai'an and Lai'an, follow her and hires mules and horses for them to ride while she rides in a sedan chair covered by curtains. According to custom, Wu burns paper money before her departure and bids the memorial tablet of Ximen Qing farewell at nightfall. The concubines prepare liquor, and they depart early the following day. The story of *Jin Ping Mei* takes place in the fictional "Qinghe County" of Shandong. In the novel, Chen Jingji travels from Qinghe to Linqing, a dock town on the Grand Canal, to tend to his inn business, and can make a round trip in a day, which suggests that Qinghe is close to Linqing.

Meanwhile, *Jin Ping Mei* continues the story of Wu Song's fight against the tiger in Yanggu County in *Water Margin*, claiming that Qinghe is the county of Yanggu. If we take Yanggu as an approximate starting point, the journey to Tai'an Prefecture would be about 200 kilometers. In *Jin Ping Mei*, Wu Yueniang and others "travel two stages each day, covering sixty or seventy *li*, and sought out village inns before dusk to spend the night, resuming their journey early the next morning."[48] It takes them several days to reach Tai'an. Hence, we can see that a distance of 200 kilometers and a journey of several days are not beyond the reach of the female traveler who can afford to travel, provided the will and need to do so exists.

Sujie's initiative to join the pilgrimage was at first thwarted by her father-in-law, who deems her mingling with the servant women in the Incense Society unacceptable for a "family of Poetry and Proprieties" 诗礼人家. Old Di's concern is not without reason. Indeed, since Di Xichen passed the entry-level civil service examination and purchased a studentship at the National University, the Dis have joined the local elite. As the Confucian proverb states, "Propriety does not condescend to commoners, and corporal punishment does not reach up to grandees." In essence, the elite are not supposed to consort with commoners. Therefore, to be seen among low women in an outer-domestic sphere would have been very improper for a young housewife such as Sujie, and it would potentially lead to a detrimental effect on her husband's career or the family's reputation. On top of that, as the pilgrimage was not to be carried out in an enclosed, controlled environment, gender segregation, the primary concern of the educated elite, could not be guaranteed. Sujie, who has been offered the alternative by Old Di to go to Mount Tai on an individual trip after the autumn harvest, is nonetheless unyielding. She insists on going with Hou and Zhang, threatening to bully her husband should he choose not to accompany her; at last, Old Di relents and lets Xichen go with her (68.524–526).

2) The Actual Pilgrimage

Each of these incense-offering activities at Mount Tai has a specific name in strict order of precedence, and some of them have evolved into folk customs. The incense offering at Mount Tai is known as *Shang Ding* (going to the mountain top 上顶), which is related to the fact that the Mother of Mount Tai is also known as "the Mother of the Top." *Jian Ding* 饯顶, the farewell dinner before leaving for the paramount, is usually given by the pilgrim's close relatives. For a medieval female, the opportunity to visit Mount Tai comes once in a lifetime. Such an opportunity brings about both thrilling expectations and tantalizing anxiety as she is to face the unknown world. The *Jian Ding* arrangement functions as a social occasion to calm her anxiety, bid her goodbye, and wish her a sound return. The term *Jian Ding* is not limited to the pilgrimage to Mount Tai but can be used to describe the farewell dinner of all who would offer incense to the deity. Sujie expects her brothers' wives to organize a banquet for her, but *Jian Ding* becomes a pretext for her brothers to trick her into returning to her parent's house for a final dissuasion.

Before setting out, the Incense Society would organize a parade called *Yan Xinxiang* 演信香, the Rehearsal of the Faithful Incense. It is aimed at displaying the sincerity and faithfulness of its members to the local community. As the parade goes along the town's major roads, holding high the image of the Mother of Mt. Tai while burning incense, they send out the message that "we are pious, and we are coming to the Mother soon."[49] Sujie attends the *Yan Xinxiang* practice, but her natal family, annoyed by her henpecking behaviors that undermine their reputation as educated elites, refuses to offer her a farewell dinner (68.526–528).

The conservatives oppose women's participation in the Mount Tai Incense Society, largely because the *Yan Xinxiang* parade is held in their villages. If the women of one's family march in the streets, "wearing a *qingtun* silk blindfold on their heads, tying a bunch of incense wrapped in blue silk above the shoulders, and running down the street in a mixed group of men and women" (68.525), they would be considered unseemly by those families with merit. The male scholars also have another concern, as Sujie's eldest brother Xue Rubian points out: the women often had to go up and down the mountain in sedan chairs.

> You have not seen the mountain sedan chair. It is fine going up, but going down, the woman will sit in an uncomfortable posture, face-to-face with the bearers. Leaning down, the woman has her feet almost on the bearer's

shoulders. The bearers are so disturbing that they deliberately shake the sedan chair, which looks unpleasant! Is this the kind of thing a family of scholars would do?

(68.525)

On the way to offering incense, the congregation of the Incense Society is required to hold a flag specially prepared for the incense offering. The Head of Society has to arrange a special incense pavilion for the worship of Yuanjun. Before the accommodation, the congregation has to *anjia* 安驾, which means to place the Mother of Mount Tai statue. The Mother has three symbols: the figure, the scroll, and the tablet. Whichever one it is, it must be placed in the middle of the room where they stay, and incense should be burned before other matters can be arranged. Whenever the congregation stays in an inn, all must "call on the Buddha" before going to bed. This means that one person sings the Buddha's verse and the others shout in unison, "Namo Goddess of Mercy Avalokitesvara! Amitabha!" The sound of this chanting is astonishing and can be heard for miles (69.259).

After reaching the mountain top, the congregation can burn incense and make wishes, offer money and give charity, and after descending from the mountain, shops will arrange for banquets and plays. When conditions permit, some Incense Societies will commission shops or temple monks to carve stones and erect steles for the Incense Society to leave its name for the ages. Associated pilgrims erected most of the existing steles of Mount Tai Incense Society during the Ming and Qing dynasties. For example, *The Stele of Beidou Shenghui Society* (Beidou Shenghui Timing Jibei 北斗盛会题名记碑) records that "the Beidou Shenghui Society has experienced hundreds of years since the Ming dynasty, which is an ancient association."[50] After descending from Mount Tai and returning to their respective homes, pilgrims would go back to the local Temple of the Mother of Mount Tai to "burn incense again" and thank the goddess for blessing their safe return. Of course, the above is only a general procedure, which varies from region to region and from Incense Society to Incense Society, but it should be more or less the same.[51]

Sujie and Xichen set out for the pilgrimage; she rides on a donkey, and he goes on foot. Unfortunately, after walking 20 *li*, he gets blisters on his feet. The very idea of denying Xichen his privilege to ride the donkey is designed to punish him for his unsupportive attitude towards her joining the pilgrimage. She finds that she is the only upper-class woman of the assembly, the others being either retired servants or wives of poor households.

The author, Xizhou Sheng, has endeavored to describe the inconveniences and embarrassments of these lower-class women's travels, including toileting, menstruation, and breastfeeding, all of which are mentioned in *Yan Xinxiang*, but not again after the actual journey starts:

A group of women, like jackals, ride about on donkeys with no order whatsoever. Some of them hold their babies on the donkeys, some have *diji* coiffures on the donkeys, some fall out of their saddles, some watch the donkey run away and scream in a strange voice, and some do not get very far before they say they have to get off the donkey to find an open space to relieve themselves as their stomachs ache, some say they are menstruating and thus have to find a piece of cloth from their quilts, some have to feed their children and ask the driver to hold the reins, some complain that their legs are numb and ask for help to get their feet out of the stirrups, some drop their gloves and ask someone to look for them along the road, and some forget their comb box so they ask someone to go home to retrieve it. The dust is everywhere, as well as a stinky smell. It is unseemly to be like this just after setting out.

(68.527–528)

Sujie feels quite at home among the womenfolk and becomes good friends with a Née Liu 刘嫂, at whose urging she allows Xichen to ride on a spare donkey. On the first day the troop advances 100 *li*, checking into an inn near Jinan, that of "Mr. Zhou Shaogang of the East Gate." Xi Zhousheng pens it so verifiably that one wonders if he has personally experienced it. After checking in, the first thing they do is to enshrine the image of the Mother in a safe and decent place, at which point the whole assembly kowtows to the image, chanting NAMO AMITABHA, their loud voices reaching for miles. After the ritual, they go to dinner and bed (69.528–529). On this day, Sujie officially kowtows to Hou and Zhang, calls them masters and becomes a member of the folk society.

The next day the incense-offering pilgrims travel another 100 *li* and stay at Wande 弯德. Finally, on the third day, after walking a few dozen *li*, they pass through a place called Huolu 火炉, literally "furnace."

Numerous small restaurants, stalls, and booths line the road from Huolu to Tai'an prefecture, striving to solicit business from the pilgrims passing by. Shop owners would pull the donkeys of the society's heads to a halt, and, half-threatening and half-beseeching, try to entice the riders to come into their shops. Sister Hou and Sister Zhang, whose donkeys are almost hijacked by a bunch of peddlers who are fervently promoting their "scalding-hot fried bread stick 油条, fragrant and crispy, fried in pure sesame oil, fresh out of the oven," arduously fight their way out from the encirclement as if they were leading a sortie. This bemusing way of soliciting business is not understood by Sujie, who, in her naivete, thinks the merchants are hospitable friends of the two heads who endeavor to offer food to their guests (69.531.532). The solicitation reminds a modern traveler of the similar experiences in tourist areas nowadays. This description also testifies that the Incense Society had brought about a considerable scale of the tourist economy in the surrounding regions of Tai'an Prefecture. The catering and hotel industries all targeted the passing pilgrims, and forcibly selling and solicitating had become a business pattern.

When finally arriving at their destination, the pilgrims are received by two dispatched servants and expediently ushered to an inn run by Master Song, an old acquaintance of Hou and Zhang. A great deal of—almost too much—hospitality is paid by the hotel owner, who greets the assembly with warm words and inquiries about the welfare of the two heads.

The man sent by Master Song comes running up to meet Hou and Zhang and takes hold of their donkey, saying, "I have been waiting for you for several days, but you have arrived so late. Did you leave on the 15th? Did it rain on the way? How are you?" The man takes the donkey straight away, and the group follows him to the inn. When Master Song sees them, he comes out to greet all the people with the flattering attitude of an innkeeper and says some unintentional pleasantries. After washing their faces and drinking tea, the assembly hire donkeys and sedan chairs according to the number of people, chant the Buddhist Scriptures, and first, all go to the Tianqi Temple for a tour and worship. Then, having returned to the inn for dinner and slept until the early morning hours, they all get up, finish freshening up, burn incense, chant the Buddhist Scriptures, and eat together. Hou and Zhang watch all the people get into the mountain sedan chairs before they get into the sedan chair to escort them. All along the way, as those who beg for money, wash tortoise [*fugui* 袚龟], and offer street lamps, the road is as bright as daylight.

(69.531)

Since the God of Mount Tai was granted the title of "King of Tianqi" in the Tang dynasty, it has been bestowed high ranks in all the later dynasties and is known as the "God of Tianqi" among the people. Due to the widespread belief in Mount Tai, the "Tianqi Temple" is built in almost every town in China, and is also known as Mount Tai Temple. *Fugui* is a divination technique, and the meaning of *fu* is most likely associated with "a ritual to remove evil spirits." *Records of the Grand Historian-Biographies of Divination Activities* states that:

> the tortoise is often washed on the first day of each month to get rid of bad luck. This is usually done by bathing the tortoise in water, rubbing an egg on it, and then taking it to use for divination.[52]

Although most ancient divination practices used tortoise shells, we believe that the *bogui* practiced by the pilgrims at Mount Tai here is done with live tortoises. Xizhou Sheng, in a satirical reference to Hou and Zhang's skillful deception, uses the metaphor of "coaxing the dull wives to follow them around like the tortoise" (68.521). The *bogui* of pilgrims at Mount Tai has very little to do with divination and everything to do with blessing. The "offer of lamps" is also an act of charity for the pilgrims, lighting the mountain path at night.

Sujie, accompanied by Xichen, ascends the mountain by taking a mountain sedan chair, which is essentially a willow chair without a footplate. The mountain sedan chair is not covered by a curtain so that all passers-by can see the person on it. If the bearers viciously shake the sedan chair on the way down, the female guest will be unable to keep her feet on the footrest but rock on the chair, which is embarrassing for someone from a noble family.

Sujie feels nauseous, vomiting along the roads, causing chaos among her pilgrim peers, who shout, "The Mother of Mount Tai is grasping her!" The crowd reaches a common verdict that the Mother is displeased because of Sujie's henpecking behaviors along the way. The spirit of the Cult of the Mother of Mount Tai, as the *baojuan* literature reveals, accords with the fundamental values of the traditional society.[53] Bixia Yuanjun, the prototype immortal of the Mother, though a feminine figure and cherished by the women of the inner chambers, does not harbor a feminist agenda of gender equality; and women's henpecking behaviors, which constitute a vice in a patriarchal society, would have been abhorred by the Mother.

Taking Sujie's previously execrable attitude towards her husband into account, Née Liu infers that it must have been the Mother punishing the virago. As a result, all the fellow women pilgrims feel ashamed to be associated with Sujie. The supposed scenario of the Mother "grasping people" is based upon the belief that good people accumulate credits of virtue during the pilgrimage, including being allowed to see the golden face of the Mother, while evil ones receive their due punishments.

Yet Sujie's sickness is caused by nothing more than the jolting of the sedan chair. As a fox fairy who had lived on Mount Tai for 1,000 years in her previous life, Sujie is not foreign to the surroundings. As soon as she gets off the sedan chair, she feels so at ease that she decides to walk her way to the peak. In a sharp contrast to her striding vigorously on her bound feet, Xichen, now deprived of the right to sit on the sedan chair because his wife is walking, has to accompany her, the plodding of each step causing him great agony (69.531–532).

When Sujie reaches the peak, she finds, to her great disappointment, that the most popular Saint Mother Palace 圣母殿, to protect its property, is now closed to practitioners of *Shuan Wawa* and *Gua Pao*. Resourceful and strong-willed, she can resort to her husband's ready self-debasement: she straddles herself over Xichen's shoulders and lifts her eyes. Xichen, on his side, clenches her feet with both his hands. Sujie can finally see the Saint Mother's true face (69.532).

These descriptions are authentic and vivid. For visits of pilgrims to the Bixia Temple as a group, it is usually in front of the main hall. The Head of Society stands at the front of the procession and leads the men and women in the Incense Society in offering incense, bowing, saluting, and reciting the prepared list of rituals before the goddess to inform her. Some also ask the Taoist priest at the temple to read it out for them. After the reading, they take out the tributes and display them one by one, asking the Mother of Mount Tai to accept them. While offering incense, some Incense Societies also have the Head of Society lead the group in chanting the scriptures and praising the deity as an expression of their devotion to the deity. After the collective ceremony, members of the Incense Society then make individual wishes or redeem their vow to the deity, depending on their circumstances. The Saint Mother Palace is crowded with heads of society, far beyond our imagination. The 18th day of April every year is the birthday of Bixia Yuanjun, when the pilgrims will be particularly numerous. According to *The Prefecture Annals of Tai'an* (Tai'an Zhouzhi 泰安州志) compiled in the Kangxi reign, a stampede occurred on April 18 in the 14th year of Wanli reign, resulting in the deaths of 61 people.[54]

For the pilgrims, Master Song's reception goes beyond general hotel hosting. He also provides a complimentary service after their return from the mountain: a receiving ritual called *Jie Ding* 接顶, which is essentially a counterpart of *Jian Ding*.

Strictly speaking, the formal procedure of *Jie Ding* is complete only when the guest is greeted at the red door with a banquet and liquor is poured in front of the feet of the Head of Society. Loosely, when the innkeeper symbolically brings out food and wine and says "congratulation" after the pilgrims return to the inn, a *Jie*

Ding can then be completed. Then, the innkeeper should order a Peking Opera show to entertain the assembly called *Chao Shan Gui* 朝山归. During the show in the evening, the picture of Yuanjun must be hung in the middle of the hall so as to "invite the Mother of Mount Tai to watch the show."[55]

The arrangement of Master Song is satisfactory. After the *Jie Ding*:

> the men and women are seated at separate tables in the canopy, where liquor and opera shows are served as a farewell. The one in the seat of honor orders *The Romance of a Hairpin*, as well as excerpts from *The Beheading of the Diaochan under the Moon* [Yuexia Zhan Diaochan 月下斩貂蝉] and *A Thousand Li Alone* [Duxing Qianli 独行千里]. When the performances are completed, everyone retreats to each of their rooms.

Having watched the plays, Sujie asks Hou, a little confused:

> Master Hou, what is the story about? How come Qian Yulian is killed by Master Guan just after she is rescued from the river? Why does Guan flee with two women after he kills Qian? Is he afraid of paying with his own life?

They all agree: "That's right. Qian Yulian is such a good woman. Master Guan does not protect her but kills her instead. It is not fair!" (69.533) Xizhou Sheng's writing reflects that the pilgrims have not seen much of the world. Even Sujie, from a wealthy family, would not have been able to see a few plays in her native Mingshui if she had not joined the Incense Society.

Before leaving, Master Song gives Hou and Zhang, the two society heads, each "an umbrella, a bamboo fan, a piece of salted pork, and a copper washbasin weighing 12 ounces" (69.533). After each visit, in gratitude, Master Song would send gifts to consolidate the relationship. The milk of human kindness certainly helps foster a solid host-client relationship, for year after year, Hou and Zhang would repeatedly bring the pilgrimage to Song's inn. The savvy marketing of this small inn is quite reminiscent of present-day China's commercial strategies, which blend the needs of worldly concerns with the pursuit of benefits.

According to Xizhou Sheng, "The first step is always the most difficult. Sujie's mind has been set free since her trip to Tai'an" (69.532), and, from then on, her desire to get out becomes unstoppable. Modern readers, however, see in this trip to Mount Tai the cultural resources, well-known mountains and rivers, temples and horses, and, most surprisingly, the still-nascent tourist organization, the religious Incense Society. Without this religious cloak, it is hard to imagine how the "wealthy women from urban and rural areas" of the Ming and Qing dynasties could have emerged from their boudoirs to travel to mountains and rivers.

3) Patterns and Selling Points of the Incense Trade Economy

Owing to Mount Tai's unique cultural and historical legacies, the imperial patronage it had enjoyed, and the appeal of Bixia Yuanjun to womenfolk as the most famous fertility goddess in China, Chinese people's zeal to visit this sacred mountain has never abated. Notwithstanding a lagging tourist infrastructure in ancient China, pilgrims, literati, wanderers, and politicians swarmed into Tai'an Zhou to climb "the first mountain under Heaven." They have formed the Taishan incense economy that has flourished to this day.

The depiction of Master Song epitomizes the centuries-old tradition of Mount Tai's inn business. Scattered records trace the history of this enterprise to as early as the Southern and Northern Dynasties. Its targeted pilgrim customers are called *Xiang Ke* 香客, or the "incense guest," whose purpose in touring Mount Tai differs little from that of Sujie and her peers. The Tang and Song witnessed a gradual expansion in the scale of this business, with the Ming experiencing its peak. The hotel business can be roughly divided into two categories: the monastery-run and the civilian-run. The civilian-run hotels enjoyed protections and tax benefits from the local government, and during the Zhengde reign of the Ming, they were even entrusted by the government to levy an "Incense Tax" or "Mountain Tax" from the incense guests. Unfortunately, the flourishing hotel business was severely impaired by the Manchu invasion in 1644 and did not regain its full scale until the Kangxi Reign.[56]

Most inns and taverns at Mount Tai had a small Temple of the Mother of Mount Tai. Upon arriving, in addition to placing their own sets of offerings for the Mother, the incense guests would also bow down in the temple inside the inn or tavern, giving incense money to show that they had "reported" to the Mother of Mount Tai at the top of the mountain.[57]

The Mount Tai Incense Society leaves an extremely full historical, literary, and inscriptional record of the mid to late Ming period. Not only does *XSYYZ* state that "in spring and autumn, hundreds of thousands of people come to Mount Tai to offer incense every day" (28.214), but *Historical Records of Mount Tai* (Dai Shi 岱史) and *Folk Anecdotes* (Tianchi Ouwen 天咫偶闻) also contain records of the prosperity of the incense offering on Mount Tai. Moreover, in local chronicles of Shandong during the Ming dynasty, such as *The County Annals of Linqu* (Linqu Xianzhi 临朐县志), compiled in the 31st year of the Jiajing reign; *The County Annals of Zhangqiu* (Zhangqiu Xianzhi 章丘县志), compiled in the 24th year of the Wanli reign; *The Prefectural Records of Dongchang* (Dongchang Fuzhi 东昌府志), compiled in the 28th year of the Wanli reign; and *The County Annals of Zou* (Zou Xianzhi 邹县志), compiled in the 37th year of the Wanli reign, voluminous accounts of people going to the mountain top with the Incense Society for a blessing when the seasons change or in late spring every year are recorded.

It is noteworthy that records of the Incense Society in the local chronicles of Shandong during the Ming dynasty were no longer limited to Mount Tai alone. During the late Imperial period, the incense trade economy experienced a boom in several of China's most famous tourist-scenic-pilgrimage cities. The well-maintained incense trade economy has survived into modern times.

The Prefectural Records of Yanzhou (Yanzhou Xianzhi 兖州府志) of the Wanli reign mentions that:

> the people of the city gather into societies. In the east, there is Mount Tai, and in the south, there is Mount Wudang. When people are free, and at leisure,

they form a society of around a hundred people to go there together, which is called the Incense Society.[58]

Prefectural Records of Dongchang, compiled in the 28th year of Wanli reign, records that "(the people) also often carry food and travel by land to Mount Tai and Mount Wudang, and by sea to Mount Putuo, to pray for longevity."[59] The three mountains, Mount Tai, Mount Wudang, and Mount Putuo, together form the subject of the famous theory of "three mountains of incense offering" in the Ming and Qing dynasties. Still, both Ye Tao 叶涛 and Liu Hui 刘慧, another researcher of the Incense Society of Lingyan Temple, believe that "three mountains" refers to "offering incense on Mount Tai for three consecutive years."[60] Regardless of the theory's validity, the incense trade economy of the Ming and Qing dynasties was certainly not confined to Mount Tai alone. The incense trade economy combined religion, travel, trade, and leisure. Its unique character and contrast between the present and the past are worth exploring.

A modern study on the incense trade 香市 of the City-God Hill in Hangzhou during the Qing and early Republic Era, done by Liping Wang, offers a parallel perspective from which to examine the incense economy. In her *Tourism and Spatial Change in Hangzhou, 1911–1927*, Wang writes:

> The annual Pilgrimage demonstrates that Qing Hangzhou was closely connected to its rural hinterland. The Pilgrimage had a significant impact on the urban economy. These Pilgrimages' needs, their trips' timing, and the volume of trade they generated in Hangzhou were critical in shaping handicraft production and urban commercial life. The items Pilgrimages required for religious purposes, such as candles, incense, and especially tin foil paper for making spirit money, constituted a significant part of the city's handicraft business. More importantly, Pilgrimages were also shopping trips for peasants. Local people observed that most pilgrims were well-off peasants who carried large quantities of cash and spent it generously.[61]

While Hangzhou's alias, "paradise on earth," signifies its unparalleled role in leisure tourist culture, characteristic of material comfort, the city image of Tai'an 泰安 (Tai'an Zhou in pre-modern times) boasts a similar attraction but is aimed at a different kind of tourist pursuit. Both cities relied heavily on tourism revenues, contrived to protect their tourist resources, and were recognized as "cultural cities" by the PRC government after 1949. Hangzhou maintains its exuberant tourist city status well into today, and tourist revenue still constitutes a vital part of its municipal economy, yet it is less fortunate in terms of the survivability of the old-fashioned incense economy.

A victim of Hangzhou's spatial transformation, the incense trade started to decline after the 1911 revolution; the tourist significance of the City-God Hill was replaced by other scenic spots deliberately shaped to meet the interests of modern tourists.[62] In contrast, the Mount Tai incense economy, having transcended its primitive stage and the formation of the Incense Society, has persisted into contemporary times, except for a hiatus during the era of the Great Cultural Revolution. Its incense economy has transcended the primitive and austere forms of the late empire, and the various service industries, represented by the hotel industry, have managed to keep pace with modern hardware and service awareness.

The Incense Tax is also mentioned in *XSYYZ*, where it is said that after Sujie and other incense guests reach the top of Mount Tai, "the one in charge of the Incense Tax is the county magistrate of Lixia county, who names the Incense Guests one by one according to the list" (69.532). The Mount Tai Incense Tax is the Incense Tax paid to the state by incense guests of Mount Tai, and mainly consists of incense money and mixed money. The Incense Tax was levied in the Zhengde reign of the late Ming dynasty to renovate the Bixia Temple. As the worship of folk gods and goddesses like Bixia Yuanjun was not in line with the Cheng-Zhu neo-Confucianism ideology of the mid-Ming dynasty, it was suspected of being an "obscene ritual" and caused considerable controversy among the courtiers when the Incense Tax was created. *The Veritable Records of Emperor Wuzong* (Ming Wuzong Shilu 明武宗实录) in *MSL* contains the following words:

> There is a temple of Bixia Yuanjun on Mount Tai, the Eastern Mountain. Li Jian 黎鑑, the Guardian Eunuch, requested the incense tax for the temple's repairs, which was granted. However, Shi Tianzhu, *Gong Ke Jishizhong*, and others stated that the rituals of worship could only be given to the God of Mount Tai rather than Bixia Yuanjun, and that the worship of Bixia Yuanjun was not in conformity with the rituals and thus could not be respected and supported. Moreover, the collection of the incense tax would consume the people's money, violate the country's canonical system, lead to corruption, and encourage sinful indulgence, and must therefore be stopped. When the proposal was reported, the division in charge of the matter was notified by delivery.[63]

Once the Incense Tax was introduced, however, the local and central governments could reap the benefits, and the tax became unstoppable. From the 11th year of Zhengde reign (1516), the Mount Tai Incense Tax was levied for 220 years until it was abolished in 1736, the first year of Qianlong reign in the Qing dynasty. *The General Chronicle of Shandong* (Shandong Tongzhi 山东通志) reads: "Tai'an Incense Tax, formerly collected by Tai'an Prefecture, was originally 5,934 *taels*. After the 4th year of Yongzheng reign, regardless of the amount collected, it was all paid to the state treasury." To be exact, the abolition of the Incense Tax took place during the transition between the Yongzheng and Qianlong reigns. Emperor Yongzheng died in the eighth month of the 13th year of the Yongzheng reign, and *The General Chronicle of Shandong* records that "the Incense Tax ceased to be collected in the eighth month of the 13th year of the Yongzheng reign."[64] After he acceded to the throne, Emperor Qianlong changed the reign title to the Qianlong reign in the following year. On the first day of the first month of the first year of the Qianlong reign, Emperor Qianlong went to the Yonghe Lamasery, where Emperor Yongzheng lived before his reign and where Qianlong was born, to perform rituals in plain clothes, and then proceeded with his first task, the removal of the Incense Tax in Tai'an. The urgency leads to a conjecture: the abolition of the Incense Tax may have been linked to Yongzheng's dying wish. Qianlong confessed in his imperial edict that:

> I have heard that there is a Bixia Temple on Mount Tai, Shandong Province. If people want to offer incense, they must pay an Incense Tax at the government office of Tai'an, which is 1.4 coins per person, costing about 10,000 per year. If the people cannot afford to pay the tax, they cannot climb the mountain and enter the temple. The tax started in the former Ming dynasty and has never been reformed. In my opinion, it is the public opinion that should be considered when commoners go to pray to the gods and goddesses, and there is no need to collect such a tax. In the future, the Incense Tax should be abolished forever. If people are willing to give money for incense, they can do so according to their means, without any restrictions on the amount. Besides, the money should only be collected and deposited by the Taoists on the mountain and used to pay for the repair of the temple and the roads. No official is allowed to handle the money. This is to be made a decree and immediately announced to all.[65]

In pre-modern times, the collection of Incense Tax enabled Mount Tai's tourist economy to support its infrastructure and leave additional taxes to the emperor regularly for other purposes. In addition to being paid to the treasury, Mount Tai Incense Tax was used in a variety of ways, mainly for the operation of the Provincial Tax Administration Commissioner's Office, the construction of temples, the building of the city walls, assistance with the imperial examinations, support for the administration of logging sites, the replenishment of the population tax of the *lijia*, the replenishment of the rice of the Mansions of Prince De, Prince Lu and Prince Heng, assistance with the construction of the river, and support for the soldier's pay and provisions.[66]

The fundamental reason for the economic prosperity of the Mount Tai incense trade economy was the Bixia Yuanjun Worship. The goddess has various supernatural powers, but one of the most powerful and attractive ones was her ability for aiding fertility. Although she was still anathema to the Cheng-Zhu neo-Confucianism scholars during the reign of Emperor Wuzong, Bixia Yuanjun radiated her power to the imperial palace in just 15 or 16 years.

Fertility concerns constituted such a vital segment of the Mount Tai pilgrimage that even the imperial house was no exception. In the 11th year of the Jiajing reign, the then Empress Dowager sent a high-ranking officer, Advisor to the Crown Prince, to Mount Tai to make an invocation, praying for the emperor's expedited luck to have a baby boy:

> It has been twelve years since the Emperor's accession to the throne, but he has not yet appointed a successor, and the state's foundations are thus not sufficiently secure. All the ministers and people are expecting. Therefore,

I have been sent to this temple to offer sacrifices and perform rituals, praying to the goddess for a gracious transit that will shelter the royal descendants and the early birth of a crown prince. This is a genuinely incomparable joy, and I wish it faithfully to the utmost.[67]

While the traditional incense economy may not have had the marketing power to devise "themed tourism," the Mount Tai Incense Trade did successfully capitalize on the imperial drive. As Bixia Yuanjun's fertility power became famous and the most powerful of all Chinese fertility deities, "child-seeking tourism," very much akin to themed tourism, took off on Mount Tai, and even as of today, still attracts childless men and women from all over China.

The most famous practice in Mount Tai, mentioned in the Novel but not given much length, is *Shuan Wawa* 拴娃娃, the fetching back of a baby by a tied knot. It has become the most influential of the Mount Tai faith folklore events.

Desperate childless women would crawl and climb from afar; step by step, they would kowtow all along the steep mountain road, seeking blessings. A general fertility goddess, Bixia Yuanjun, also known as the Mother, is believed to have fertility power on top of many of her other magic capabilities. She attracts infertile couples from all over China. She also has eight attendants, of whom two are principal: one in charge of giving children (Songzi Niangniang 送子娘娘) and another protecting the vision of the elderly and the very young (Yuanguang Niangniang 圆光娘娘). The other six take charge of each part of the reproductive process from conception to breastfeeding.[68]

There are three famous places on Mount Tai where *Shuan Wawa* is done: the Songzi Niangniang Hall at the Bixia Temple at the top of the mountain, the Wangmu Pond at the bottom, and the Doumu Palace halfway up the hill. Apart from these three places, almost all the halls on Mount Tai dedicated to Bixia Yuanjun also serve the function of giving children. Many mud babies painted in gold are placed on the shrine tables of Bixia Yuanjun, Songzi Niangniang, and Wangmu all year round. Anyone who comes for *Shuan Wawa* must pay money to the Taoist priests, known as "happy money." Women who have been infertile for many years after marriage are usually accompanied by female relatives to the shrine, where they burn incense, bow down, pray, and take a mud baby from the shrine table and hand it to the Taoist priest who conducts the ceremony. In ancient times, most people sought only boys, so early mud babies were of only one gender: naked, some wearing necklaces, sitting or crawling. All were boys and showed their male genitalia deliberately and dramatically. Nowadays, to cater to the modern incense guests seeking girls, there are also female mud babies on the shrine table.

The Taoist priest ties a red cord around the neck of the mud baby while he chants, "a fortunate boy follows his mother, and an unfortunate boy sits on the counter of the temple; go to neither your aunt's home nor your grandma's, and just follow your dear mother to go back home." At last, he chooses an auspicious name for the future baby, telling the barren woman to store the mud baby in her bedroom. The woman wraps the baby in a red cloth wrapper and takes it away. Thus ends the ritual.[69]

If the goddess helps them get a baby, the woman must put red and colorful silk on the mud baby and return it to its original place, "returning the baby." The woman should also offer incense to the Mother of Mount Tai. It is important to note that the child born after the journey is not allowed to climb Mount Tai for his or her entire life. Otherwise, the goddess may take them back. If one's wish is not granted, she can come back again, but "no more than three times." There are many ways to redeem one's vow, including making offerings and gifts, putting on robes and presenting plaques, donating money to repair the temple, and planting trees in recent years.

Another notable incense activity is *Gua Pao* 挂袍, literarily "putting on a robe." Pondering the possible needs of the Mother of Mount Tai, believers decided that she wanted new clothes at the change of the seasons, much as an earthly woman did. The ritual of offering robes to the Mother occurred twice a year, in spring and autumn, respectively. The spring robes are of thin, flimsy silk, and the autumn ones are cotton-quilted coats. Before the anti-footbinding movement in the late Qing, shoes offered were in varied colors, but all in the standardized size of three inches: a perfect illustration of the Chinese aesthetics towards the Golden Lotus.

The various head crowns, embroidered shoes, flower ornaments needed by women, and even snacks and fruits are sincerely offered by incense guests.

Although the Great Emperor of the Eastern Mountain (Yu Huang 玉皇) Worship has declined, incense is frequently offered to this male deity. Generally, incense guests come out of the Bixia Temple, bypass the Qingdi Palace, and arrive at the Jade Emperor Summit. The Jade Emperor is worshiped in the Jade Emperor Hall and has a similar procedure to that of Bixia Yuanjun, with the only difference being that the Jade Emperor is a male, so modern incense guests often offer full packs of cigarettes, as it is often assumed that he likes to smoke.[70]

The Incense Society functioned as a tour group, a substitute in a pre-modern society in which the mechanism of tourism was not yet well developed. Incense-offering brought the gods and goddesses closer to the ordinary people, satisfying their religious sentiments. Bixia Yuanjun, with her divine power of fertility, had a solid appeal for childless people, especially women. Her blessings for grain harvests, safe travel, and good health were well received. The collection of the Incense Tax resulted in economic benefits for both the local and the central governments. The opening of the incense trade boosted local trade. In his essay "The Incense Trade," Mao Dun, born in Wuzhen, lamented in 1933 that "once upon a time when the countryside was still a fictitious land of peace and happiness, this incense trade was a rural carnival."[71] We find this perspective invaluable. The incense trade provided an opportunity for rural people, who had to work hard all year round in pre-modern society, to "escape" from the orbit of everyday life and have fun—an "escape" that could have nothing to do with religion, shopping, or tourist aspirations. The prosperity of the incense trade economy was blessed with many of these elements.

However, there is also a difference between famous mountains and deities. When the countryside emerged from the "peaceful and happy" pre-modern society, the religious significance of the incense-offering faded, the tourist and trade functions of the Incense Society were replaced by the modern division of labor, and the rural population could no longer rely on the incense trade to "escape" from the trajectory of everyday life. Thus, the incense trades that had not been home to famous gods and goddesses and have no longer a powerful blessing function, such as Mount Chenghuang, could not withstand the competition of modern tourism and inevitably declined, as the conditions that had made them prosperous in the pre-modern society were no longer there. On the other hand, the incense trades of famous mountains boasting gods and goddesses with powerful blessing functions, which still satisfy the religious sentiments of the people and appease their anxieties about childlessness, traveling risks, and illness, have become more and more prosperous in modern society.

4) Yinyang *Theory and the Right of Women to Travel*

Sujie "steps on both of Di Xichen's shoulders" to get a good view of the golden face of the Mother at the Saint Mother Palace.

If we pause our reading here and start to envision the scenario depicted, we see a curious reversal of the classical Qian-Kun norm, a famous Chinese cultural matrix that defines the attributes of genders. Sujie, against the conventional cosmological characterization of women as earth, or *Kun* 坤, which belongs to an inferior, soft, yielding *Yin* 阴, is literally squatting over her man, the embodiment of heaven, or *Qian* 乾, whose attributes belong to a superior, masculine, dominant *Yang* 阳.[72]

How *Yin* and *Yang* are construed in a gender-defining context has been a vexing question to China historians. By referencing pre-Qin cosmological works, we know that *Yin* and *Yang* used to be regarded as equal and complementary to each other. However, since the Han scholar Dong Zhongshu's 董仲舒 syncretic version of Confucianism was made orthodox, *Yin* had been addressed as an insufficient, incomplete element, constantly waiting for *Yang's* fulfillment. It was thus deemed inferior to *Yang*. The theory regarding women's submissiveness and inferiority, defined as their fundamental attributes and reinforced over the past 2,000 years, helped to confine women to an immobile, auxiliary, domestic position.[73]

In the case of Sujie, the author intends to portray a virago who steps out of her social role, violates the Confucian ideal of matrimony, and upsets familial harmony. In writing, though, the logic of the literary narrative inevitably requires the author to explain the reasons for Sujie's rebelliousness and disagreements with the patriarchal system. It turns out that nine out of ten times, Sujie's family conflicts with her parents and husband's families are due to her struggle for personal freedom of movement and the suppression of her battle.

A modern reader would find it relatively easy to sympathize with her, recognizing her as a frustrated woman who has difficulty accepting her feminine role.

Chen Dongyuan, a researcher of the history of ancient Chinese women, puts forward a theory. He believes that the suffering of Chinese women had reached its peak in the Qing Dynasty, so there had to be a counter-reaction. Chen virtually renounces the happiness index of Chinese women in the Ming and Qing dynasties and ascribes the situation to "the evil Confucian ethics." Contemporary Western Sinologists often hold opposite opinions and frequently depreciate Chen's theory on the "eternally men-victimized Chinese woman" in the Ming-Qing Dynasties.

There are intrinsic connections between Sujie's henpecking behaviors and her drive to breach the confined situation. As a vibrant, animated character, she strives to have a social life not restricted to familial patterns, such as joining religious worship groups and partaking in folk festivals. However, her wish to tour scenic spots in outings and excursions, a seemingly harmless, natural desire for a modern woman, has been repeatedly thwarted.

Mann notes a paradox: while the official discourse constantly denies women's traveling rights, it was often the government that vigorously built and renovated temples, which in effect, constituted an attraction for women to travel.

> Often, women's religious practices were the subject of critical official discourse, yet the temples they visited were endowed by government funds. Even so, women's religious lives seemed remarkably free of state hegemony or official control. The politics of temple endowment and restoration were almost completely separate, socially and culturally, from the pious world of the female devotee, even though female devotion inspired it . . . however, the reach of the state was limited, because the government manipulated and shaped family relationships mainly through Confucian learning.[74]

A patriarchal society's great fear was that women should be sexually seduced by men other than their husbands. Women attending religious activities were often seen as having opportunities to have affairs with random men; or, at least, these trips were seen as occasions for women to be "molested" by street hoodlums. In the traditional male imagination, the most frightening thought was that a woman visiting a Buddhist temple or Taoist monastery was bound to have her body defiled by a monk or Taoist priest.

Except for Sujie's pilgrimage to Mount Tai, the right to which she has bargained for by bluffs and threats, most of her outings are quickly vetoed, denied, or frustrated. The resulting conflicts are grave, and both sides suffer. For example, when she plans to go to a local Buddhist festival, both her mother-in-law and her father demonstrate their strong objection; as she proceeds, the two elders are so upset that they simultaneously have strokes. On her Beijing trip, when she is desperate to visit the Imperial Aunt Nunnery 皇姑寺,[75] but is denied the opportunity repeatedly by her host, Xiang Yuting, cousin of her husband, she tries to commit suicide in defense of her free will. After she is rescued, she cries out in grief:

> They guarded me like a thief and wouldn't let me out the door! If I would like to go to other temples, they could say that I was not allowed to go as there are monks and Taoist priests. But in the Imperial Aunt Nunnery, there are only nuns, and even the doorkeepers are eunuchs. Can they even pinch or defile me? I am not even allowed to go there! I beg him again and again, but he refuses me. I will now give him my life. No one can control my ghost. I must have my spirit stay in the capital for a few days before I'm reborn.
>
> (77.596)

The stereotype that monks and priests would seduce virtuous women who visit the temple had been festering in traditional society for so long that almost every adult male would include it in his dirty jokes. When Xiang Yuting and his cousin Di Xichen have a drink, they mention that Sujie is too spirited for Di Xichen to control, so Xiang, a prankster, has a unique plan for Di:

> Xiang Yuting says: "Why don't I give you another idea, cousin? My sister-in-law is not a chicken, a cat, or a dog. You always defy her wishes, so you are at odds with her. You should be more obedient in everything in the future. Don't squirm. Don't go against her wishes. If she says she wants to go to the temple, prepare a sedan chair or horse. If she asks you to follow, follow her obediently. If she does not ask you to follow, wait at home patiently. If she stays at the temple, do not hurry her home. If she says a monk is good, do not ask about another Taoist priest. If she loves a Taoist priest, do not persuade her to love a monk. If you listen to her in everything, will she still dislike you?"
> (58.446)

Xiang Yuting uses the joke to satirize Sujie's travels and the suspicion that her travels will make Di Xichen a cuckold.

Maram Epstein, whose research focuses on gender issues in the Ming-Qing vernacular novel, notices the relationship between the theme of the shrew and the "yin-yang symbolism" in *XSYYZ*. She argues that the author's purpose in creating the image of Sujie, the reincarnation of the fox spirit, is to demonstrate the danger posed by the excess of *yin* that she embodies. The destructive aspect of Sujie's sexuality is brought out most clearly in her identity as a fox spirit since it had long been associated with the dangers of sexual desire. In the author's mind, the triumph of *yin* over *yang* threatens the integration of the individual, the family, and the natural world, leading to chaos.[76]

We can comprehend her plight if we shed enough light on her outgoing nature and her desire to engage in fun-loving pursuits. Caught between complying with the patriarchy's ethical code, subduing her will, or behaving rebelliously to secure a certain degree of personal freedom, she chooses the latter.

To explore the women's traveling patterns as reflected in the Ming and Qing literature, we cannot ignore the image of Yunniang, created in the biographical work *Six Chapters of a Floating Life* 浮生六记, by her husband Shen Fu, an unsuccessful Qing literatus.[77] Lin Yutang's translation has rendered a Chinese feminine figure beaming with charm into the English literary world: she is beautiful, intelligent, humorous, and poetic, yet faithful and convention-abiding. She loves her husband to the extent that she would spend years encouraging him to have a concubine. Calling her "one of the loveliest women in Chinese literature," Lin Yutang denies the possibility that her husband had idealized her.[78] However, the *Six Chapters* is comprised of only four chapters, two of which have either been lost or are incomplete. We particularly notice that Yunniang is not portrayed as a typical "female talent," whose travels and whose publication of her travelogue, diary, or poems would either be sponsored by, or would likely end up soliciting financial support from, the male literati who admire her.

Yunniang distinguishes herself from the female talents by her unpretentious display of a passion for life; not only does she crave opportunities for outings and excursions, but she also appreciates tasting good food, delights in viewing blossoms and the moon, and loves such things as spending time with girlfriends and playing practical jokes on her husband. Her fondness for the beauty of life even extends to other women. For example, in selecting a concubine for her husband, she insists the potential concubine be physically beautiful and spiritually charming.

Yunniang and Sujie have much in common in terms of breaking domestic restraints. Both have dominant in-laws and must fight their way out to reach the outer world. It is indeed fortunate for Yunniang that she has a husband who understands and supports her, tolerating her mischievous disguise as a man on their travels. Yet her outings beget as much distaste from her mother-in-law as Sujie's do from hers. Shen Fu makes it explicit that his lovely wife's penchant for venturing out of the inner chambers has made her a target of domestic jealousy, hatred, and misunderstanding, which eventually crushes her health and dispirits her vibrant life.

The postcolonial theorist Edward Wadie Said criticizes the history of the white race as the "history of the victors" and "history of the survival." He criticizes the lack of a "contrapuntal perspective" in such historiographies. The same is true for women's studies. Let's look at Sujie and Yuniang from a "contrapuntal perspective," free from aesthetic and moral preconceptions about literary characters and consider the similarity of their situations in many respects. We may wonder whether the sharp contrast between the images of Yunniang and Sujie is a consequence of two very different narrative perspectives: one by an affectionate, bereaved husband who recounts the endearing moments of his happy married life, and another by an author who always makes prominent his main mission of skewering henpecking viragos through his pen.

Labeled a "shrew," Sujie is tough and bellicose, confronting opposing forces directly. Yunniang is soft and meek, pursuing opportunities to go out secretly, and when she is discovered, she becomes entangled in a maelstrom of family slander and praise, and eventually dies of her illness. If the emotions and preconceptions of the authors of the two texts can be set aside so that the aspirations of the two literary female figures concerning their travels can be viewed objectively, we find the two women are both goaded by a freedom-loving nature. Therefore, the idea that Yunniang is so lovely and Sujie so detestable is really no more than a prejudice, and it should not be given serious consideration.

Notes

1 Timothy Brook, *The Confusions of Pleasure: Commerce and Culture in Ming China* (Berkeley: University of California Press, 1998). Also see Susan Naquin and Chun-fang Yu, *Pilgrims and Sacred Sites in China* (Berkeley: University of California Press, 1992).
2 Chun-fang Yu, *The Renewal of Buddhism in China: Chu-Hung and the Late Ming Synthesis* (New York: Columbia University Press, 1981).

3 Zhenhua, Chun-fang Yu, and Denis C. Mair, *In Search of the Dharma: Memoirs of a Modern Chinese Buddhist Pilgrim* (Albany, NY: State University of New York Press, 1992).
4 Chun-fang Yu, *Kuan-Yin, the Chinese Transformation of Avalokitesvara* (New York: Columbia University Press, 2001).
5 Daria Berg and Chloe Starr, eds., *Quest for Gentility in China: Negotiations Beyond Gender and Class* (Hoboken: Taylor & Francis, 2007); Dorothy Ko, *Teachers of the Inner Chambers: Women and Culture in Seventeenth-Century China* (Stanford, CA: Stanford University Press, 1994); Susan Mann, *Precious Records: Women in China's Long Eighteenth Century* (Stanford, CA: Stanford University Press, 1997).
6 Susan Mann, "The Virtue of Travel for Women in the Late Empire," in *Gender in Motion: Divisions of Labor and Cultural Change in Late Imperial and Modern China*, ed. Bryna Goodman and Wendy Larson (Lanham, MD: Rowman & Littlefield Publishers, 2005), 70.
7 Ibid., 65–70.
8 Ibid., 70.
9 Francesca Bray, *Technology and Gender: Fabrics of Power in Late Imperial China* (Berkeley, CA and London: University of California Press, 1997), 143.
10 Philip A. Kuhn, *Rebellion and Its Enemies in Late Imperial China: Militarization and Social Structure, 1796–1864* (Cambridge, MA: Harvard University Press, 1970), 8.
11 Yulan Chen, "The Literary Life of Women in Jiangnan in Ming and Qing Dynasties," *Chinese Social Sciences Today* 392, December 14, 2012. 陈玉兰：《明清江南女性的文学生活》，《中国社会科学报》，2012年12月14日第392期。
12 Daria Berg, *Women Writers and the Literary World in Early Modern China* (London: Routledge, 2013), 11.
13 Tani E. Barlow, *The Question of Women in Chinese Feminism* (Durham, NC and London: Duke University Press, 2004), 21–22.
14 Paul S. Ropp, *Banished Immortal: Searching for Shuangqing, China's Peasant Woman Poet* (Ann Arbor: University of Michigan Press, 2001).
15 Ibid., 5.
16 Jen-shu Wu, *Women's Consumer Culture of the Jiangnan Region in the Ming-Qing Period* (Beijing: The Commercial Press, 2016), 143–45. 巫仁恕：《奢侈的女人：明清时期江南妇女的消费文化》，北京：商务印书馆，2016年，第143–45页。
17 Quote from Patricia Buckley Ebrey, *Women and the Family in Chinese History* (London and New York: Routledge, 2003), 207.
18 Paul S. Ropp, "The Seeds of Change: Reflections on the Condition of Women in the Early and Mid Ch'ing," *Signs: Journal of Women in Culture and Society* 2, no. 1 (1976): 5–23.
19 Dorothy Ko, *Cinderella's Sisters: A Revisionist History of Footbinding* (Berkeley: University of California Press, 2005), 5.
20 Ko, *Teachers of the Inner Chambers*, 149.
21 Many scholars nowadays still insist that "the most painful symbol of subordination of women to the sexual tastes of men was the practice of footbinding." They are obviously standing on the opposite side of Ko's idea. Ropp, "The Seeds of Change," 5–23.
22 Bray, *Technology and Gender*, 146.
23 Wendy Larson, "Women, Writing, and the Discourse of Nationalism," in *Women and Writing in Modern China* (Stanford, CA: Stanford University Press, 1998).
24 Bray, *Technology and Gender*, 237.
25 [Qing] Liuhong Huang, *The Complete Collection of the Benevolence*, proofread by Baoming Zhou (Yangzhou: Guangling Press, 2018), 353. [清]黄六鸿著，周保明点校：《福惠全书》，扬州：广陵书社，2018年，第353页。
26 Yenna Wu, *The Chinese Virago: A Literary Theme* (Cambridge, MA: Council on East Asian Studies distributed by Harvard University Press, 1995), 24.
27 Hai Ren, "The Landscape of Power: Imagineering Consumer Behavior at China's Theme Parks," in *In the Themed Space: Locating Culture, Nation and Self*, ed. Scott A. Lukas (Lanham: Lexington Books, 2007), 97.

28 Sima Qian, "The Fengshan Book," in *Records of the Grand Historian* (Beijing: Zhonghua Book Company, 1959), 1361. [汉]司马迁：《史记·封禅书》，北京：中华书局，1959年，第1361页。
29 Junzuo Yi and Delin Wang, "On Making Mount Tai a National Mountain," first published in *Jiangsu Education Magazine* 2 (1933): 311–20; revised and proofread by Ying Zhou, reprinted in Junzuo Yi, *Tai Shan Guo Shan Yi* (Beijing: China Intercontinental Press, 2013), 135. 易君左、王德林《定泰山为国山刍议》文，初刊于1933年《江苏教育》杂志第2卷，同年由泰安县立师范讲习所翻印为单行本，但其中不少讹误。下书由周郢校订和续纂而成。易君左：《泰山国山议》，北京：五洲传播出版社，2013年，第135页。
30 [Ming] Xijue Wang, "The Monument to Bixia of Mount Tai," in *The Recompiled County Annals of Tai'an*, revised by Yanying Ge and Yuanlu Wu, compiled by Zhaozhang Meng, vol. 14 (Tai'an: Tai'an County Chronicles Office, 1929). [明]王锡爵：《东岳碧霞宫碑》，见葛延瑛、吴元禄修编，孟昭章纂：民国十八年泰安县志局排印本《重修泰安县志》卷十四，泰安：泰安县志局，1929年。
31 [Ming] Zhaozhe Xie, "Land II," in *Five Miscellaneous Morsels*, vol. 4 (Shanghai: Shanghai Bookstore Publishing House, 2001), 66. [明]谢肇淛：《五杂俎》卷四《地部》（二），第66页。
32 Daria Berg, "Reformer, Saint, and Savior: Visions of the Great Mother in the Novel Xingshi Yinyuan Zhuan and Its Seventeenth-Century Chinese Context," *Nan nü: Men, Women, and Gender in Early and Imperial China* 1, no. 2 (1999): 246.
33 Tao Ye, "A Study of the Incense-offering Ritual by Tai-Mount Incense Society Mount Tai Incense Society," *Thought Battlefront*, no. 2 (2006): 80–90. 叶涛：《泰山香社传统进香仪式研究》，《思想战线》，2006年第2期，第80–90页。
34 Hui Liu and Li Tao, "About Incense Societies of Mountain Tai in Song Dynasty Mount Tai Incense Society," *Folklore Studies*, no. 1 (2004): 120–28. 刘慧，陶莉：《关于宋代的泰山香会》，《民俗研究》2004年第1期，第120–28页。
35 Zhou, "Book of Incense, vol. 11," 10. [明]周嘉胄：《香乘》卷十一，第10页。
36 Naquin and Yu, *Pilgrims and Sacred Sites in China*, 337.
37 [Ming] Ruoyu Liu, "A Brief Account of Eating Habits, the Fourth Month," in *A Weighted and Unbiased Record*, vol. 20 (Beijing: Beijing Classics Publishing House, 1994), 180. [明]刘若愚：《酌中志》卷二十《饮食好尚纪略·四月》，第180页。
38 Ibid., [Ming] Ruoyu Liu, "A Brief Account of Heitou Yuan Li (attached)," in *A Weighted and Unbiased Record*, vol. 24 (Beijing: Beijing Classics Publishing House, 1994), 218. 同上，卷二十四《黑头爱立纪略附》，第218页。
39 [Ming] Dong Liu and Yizheng Yu, *A Brief Record of the Scenery of the Imperial Capital* (Beijing: Beijing Classics Publishing House, 1983), 133. [明]刘侗，[明]于奕正：《帝京景物略》，北京：北京古籍出版社，1983年，第133页。
40 Xiaoqun Wu, "A History of the Study of the Belief in Bixia Yuanjun in Mount Miaofeng, Beijing," *Folklore Studies*, no. 3 (2002): 42–51. 吴效群：《北京妙峰山碧霞元君信仰研究史》，《民俗研究》，2002年第3期，第42–51页。
41 Xuedian Wang and Yanjie Sun, *Gu Jiegang and His Disciples* (Beijing: Zhonghua Book Company, 2010), 29. 王学典，孙延杰：《顾颉刚和他的弟子们》，北京：中华书局，2010年，第29页。
42 Jiegang Gu, *Mount Miaofeng* (Guangzhou: Institute of Language and History of National Sun Yat-sen University, 1928), 1027. 顾颉刚：《妙峰山》，广州：国立中山大学语言历史研究所，1928年，第1027页。
43 Ibid., 1026. 同上，第1026页。
44 [Yuan] Zongyi Tao, "The Three Gu and Six Po," in *Farming in Nan Village I*, proofread and annotated by Xueling Wang (Shenyang: Liaoning Education Press, 1998), 125. [元]陶宗仪：《三姑六婆》，见王雪玲校注：《南村辍耕录（一）》，沈阳：辽宁教育出版社，1998年，第125页。

45 Ruolan Yi, *The Three Gu and Six Po* (Taipei: Daoxiang Publishing House, 2002), 137. 衣若兰：《三姑六婆：明代妇女与社会的探索》，台北：稻乡出版社，2002年，第137页。
46 Glen Dudbridge, "A Pilgrimage in Seventeenth-Century Fiction: T'ai-shan and the 'Hsing-shih yin-yüan chuan'," *T'oung Pao* 77 (1991): 234–35.
47 Arthur H. Smith, *Village Life in China: A Study in Sociology* (New York: F. H. Revell company, 1899), 141–42.
48 Hsiao-hsiao-sheng, *The Plum in the Golden Vase or, Chin P'ing Mei, vol. 5, The Dissolution* (Princeton: Princeton University Press, 2011), 161.
49 Ye, "A Study of the Incense," 81–82. 叶涛：《泰山香社传统进香仪式研究》，第81–82页。
50 Dong Liang, "Climbing the Famous Mountain, Praying for Great Happiness: The Mount Tai Incense Society Carries on the Culture of Praying for Blessings," *Taishan Evening News*, February 12, 2014. 梁栋：《登名岳，祈洪福：泰山香社传承祈福文化》，《泰山晚报》，2014年2月12日。
51 Tao Ye, *Study on Mount Tai Incense Society* (Shanghai: Shanghai Classics Publishing House, 2009), 107. 叶涛：《泰山香社研究》，上海：上海古籍出版社，2009年，第107页。
52 Sima Qian, "Biographies of Divination Activities 68," in *Records of the Grand Historian*, 3239. [西汉]司马迁：《史记·龟策列传第六十八》，第3239页。
53 Bingwen Nan, *The Secret Religion of Buddhism and Daoism and Ming Society* (Tianjin: Tianjin Classics Publishing House, 2001), 163–65. 南炳文：《佛道秘密宗教与明代社会》，天津：天津古籍出版社，2001年，第163–65页。
54 [Ming] Honglie Ren, "The Prefecture Annals of Tai'an, vol. 1, Omen of Good or Bad," in *Chinese Local Chronicles Series, North China*, no. 10 (Taipei: Cheng Wen Publishing Company, 1936). [明]任弘烈：《泰安州志》卷一《灾祥》，《中国方志丛书·华北地方·第十号》，台北：成文出版社，1936年。
55 Ye, *Study on Mount Tai Incense Society*, 276. 叶涛：《泰山香社研究》，第276页。
56 Ying Zhou, "The Textual Research About Ancient Incense Guest Hotels in Mount Tai," *Journal of Taian Institute of Education*, no. 2 (1999): 7–9. 周郢：《泰山古代香客店考》，《泰安教育学院学报岱宗学刊》，1999年第2期，第7–9页。
57 Ye, *Study on Mount Tai Incense Society*, 271. 叶涛：《泰山香社研究》，第271页。
58 [Ming] Shenxing Yu, "Geography," in *The Prefectural Records of Yanzhou*, vol. 4 (Jinan: Qilu Press, 1985). [明]于慎行：《兖州府志》卷四《风土志》，济南：齐鲁书社，1985年。
59 [Qing] Menglei Chen, ed., "Systematic Textual Research of Dongchang Prefecture VI," in *Ancient and Modern Book Collection, vol. 83, National Territory* (Shanghai: Zhonghua Book Company, 1934), 13. 《东昌府都汇考六》，收录于[清]陈梦雷编《古今图书集成》第83册《职方典》，中华书局1934年版，第13页。
60 Ye, *Study on Mount Tai Incense Society*, 95. 叶涛：《泰山香社研究》，第95页。
61 Liping Wang, "Tourism and Spatial Change in Hangzhou, 1911–1927," in *Remaking the Chinese City: Modernity and National Identity, 1900–1950*, ed. Joseph Esherick (Honolulu: University of Hawai'i Press, 2000), 111–12.
62 Ibid.
63 "Jiashen Day of July, The Eleventh Year of the Zhengde Reign," in *MSL—The Veritable Records of Emperor Wuzong*, vol. 139. 《明实录·武宗实录》卷一三九《正德十一年七月甲申》。
64 [Qing] Zhao Du, "The General Chronicle of Shandong, vol. 12, Mount Tai Incense Tax," in *Complete Library of the Four Treasures, Photocopied Wenyuan Pavillion Edition* (Taipei: Taiwan Commercial Press, 1986). [清]杜诏：《山东通志》卷十二《泰山香税》，《影印文渊阁四库全书》，台北：中国台湾商务印书馆，1986年。

65 [Qing] Gui Qing, "The Veritable Records of Emperor Gaozong I, the 13th year of Yongzheng reign, November, (Part II)," in *The Veritable Records of Qing Dynasty* (Beijing: Zhonghua Book Company, 1985), 285. [清]庆桂：《高宗实录》（一）《雍正十三年十一月》（下），《清实录》，北京：中华书局，1985年，第285页。
66 Taibin Cai, "Incense Tax Collection, Management, and Usage of Mt. Tai and Mt. Taihe during the Ming and Qing Dynasties," *Humanitas Taiwanica*, no. 74 (2011): 127–79. 蔡泰彬：《泰山与太和山的香税征收、管理与运用》，《台大文史哲学报》，2011年第74期，第127–79页。
67 Mingchu Ma and Chengfei Yan, *Annotated History of Mount Tai* (Qingdao: Qingdao Ocean University Press, 1992), 149. 马铭初，严澄非：《岱史校注》，青岛：青岛海洋大学出版社，1992年，第149页。
68 Theodore Huters, Roy Bin Wong, and Pauline Yu, *Culture & State in Chinese History: Conventions, Accommodations, and Critiques* (Stanford: Stanford University Press, 1997), 193.
69 Ye, "A Study of the Incense." 叶涛：《泰山香社传统进香仪式研究》。
70 Ye, *Study on Mount Tai Incense Society*, 170–71. 叶涛：《泰山香社研究》，第170–71页。
71 Dun Mao, "The Incense Market," in *China on the Fingertips: The Original Landscape of the Hometown*, ed. Ziqing Zhu (Tianjin: Baihua Literature and Art Publishing House, 2014), 174. 茅盾：《香市》，见朱自清主编：《指尖上的中国：故乡的原风景》，天津：百花文艺出版社，2014年，第174页。
72 Lisa Ann Raphals, *Sharing the Light: Representations of Women and Virtue in Early China* (Albany, NY: State University of New York Press, 1998), 2.
73 Chia-lin Pao-Tao, "The Yin-Yang Theory and Women's Status," in *the 2nd Volume of the Collections of the Studies of Chinese Women's History*, ed. Chia-lin Pao-Tao (Taiwan: Dao Xiang Publisher, 2008), 37–54. 鲍家麟：《阴阳学说与妇女地位》，见鲍家麟编著：《中国妇女史论集续集》，台北：稻香出版社，2008年，第37–54页。
74 Mann, *Precious Records*, 199–200.
75 The Imperial Aunt Nunnery, officially known as Bao Ming Temple 保明寺, was allegedly founded by the reinstated Emperor Yingzong to commend a nun who tried to, although in vain, thwart his ill-fated military campaign against the Mongols which later led to the catastrophic Tumu Fort Incident. Its ruins now located at the foothills of the Western Hills in a small settlement called West Huang Village, a dozen kilometers west of Beijing. Throughout the fifteenth century, the temple received repeated imperial patronage. See Thomas Shiyu Li and Susan Naquin, "The Baoming Temple: Religion and the Throne in Ming and Qing China," *Harvard Journal of Asiatic Studies* 48, no. 1 (1988): 131–88.
76 Maram Epstein, *Competing Discourses: Orthodoxy, Authenticity, and Engendered Meanings in Late Imperial Chinese Fiction* (Cambridge, MA: Harvard University Press, 2001), 136–41.
77 [Qing] Fu Shen, *Six Chapters of a Floating Life*, trans. Yutang Lin (Beijing: Foreign Language Teaching and Research Press, 1999).
78 Yutang Lin, *The Wisdom of China and India* (New York: Random House, 1942), 966.

Conclusion

This book deals with Ming clothing, food, and travel institutions, conventions, and practices reflected in the profound yet understudied seventeenth-century novel *XSYYZ*.

By the seventeenth century, some significant developments were taking place that began to change the shape of the genre. The last few decades of the Ming saw the gradual growth of a more broad-based audience for printed colloquial fiction, which included fine editions of vernacular plays and short stories published by the studios of Feng Menglong. As to saga novels, while the Jiajing and Wanli reigns of the sixteenth century witnessed the completion of the four undisputed Ming masterpieces, the seventeenth century was by no means a slack period, due to the appearance of *XSYYZ*. Its major plot, a henpecked husband being tortured by his shrewish wife because of karmic retribution for the sins he had committed in his previous life, is already known to most readers. However, despite a few experts who uphold it as "upwardly carrying on the legacy of *Jin Ping Mei* and downwardly enlightening *A Dream of Red Mansions*" and propose to boost it into the "top five" tier of classical novels, *XSYYZ* has not received its due attention. On the contrary, it has long been undervalued and misconstrued, probably due to its flaws, such as the excessive use of vernacular dialogues, moral didacticism, and prejudice against women.

Assessing the Novel's literary value can be difficult.

The theme that runs through the entire composition remains a satire on the reversal of proper marital relationships and the curious phenomenon it results in: henpecking. To put it more concretely, had a man committed heinous crimes in his previous life, the worst karmic retribution that could have befallen him was to marry a horrible wife. Aside from elaborating on this theme, the author also lends his pen to expound on other facets of the karmic law, such as how the abuse of food and drink leads to fatal disasters.

XSYYZ is the first saga novel to render karmic retribution a cardinal structural principle.[1] In its finely designed fictitious world, everyone acts on the Law of Karma: sins are punished, virtues rewarded, old scores paid off, and victims get revenge on their victimizers.

The grand, thematic design of a world centered on the Law of Karma is not foremostly Buddhist, but Confucian. Karmic retribution functions only as a narrative tool,[2] used by the author to permeate the reader's mind with Confucian morals.

Embracing literature's social mission, Xizhou Sheng believes that "for most of the fictional, unorthodox works, the only case in which they can prevail in the future and be remembered by later generations is when they help to correct the ethos of society." Therefore, he painstakingly adopts a didactic tone, notwithstanding an awareness that "my garrulous insertion might sound tedious."[3]

Having enumerated the "three ultimate pleasures for a gentleman" as defined by Mencius—"to have both parents alive, and brothers living free of rancor; to be free of guilt before heaven and shame before men, and to gather the talented men of the empire and educate them."[4] Xizhou Sheng petitions to differ with the Secondary Saint. One more important pleasure is missing, says he, "That is, to have a virtuous wife."[5] He stresses that the fourth criterion ought to be added to the list to make a gentleman wholesome, for if this one condition is not met, none of the three above can be attained.

> Even if your parents were alive, their lives would be so miserable that they would wish they were dead. Even if you get along with your brothers now, you guys will become bitter enemies in the long run. You wouldn't be able to face heaven without guilt or men without shame, let alone teach the talented men of the empire.[6]

It Is from this point on that moral didacticism steps in. Convinced that society awaits moral corrections and cautions, and that a worthy writer should take up the responsibilities of preaching morals to people between catering to the reader's desires for uncanny plots and delivering his sermons, Xizhou Sheng establishes a delicate balance. If the stories expounded inspire awe, and if the narrative tool of karmic retribution works and the ethics indeed permeate the reader's mind, then, in the end, the reader, upon finishing reading them, would be very soul-troubled and, with a reformed heart, would never have been so eager to embrace Confucian doctrines.

According to the Confucian doctrines illustrated in *The Great Learning*, one should first cultivate himself, regulate his family well, propel the good order to govern the state, and ultimately apply it to the Under Heaven.[7] A world where doting husbands and shrew wives prevail poses a subversive threat to the patriarchal society and must be corrected. Beneath the veiled karmic theme, playing up a Confucian agenda to uphold the proper social and gender hierarchies is the Novel's sole concern.

While *XSYYZ* deals primarily with the distortion and inversion of proper conjugal hierarchies, it also lavishes no less ink on the Ming material life.

As stated in the opening chapter, this study does not seek to address, solve, or debate textological issues regarding its unknown authorship or unspecified periodization. Nor does it intend to follow the lead of the preceding Western scholarship, which is overwhelmingly comprised of literary critiques or gender studies. This work is not interested in construing literary techniques or constructing feminist agendas.

Without sufficient raw materials to support a study of housing, this research leaves out the housing, *zhu* 住, component of the people's four primary concerns, *yishizhuxing*, addressing only the remaining three: clothing, food, and travel. Following the clothing chapter and preceding the food chapter, an independent chapter embedded in the context of Ming luxury consumption and financial institutions is conceived. It raises an inquiry into a counteractive factor of the Ming's consumerist culture: the sumptuary ethos.

The study of sumptuary laws, a well-trodden academic area, is composed of the study of the following elements, which also happen to be the components of the subtitle of Lambert M. Surhone, Miriam T. Timpledon, and Susan F. Marseken's edited work, *Sumptuary Law: Social Stratification, Morality, Clothing, Food, Luxury Goods, Discrimination, Nobility, Privilege, Bourgeoisie, Dress Code.*[8] The causes and effects of the Ming sumptuary legislation have been amply discussed by Brook, Clunas, and Appadurai; its societal derivative, the sumptuary ethos, has not received as much attention, though. Scholars differ over how to construe the highly commercialized late Ming economic pattern. Still, few disagree that in so materialistic a society, the sets of sumptuary laws devised in the early Ming had already crumbled. The weakening of sumptuary laws was reflected in the outright defiance of them by the rich; their purchasing power had far surpassed the modest earlier standards. It was also embodied in the incompliant dressing practices by opera actors, pimps, prostitutes, concubines, and eunuchs—all professions or statuses required by law to distinguish themselves from commoners in appearance by wearing denigrating clothing or headwear as reflected by style, fiber, or color. Laws had become so powerless that virtually any commoner could trespass them in one way or another. The impracticability, complexity, and ease with which people violated the laws all contributed to people's disregard for them.

Yet to claim that the Ming sumptuary legislation simply evaporated into thin air would be erring into over-simplification. There were, unmistakably, forces outside the framework of the sumptuary laws. They deformed the commercial rivalries between the North and South, deterred a booming consumerist economy, and polarized the urban and the rural. Even when we discount factors of the unbalanced transportation means and local wealth, we still must acknowledge the potency of the forces. We call these collections of mentalities, psychologies, practices, and customs that worked against consumerist culture "sumptuary ethos." Without ascribing all powers external to sumptuary legal codes that are against consumerist culture to this sumptuary ethos, and without labeling the sumptuary ethos Ming-generic, we argue that it permeated most pervasively in the Ming. The regime (at least at its commencement stage) had worked most diligently to establish an elaborate sumptuary legal structure to uphold its desired hierarchies. The sumptuary ethos was protected, encouraged, and made orthodox by sumptuary laws but revealed itself to the people in a much less rigid form. It frowned upon the consumption of luxury goods, dissuading one from, instead of directly punishing one for, accessing material comforts to which one's social status was not permitted.

194 *Conclusion*

The reservation by Confucian moralists to mobilize laws to punish transgressors further enhanced its validity and vitality. Fueled by an autarkic economic society's disapproving sentiments regarding trading and commerce, it went along with the paramount virtue of the agricultural society: frugality. It was endorsed by the state's agenda to deemphasize the roles played by merchants. In general, it had strong adverse effects on the development of the nation's spirit of entrepreneurism, which, if given ample nourishment, might have gained socio-economic momentum to grow into capitalism, leading the dynasty to embark on a route taken by the post-Glorious Revolution Britain.

Despite the universality of this research theme, namely, to discover and present Ming material culture, each of the four research chapters centers on different focal points. Nevertheless, the connectedness among the chapters extends beyond the four "people's primary concerns." Each chapter associates a facet of the Ming material life to its correlated worldly realm. From that lens, we observe how Ming legislative measures, customary practices, and ethical norms combined to take effect. This coextension into socio-economic dimensions ensures the consistency of the chapters.

The clothing chapter covers the kaleidoscopic world of Ming raiment. A glimpse into this world finds social boundary-crossing: coin money trampling over the noble, people of low status usurping the rights reserved for the dignified, concubines taking precedence over legitimate wives. Yet a closer examination still finds obeisance to the older codes devised two centuries before. The eschatological world of the late Ming, notwithstanding its disorderliness and rampant materialism, even in its utmost moment of dolce vita sentiment, was still governed by the gravity of laws initiated by its founder. The instituted dress codes were indeed being ignored, trespassed, and disregarded, but the transgressors were not spared moral reprimand or legal retribution. To probe the reasons for the coexisting orderliness and disorder of the Ming people's clothing, one must trace back and examine how the functions of clothing were perceived at the dynasty's inception.

The elaboration of the Ming clothing institution is fundamentally a reflection of the regime's excessive concern with differentiating people by dressing them differently. Emperor Hongwu, whose parochial mindset, despotic maneuvers, and strong-willed character were of immense faculty in molding the shape of the dynasty, was obsessed with the idea of hierarchizing the populace. Unlike other founding emperors of preceding dynasties who had either sonorous names or titles to fall back on, he rose from poverty and obscurity. He had witnessed his parents and siblings starving to death, worked for his proprietor as a cowherd, and scratched out his living by turning himself into a monk, a beggar, and eventually a rebel. The sole survivor among his fellow rebels, he practically embodied the social Darwinist rule of "survival of the fittest." His animal-like survival instinct had goaded him to propel himself forward until he stood alone as the ultimate winner in a series of civil and ethnic wars. But the prolonged instability and the brutality he experienced wrought paranoia and parochialism into his mind, which led him to trust no one—perhaps except for his wife, the virtuous Empress Ma.

Moreover, he harbored no illusions about the innate goodness of human beings, a fundamental theory held by Mencius and his followers. To rule his people in a pro-Daoist, laid-back way, as was done by the early Han emperors, had never been an option for him. Indeed, in agricultural policies, he did take many measures to encourage the rehabilitation of farming. Still, his ultimate design of Ming society went far beyond adequately clothing and feeding his subjects. In his mind, a society ought to be trimly hierarchical, which in turn would bring order, and order would, in turn, bring stability, which was essential to the longevity and perpetuation of the regime.

Major imperial dynasties of grand unification, from a need to have people conform to its governing order, usually stood ready to embrace imported ideologies that might safeguard social stability. If a notion, a cult, or a religion should lessen the regime's burden of mobilizing legislation, police, and the army—in brief, the machinery of the state apparatus—a worldly ruler might endorse or go so far as to promulgate it. If it went well with China's generic socio-cultural norms, it might even gain popularity without the regime's promotion.

The quick demise of the Qin taught a weighty lesson to practitioners of Chinese politics. In *Disquisition Finding Faults with Qin*, Han Confucian scholar Jia Yi ascribes the collapse of the Qin to its adoption of harsh legalist enforcements, cautioning sovereigns of subsequent dynasties against the overuse of state power.[9] Heeding that critical warning, even the most autocratic rulers wanted to shun being called legalists, a political paradox most clearly embodied in the person of Hongwu. When Timothy Brook describes the founding emperor's ideal agrarian society as a "Taoist model of a little elite of virtuous elders supervising self-sufficient villages,"[10] he is right about the self-sufficiency part but wrong in ascribing the emperor's utopian vision to Taoism. Hongwu never stinted Draconian measures to strike out at his political opponents or the discontented populace, yet identifiably legalist as he was, he still strove to ward off an appearance of having succumbed to legalism. Scheming to awe the masses yet avoiding the use of force, he devised a delicate institution based on an existing popular belief, the City God cult.

The "What Drives People to Sell their Daughters" section of the clothing chapter examines the clothing situations of the Ming destitute and the social mechanisms behind their poverty. The price of labor was so appallingly cheap that the cost of purchasing a maid was not much higher than that of clothing her with a set of winter garments. The destitute succumbed to financial adversities and were reduced to selling themselves. In a bad year, impoverished parents were virtually left with no choice but to sell their daughters into wealthy households to secure them a warm winter.

The same rationale underlying the Ming dress codes also prevailed in devising Ming sumptuary laws. The spirit of the sumptuary legislation was ultimately not concerned with material culture but with the permanence of hierarchical social order. The study of the sumptuary ethos unpacks an important socio-economic factor independent of law enforcement but potent in deterring people's luxurious consumption, discouraging entrepreneurism, and harboring prohibitive prices.

Derived from the famous Chinese idiom "the masses regard food as their heaven," those seemingly loose but logically coherent subtopics endeavor to cover an array of socio-economic facets on issues of food, including crop planting, food processing, catering food for field laborers, morals on food consumption, and the salt franchise. Social responsibility, ethical values, and moral economy are all mirrored in one's attitude towards food and water, which echoes the call to venerate frugality, a good-karma-generating virtue. In this sense, food is regarded as a heavenly sustenance for the populace and a treasured commodity in an agrarian society, which abhors the desecration of its primary product. Through a short anecdote, the food chapter also examines the Ming Salt Franchise policy, discussing its ineffectiveness in halting salt smuggling, and then moves to a review of the comprehensive Beijing food culture.

In the opening chapter, we mentioned that both *Jin Ping Mei* and *XSYYZ* are obsessed with the "portrayal of things." The material fetishism in the latter's case is best exemplified by the Novel's narrative economy in listing varieties of foods, especially when it comes to the depiction of the food culture in Beijing, whose political, cultural, and economic significance rendered it a place of assemblage of different local flavors.

The traveling chapter singles out and examines a leisure-oriented pilgrimage to Mount Tai undertaken by Sujie and her husband, Di Xichen, to research Ming traveling culture. Unlike the much recorded and culturally sanctioned *guixiu* adventures, Sujie has to resort to alternative means, the Mount Tai Incense Society, to achieve her tourist goals. Headed by sophisticated town women with Buddhist and Taoist backgrounds, the society arranges transportation, food, and accommodations, and is flexible in policies to cater to various needs. The relationship between the leaders of the society and the innkeeper benefits both parties.

This chapter visits a tradition that customarily frowned upon commoner women's travels, which were deemed legit only under certain circumstances such as family reunion. Paradoxically, the same tradition embraced the travels of elites, regardless of gender. Therefore, we introduce some Western scholarship on Ming-Qing *guixiu* adventuresses, a group of culturally prestigious female elites. A brief comparison between Sujie and the stereotypical *guixiu* adventuresses raises questions on the traveling rights and practicalities for a woman of lower-class status. How would she manage to break out of familial, societal, moral, and physical confinement to reach the outside world? How did the footbinding practice and a cloistering culture affect her initiatives to travel, both physically and psychologically? What role would her husband take in accompanying her on her journey?

The chapter also tries to compare the traveling images of Sujie with another unorthodox adventuress, Yunniang, the heroine of *Six Chapters of a Floating Life*, and points out that, in pursuing liberty, the right to travel at one's free will is a critical component. At this point, the two women are indeed not that different. While Yunniang enjoys the status as one of the most beloved female images in classical Chinese literature, and her sneaking out to join her husband on leisure-oriented trips wins her much charm in the eyes of readers, Sujie is repeatedly studied, represented, and anatomized as a specimen of a traditional virago by modern researchers. To construe Sujie's rebellious behaviors, the chapter briefly resorts to a feminist-modernist lens. We argue that her shrewdness should not be ascribed to her character as a "roaring lioness," as the author explains. Sujie is a free soul who longs to visit the outside world. Her repeated frustrations in acquiring freedom of mobility ought to be noticed.

We find that the travels of Sujie and Yunniang are both external to the *guixiu* pattern; they can hardly expect to receive cultural sanction from their social surroundings. They both have bigoted in-laws and gossiping relatives, and both must fight to break with a highly disapproving tradition of women's excursions to the outside world. In pursuing the same category of physical freedom, the coarse, strong-willed, defiant Sujie wins, but she is labeled as a shrew; the meek, social-protocol-abiding Yunniang becomes a victim of domestic hatred and slander and dies in repentance. Suppose a reader adopts the modern perception that a woman's ability to travel at her free will is one of the unalienable rights essential to the fullness of her liberty. In that case, he might come to comprehend Sujie, a defensive character who fights tooth and nail to bargain for freedom that is usually not allotted to women.

This study repeatedly accentuates the great, and usually negative, influence the founding emperor Hongwu had on Ming social institutions and practices. In fact, this author would acknowledge that measures devised by this emperor had restricted the rules and practices of economics to the degree that would have amazed Adam Smith. Hongwu was a character of extraordinary diligence and frugality, yet a historical figure is not to be weighed on the scales of history merely by such virtues. On the other hand, when a historical figure's personality and temperament cast a mold on history, his flaws always tend to leave deeper marks than his virtues. To what extent the severe poverty of the emperor's early childhood and the blood-shedding of his adulthood before he seized his throne had traumatized his mind, we do not know, but the frequent references to him as a "paranoid autocrat" in Western scholarship, including that of Frederick Mote and Denis Twitchett, the authors of *The Cambridge history of China. Vol. 7, The Ming dynasty, 1368–1644*, are not made without reason. Similar criticisms can also be found in Chinese scholarship. Wu Han, the famous Ming historian who had authored the *Biography of Zhu Yuanzhang*, was ordered to revise his book in 1965 on the eve of the Great Cultural Revolution, during which he was persecuted to death. The revision, made under Mao Zedong's direct attention, was meant to beautify the peasant rebels following the then national discourse. Because of all the antipathy Wu Han held towards Emperor Hongwu's autocracy, this revised version thus contained a strong flavor of paradox. Aside from the added contents complimentary to the beggar-turned-emperor and the premise that his rebellion emancipated the poor people, we find Wu Han harshly criticizing Hongwu for his stubbornness, narrow-mindedness, and shortsightedness:

> Political measures must change along with the movements of society and time. Zhu Yuanzhang, nevertheless, institutionalized his imperial edicts, made decisions for his descendants hundreds of years later and ruled out

possibilities of any changing in his policies. These measures greatly fettered political reform and blocked the advancement of the era.[11]

By comparing the sumptuary legislation and sumptuary ethos, we can safely boil down our conclusion to this: the sumptuary legislation failed. It had ramifications far beyond Hongwu's initial design. Yet the sumptuary ethos sustained, reaching a stalemate against a booming consumerist culture. In rural areas of northern China, where the ethos remained most resilient, it was often lent legitimacy by Confucian ethical norms, which took a heavy toll on the fundamental rules of fair exchange and had arguably deterred the trend of burgeoning commercialism.

Notes

1 Yenna Wu, "Repetition in Xingshi Yinyuan Zhuan," *Harvard Journal of Asiatic Studies (Cambridge, MA)* 51, no. 1 (1991): 62.
2 For narrative tool theory, please see Andrew H. Plaks, "Issues in Chinese Narrative Theory in the Perspective of the Western Tradition," *PTL: A Journal for Descriptive Poetics and Theory of Literature*, no. 2 (1977): 341.
3 Xizhou Sheng, *Xingshi Yinyuan Zhuan*, proofread by Bing Zhai (Jinan: Qilu Press, 1993), Preface.
4 Ibid.
5 Conjugal harmony has always been emphasized in Confucian codes, though the state of harmony is defined patriarchally. The husband-wife relationship is positioned as the primary of the "five cardinal relationships," more important than those of emperor-vassal, father-son, elder brother-younger brother, and friend-friend. Wei-ming Tu, "Probing the 'Three Bonds' and 'Five Relationships' in Confucian Humanism," in *Confucianism and the Family*, ed. George De Vos and Walter Slote (New York: SUNY Press, 1998), 129.
6 Xizhou Sheng, *Xingshi Yinyuan Zhuan*, Preface.
7 James Legge, *The Great Learning in The Four Books* (Hong Kong: Wanguo Publisher, 1947), 11–15. 理雅各：《华英对照四书·大学》，香港：万国出版社，1947年，第 11–15 页。
8 Lambert M. Surhone, Miriam T. Timpledon, and Susan F. Marseken, eds., *Sumptuary Law: Social Stratification, Morality, Clothing, Food, Luxury Goods, Discrimination, Nobility, Privilege, Bourgeoisie, Dress Code* (Beau Bassin, Mauritius: Betascript Publishers, 2009).
9 Robert Joe Cutter, "Chia I (贾谊)," in *The Indiana Companion to Traditional Chinese Literature*, ed. William H. Nienhauser (Bloomington: Indiana University Press, 1986), 254–55.
10 Brook, *The Confusions of Pleasure*, 19.
11 Han Wu, *Biography of Zhu Yuanzhang* (Tianjin: Baihua Literature and Art Publishing House, 2000), 325. 吴晗：《朱元璋传》，天津：百花文艺出版社，2000 年，第 325页。

Index

Note: Page numbers in *italics* indicate a figure on the corresponding page.

agriculture 117–20
*Ameliorative Satire and the
    Seventeenth-Century Chinese Novel*
    (Wu) 16
Ancient and Modern Wonders
    (Xiaohua Zhuren) 18
Anecdotes from the Political Turmoil 142
Annales School 10
artisans 59–62

bamboo raccoon 126–7
bamboo-strip cases 80–1
Ban Gu 11
baotou 60
Baoyuan Bureau 96, 100–1
Beihu Record, The (Duan Gonglu) 129
Beneath the Red Banner (Lao She) 48–9
Berg, Daria 17, 19, 150
bianshi 116
Biography of Zhu Yuanzhang
    (Wu Han) 197
Bixia Yuanjun 160–1, 164, 174–5, 179–82
Bloch, Marc 85
Bonds of Matrimony, The (Nyren) 15
Book of Siyouzhai 132
Braudel, Ferdinand 10, 114
Bray, Francesca 19, 151, 157–8
Brecht, Bertolt 12–13
Brief History of Chinese Fiction, A
    (Lu Xun) 3–4
*Brief Record of the Scenery of the Imperial
    Capital, A* (Liu Dong and Yu
    Yizheng) 163
Brokaw, Cynthia 19
Brook, Timothy 19, 150, 193, 195
Buddhism 143, 150, 165, 192

Cai Wenji 34
Cai Yuanfang 18
*Cambridge history of China. Vol. 7,
    The Ming dynasty, 1368–1644,
    The* (Mote and Twitchett) 197
Cao Xueqin 5, 6
Capable of Doing All Sorts of Vulgar Things 132
Carnival in China (Berg) 17
Certeau, Michel de 36
Chang, Chun-shu 5
Chang, Eileen 10, 49
Chang, Kang-i Sun 154
Chang, Shelley Hsueh-lun 5
Changing Clothes in China (Finnane) 32
Changqing Collection (Yuan Zhen) 128
Chen Bingzao 6
Chen Cheng 130
Chen Chunsheng 107
Chen Dongyuan 183
Chen Hongmou 159
Chen Jingzong 45
Chen Jiru 79, 132, 134
Chen Rikun 130
Chen Shubao (Emperor) 128
Chen Shunxi 142
Chen Yinque 34
Chen Yuanyuan 154
Chen Zilong 86–7, 106, 154
Chenghua reign 137
Chengzu (Emperor) 124
chensu 62
chicken 128, 141–2
children 64–6
Chinese Classical Novels 3
Chinese Culture and Chinese Soldiers
    (Lei Haizong) 30

Chinese Virago, The (Wu) 16, 158
Chongzhen 7
Chronicles of the Eastern Zhou Kingdoms (Cai Yuanfang) 18
Cinderella's Sisters (Ko) 58
City God 54–6, 195
civil officials 52
Civilization and Capitalism (Braudel) 114
Classic Selections of the Ming (Chen Zilong) 106
clothing: *banbi* 37–8; and entertainment 38–9; and funeral preparations 46–7; headdresses 40–2, 46, 50–1, *61*; historical background 29–32; Kylin coat 39; legislation of 82; Ming costume 42–6; in Ming dynasty 194–5; overview 20; and social class 33–44, 49; symbolism of 63–4; Zhaojun 33–4
Clunas, Craig 19, 193
Codes of the Great Ming Dynasty 138–9
color 46–7
commerce 82
Compendium of Materia Medica (Li Shizhen) 125–6, 127, 129
Compilation of Convenience Atlas 132
Compilation of Histories in the Wanli Region (Shen Defu) 82
Complete Collection of Essential Things at Home 132
Complete Collection of the Benevolence (Huang Liuhong) 159
Concise History of International Finance, A (Neal) 88
concubines 46–7, 51–2, 63–4
Confucianism: consolidation with Buddhism and Taoism 143; doctrines of 192; and Emperor Hongzhi 139; and folk gods 179; and Law of Karma 192; and morality 194; and social class 32, 170; and status of women 158–9; *Yin* and *Yang* in 183
Confucius 32
congee 119
cotton 66, 79, 117
crabs 128
Criticism at Taowu 131
Cultural Revolution 4
currency: circulation 92–6; coinage 21, 96–108; paper money 85–7, 90

Daoism 32
daughters 65–7, 69–70, 195
decuple coins 102–6

Deep-Fried Whole Scorpion 126
Deng Yuanxi 139–40
dianzhu 52–3
diji 48–9
Ding Yaokang 5–6
Disquisition Finding Faults with Qin (Jia Yi) 195
divination 174
Dong Zhongshu 183
Dream of Red Mansions, A: clothing in 33, 65–6; and gold 93; importance of 3; legacy of 191; quality of 8; study of 6
Duan Gonglu 129
Duan Jiangli 7, 16
duck eggs 128–9
Dudbridge, Glen 6, 9, 167

Eight Beauties of Qinhuai 154
embroidery 78
Emperor Hongzhi's Speeches and Edicts 139
Epstein, Maram 185
Essays of Wangxiangtang 132

face-plucking 48–9
Fan Lian 89–91
fangbo 53
fans 80
Fate in Tears and Laughter (Zhang Henshui) 3
feminism 156–8
Feng Chengjun 129
Feng Menglong 3, 191
Feng Yuanjun 38
fertility 180–2
finance: in China 85, 88–9, 92; in Europe 88–9; in Ming dynasty 102–8
Finnane, Antonia 32
Five Miscellaneous Morsels (Wu Za Zu) 76, 80
Flowers on the Sea (Han Bangqing) 154
Fong, Grace 154
food: books about 132; culture of 114–15, 132–44; imported 119–20; and labor 120–3; local specialties 125–32; northern Chinese 115–17; overview 22, 196; for pregnant women 129–30
foot binding: and freedom of movement 156–9; importance of 47; practice of 58; and sleeping shoes 58
Frank, Gunder 85
Franke, Wolfgang 17, 18
Fu Chai 60
Fu Jingbing 85

Fu Sinian 11, 19
Fu Yanchang 164–5
Fu Yiling 121
fugui 174
funerals 52

Gazetteer of the Capital (Shoudu Zhi) 81
General Chronicle of Shandong, The 179
Gibbon, Edward 12
globefish 127
gold 92–3
Gonzalez de Mendoza, Juan 157
Great Learning, The 192
Gresham's Law 104
Grieder, Jerome 5
Gu Bingqian 52
Gu Jiegang 164–5
Gu Jiguang 86
Gu Lin 76
Gu Yanwu 85, 100
Gua Pao 182
Guang Zong (Emperor) 104
Guangyou Temple 90
guixiu 150–1, 154–6, 196
Guo Chao 8
Gushan Notes 90
Gushi goose 128

hairstyles 49, 65–6
Han Bangqing 154
Han Fei Zi—Outer Congeries of Sayings, the Upper Right Series 121
handkerchiefs 57
Hanlin 138
He Liancheng 86
He Liangjun 132
He Shuangqing 155
High Qing period 159
historiography 9–12, 17, 32
history 12–13, 17–18
History of Chinese Literature, A 4
History of Chinese Monetary Theory 86
History of the Ming Dynasty, The 41, 76, 97
History of the Sui Dynasty 128
History of the Yuan Dynasty, The 30, 32
Honey Chirp 125–6
Hong Chengchou 7
Hongwu (Emperor): character of 194–5; and City God cult 54; and clothing 35; and Daoism 32; and gastronomy 137; influence of 197–8; and modern culture 13–14; and sumptuary laws 135
Hongzhi (Emperor) 137–40, 143
Hou Zhenyang 106

housing 193
Hu Shih 2–3, 4, 5, 7, 14
Hu Wenkai 154
Huang Liuhong 159
Huang Yunmei 45–6
Huang Zongxi 85, 86
Huang, Ray 19, 70, 104, 124

Idle Talk Under the Bean Arbor 87
Impeachment of Qie (Hou Zhenyang) 106
Imperial Academy 45–6
Important Arts for the People's Welfare (Jia Sixie) 128
In Search of the Dharma (Yu) 150
incense 77–8, 161–4, 170–1, 176–83
"Incense Trade, The" (Mao Dun) 182
ink 80
Introduction to the Sources of Ming History, An (Franke) 17, 18
ivory 76

Jade Emperor 182
Jia Sixie 128
Jia Yi 195
Jiang Yingke 83
Jianwen (Emperor) 136
Jiaozhi 129–30
Jin Ping Mei: as cautionary work 136; and clothing 49, 56, 58–9; and coinage 101; and economics 83–4; and food 133–4; importance of 3; legacy of 191; and luxury goods 77; materialism in 14, 196; quality of 8; study of 6; and traveling 92, 170
Jin Xingyao 4
Jingling School 163
Johnson, David 54
Journey to the West 3

Kai Zhong Law 124
Kangxi (Emperor) 159
Ko, Dorothy 19, 58, 150, 154, 157
Kong Ji 104
Kong Shangren 154
Kozo Yamamura 85
Kuan-yin, the Chinese Transformation of Avalokitesvara (Yu) 150
Kublai Khan 30
Kuhn, Philip 66, 153

Lan Dingyuan 159
Lang Collections 132
Lao She 48–9
Larson, Wendy 158
Lasting Words to Awaken the World 3

Law of Karma 191–2
Leach, Edmund 66
Legend of Heroes and Heroines 92
Lei Haizong 30
Li Cuiran 4, 7
Li Dazhao 10
Li Guoqing 15
Li Jiannong 104
Li Jinghan 164
Li Kui 117
Li Longsheng 85
Li Shimian 45–6
Li Shizhen 125–6, 127, 129
Li Wenzhong 52
Li Yu 128, 134
Li Zhen 90
Liang Fangzhong 107
Liang Qichao 10, 18
Liang Shiqiu 132
Liang Tongshu 80
Lin Yutang 48, 185
lion leg of Jiaozhi 129–30
Liping Wang 178
Little Reunions (Chang) 49
Liu Dong 163
Liu Gongquan 80
Liu Guanglin 107
Liu He 77–8
Liu Hongqiang 4
Liu Jieping 4
Liu Ruoyu 106, 163
Liu Rushi 34, 154
Liu Xun 129
Liu Zhiwei 107
locks 80
Lu Dahuang 4
Lu Ji 83
Lu Rong 97
Lu Shiyi 86–7
Lu Xun 3–4
luxury goods: and food 142–4; in Ming dynasty 75–82, 193–4; overview 20–1; and women 155–6

Ma (Empress) 137, 194
Ma (merchant) 89–90
Manchu conquest 157
mang 29
Mann, Susan 37, 150–1, 154, 159, 184
Mao Dun 182
Mao Lianquan 6
Mao Pijiang 6, 132, 154
Mao Zedong 197

marriage 63
Marseken, Susan F. 193
May Fourth 157–8
McMahon, Keith 16
Méditerranée et le Monde Méditerranéen a l'époque de Philippe II, La (Braudel) 10
Meigong cloth 78–9
Memories of Yingmei An 132, 154
Meng Sen 105–6
methodology 14–20
Ming dynasty: and capitalism 21–2, 107; culture of 8, 134–6, 191, 194; dates 7; economy of 83–93, 122–3, 155, 193; founding of 32; historical sources 18–19; legal code 123; and luxury goods 75–82; official costume 42–3; and salt trade 123–5
Ming Emperors' Speeches and Edicts 139
Miscellaneous Records of Wanping 142–3
Mo'e Records 132
Moment in Peking (Lin Yutang) 48
Monetary History of China, A (Peng Xinwei) 107
Mongol conquest 30–2, 136–7
Morgan, David 32
Mote, Frederick 197
Mount Miaofeng 164–5
Mount Miaofeng Incense Society 165
Mount Tai 160–1, 176–8
Mount Tai Incense Society 23, 161–76
mountains 159–60
My Re-conception of Wage Labor after the Mid-Ming Dynasty (Fu Yiling) 121

Naito Konan 21
Naquin, Susan 19, 150
Neal, Larry 88
Ni Gu Lu 80
Ning Zhi 122
Notes in Xiqing (Shi Zhenlin) 155
Nyren, Eve Alison 15

Occasional Notes with Leisure Motions 132
Ode to Lions (Chen Cheng) 130
On Making Mount Tai a National Mountain (Yi Junzuo) 160
On the Ancient Entertainer (Feng Yuanjun) 38
On the Tombstone of the Five (Zhang Pu) 105

Pang's Family Discipline 122
Pao Xiaolan 19
Papal Remittance 88
Peng Xinwei 107
phoenix meat of Baoji 129
pianshan 64
Pilgrimage in Seventeenth-Century Fiction, A (Dudbridge) 6
Plaks, Andrew 5, 9, 16
Polo, Marco 137
polygamy 16
Posthumous Collections of Pinluo An (Liang Tongshu) 80
Practice of Everyday Life, The (Certeau) 36
Prefectural Records of Dongchang, The 178
Prefectural Records of Yanzhou, The 177–8
Prefecture Annals of Gaoyou, The 128–9
Prefecture Annals of Tai'an, The 175
prostitutes 56–9, 154
Provincial Administration Commission 123–4
psychedelic fish 129
Pu Songling 4, 5–6, 7, 122

qi snake 126
Qian Pu 140
Qian Qianyi 154
Qianlong (Emperor) 159, 179–80
Qiantang Tide 13
Qing dynasty 7, 81, 87
Quan Hansheng 85

rank badges *43, 44, 45*
Ranke, Leopold von 11, 85
Records of Shanxi (Shen Sixiao) 86
Records of the Grand Historian-Biographies of Divination Activities 174
Records of the Taiping Era 127
Records of Things 142
Records of Unusual Things in Lingbiao (Liu Xun) 129
Records of Winds and Rains in Qingxi (Xieqiao Jushi) 154
Rectifying Matters of Temporary Action (Tian Wenjing) 128
Red Pill Case 104
Regular Supply 137
Rehearsal of the Faithful Incense 171
Reminiscences in Dreams of Tao An 132

Renewal of Buddhism in China, The (Yu) 150
Reorient (Frank) 85
Reorientation of Jinpingmei and Xingshiyinyuan (Yang) 16
"Repetition in *Xingshi Yinyuan Zhuan*" (Wu) 16
Request for Ceasing the Coin Casting of the Baoyuan Bureau (Xu Jie) 100
Research on Xingshi Yinyuan Zhuan (Xia Wei) 15–16
rhinoceros girdles 76–7
roast elephant trunk 129
Robertson, Maureen 154
Romance of the Song Dynasty, The (Xiong Damu) 17–18
Romance of the Three Kingdoms 3, 8
Ropp, Paul 154, 155, 157
Rou Putuan 3
Ruyijun Zhuan 3

Said, Edward Wadie 186
salt 22, 123–5, 196
satin 79
Scholars, The 3, 18
School of Mind 143
Seeds of Change, The (Ropp) 157
Shen Bang 142–3
Shen Congwen 34
Shen Defu 82
Shen Fu 185
Shen Shixing 52
Shen Sixiao 86
Shen's Book on Agriculture 122
Shi Zhenlin 155
Shizong (Emperor) 105
shoes: and commerce 82; *geweng* 34–5, *36*; sleeping 57–8
Shu Wu 155
Shuan Wawa 181
silk 79, 81–2
silver 83–5, 92–6, 106–7
Sima Qian 12
Single Whip Law 107
Sinology 19, 154
Six Chapters of a Floating Life 185–6, 196
Smith, Adam 197
Smith, Arthur H. 168
social classes 60, 69–70
Song dynasty 158
Song Lian 54
Songzi Niangniang 181
Special Decrees of the Ming Dynasty 39

Starr, Chloe 150
Stele of Beidou Shenghui Society, The 171
Story of a Marital Fate to Awaken the World, The see *Xingshi Yinyuan Zhuan*
Story of the Pearl 131
Strange Tales from a Chinese Studio 3
Study of Late Ming Historical Texts, A (Xie Guozhen) 18
Su Kewen 90
sumptuary laws 82–3, 135–6, 193–5
Sumptuary Law (Surhone, Timpledon, and Marseken) 193
Sun Kaidi 5
Sun Qiang 86
Surhone, Lambert M. 193

tadpoles 126
Taichang Tongbao 104
Talking about the Past 87–8
Tang Te-kang 13
Tang Wenji 107
Tao Zongyi 166
Taoism 143, 160–1, 165, 174–5, 181
taxation: Incense Tax 179–80; remittance of 89–90; and salt trade 123; silver taxation 84; system of 107, 158
Taxation and Governmental Finance in Sixteenth-Century Ming China (Huang) 124
Temple of Heaven 82
Tetsuo Kamiki 85
textiles 55–6, 66, 78–9 see also specific fabrics
Textual Research on A Dream of Red Mansions (Hu Shih) 5
Textual Research on Women's Works of Past Dynasties (Hu Wenkai) 154
"Textual Research on *Xingshi Yinyuan Zhuan*, The" (Hu Shih) 2–3
Three Gu and Six Po, The (Yi Ruolan) 166–7
Tian Pu 4
Tian Wenjing 128
Tianqi (Emperor) 106
Tianshun reign 139
Timpledon, Miriam T. 193
tofu 137–8
Tokugawa period 135
Tong Wanzhou 4
Tourism and Spatial Change in Hangzhou, 1911–1927 (Liping Wang) 178
travel: as leisure 150, 196; overview 22–3; reasons for 168–70; and tourism 159–61, 176–8; by women 150–6

Travels of Lao Can, The 92–3
Travels of Marco Polo, The 129
Treatise on Superfluous Things 132
Tumu Fort Incident 47
"Twenty-Four Histories" 10
Twitchett, Denis 197

Unofficial Biography of Liu Rushi (Chen Yinque) 34

velvet 81
Veritable Records of Emperor Wuzong, The 179
Village Life in China (Smith) 168
viragos 16, 158, 183
Von Glahn, Richard 85

Wan Ming 107
Wanfang Data 3
Wang An 105–6
Wang Huizu 159
Wang Saishi 127
Wang Shixing 83
Wang Shizhen 39, 52
Wang Shouyi 88
Wang Sucun 4
Wang Yangming 143
Wang Zhaojun 34
Wang Zhen 39, 47
Wangmu 181
Wang's Witnesses 127
Water Margin 3, 8, 97, 170
Wei Shuo 80
Wei Zhongxian 39, 105–6
Weighted and Unbiased Record, A (Liu Ruoyu) 106, 163
Wen Zhenheng 132, 134
Widmer, Ellen 154
women: behavior of 174–5; and clothing 34, 46, 50, 55–6, 65–6; elite 150–6; and hygiene 57; lives of 155–6; and power 166; status of 158, 197; and traveling 23–4, 172–3, 183–6
women's studies 19–20
World Browsing Series (Yueshi Bian) 56
writing brushes 79–80
Wu Han 197
Wu Jen-Shu 82–3, 155
Wu Meicun 154
Wu People's Revolt 105
Wu Shilai 122
Wu Xiaolong 16
Wu Za Zu 76
Wu, Yenna 16, 19, 158

Xi Shi 60
Xia Wei 7, 15–16
Xia Yan 52
Xian Zhai Lao Ren 18
Xiaohua Zhuren 18
Xie Guozhen 18
xiku 56
Xingshi Yinyuan Zhuan: authorship 4–6; influenced by *Jin Ping Mei* 134; legacy of 3–7; as morality book 136; outline 1–2; study of 6, 14–20; timeline 7, 120; value of 7–14, 191–2
Xingshi Yinyuan Zhuan and the Secular Life of the Ming Dynasty (Wu Xiaolong) 16
Xiong Damu 17–18
Xizhou Sheng: authorship of *Xingshi Yinyuan Zhuan* 1, 6, 8; and clothing 40; life 7; and morality 167; views of 192
Xizong (Emperor) 104, 105–6
Xu Fuling 7
Xu Guangqi 87
Xu Jie 52, 89, 100
Xu Zhimo 3, 4, 155
Xue Huigong 78
Xueqiao Jushi 154

Yan Song 52
Yan Suozhu 35
Yan Xinxiang 171
Yan Zhong 6
Yang Chunyu 15
Yang Dongfang 7
Yang Lian 105
Yang Weizhen 42
Yang, Yu-chun 16
Yao Congwu 11
Yasushi Oki 134–5
Ye Mengde 127
Ye Mengzhu 81
Ye Shichang 86
Ye Xiaoluan 155
Ye Xun 90
Yellow-Fringed Coin 98, 101–2
Yi Junzuo 160
Yi Ruolan 167

Yin and *Yang* 183–6
Yin Huiyi 159
Yingzong (Emperor) 32, 39, 47, 84
Yongle (Emperor) 136
Yongzheng (Emperor) 159, 179–80
Yu Dafu 155
Yu Qian 127
Yu Shenxing 89–90
Yu Yizheng 163
Yu, Chun-fang 150
Yuan conquest 29–32, 137
Yuan Mei 154
Yuan Zhen 127, 128
Yun Zhong Ji Shi (Yu Qian) 127
Yunjian Authentic Records 89–91
Yunniang 185–6, 196

Zarrow, Peter 158
Zelin, Madeleine 123
Zeng Guofan 140
Zha Jizuo 140
zhang 54
Zhang Dai 132–3
Zhang Guiyong 11
Zhang Henshui 3
Zhang Juzheng 52, 76–7, 140
Zhang Lihua 128
Zhang Pu 105
Zhang Qingji 4
Zhang Wanying 151
Zhang Xiaoxiang 32
Zhangqiu 4
Zheng He 96
Zhengde (Emperor) 135–6
zhisun 30, *31*
Zhou Guang 96
Zhou Jiazhou 161
Zhou Shunchang 105
Zhu Guozhen 139
Zhu Yanjing 5
Zhu Yuanzhang 96, 123
Zhuang Guotu 85
Zhuang Tinglong 140
zhusi 79
zhuyao vests 66–8
Zi Xia 11
Zou Zongliang 7
Zuo Guangdou 105

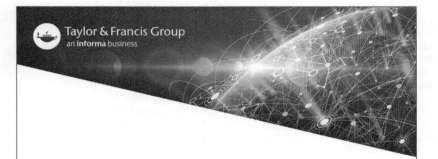

Taylor & Francis eBooks

www.taylorfrancis.com

A single destination for eBooks from Taylor & Francis with increased functionality and an improved user experience to meet the needs of our customers.

90,000+ eBooks of award-winning academic content in Humanities, Social Science, Science, Technology, Engineering, and Medical written by a global network of editors and authors.

TAYLOR & FRANCIS EBOOKS OFFERS:

- A streamlined experience for our library customers
- A single point of discovery for all of our eBook content
- Improved search and discovery of content at both book and chapter level

REQUEST A FREE TRIAL
support@taylorfrancis.com